They Called Me
Teacher

**Stories of Minnesota
Country School Teachers and Students
1915 to 1960**

by
Tom Melchior

Mora Normal School Training Class of 1936.

Library of Congress Catalog Card Number   97-92748

ISBN 0-9661613-0-0

Publisher's Cataloging-in-Publication

Melchior, Thomas
        They called me teacher : stories of Minnesota country school
teachers and students (1915–1960 / Tom Melchior.–1st ed.
        p. cm.

    1. Rural schools–Minnesota–History. 2. Teachers–Minnesota.
3. Minnesota–Rural conditions. 4. Education, Rural–Minnesota.
I. Title

LC5147.M6M45 1997   371'.00976
                                          QB197-41304

Melchior Publishing
1901 West 125 Street
Shakopee, MN 55379
1 (612)-445-4109
Published: 1998

Acknowledgements

Mining for stories requires the generosity of many people. Thanks to all of you for your help:

The Country School Teachers and Students who contributed their stories.

My friend and teaching colleague, Mary Ronzani, for her unrelenting commitment to editing the text. She has read the stories so often she has them memorized.

Gloria Borchert of Baudette, Margaret Sandberg of Kennedy and all the other people who helped me locate the storytellers. Thanks for writing, calling, and setting up all those interviews.

Kaaren Fleischer for her help in transcribing hours of interview tapes and editing.

Barb Roell, Ralph Schmidtke and Jill Woodruff-Gerold, deities of Hennepin Technical College, for their wizardry.

Saundra Schaitberger, owner of Pines-n-Tiques in Plato, for the cover photograph.

Jane Hodgins for her editing help and layout suggestions.

My wife Sue for reading, reading, reading, and never doubting that the journey was worth taking.

Contents

The author and his chief-of-staff, grandson Sam. Tom Melchior taught English for thirty-four years, twenty-eight in the Burnsville system.

Dedication

Susan Heselton c. 1924

Albert Maas remembers the day Basil Heselton pulled into the school grounds to drop off his wife Susan for the first day of school. Always in a hurry to supervise his dirt contracting business, Basil tore out in a cloud of gravel and dust.

The year before, the most notorious members of Albert's class had mud-balled the school and tormented the teacher by dangling a mouse in front of her face (stories in Chapter 17: Shenanigans and Stuff). These were just two of the devious tactics used by the students of District 104 which resulted in the teacher's dismissal for her inability to control the students. The teacher before her had also succumbed to the infamous class's rowdy behavior and quit.

Mrs. Basil (Susan) Heselton inherited this group of ne'er-do-wells at District 104, Rice County, in 1928. To make matters worse, a farm family in the district had taken in a foster child to help with their chores. This sixteen-year-old had honed his rowdiness in Minneapolis and thought he had "easy pickin's" at Mrs. Heselton's country school.

Albert Maas tells the story.

We Respected Her!

The first day Mrs. Heselton came she said, and I can remember it very clearly, "OK, I've heard we've had a little trouble in the past here with discipline, and I'm going to try to straighten that out. I think I can. Of course, I need your cooperation. And I will.

"If you do everything the way I tell you, we'll get along fine. But if you do something wrong, I'm going to have to punish you."

Well, at the first recess, Frank said, "She talks tough, but I'm going to test her out." We get back in school and everybody is watching him. He's sitting up about two seats ahead of me. He looked around. Mrs. Heselton was looking down. I think she was watching, but she was looking down. He got up, unzipped his pants, pulled his tool out, and peed on his geography book and also hit my leg.

Mrs. Heselton got up, walked around to the back, and come up his aisle. She didn't want to call too many students' attention to it, ya see. "Frank, I saw what you did. You desecrated your geography book. One hour up in the corner. See that stool up there? One hour on that stool facing the corner."

She led him up there and then said a little louder so everyone could hear it, "If you turn around before this hour is up, it will be fifteen minutes more."

Well, he did look around and she said, "OK, Frank, you just lengthened that to fifteen minutes longer." When the hour and fifteen minutes was over, she went up and said, "Well, that's good. You absorbed your punishment. Do you know what it was for? Now go back to your seat."

Frank was pretty good for two weeks, but then he shot some spit balls through a tube. She kept him after school for an hour. And that was the end of his meanness.

We liked her and had great respect for her. We became a very changed group of children.

Susan Marie Heselton was the mother of my wife, Suzanna Marie Heselton. Susan Heselton died when my wife was seven years old. I know Susan Heselton only through stories. After Albert had told this story to my wife and her sister, I began my journey to find Albert, who spins a good tale. He also helped my wife and me get to know her mother, Susan Heselton, Country School Teacher.

Susan Voegele Heselton (back row, right) c. 1927

Cecile Cowdery

Cecile Cowdery is the eighty-nine-year-old grandmother of three of my former students at Burnsville High School. Perhaps no one knows the life of a Country School Student better than Cecile. She is one of thirteen children who attended District 1 near Long Prairie. Over the years Cecile's parents also cared for thirty-nine foster children. Cecile's story as a Country School Student is told in Chapter 20.

I had finished interviewing teachers and students and had written the rough draft when Cecile's granddaughter Jackie and I went to interview Cecile. Jackie told me about Cecile's artistic talent. After we had finished our interview and as I was walking out the door, I asked Cecile if she would consider illustrating two of her stories. Thankfully, she did not stop with those two. Her whimsical characters seem to dance on the paper.

Cecile has been one of the luminous golden treasures I have been blessed to meet in this story mining adventure.

Story Mining

At any moment in our lives, we can look back and discover that the stories of our lives are following us. They seem at first glance to be scattered haphazardly, bouncing along the ground, dancing like kites in the summer breeze, or tangling themselves in thorny bushes.

Our stories seem detached, disjointed pieces from unrecognizable puzzles. Some look like realistic paintings while others are shimmering mirages. But when we move, they follow us, these stories of our lives. Some are tied together with silken threads, love stories, that reach out to touch the rainbow. Others hook us with log chains, heavy memories, weighing us down like lead. Some are as mesmerizing as yesterday's sunrise. Some are shrouded in a mist of time and pain.

If we want to know who a person is, we must listen to that person's stories, all of them, if possible. Oh, we could say, "Country School Teachers were dedicated, creative, hardworking, compassionate, caring, and sometimes angry and cruel." But those words tell us nothing about who these people really are. If we know their stories, then we will know their hopes, fears, loves, and dreams.

To find these stories, I became a story miner. I traveled approximately 15,000 miles throughout Minnesota, interviewing more than 200 teachers and students to mine these stories. Some stories were pasted in aging, fading scrapbooks. Some were stored in frayed leather shipping trunks, smothered by piles of junk and forgotten in dusty attic niches. Others moldered away in cardboard boxes, stacked in unexplored basements.

I found many stories in young faces, smiling out of old photographs arranged neatly on the pages of black paper albums.

Once-precious stories scattered themselves among friends, relatives, or casual acquaintances—unprized possessions, forgotten as quickly as the people who told them. Tragic moments that scarred teachers and students, kind words that inspired heroic journeys, embraces that stilled fearful hearts—too many of these stories have been lost in the fog of indifference. Vital stories, bursting with the pride of battles won, have withered from want of telling, disintegrated for want of a listener. Unappreciated and unheard, they vanished with the tellers.

And what do we know about Country School Students, who walked through blizzards, husked corn in the fall, fought playground battles, ate lard sandwiches, and lost themselves in the wonders of nature? Were Country School Students occasionally misguided angels, disciplined by strict parents as well as Country School Teachers who kept "the rulers of righteousness" in their desk drawers for such emergencies?

Sometimes I found stories as fragile and thin as fine muslin hiding in the memories of Country School Teachers and Students. We mined them together, gently peeling away bits and pieces that sparked forgotten tales.

When Country School Teachers and Country School Students mined their stories and warmed them in the sunlight of memory, they told them with passion, pride, and humor.

His-story and Her-story:
Ode to Country School Teachers

History, my friend, you're in a pickle
For being naive and downright fickle.
You pat your back for a job well done.
It's out of town you should be run.

Cowboys, Cheesecakes, and Chicago Crooks,
All have a place in your textbooks.
Rosie the Riveter and the Babe got fame.
Desperadoes and heroes are mentioned by name.

Villains and Varmints fascinate you.
To tyrants and despots you stick like glue.
And Heroes abound in bold type and glitter,
But words about me you never would fritter.

'Bout Saints and Sinners you love to print.
To War and Envy and Greed you sprint.
My starbursts you never could find.
Fireworks bursting in children's minds.

I'm Country School Teacher. Remember me?
My life on your pages I never see.
I taught farm children for ten generations,
Who danced the dance of this great nation.

We did our work for little pay.
Is that why we were filed away?
Our names are listed with dusty propriety
Boxed away by Historical Society.

Rogue, Riffraff, Scoundrel and Knave—
History, are these the friends you crave?
Renegades pique your curiosity
More than Teachers' generosity.

Shame, History, we're omitted!
For this faux pas you'll be committed.
We school teachers were also heroes.
Forgetting us earns you a ZERO!

You skipped our chapter, how absurd!
Come now, History, not a word?
You mourned the passing of Golden Years
And wept for heroes with words of tears.

Who grieved when Country Schools had died,
Sculpted a statue or even cried?
The tireless silent are easy to bury
As whispering winds across the prairie.

George, Abe, and JFK,
And all the Vets who passed our way,
Your Heroes all get glorification,
Well-deserved pages of adulation.

But even Superman with kryptonite,
Couldn't beat bed bugs every night!
Would Wonder Woman, looking so nice,
Dig in scalps for leaping lice?

Would Roy Rogers and Old Tom Mix
Wrangle with all those schoolboy tricks?
Or Skywalker with his flashy light saber,
Solve the feud of angry neighbors?

You think we never went to war?
Toughie strutted through our school doors.
We didn't whine or cry or bawl,
Kids? We loved 'em warts and all!

His-tory, with your male order pen
Can't you tell tales of us women?
Country School Teachers were Mr. _and_ Marm.
Her-story, too, is filled with charm.

Country School Students can sing our fame,
Praise our worth, recall our names,
Recite their tables and rules of phonics,
Describe our habits and histrionics.

They know the date the stove exploded
And when they came to class half loaded.
Sixty years later with jabbering publicity,
They gossip 'bout our eccentricities.

"I fell in the creek, was cold and wigglin'
She gave me her coat an' couldn't stop gigglin'."
"One teacher laughs, the another one rants
At all those times we wet our pants."

"When Tragedy knocked, how I cried,
But Teacher hugged me when Papa died."
"I remember how they wept and swore
For kids they loved killed in the war."
        Our Cheer
His-tory, Her-story, we proclaim,
Country School Teacher was our name!
We want to holler and ring the bell
So in this book our stories we'll tell.

From woods and prairies, valleys and hills
These pages with our tales we'll fill.
And if you remember, give a cheer
For every teacher you hold dear!   -TM

Dear Country School Teachers,

Congratulations on your book! Since we played such an important role in your lives, we are pleased that you included some of our stories. Here is a reminder of what your life was like in those "golden" years.

Sincerely,

Country School Students

I'm Margaret Liebsch and this is a picture of my school, District 126 north of Albany in Stearns County. We called it the Roesch School. One Sunday in 1910, my mother took me to the school to have my picture taken with my class. I was so scared. They were talking about "shooting a picture," and since I spoke only German, I thought they were going to shoot me. I tried to hide behind the girls in front of me. You can see my head. The photographer took our picture with one of those old-time cameras, the ones with the cloth on top and you throw that over your head to keep the light out.

There were eighty-three kids in my school, and we had just one teacher, Anton Theisen. We were all in one room. We sat two in one desk. The boys sat on one side of the room and the girls on the other.

We didn't know any English when we went to school. The teacher taught us in both German and English. I remember I had a German reading book. One time the teacher asked us to bring a newspaper from home to use as a napkin on our desks when we ate. Years back the ink in the paper did not come off. I asked the other students, "What is a newspaper?" I didn't know the English word.

At lunch time the teacher ate at the house where he was living. We were well behaved except for the bigger boys who ran on top of the desks. It's a wonder they didn't fall and break their necks. We girls sat and ate our lunch. Every day we had brown syrup on bread. On warm fall and spring days when I opened the top of the syrup can, the bread was soaked with syrup and the fumes came out so bad. I didn't eat anything—no dinner.

I walked to school every day. Dad never harnessed the horses to take me. I went through a pasture, down a hill, across a meadow, and through a woods that had a mud road for a horse and wagon. The neighbor kids told me there were wolves in the woods. In the winter, the trees cracked and I listened. I ran as fast as I could. No wolf was going to catch me. When the weather was bad, I was not sent to school. After I finished grade school, I went home and spoke only German again.

Congratulations, Country School Teacher. You did a good job.

Margaret Liebsch, age six, 1910: In the picture above, Margaret is hiding behind two of the older girls.

Margaret Liebsch

The Opening Bell

By 8:30 the September sun had lit up the golden maple leaves and turned the east windows into silvery mirrors. Mothers Clubs had spit-shined their country schools for the new year.

Dressed in their opening day finery, Country School Teachers from St. Vincent to Freeburg stepped out on the front stoops and shook their handbells, calling their charges to class.

From Mineral City to Round Lake, kids yanked the ropes that sent bells in the schools' towers clanging and banging. Within a few minutes, the largest bell choir ever assembled, one every two square miles throughout the state, was playing the *Time for School Symphony*.

The bells chimed across the northwestern prairie, through northern forests, over the waves of rivers, lakes, and ponds, and up and down the great iron ore mines. Then in one resounding chorus, the bell ringing swept over the rich, black soil of central and southern Minnesota.

As Country School Students before them had done for years, farm children followed the ringing bell into the one- and two-room schools to meet their new teachers.

Marm

When I went to high school, I took four years of Latin and two years of chemistry because I wanted to be a doctor. But my mother said, "You'll never be a doctor, not while I'm living!"

"I thought that was a wonderful thing to be."

"You have to go out at all hours and go whenever you are called. No, you can't be a doctor!"

"Well, then can I be a nurse?" I asked.

"Oh, no!" she said. "When I was in the hospital, they had to scrub the floor and do terrible jobs. You can't be a nurse. Will you be a teacher?"

"Yes," I said, "but teachers have to scrub the floors."

"Yes, but that's not as bad as being a doctor or a nurse." That's how I became a teacher. **Elida Farber Berg, 1925: Elida taught for sixteen years at the Hagen School in Lake of the Woods.**

Mister

My mother was a teacher, and she was interested in having us further our education. We were so poor we couldn't go to college so my brother and I went to teachers training in Thief River Falls. I was only sixteen.

Harry Sjulson, 1938, Kittson County

Completing teachers training was a grueling nine months with a demanding instructor. Charles T. Steenblock completed his teachers training in 1950–1951 in Austin, in Mower County.

She Who Must Be Obeyed

Our teacher training teacher was very strict. She had to make teachers out of teenagers. At that time the girls wore bracelets around their ankles. On graduation night one of the girls wore one of these bracelets. Our supervisor was sitting in the back of the auditorium. Suddenly a slip of paper was passed on down the aisle to this girl: "You get that ornament off your leg or you will not graduate."

My writing was poor. I had to stay after school the night of graduation and write the alphabet, I don't know how many times. She had been after me all year to improve my writing. Then I hitched a ride home to Dexter, about sixteen miles away. I did the chores and then I went back for graduation.

She was a hard teacher, but we were very immature and undisciplined. She did have an interest in us, but she had to iron out a lot of things. I received Christmas cards from her for years.

As part of their teachers training program, Country School Teachers often taught for a week or two in a school in their district. Most of these experiences were uneventful, but sometimes they held unusual surprises.

Sackin' Out

One night we were getting ready for bed. I suppose we lit the kerosene lamp. There wasn't much light in the room. We jumped in surprise. There under our covers was someone sleeping! We were quite alarmed. Then we got up the courage to lift the covers. Instead of a person, we found a sack of potatoes! The hired man had lugged the sack up the stairs and put it in our bed. My instructor eventually married him. **Ida Haukos practice taught near Fergus Falls in Otter Tail County in 1946.**

Most Country School Teachers taught in one- or two-room schools built by their students' fathers.

Hilda Benedict Hendrickson: My dad moved to Lake of the Woods County in 1914, and they didn't have a school for a year. My dad donated a piece of his land and the shingles.

Leora White: My father ran a saw mill so he donated the lumber. He sawed all the lumber, flooring, and window casings.

Another neighbor, Mr. Searls, a carpenter who had no children, built the school. Mr. McGee was a superintendent from Bemidji. He came there and he saw what they had done, and they were just going to make some board seats that we could sit on. He said, "No I'll send the seats, and the desks, and the teacher and the teacher's chair out on a truck."

Hilda: The first day of school my dad gave a little speech and told them that if they worked hard they might even become President of the United States. Of course they never did.

Country School Teachers taught readin', writin', and 'rithmetic to students ages five to sixteen. It wasn't always easy.

"There's a Friend!"

In 1936, I was seventeen years old on my first day of school. This mother hauled her son into the building for his first day. Screaming and yelling, he didn't want to leave home; he didn't want to come

to school. She was beating the tar out of him. Finally I picked him up. He was such a little guy, so dirty and uncared for. He screamed and squirmed, trying to get out of my arms to get back home to his mother. So there's a good lesson in that: No matter what the home is like the child thinks it's OK. Finally I said to his mother, "Why don't you just go and let me handle it." I sat in my chair, swiveling back and forth with thirty-nine other students in the room.

I tried to comfort this crying child and conduct my classes at the same time. By afternoon I had gotten enough playthings that he settled down. The next morning was a repeat of the first morning, but when he saw me, he seemed to think, "There's a friend." In about a week he was satisfied to come to school like everybody else.

Now he's a big buddy of mine; every time I see him we stop and visit. We talk about that day very often. He said to me one day, "And I'm sure I had wet pants while I was sitting on your lap!" In a way it was a good lesson for some of those kids. They saw this hysterical child I was able to quiet down, and he became one of the group. They learned "That's life." **Marietta Moore Sharkey, 1937, District 77, St. Thomas School, Le Sueur County**

School Teachers fought blizzards, snow banks, and bone chilling cold weather to reach their schools. Somehow they found a way to be there before the children arrived.

Rockin' and Rollin'

The winter of 1936 was ferocious. I lived four and a half miles from school. I had a road for only one mile so I rode horseback. My horse was a little short legged thing, so I had to get off once in a while and give him a breather. I used any way I could to get to that school. There was a very steep hill above the school. One morning I was so tired I lay down and rolled down the hill right up to the school. I don't think any one saw me because it was a pretty isolated territory. **Blanch MacAllister Swift, Klatt School, Cass County**

My Knight

Part of the time I stayed in the district and part of the time I rode with two other teachers. We had our first snowstorm and the roads were blocked and the snowplows had not been out. We made it to the first teacher's school. I wondered what I was going to do. I was too cold to go much farther.

I looked up and saw the neighbor man coming on a white horse. He said, "You'll never get through, but your pupils will be waiting for you, Helen, so why don't you take my horse." He took

off his outer overalls and I put them over my coat. I climbed up on the horse. I had not ever ridden horseback in my life. However, I could have walked faster than the horse so I tried to make it trot. Well, I just about fell off. I walked that horse three miles to school. He was right. The pupils were all waiting for me. **Helen Christofferson, 1936-1938, District 54, Stevens County**

There was no job Country School Teachers hated more than hauling wood, building a fire in the jacketed stove on Monday morning, and keeping it banked and alive during the week.

How Cold Can It Get?

One Monday morning when I arrived at the school the temperature was fifty-one degrees below zero. All I had to make a fire with was green birch. I finally managed to make a fire, but it didn't get started right away. All the youngsters walked to school. I had to walk a mile to get to the school, and it was COLD! **Mae Wilson, 1931, Algoma School, Roseau County**

Country School Teachers loved their students and many claim, "Children were different then. They were better disciplined and they respected their teachers. But they weren't all angels."

The Pocket Mouse

We killed a field mouse out behind the school during recess. Roy dared me to put it in my pocket and take it in school. Afterwards, when all the boys would be watching me, I'd take it out of my pocket, and swing it by the tail. He taunted me. "You ain't got nerve enough, Albert."

I said, "Oh, yes, I'll do it. You've done some goofy things. That isn't too bad. I'll do it." I put it in my pocket, and of course, the boys were all watching me and some of the girls. I sat there awhile, and pretty soon I reached in my pocket and pulled out the mouse and dingled it around. It took pretty long for the teacher to see it.

"Albert, what have you got there?" she said.

"Just a mouse."

"Eeeeeek! Open the door. Throw it in the fire."

"I threw the mouse in the stove, but she didn't see me." She had one of the boys search my pockets and that took some time, so we got out of about fifteen more minutes of schooling. **Albert Maas, c. 1928, District 114, Rice County**

The Big Bang!

My oldest brother had a sixteen-gauge shotgun. My second brother brought a brace and bit from home and they bored a hole in a log and put the shell in there. Of course they took the BBs out. Then they put the log on the wood pile in the school. Then we went into the school for class. Every kid knew the log had the shell in it and we just waited. When the fire died down, the teacher went to poke up the fire. She walked over to the wood pile and picked up that log. We knew what was coming.

Suddenly that darn thing exploded. It blew the cover off the jacket. It blew the draft wide open and shot ashes all over the room. It blew the pipes apart.

The jacket had kind of a catch on the door and that blew open. Ashes flew all over. There was smoke everywhere. My god, she was scared. But the whole school was in an uproar. We cleaned up the ashes, put the pipes back together, and went back to work. **Julius Schneider, c. 1918, Credit River School, Scott County**

The Cat's Away

The first year I went to school they hired a teacher, but they found out she didn't have the right papers so they fired her. They hired a new teacher, who did not bring her lunch to school. She walked to the place where she boarded to eat dinner. While she was gone, we had a great time. One of the guys took his violin and climbed up through the trap door. He sat up there and played. The rest of us square danced below. One of the students did the calling. We had someone watching to see when she started to come back. Then we'd put down the trap door and stop dancing before she got back to school. We did a lot of square dancing in that school. **Hazel Henschel Benson, 1906–1912, Gates School, District 32, Isanti County. Hazel taught in the country schools for thirty-four years.**

Puff

There was a creek a ways down, so we would go down during the noon hour, mostly in the winter when the creek was frozen and we would skate. There were trees on the edges and roots would stick out from the creek banks. Some were the size of cigars and were dried up.

So we lit them and smoked them like cigars, but boy, were they strong! When we got back to school, we smelled like retired firemen. Our teacher, Ann Daleiden, was curious why we smelled so bad. We told her why and then we had a bonfire. But she was too smart and experienced to believe that story.

John T. Flicek, 1929, District 71, Scott County

No one was more interested in the new schoolmarms than the eligible young bachelors. These suitors used many ingenious ways to try to win the hearts of Country School Teachers.

The Singing Plowboy

I was single during my first five years of teaching. I had a boyfriend who would be plowing in the field beside the school house and I could hear him singing his love songs out there. He sang "You Are My Sunshine" and "May I Sleep in Your Barn Tonight Mister? It's so cold lying here all alone."

He would stop plowing and come under the window and start singing like crazy during school time. I just laughed and tried to ignore it. I didn't like him. When I went to dances, he would always try to dance with me. I really wasn't enamored with him. I tolerated him. It ended when the war came and he was drafted. **Gladys Lundstrom, 1942, District 70, east of Clara City, Chippewa County**

Cupid's arrows sometimes hit younger hearts.

No Syrupy Romance!

When I was in the fourth grade, a boy I did not like tried to hug me on the way home. I hit him on the head with my syrup pail and cut a good-sized gash in his head. He bled profusely. The next morning Lily, his mother, was waiting for me at the road. When I walked by, she said, "You could have killed my son!"

All I said was, "Tell him to leave me alone and I won't hit him." **Luva Wilson attended District 87-181, Mt. Hope School, in Meeker County, from 1921 to 1928.**

He's Got the Whole World

Gladys DeFrance Sutherland was my first grade teacher. One Friday her boyfriend came to pick her up. He was sitting in the big orange chair under the globe that hung from the ceiling, waiting for class to be done. Suddenly that old papier-mache globe broke and hit him on the head and he took off for the front door. He ran down the aisle with that globe on his head, and we kids had a terribly difficult

Help! Help! The sky is falling!

time to keep from laughing. Even though that silly thing happened, she married him anyway.

Martha Lindstrom, District 45, Kittson County

Country School Teachers completed rigorous teachers training programs, lived away from home, battled Mother Nature, confronted cantankerous school boards, rose in the dark, and corrected papers by kerosene lamps because they needed to make a living and because they loved children.

In 1935, Phyllis Van Buren Rupp, who had never attended a country school, was hired to teach in a prairie school between Breckenridge and Fergus Falls in Wilkin County. No teacher had ever completed a full year at this school.

Be My Valentine

One family of three little girls rode their horse to school, but they were very poor. They had this beautiful riding horse because the horse had run into a fence and was quite torn up. The owner said that if

the mother could save the horse, she could keep it. Their mother was a horse lover so she took the horse home and nursed her and healed her.

So the kids had a beautiful horse to ride to school. When it got too cold to ride the horse, the children had a team of mules with a long wagon that was just boards—boards on a frame of four wheels and those mules brought the children to school.

Their father was not held in high regard in the community. He was rough and tough with his wife and, I suppose, the children too, but they never did tell about it.

I looked out the window late one afternoon and coming across the prairie from the direction where they lived was their father, riding the horse and holding a long gun. I thought, "My gosh, I wonder if he's coming over here to scare me about his children." But he just came in to ask about the children, how they were doing. He was just an interested parent checking on his kids.

In February we had had a lot of snow, so the three girls didn't come to school because it was too cold—forty below, and they were little frail things and poorly clothed.

On Valentine's Day I thought I had better go to see them. Instead of going by the road, I went cross country, through hay fields. I was lucky to have made it. I thought about the Rolvaag story, *Giants in the Earth,* the one where they find the man frozen to death in the haystack in the spring. I thought about that as I was plowing through that hip high snow in that terrible cold. What a foolhardy thing to have done!

When I got to their farm, their dog charged at me like it was going to eat me up, but Marion, the oldest girl, called him off and I went in. It was warm in the house, but one of the windows had a pillow stuffed in it. The father thought he heard someone fooling around with his oil drums out in the yard so he shot through the window. He didn't bother to open the window. He shot right through the glass so they had to stuff a pillow in the open window.

I had brought the children's valentines to them. That's why I went.

I really was very foolhardy. But I had heard the mother was in the hospital. I can't remember why, but I think she had lost a baby. The father was with their mother, so I thought it would be a good idea to check on them.

I shouldn't have done it, but I just had to give them their valentines. I had a candy treat for them in each one. I was so very fond of those beautiful children. They were just the most beautiful children, with blue eyes, curly eye lashes—so sweet, and such pretty faces.

I didn't know how cold it was, and I had no idea how deep snow is in a hay field because the hay was very high. I wore my dad's heavy trousers and a heavy coat and scarf, but I still froze my feet. I wore overshoes, but not the nice lined ones we have today. After my visit I still had to walk home.

Phyllis Van Buren Rupp, 1935–1936, District 82, Wilkin County

When she had finished her valentine story, I asked Phyllis why she had put her life in danger for three valentines. She said, "Oh, they were such wonderful girls. I can still see their blue eyes. I loved those three girls so much!"

Chapter 1

Country School Teachers

Julitta Schmitz Pearl was born in 1901 in Caledonia. She taught her final three years from 1922 to 1925 in the Brownsville district, Houston County, one and one-half miles east of Freeburg, her home school.

Cecelia

Cecelia Rover was sixteen, just four years younger than I. She had a speech defect; she lisped. I got her interested in stories. She could read a little, but she could not get the idea of the story. I would tell her the different things I had read to her and work with her to have her tell me what she had really read. Reading aloud and pronouncing the words was difficult, but

Cecelia and Julitta c. 1925

she did better when she didn't have to read aloud to the class. She was a very hard worker. Cecelia was such a kind student. I felt as if she really cared for me. She even packed my lunch. I left after my third year, 1925, which was my last year of teaching.

Julitta and her daughter Richelle Pearl Koller attended a funeral in Freeburg. Richelle describes what happened after the service.

The funeral for Lena Ernster was over. Mother and I were walking the path from St. Peter's Church to the parish hall for the funeral luncheon. The crowd was beginning to lessen. Suddenly a tall, thin, elderly, white-haired woman hurried toward us, almost running up to mother. In a lisping, unclear voice she cried, "Teacher! Teacher! My teacher!" She hugged Mother and said with the same lisp,

"You are still alive!" She held my mother and looked at her with a beaming smile.

The woman was Cecelia Rover. Over seventy years earlier mother had taught her. Cecelia was about seventeen when mother came to teach in Freeburg. Cecelia had a speech impairment, and the former teacher had her crochet during school hours because she didn't believe Cecelia could learn.

Mother didn't think that was right. So mother began helping Cecelia to read and do her numbers. Cecelia wasn't dumb; she just couldn't speak well. Long before special education classes or the recognition of varieties of learning styles, my mother had an instinctual sense that every person can learn and has a right to have their world enlarged with the skills education provides.

Some seventy years later on December 16, 1993, Cecelia recognized, remembered, and honored my mother with the salute—"Teacher!"

After we had finished the interview, Julitta said, "Tom, are there any stories that I have told you that you think you might use in your book?"

I said, "Julitta, I have a teacher friend who says that every teacher should plant a garden. You could prepare your soil, plant whatever kinds of seeds you want, vegetables or flowers, water the seeds and nurture the plants. Then you could see the fruits of your labor, which you may never see as a teacher."

"Just think, Julitta, the seeds of self-esteem that you planted in Cecelia seventy years ago blossomed into that wonderful person. She could have called you Miss Schmitz, but...."

Julitta took off her glasses and began to cry. "But she called me teacher," she said proudly.

Miss Julitta Pearl's pearls, the Brownsville class, 1924

Country School Teachers

This book is about Country School Teachers like Julitta Pearl and Country School Students like Cecelia Rover. Their biographies are composites of all the stories told by the country school teachers and students I interviewed or who sent me their stories.

No one is sure when students first called out "Teacher," or where or when Country School Teachers were born. Official historical records are unable to document the birth because somewhere a few parents gathered their children in a log cabin hidden beneath towering virgin pines or in a sod house on the windswept prairie and called it "school."

Country School Students were born between the hills of Freeburg, in Mineral City, next to the Pigeon River, on the Angle Inlet, on the rich, black farm land of Martin County, and along the Minnesota, Mississippi, and Rainy Rivers.

Because Country School Students' parents knew the importance of education, wooden frame schools sprang up near towns like Starbuck, Adrian, New Prague, Goodhue, St. Vincent, Mountain Iron, and Finlayson.

Country School Students, speaking Swedish, German, Norwegian, Finnish, Icelandic, Czech, and many other languages carried their syrup pail lunch buckets on the famous walk to school.

Country School Teachers lived for more than one hundred years, dying whenever the county schools consolidated. Schools tucked away in remote places escaped consolidation until the 1970s.

Who were these teachers? Why have their biographies received so little fanfare in our efforts to research and document our history? Most counties have preserved at least one country school, designated it as an official historical site, dressed it with white paint, and filled it with desks and memorabilia of times past.

But teachers are not buildings. What *do* we know about the lives of Country School Teachers? No politician, professional athlete, or movie star gave Country School Students the gifts which Country School Teachers placed in their students' imaginations. Country School Students became farmers, teachers, artists, and leaders in all professional fields.

And They Called Them Teacher, Too

The earliest stories in this book are about Mona Brecker, age 101, Clare Wivell, age 100, Elvice Bloom, age 101, and Lillian Thisius, age 100. When these women began their careers, County School Teachers had existed for approximately seventy years. Therefore, the stories in this book date from 1915 until the 1960s when Country School Teachers died, retired, or took a different title.

From the moment five- and six-year-old first graders entered school until the eighth graders completed the dreaded state board tests, these rural students called this person "Teacher." Over the span of those one hundred and thirty years, Country School Teachers were counselors, disciplinarians, confidants, custodians, hygienists, and nurses.

The shadows cast across the room by the setting sun engraved images in Country School Teachers' memories. These shadows were filled with wonderful stories. Many nights they corrected papers by this light, recalling the day's adventures.
The Pink Schoolhouse outside Wells, Faribault County

Faces—what a place to mine stories!
Viola O'Day's class celebrates with a marshmallow outing: 1935, Loftness School, Marshall County.

Imagine the stories told on those rides home. "Today Dale came smelling like a skunk!" "Billy kissed Mary during recess!" "Eddie failed the State Board Examination in spelling. He spelled love, l—u—v!" **Evelyn Halverson's Grove Lake Consolidated School, 1926, Pope County**

The playground—what a stage for drama! "One day Billy climbed to the top of the bell tower and then screamed for help to get down." "Tony dug a pit by the outhouse the night before our game and you will never guess what happened." **School and playgound in Sauk Centre, Stearns County**

However, playgrounds, cars, and desks cannot tell stories. The history of Country School Teachers and Country School Students lives only in their memories. This book belongs to all the wonderful people who shared their stories—people like the five storytellers above who met at Doris Callahan's home in Albert Lea: (left to right) Doris Callahan, Blanche Olson, Nora Hendrickson, Mildred Dahl, and Mildred Jensen.

Country School Teachers seldom forgot shiny little nuggets that made them laugh and shake their heads in wonder.

Yikes!

I was teaching at a school three miles southwest of St. Thomas called the Meyer School. I went to school to get the fire started. As I opened the door, out pops this face covered with soot except for his white eyeballs, and a voice says, "Good Morning!" It took a while for me to catch my breath and gain my composure, but then I helped Clem out of the stove and sent him home to get some clean clothes.

Alice Burns Ronayne, c. 1920, Le Sueur County

Often Country School Teachers' stories capture moments that both teachers and students will remember for the rest of their lives.

I Hugged Her!

I always liked giving the kids a nice hug if they weren't feeling well. Something happened at Union Hill at the end of my teaching career that I had never experienced before. One day someone rapped on the door, and I went to answer it. The young girl said, "Is Joanie here?"

I said "yes" and she asked if she could speak to Joanie, who was only nine. The girl, who was Joanie's older sister, said, "Joanie, Pa died." Just "Pa died," nothing else. When Joanie left for school, her father was fine. Then at 11:00 her sister came and said just, "Pa died."

I took care of Joanie and helped her get dressed. Then I hugged her. She knew I felt bad. I can remember those two words—"Pa died." Her sister said them so matter-of-factly, like it was a chicken that had died, not a father. To a nine-year-old that could be a blow that would last forever. Evidently her sister was in shock, but their mother sent her to tell Joanie what had happened.

Years later she said, "That hug meant so much to me."

I believe in that stuff. I'm sorry. Now hugs like that are called harassment. Those two words, "Pa died," changed that girl and they also changed me.

Bea Slavik, Union Hill School, Le Sueur County: Bea Slavik lives in New Prague and taught for many years in the rural and public schools. If you want to hear more of Bea's stories, drop by the New Prague Hotel some morning for breakfast.

Chapter 2

District 57

Story Mining Begins

On a brilliant harvest morning two years ago, my Uncle Merlin Moore backed his 1928 Ford coupe out of the garage on his farm southwest of New Prague. He flipped down the rumble seat and my daughter, an elementary music teacher, and I climbed into that infamous "sin seat."

We headed for Verna Ziegenhagen's farm. Verna taught for fifty-three years, starting her career in a one-room school and ending those five decades in Le Sueur's public schools. My Aunt Evelyn, who sat in the front seat with her husband, was a third or fourth grader in Verna's first class in 1934.

My uncle shifted his coupe into gear and we headed for Verna's school. Through the cab window I watched the needle on the speedometer jiggle back and forth between thirty-five and forty miles per hour. We headed west past Heidelberg and then south toward Verna's farm, a short jaunt down a gravel road west of Lexington.

We pulled into a typical midwestern farm—a farmhouse, towering trees, and out buildings, all long abandoned by milk cows, chickens, or pigs. However, Verna's farm holds another treasure.

Verna walked out of the house as if she were ready to begin another day of teaching. She greeted us and led us through the trees out to several acres of neatly mowed grass. We turned the corner past the grove and there stood country school District 57, Le Sueur County.

The School

Verna bought the District 57 school building, which had been used as a corncrib for thirty-five years. The school is over one hundred years old. Although Verna never taught in this building, she has created a virtual replica of other country schools she taught in throughout the county.

Photographs documenting the rebirth of old District 57 line Verna's desk. The school was located about a mile and one-half from my grandparents' farm. Today it sits as it might have the first day it opened.

In the entry hang Verna's dresses. On the floor sit two syrup buckets used in the 1920s and 1930s as well as three modern-day lunch buckets, a miniature chronology of Verna's career.

On one side of the entry stands a sink which Verna purchased and her dad installed. Next to the sink sits a water crock, not the original one, but still an antique treasure, a gift from some of her students. The real thing was a five-gallon can which her students carried to the school. On the right side of the entry rests the wooden sled used for hauling firewood. Next to the sled stands the woodbox.

On the east side of the room is the pump organ. The schools had few pianos. They did not hold their tune when the temperature changed, and the schools got frigid on those bitterly cold winter nights. The pump organ, which is more than one hundred years old, was donated by a jeweler from Le Center who had it pulled in by covered wagon.

Old District 57 is filled with memorabilia from Verna's career: a picture of her entering the school on her first day, *McGuffey Readers*, and a picture of her first class. One of the students in the picture is my aunt, Evelyn O'Malley.

Spirits from the Past

The first thing that caught my attention was the threshold, worn down two or three inches from students stepping there as they moved from the entry into the one-room school.

What made this one-room school special was that sometime around the year 1900, my grandfather had stepped on that threshold as he entered school for the first time. Several years later a feisty five-year-old who would become my mother stepped on the threshold, and she was followed by my three aunts and three uncles.

That day as my uncle squeezed into one of the desks, I tried to imagine them as children, writing on the blackboards mounted near the six windows, reciting their alphabet and multiplication tables, and eating their lunches out of their maple syrup cans.

I wondered what tales they told as they ate their sandwiches. What ghosts were listening, waiting for just the right moment to speak through my uncle and aunt's stories? I wondered what they could say about my mother. Where had she sat and what did her voice sound like as she shouted "pig's tail, pig's tail" in frustration when she couldn't throw the ball over the school?

In 1934 at the age of seventeen, Verna Ziegenhagen began her teaching career.

The Long Mile

There were ten students in my first class. Those first ten children were always very dear to me because I was scared to death when I walked into the school. It seemed as if it was a mile from the back of the school to the front on that first day. I thought they were going to eat me alive, but even now we get together every year or two for dinner.

I was paid fifty dollars a month for the eight-month school year. With my first check I bought my dad a new suit and my mother a new winter coat, and I still had money left over for myself.

Suddenly Verna's demeanor changed. She put on her "time-to-get-down-to-business Country School Teacher's face." Magically, she swept us back to the 1930s. We took our places in the best fitting desks as Verna rang her bell, slapped her ruler on the desk three times, and announced:

"This school will come to attention." This is how all country schools began the day. First, I would ring the bell on the outside of the school about five minutes before school started which meant that everyone should hurry and get to school. The boys needed to put down their frogs and snakes and stop chasing the girls.

Then I would ring the bell again, tap the ruler three times, give the pledge to the flag, and then have some form of opening exercises—a Bible passage, a story or a song.

All the assignments were written on the board. There was to be no whispering, no wiggling in their seats. The boys sat on one side of the room and the girls on the other. All the children from one family went to the same school—brothers and sisters from five to eighteen were in the same school.

Students had to raise their hands to speak or answer questions. They would stand behind their desks with their hands behind them and wait to be called on. If it was a yes or no question, they had to say "yes, ma'am" or "no, ma'am"—not "ya" or "ya, I guess so." They showed respect.

When it was time to recite, they would again stand, come to the front of the room, face the chalkboard and the teacher, and then recite their work.

Day One

Verna began her first day of teaching in 1934 at the age of seventeen. Like every first-year teacher, she was nervous, but she also believed she was prepared for whatever the day might bring.

The photograph (upper right) shows Verna opening the door for her students on her first day of teaching in 1934.

I had just begun my lessons. It was the day after Kolacky Day. They sold beer on the streets and people got pretty well sloshed. This man was driving home from Kolacky Day and he was still hung over. He thought his car had stopped, so he opened the hood and stuck his fingers into the fan. The blades cut off one of his fingers. He came up to the school and knocked on the door. I opened the door and he held up his hand with the finger bleeding. Of course we didn't have any first aid supplies.

Verna got some rags from her home and dealt with her first teaching emergency. After teaching for fifty-three years, Verna has many stories to tell about life in the country schools.

He Flies Through the Air

In the winter time Vernon B. came to get his brothers and sisters. He had on his dad's coonskin coat. He backed up his sled and of course the runners went sideways. Then he loaded the kids into the sled. When he yelled at the horses to go, the sled straightened out. Well, he had such a tight hold on the reins, the horses yanked him right out of the sled. He just flew, flipped a complete somersault and landed in a huge snow bank. **Vernon flew about 1930.**

Another young man fell "head over heels," but this time it was a case of student-loves-teacher.

Love Is a Waiting Game

One of the boys in third grade was almost as tall as I was. He fell in love with me and he wrote me a note that said, "Will you marry me? I'll be waiting for your answer outside the window during recess."

At first I thought I wasn't going to answer him. Then I thought, "No, that wouldn't be very nice," so at recess time I went to the window and said, "Are you out there, Paul?"

"Yes," he said.

Then I said, "If, when you grow up, you still want to marry me, you come back again and then I'll give you an answer."

"OK," he said.

Of course, he never came back!

Then my Uncle Merlin Moore took over the storytelling. He attended District 57 from 1924 to 1929. His desk had shrunk and it pinched and squeezed him as he tried to get comfortable.

Shell Game

It was about 1927 and I was in the sixth grade. One day County Superintendent Poehler came to school. Gerald, an eighth grader, was a devil! There was a cornfield right next to the school. It was fall, so the corn was pretty mature. Mr. Poehler would usually stay during the recess and visit with the teacher while the kids were out playing.

Gerald got a cob of corn out of the field, shelled all the kernels, and shoved the cob up the exhaust pipe of the superintendent's car. The car killed again and again as

Merlin Moore, Evelyn Moore, and Verna Ziegenhagen.

he tried to drive it. More than once Gerald wore the print of the ruler across his ear. His teacher then was his cousin. She couldn't let him get out of hand. She had a ruler about a foot long and yea wide, real thin, and boy, she'd let him have it across the ear. That ear would get just as red as a beet, and after awhile a white welt would be rising.

He Kept on Writing

J. was writing on the blackboard next to a west window. I suppose he was probably in the second grade. Now the fall of the floor happened to be toward the back of the room. He was standing here writing and he didn't make a move at all. All of a sudden I saw this streak of yellow water running down the floor. Nobody said a word; nobody knew that he had just wet his pants. He was writing at the board and at the same time he wet his pants. He kept working on the blackboard.

They Were Real Devils!

About 1900 or so my dad had a man teacher who chewed tobacco who stayed about a half mile from the school. At noon time the teacher would go out while the kids were playing, and he'd walk that half mile and chew his tobacco. Dad was an altar boy at St. Thomas and these two brothers were devils. Well, the teacher wouldn't lock the school when he'd go out. Then they'd start ridiculing Dad about being an altar boy. When you were an altar boy, you'd come out and light the candles before Mass.

One day these brothers got mocking Dad being an altar boy. They took the broom and lit it on fire and they let on they were lighting a candle. They marched around and genuflected at the teacher's desk and pretended to light a candle up over it. They made like they were so holy and started praying. It's a wonder they didn't burn the school down.

Dad said that the teacher would be out walking and chewing, just walking and chewing. He had no idea what was going on in there.

Aunt Marietta (Moore) Sharkey

For years my aunt Marietta and I have exchanged stories about teaching. In the fall of 1995, I took her back to St. Thomas, where she began teaching as a teenager. Then we went to District 57, where she had been both a student and a teacher.

I was born in 1918, and I started school when I was five years old in 1923. We lived two and a half

Marietta Moore Sharkey

miles from school so we were taken to school every day of the year. Winters were so severe. I can remember going to Schumaker's Bridge and the snow was so deep the horses could not go through. We all sat on hay in the sleigh and covered ourselves with a blanket. Before we left home, Dad went down to the furnace in the basement and filled a little asbestos-covered container with hot coals. He put it in the middle of the sleigh and we sat in a circle with our feet against this hot heater.

We usually got to school at a quarter to nine and school started at nine. The big round stove was in the back of the room. The stove inside the jacket was red hot so we all huddled up against that jacket. Then we'd all take off our overshoes and put them under the jacket of the stove so when we went to get dressed in the evening, they'd be warm. We put our syrup pail lunch pails on the floor, and when we ate at noon, the sorghum bread was frozen.

Itching

The school was known as the "home of the itch." I had the itch from the time I started there until I graduated from high school. Nobody really knew what it was and no doctor ever came to check on us. Also we had some problems with lice. We'd be sitting there and a louse would drop out and run around, but we all survived. My poor mother took all the wool blankets and she treated us with this horrible, brown, smelly, god-awful stuff—sulfur. She put long underwear on us and we itched from the scratchiness of the wool and the sulfur. She'd just get us over the itch when somebody would come up with it again.

Little Devils

Everybody would like to think that we had a bunch of angels that went to school here. We had a gray-haired teacher by the name of Mabel Osborne. There was a spot here behind the stove where the boys used to stand when they were outside playing. Then they sang this little ditty:

> The rock upon the mountain,
> The fish upon the sea,
> The gray-headed teacher
> Is making a wreck out of me.

I often think of the torment she went through from those little devils.

The Queen of Sheba

When I was in the first grade, I could carry a tune better than anyone else in the school. When Miss O'Connell had the box social, the grand finale was me. Dressed in a white gauze dress, I sang "God Bless America." Then old Jim O'Connell bought my box. There was an orange in it, and when he peeled it for me, I said, "You know you'll have to be very careful because I can't get any spots on this dress." I was probably five years old then. I remember standing up on that stage as if I was the Queen of Sheba because I was dressed to kill. I had a crown on my head and there were flags behind me. I thought I had it made in the shade.

Like hundreds of children who were educated in the country schools, Marietta Sharkey completed teachers training and returned as a Country School Teacher.

Tight As a Fiddle String

In the fall of 1937, I started teaching in a one-room schoolhouse, District 77, in St. Thomas in Le Sueur County. I had forty children in one room. I was seventeen. I turned eighteen on the ninth of September. I had two or three days of teaching over when I turned eighteen because I had graduated from high school when I was sixteen. I made thirty dollars a month. The most I ever earned was forty. Each district had its own pay system. They got you just as cheaply as they could. My uncle was on the school board, and he was as tight as a fiddle string. Of course, if they could get me for thirty dollars a month and work me to death, that was OK. Even though I was his niece, I got no special treatment.

Marietta taught in St. Thomas for two years and then from 1939 to 1940, she returned to teach in her home school, District 57.

St. Jelly and Jam

One of my little girls was a real saint. Her family had six children in school at the same time. A. was the oldest girl but not the oldest of the children. I think she was in the fourth grade. She came with a loaf of sliced bread and a jar of jelly. When it came time for everyone else to get their dinner pails, she collected her little brood around her and jellied slices of bread and fed those kids. You talk about someone being a mother when she was in the fourth or fifth grade. She unabashedly, unashamedly cut this loaf of bread and they scarfed down their meal. They were just as much at home as if they were in their little two-room house.

On the way home I drove past what used to be my grandparents' farm—the most sacred place of my youth. Someone else now owns this land. The house, barn, and outbuildings were burned and bulldozed. The gravel road that sloped up the hill and twisted around the gigantic elm in the front yard is now a road to nowhere, fenced off by towering rows of corn. This place of birth and death, joy and pain, is now just moneyed dirt.

I stopped near the barren spot where District 57 had once stood. I looked toward my grandfather's farm and imagined my aunts and uncles on

Mother, back row left, first grade, age 7

their morning trek to meet Country School Teacher. Out in front, her blond hair dancing in the wind, Frances would be skipping along, waving her lunch bucket, and chattering away at any bird, cloud, or creature that would listen. In my mind the Moore children would always be young and carefree. Frances Irene Moore, the child, would grow up, marry, and become my mother. The shadow dancers disappeared and I drove on.

Chapter 3

Why Teach?

At the end of each interview, I asked every teacher, "Why did you become a teacher? When did you realize that you truly loved children?"

Malinda Wacholz Heaney attended Cloverdale School in Freeborn County from 1909 to 1917. She began her teaching career in 1924 at Sunny Brook School, District 118, Faribault County.

Malinda Heaney

All the World's a School
I always wanted to be a teacher. When I was in the first grade, I taught the pigs and the cows. I studied hard to reach my goals. When I first learned to write the numbers and letters of the alphabet, I pretended to be a teacher. I sneaked into the barn when no one else was there and pretended that the cows and horses were my pupils. I taught them what I had learned.

With a large nail I scratched the letters and numbers in front of the cow manger. I scratched

problems into the boards: 1+1=2 and 2+1= what? I also etched my spelling words with that nail. If the weather was nice, I used the east side of the granary for my blackboard, and the pigs in the nearby pen were my imaginary students. I thought they were answering me. They liked my teaching.

One day my dad discovered my handiwork, and I was informed in no uncertain terms that the walls of the buildings were not to be used as blackboards. When I was prohibited from going to the cow barn

or the horse barn or the pig barn, I moved my classroom to the maple grove. The trees and bushes were a more receptive audience. They nodded their heads if there was a gentle breeze. **Malinda Heaney, c. 1911, District 87, Cloverdale School, Freeborn County**

For forty-two years, Norma Jane Peterson Hollen comforted scared first graders on their first day of school. She taught for ten years in the country schools of Swift, Kandiyohi, and Pope Counties. She remembers her first day vividly.

Betrayed
I think I became a first-grade teacher because first graders usually cry on their first day, and I remember what my first day was like.

I didn't want to go to school. My birthday was in November, so I was five. My brother said, "I'll

give you a ride to school in my Model A. I'll drop you off, and you go in. I'll go up to the turnaround and come back to get you." They took me into the school and gave me this nice workbook. I remember what it looked like. It was black with red print and it said *Read* and then something else. And

Norma Jane Peterson

there were colored pictures in there and I did enjoy doing it. Then suddenly I closed the book and said, "No, he must be coming back now." I ran out of the school. I insisted I was going home. Then I saw my brother go by. I was so disgusted. He told me a lie. It wasn't that I didn't want to go to school. I didn't want to leave my mom. I was from a family of ten. After that day everything was fine. **Norma Jane Peterson Hollen, 1937, District 2, Pope County**

Hazel Amlie, Norma Jane's teacher on that day, was sitting next to her during this interview. Hazel had a few details to add to Norma Jane's attempted escape. Hazel taught for thirty-two years, fifteen in the rural schools of Pope County.

Gotta Get Goin'
It was 1936 and my first day in that school. There were no screens on the windows. At lunch I followed the procedure I had learned in teachers training: Put your hands on your desk. Turn. Stand.

Pass. That was the military way of leaving the schoolroom. I was busy following this procedure when suddenly a blur passed before me, and this first-grade girl jumped out the window and sprinted

Hazel Amlie, c. 1934

for home. Everyone ran after her to bring her back. She ran into a pasture where there was a bull. I sent her brother after her and he brought her back. Now the next year on the first day, I had Norma Jane as a first grader. On the first day she ran away from school. But she ran the wrong way. She was going north. She insisted she was going home, and I thought, "Oh, no, not another one after I had the problem with the other one last year who ran away."

I sent Norma Jane's sister after her and she brought her back. She became a wonderful student.

Hazel Amlie, 1937, District 2, Pope County

Louise Gruska
Louise attended grade school in Eveleth. In 1937 she began teaching at Buyck School in St. Louis County. In 1918 at age six, she learned her first letters. She made her four-year-old sister Olga sit next to her and they warmed their feet under the stove. Louise pointed at the letters RADIANT HOME embossed on the stove and made Olga repeat each letter. However, Olga often forgot the letters and became Louise's first disciplinary problem. When the frustrated four-year-old couldn't remember how to form the letter O, she rebelled, saying, "I'm not gonna play any more."

Cucumber School
I wanted to be a teacher from the time I knew what a teacher was. I had a school in my backyard all the time. Every summer I had this alarm clock going, ringing the bell and all the kids came down to our shed to play school, and I was the teacher. Once in a while I was the principal, but not usually because I wanted to be the teacher. We had some boxes for desks, and we put all the paper that we had saved from school in a little box, so we had plenty of

paper and all the bits of crayons the teacher let us take home, so those were our supplies. We sang and had a good time in there.

One summer day it was very hot and we were closeted in this woodshed. It got dark and all of a sudden there was this terrible storm. The hail came down and pounded on the roof so hard that we were all afraid. Then one little girl got hysterical and said, "Oh, I want to go home! I want to go home! I'm scared and I want my mother."

"Well," I said, "you can't go home. You'll get hurt if you go into that hailstorm. You stay here. Let's pray." So we all knelt down and we prayed. As soon as the storm was over, my mother came to see how we had fared. We were all right, but Ellen was still a little scared and crying, but she got over it. She was just scared of the storm.

Olga and Teacher Louise

I suppose I was ten or twelve years old. I was strict. Some of the boys escaped. They wouldn't stay but they came back the next day. I had adding and words. We didn't have much in the way of materials. I used to regret that later on because times were hard. We didn't subscribe to all kinds of periodicals the way people do now and we had very few magazines. I think it was more of a repetition of what they had learned already but it probably helped them because they weren't forgetting in the summer.

My mother always had a big garden, all kinds of veggies out there. Some boys said, "We'll come to school if you'll let us eat some of those cucumbers." I let them have all the cucumbers they wanted. And carrots. A few did come, not too many. They were foxy. They weren't too happy about sitting on a little box. They weren't that comfortable. I was pretty grown up, I suppose. When I was in junior high, I was still having a school every now and then. In the winter I'd have a couple of little girls come over and play school in the house. I wanted to be a teacher. That's all I had in my mind.

Vivian McMorrow completed her teachers training in Buffalo in 1939.

Not Just a Student

I'm not sure when I realized that I really loved children. During the Depression there was a family that

Vivian McMorrow leans against her trusty 1931 Chevy, which she bought in 1939 for sixty dollars.

had less than we had. I think I was a ninth grader. It was about 1934. This family's little girl must have been six or seven. She lived close to us so we often walked together. One day we were walking down the street, and she told me it was her birthday. I had a nickel, so I gave it to her. I felt good that I had something I could give her for a

birthday present. From that time on, her family fell all over me. They gave us molasses. They did everything for us because I had given her that nickel.

When I started teachers training, I was captivated by the glamour of being a teacher, not the love of children. At the end of the year, I was practice teaching. I had a little first-grade girl to work with for six weeks. I got to be so proud of her. I came to love her dearly.

That was my first feeling that she was a person, a child, not just a student. What an awakening! I loved the little girl, not the student.

Elaine Nelson taught from 1936 to 1937 in District 16, Arlington Township, Sibley County.

Inspiration

My first-grade teacher, Hazel Axeen, inspired me to become a dedicated teacher, and I was only five years old at the time. Ever since that time I knew I wanted to teach.

She did two things I remember vividly, which inspired me to feel this way. When the whooping cough epidemic hit the area in 1936, schools were closed for the whole month of December. She went from home to home, helping the students keep up

with their homework. There were twenty-two students in that one-room school, all eight grades. Needless to say, she was always very busy.

Then when she went home on weekends just fifteen miles away, she would take one student home with her for a visit. We got to sleep in her bed. I remember waking up in the morning with my feet in her face.

On Sunday morning we would go with her to church and attend eighth-grade Sunday School class, which she taught. The class was all boys, and I sat on a chair right next to her.

In 1928, Bertha Everson attended District 111 in Freeborn County. Bertha taught for ten years in the rural schools in Mower and Freeborn Counties between 1940 and 1956.

She Had Style!

I decided to become a teacher because when I was in third grade, I had a teacher who was so pretty and

Bertha Lunt Everson and Ardel Ward celebrate the end-of-the-year picnic, 1945, District 100, Freeborn County.

she wore quite short dresses and she always wore pleated skirts. She'd slither down the aisle, sashay, and all those pleats would swish back and forth, and I thought that was so neat. She also wore high heels, which was not very common for teachers in those days. I thought, "That's what I'm going to be, a teacher." She had a boyfriend who picked her up and we thought that was "swell," which was the expression used in those

days. I have talked to her and she says she had no idea she made that impression.

Arvalla Smith was a country school student in 1940 in District 1, Big Stone County. She taught from 1943 to 1946 in District 20, Golden Prairie School, in Traverse County. Throughout Arvalla's career she celebrated two "flag days."

Flag Day

I was a short, fat kid with a lot of allergies, not pleasing to look at. So at an early age my mother had to instill in me that "You are a person regardless if you have these things." So from day one I had to overcome these feelings and believe that "I am someone. I am important."

Once I was expelled from school because I had eczema with itching and that made the teacher nervous, so she sent me home. Mother took me back because she was determined I was going to have an education. So the teacher had me sit in the hall for the rest of the year, away from her and the other students. At that time I looked around and realized there were many kids that had troubles that prevented people from accepting them as they were. So I became determined that teaching was going to be my profession. I was going to help other people while at the same time helping myself.

Arvalla, fourth from left in the front row, toots her horn as a fourth grader in 1932.

My biggest disappointment was that my grandma didn't like me. I don't know if my looks made a difference to her, but one time she said to me, "Arvalla, if you get to be a teacher, I'll raise the American flag."

Well, the first day I taught in District 20, I called my grandmother and said, "Grandma, raise the flag! I am a teacher!" **Arvalla Smith, 1943, District 20, Traverse County**

Mom's Interview

When I was a senior, I applied for teachers training at Fergus Falls. The day I was supposed to have my interview, I became ill. The doctor sent me to the hospital. I went for lab tests at 7 a.m. so I couldn't go to my interview.

Mother said, "While you are having surgery, I'll go for your interview." Mrs. Kjaglien, who is the teachers training instructor, said it was the only interview she ever had with a parent. My mother wasn't keen on my becoming a teacher, but I wasn't going to let her tell me I couldn't be a teacher. I was surprised when Mother came to the hospital. She said, "I was really impressed. I'm glad you're going into teachers training." **Dia Ann Smidt**

Dia Ann Smidt completed her teachers training at Fergus Falls High School in 1950. Her mother may have passed the interview, but DiAnn became the teacher. This is Dia Ann's District 221 class in Otter Tail County in 1956.

Country School Teachers' response to the question, "When did you realize you loved children?" was nearly unanimous: "I have always loved children."

Chapter 4

Teachers Training

In the early days of the rural schools, it was possible for a student who had completed the eighth grade to begin teaching the following year with no formal training. Later, teachers were required to complete two years of normal school. Many normal schools held classes in local high schools. Eventually, most teaching candidates attended one of the state teachers colleges. After a rigorous nine months of training and a few weeks of student teaching, the seventeen-year-old to twenty-year-old graduates began the search for jobs. Many began in their "home schools," which were close to mom and dad and provided less expensive room and board.

Helen Haugen Lodes Merville attended the teachers training program in New Ulm from 1926 to 1927. Her instructor was Ida Koch. Ida's students all agree that she was a wonderful teacher but a stern taskmaster. According to Helen, Ida was "busy" and "tough."

'Fessin' Up
I was just sixteen when I started teachers training. Each one of us was appointed to take charge at one of the schools. Well, from the time I was a kid, I always did things I wasn't supposed to do. Because Ida knew I knew how to play the organ, she chose me to give the music lesson when she was gone for the day. She was checking other schools.

Helen Merville

Ida was very active when she played, feet pumping and arms swinging. Naturally, I tried to play as dramatically as she did. Trying to be smart and show off, I climbed up there and really pumped those pedals. Suddenly the strap on the pedal snapped. I was scared to death because she was so tough. I went down to the manual arts department and asked the kids—I didn't ask the instructor—if they knew how I could fix that pedal so she wouldn't know I had broken it. He put a nail through the broken strap, just enough to hold it.

The next time she played she stomped the pedals and dramatically pounded the keys. One day that nail popped up. All of us were petrified. I thought sooner or later she would find out so I confessed. I think she was so surprised by my confession that she couldn't get angry. She was tough, but I think she actually felt sorry for me.   **Helen Merville**

Doris Sather Erdahl completed her teachers training from 1929 to 1930 in Wheaton in Traverse County.

The Nasty One
Our teachers training instructor was harsh. She picked on one student constantly. If the girl didn't

give the right answer, she made a sarcastic remark about her not being very smart. The girl was just as good as the rest of us.

Our instructor was going with the dentist in town. When they had a fight, she would take it out on us, so we knew exactly when they were fighting. We could tell by her attitude when she walked in

Doris Erdahl, 1929–1930 the door. She was so belligerent. We could tell by the look on her face. She was very sarcastic and nasty. We didn't look for any kindness in her. She gave us low marks, mostly *C*s. When I went up to Moorhead with those low marks, the college teachers said, "Yes, we know her."
Doris Erdahl

Luva Wilson attended St. Cloud Teachers College from 1932 to 1933.

No Stopping Me
I completed my eighth-grade year during the Depression. My parents thought we were much too poor to go on to high school. I wore the same dress

to high school every day until Thanksgiving. On the weekends I laundered that dress and ironed it, and then I wore it again every day the next week.

When my parents saw how serious I was about going on to school, my aunt made me some more dresses. The times were so hard. I walked three and a half miles to school in Kimball. Sometimes if I got to the neighbor's house by 8:30, I could get a ride with him. That was wonderful!

But I loved school and I loved education. I wanted to get an education so I could make some money and help my parents. Nursing or teaching were the only options. **Luva Wilson**

Puff

When I went to practice teach, I was put with a smoker and in those days, smoking just wasn't done. She eventually got into trouble. I wanted to graduate so badly that I just couldn't put myself into that situation. I don't know if she ever completed school. I know they threatened her with not graduating. I did everything I could to separate myself from her. It was so bad. She must have really been addicted. She would open the window and then blow out the smoke. I don't know how she could take that chance. Sometimes it got very cold with the window open. **Luva Wilson**

In 1934, Pearl Jacobson Hanse completed normal training at the age of seventeen.

No Calculators!

When I went out to do my teachers training, the teacher gave the students a little arithmetic exercise. When the teacher stood up, all the kids stood up as well. Then she said, "Are you ready?"

"Yes!" they yelled.

At this time to dramatize her point, Pearl looked at me with her "teacher look," but I didn't realize I was to be the student.

In rapid fire Pearl said, "Here we go. Five times six, take away six, divide by three, add eight.

Pearl Hanse What's your answer?" Pearl looked at me for the answer. I sat there dumb as the proverbial doorknob. "Yes, you, now try it again."

Once more she gave a whirlwind of calculations. I hunched my shoulders in that "I haven't a clue" gesture.

Well, I couldn't do it either! The student teacher couldn't keep up with the children. Soon I learned how to do it. When I taught, we played that game every day. My students could do arithmetic with lightning speed. **Pearl Hanse, 1934**

Burt mastered the art of discipline on his parents' farm. There was no horsin' around with Mr. Kreitlow!

In 1935, Burton Kreitlow completed Cokato Normal School in Wright County.

Good Grammar

One day when I was in normal training, the state supervisor came to visit us. Everybody had been prepared by our teachers training teacher. The supervisor had me tell a story that was in the book. I'm certain the book was written with good grammar. This frog was blowing itself up and huffing and puffing. The frog blew itself up until it burst. Then I told my version of the story: "This frog got so big it busted and slammed all over!" Unfortunately, our teacher was in the room also. Boy, did I get it for using bad grammar. Well, did they want a good story or good grammar?

Burt Kreitlow became a master storyteller who has been spinning yarns to students of every age for over fifty years.

Laurabelle Martin completed the teachers training program from 1934 to 1935 in Renville.

Surprise!

Our instructor, Martha O'Connor, was very stern and strict. Once she told one of the girls in our class not to talk so much. One of the boys quit after the first few weeks. I remember he couldn't learn the difference between transitive and intransitive verbs. Right after that he never returned.

One day I was practice teaching. When Miss O'Connor walked in, the students began to change immediately. She sat for awhile and then walked up to me and said, "You look so tired. Let me finish teaching the assignment." I went to the back of the room and listened.

What really surprised me was what happened afterward when all the student teachers were gathered after we had finished teaching our classes. Miss O'Connor commented about how well I had presented and taught my lesson. She never mentioned that she had taught most of it. I didn't know whether to tell my friends or keep quiet. I thought it best to take the compliment and keep it to myself.

Laurabelle Martin

Ruth Domingo completed her teachers training at Appleton Normal School in 1936.

Revenge

My teachers training teacher made a great impact in my life. Maud, our teacher, was stern, demanding, but loving, too. The entire experience was very difficult. Our day was so full we didn't have time for anything else and this angered some of the people. She kept us working from eight in the morning until six at night. Then we had homework. But I thought she was a wonderful teacher. She gave me everything I ever needed to be a good teacher.

One gal hated Maud. On Valentine's Day, she made a batch of chocolate candy filled with Ex-lax. Our bathroom was on the third floor. Usually our teacher never left our classroom. But that day she had to make trip after trip to the third floor.

The girl brought candy for everyone and passed it around. She brought a special little box for Maud and put it on her desk. She never expected her student had laced the candy with the laxative. The girl got quite a kick out of Maud having to go up to the bathroom many times that day.

We had no idea what was causing this until the end of the day when our classmate told us what she had done. I thought it was a dirty trick. Maud sensed that this girl was the cause of her problem and that put her out of Maud's good graces for the rest of the year. That girl never did learn to be a good teacher. But I loved Maud. **Ruth Domingo**

In 1936, Marge Abbott completed her teachers training in Pine River in Cass County.

It's Show Time

One evening a group of us girls in the teachers training program decided we were going to go to

Marge Abbott, c. 1937

the show instead of doing our lessons for the next day. When we got to the show house, there was Miss Henry, our teacher. We didn't think too much of it until the next day. Of course she pointed out to the rest of the class where we had been and that we were really in trouble. Every time she asked a question she pointed to one of us girls. We weren't prepared so we had a very rough day that day. We learned never go to a show or any thing else on a school night because we had so much studying.

Make or Break

When I went out to do my student teaching, I went back to Crow Wing County for the two weeks. We were told that we were to observe one week and then teach one week. When I got back here to do the student teaching, I was sent out to a little school on Highway 45, which was Mr. Wooden's, my cousin's, school. When I found that out, I stayed in town with his family. The first day he took me out there and said, "This is my school and you have all eight grades to teach. I want you to observe what I'm doing today."

There was a family that went to the school, and these children were just as happy as could be until the school bell rang. Then one little guy started in crying and he cried for hours and hours. My cousin said, "You're going to have to contend with this."

I thought, "This is going to be something. My cousin has been here for so many years and still that child is crying." The next morning he took me out there and said, "This is it! You're either going to make a good teacher or a poor teacher."

I argued that I was supposed to observe for a whole week. "No," he said, "you had your day."

Well, the same thing happened. This poor little

guy began crying just as soon as that bell rang. He cried and fussed every minute of every day. Every day I went home and told Aunt Liz, "Clarence is really mean. He shouldn't put me through all this."

Then she would say that if I really wanted to be a teacher, I would have to do what her brother tells me to do because he had the experience and he knew how to teach. Then I'd argue, "But he's doing all kinds of things he isn't supposed to be doing, things that I was told wouldn't be happening in my student teaching."

Well, I didn't get anywhere with the boy. I tried everything under the sun to get him to stop, but when the two weeks were over, he did the same thing. My cousin said, "Don't worry about it. He's done that for four years with me."

I have thanked my cousin for many years because he really made a teacher out of me. It was make a teacher or break a teacher, and I became a very good teacher in my day!   **Marge Abbott**

Vivian McMorrow learned about "the way it should be" during her teachers training in Buffalo from 1938 to 1939.

A Muddy Lesson

When I was doing my teachers training, my supervisor visited to see how I was doing. I wanted everything to be perfect. One of the kids tracked in some mud and I picked it up. One of her criticisms for the day was that I should not have cleaned up the mud. I should have made the kid do it. I wanted to make sure it was done. I wanted to impress her that I had a clean school and that I had control.

That lesson stuck with me. If she said, "That's the way it should be," then I believed that's the way it should be. It made me realize it was my students' job as well to take pride in the building, not mine alone. They had to learn to be responsible.

Vivian McMorrow completed her teachers training in the spring of 1939 and began her teaching career that fall.

In 1941, Yvonne Gagnon completed her teachers training in Buffalo in Wright County. Yvonne's training was conducted by a tyrannical instructor, who struck fear in her students. Many of her students withered under the teacher's imposing stature and unrelenting stare. Yvonne soon discovered why she was called "The General."

The General

On Monday morning my father took me back to school. For some reason we were delayed a bit.

Yvonne Gagnon, c. 1941

School had just started when I walked into the room. "Miss Sexton," the General said, "pull a shade down so I can murder all of you in peace this week." Then we knew it was really going to be a challenging week! One of the first things she said was that we were going to work very hard and if we weren't prepared to do that, we should drop out right then. She said that she would give us four years of education in a year. If we didn't want to take that, this was no place for us. We worked until two o'clock each night, and we worked all weekend. During Christmas vacation she gave us enough assignments to keep us busy for two weeks. She was a very intelligent tyrant. She taught us so much. We knew when we left, we were well prepared and we could go out to the country schools and know how to teach.

Yvonne learned more than teaching methods from the General. On November 11, 1941, Armistice Day, Yvonne learned something about herself and the General.

Obsession

I had gone home for the weekend. I had packed my clothes the night before and left them near an open window. The rain and snow had blown in, so I had to dry the clothes above the kitchen stove before Dad took me to town. When we left home, the weather wasn't too bad. By the time we got to Buffalo and I left my things at the boarding house and got to school, it was quite unpleasant. As the storm grew worse, someone knocked at the door of the teachers department.

The General

They said they were going to let all the children go home because the furnace had gone out.

Our teacher turned around and said, "Good teachers stay in their position. You stay right here." She kept us there until four o'clock. By the time we left, the drifts were hip high. I had a satchel of books and another arm full of books. I had to walk four blocks and another girl walked with me for three blocks.

We got about halfway home and she said, "I just can't go on any farther. You just go on. I can't." She laid on the snow. Well, I knew I couldn't leave her there, so I half carried her. Some of the snow was hard because it had drifted, so we just lay on the snow and rested a few minutes. Then we trudged on a few more yards and rested again. We both held onto our books. Somehow I carried her to the place. She would have frozen to death.

The next morning I stayed in bed. I thought there wouldn't be any school because it had snowed so much. After we had eaten breakfast, my landlady said, "Well, now, I'll give you your books and you'll have all day to work on them." About four o'clock she told me that the teacher had called her in the morning and told her that the teachers training students were having school, but my landlady didn't tell me because she didn't want me to walk back to school.   **Yvonne Gagnon**

Arvilla Hinseley was eighteen when she completed her teachers training in Le Center in Le Sueur County.

Too Much "Noise"
Our teachers training instructor had been a professor at the University of Minnesota before coming to Le Center. She was a typical college professor. One day one of the girls was presenting a class in geography and using the map. She pronounced *Illinois* as *Illinoise*. Our instructor cut right in with her gruff voice, shook her ruler at the girl, and said, "There is no *noise* in *Illinois*." The girl then continued her presentation, but whenever she had to say *Illinois*, she again said *Illinoise*. She tried to say *Illinois*, but she couldn't break her habit. No doubt her teacher in grade school had not corrected her. Every time she had to say *Illinois*, she became very upset. She had a difficult time finishing her lesson.   **Arvilla Hinseley**

In 1946, Geraldine Massmann earned her teachers training certificate in Canby in Yellow Medicine County.

Boarding House Banter
When we were in teachers training, five of us girls lived at the boarding house. We shared one large room. Our landlady thought a 25-watt bulb was bright enough for us to do our homework at night. We knew it wasn't so we put in a bigger light bulb but that disappeared every morning. Our landlady thought it cost too much to use a larger bulb. So we removed our big light bulb every morning and put in the 25-watt bulb. Then as soon as we got home at night, we screwed in the big bulb, did our work, and then screwed the 25-watt bulb back in before we left for school. Our landlady thought she had won.

We played tricks on one another. We put all our school materials in paper bags. They were filled with our pictures, worksheets, supplies—everything we used in class. When we had gone to bed, we heard a noise that sounded like a mouse in our bags. We listened. It was a mouse! We got up and went through everything to find that mouse.

We went back to bed again and heard the noise again. Two of the girls had taken a piece of string and a spool, stuck the spool in a bag, and when we got into bed, they pulled the spool. It rattled the paper just like a mouse.   **Geraldine Massmann**

Nolan Sorenson farmed for eight years before he began teachers training. His mother, a teacher, and the county superintendent recommended teaching as a career. In 1948, Nolan began normal training. Nolan said, "They evidently thought that anyone who wished to teach in a one-room school

would need training in order to be normal."

Nolan's classmates, ten young women, had been fourth graders when he graduated from high school, making him feel like an aging senior citizen. Nolan entered the classroom to begin teacher training in East Grand Forks in the fall of 1948.

Nolan Sorenson, c. 1948

Nolan wrote the following poem to celebrate his initiation into the teachers training program.

Alone

This was the plight of a farm boy—
He had been for the past ten years.
Should he casually walk into the room
In spite of all his unanswered fears?

He paused briefly at the classroom door
To wonder who he would see.
This was all so new to him
But today that him was me.

It was certainly a possibility—
Could it really happen to him?
The sound of voices from the room
Made prospects seem mighty dim.

He shyly looked into the gathering.
The door opened "to his doom,"
Classes to tolerate for a year—
Only girls were in that room.

Nolan Sorenson must have made a good decision. He taught for thirty-six years, four in District 24C, Abel Nelson School, Clearwater County.

George Klomp taught in Fillmore County from 1949 to 1950.

Don't Do It My Way

I was working with a group of third graders during my normal training. Arthur just would not sit where he was supposed to. He turned around in his seat and did anything and everything. My teachers training instructor came in and watched me. I had Arthur sitting next to me. When he moved, I reached over and put my hand on his shoulder and told him to sit down. My instructor said, "You shouldn't have to do that. Let me teach the unit."

Well, she put Arthur right across from her. He began twisting and turning around. She reached out and pulled him closer to her. Well, he stood up. She reached over and grabbed him by his hair—he had a little butch haircut—and picked him right off the ground and set him down.

He looked up at her and said, "You think you're tough, don't you?" She turned and walked out.

George Klomp, Fillmore County

Norma Jane Peterson Hollen attended teachers training in Glenwood in Pope County from 1949 to 1950.

Line Drawings

We had to make sure we were wearing nylons. Our teachers training instructor always inspected our legs to make certain we were. At that time the nylons had seams up the back. One of the girls could not afford nylons. When she came to school without them, the instructor told her, "You must go home and put nylons on."

Well, she didn't have any. So we went to the bathroom and drew what looked like seams up the backs of her legs with an eyeliner. She looked as if she were wearing nylons. The instructor thought she was wearing them so she got to student teach.

Norma Jane Peterson Hollen, 1950

Mmmmmmm, I'm just egging you on, Miss Peterson.

Glug! Glug! Glug!

When I was student teaching, one of the boys ran home for lunch. When he came back, he had three raw eggs. He cracked an egg, held it about six or eight inches above his mouth and let the raw egg slide down into his mouth. He had it down to a real science. I'm certain he wanted to gross us out, and of course he did. Everyday he ate those three raw eggs. He went home and brought them back to school every day. He wouldn't eat the eggs at home because he wanted to make certain the other gal who was student teaching and I saw him.

Norma Jane Peterson Hollen, 1950

Chapter 5

I'm Just a Bit Past 100!

The teachers in this chapter are all over one hundred years old. They began their teaching careers while World War I raged throughout Europe. Some taught for more than forty years.

1915

About the time Country School Teachers were preparing their teaching materials for the fall, the German submarine U-20 sank the *Lusitania*. While they taught that year, British and Australian troops suffered severe losses at the Gallipoli Peninsula and German submarines blockaded Britain. D.W. Griffith's *Birth of a Nation*, starring Lillian Gish, made film history. The Joseph Campbell Company bought Franco-American, Kellogg introduced 40% Bran Flakes, and the one millionth Ford rolled off the assembly line. In 1915, Elvice Bloom from Chisago Lakes began her great adventure.

Elvice Bloom

Elvice Bloom was born in November of 1895. She graduated from St. Paul Central High. She then went to St. Cloud for normal school training. Once twenty-year-old Elvice Bloom stepped on the train to her first teaching job, she lost touch with the world of international politics, movie theaters, and anything outside the "Big Woods."

A Trip North

My first school was in Floodwood in St. Louis County. I didn't know where Floodwood was or that the people were all Finnish. I took the train from St. Paul to Duluth and then to Cloquet. Then I took another train from there to Floodwood. The place where I was staying sent their oldest son to meet the train. He said, "Are you the new teacher?" He took my trunk and took me to the house. The people up there were all lumberjacks. I made sixty-two dollars a month. They had to pay well because Floodwood was way up in the woods. It was a one-room school. I had sixteen students and they were all Finnish.

They talked Finnish, but they had to learn to speak English; however, when they got out on the playground, they spoke Finnish. Sometimes the children would come in to me and say, "The big boys are talking about you." The teacher who had taught them the year before—nobody stayed more than one year because of the conditions—told them, "Don't talk Finnish out on the playground."

The parents did not speak English. I was expected to visit every home. When I came, the children would be interpreters. I talked to the mothers through the children. The parents wanted their children to learn English. They knew they had to learn English, but they wanted them to keep up with their Finnish, too. There was also one English family and one Polish family.

The automobiles were so new, and when they could hear an automobile come, everybody ran to the window to see the car go by.

I had no information about the war because there were no radios or television and nobody took a newspaper. My mother wrote to me every week. I had a long letter from her, and she would tell me if someone I knew had died in the war.

The Great Outdoors

I had never been in those big woods and I was really nervous. I had another girlfriend, who taught in another rural school about eight miles away. I had walked over to visit her so when I came home, it was dark. I walked eight miles over and eight miles back. When I came into the house, the people said, "Wohhhhhh, did you know you went under a tree and there was a big bear right up in the tree?" One night when I came home from school, it was dark. I walked the half mile, and I could hear something running on the other side of the fence. I said, "I wonder what was following me home?" They said, "It probably was a wolf." Once I was walking through a pasture and I was chased by a ram. I thought he was going to butt me. I had to crawl under the fence in a hurry.

Plenty "Colt"

I boarded in a great big house. The living room was so big they held dances in it. I had a little tiny bedroom. I had to do my own cooking. I had a packing box for a table and a spring cot for a bed and a little wood-burning stove with a top on it. The mother, who was a widow, used to come in before I got out of bed and build up the fire. It was really cold at night. And then she'd come in and she'd say—she just talked Finnish, she couldn't talk English, and she'd say —"Colt, it colt, nort wind."

She really didn't need to tell me it was "colt."

Surprise!

I came home only once that year, at Christmas. At Thanksgiving I had a big surprise. The guy I was going with at St. Cloud came walking down the country road carrying his suitcase. Another rural teacher, who was a friend of mine, had come over to spend Thanksgiving with me, and we were riding on a sleigh, pulling a pile of wood. I was embarrassed to see him walking along the road. I wasn't very serious about him, but he was about me.

I stayed in Floodwood one year.

Elvice Bloom began her teaching career in 1915 and she retired in 1963. She taught first grade for forty-four years.

A Grand Career

I always enjoyed teaching. I got a good feeling from it. I always prayed for patience. On the way to school I prayed for patience. I did a lot of praising. I think that helped with the first graders. Well, I worked hard and I loved my teaching and I loved my children. I went home for noon lunch, and sometimes all the little kids would come over and sit on my porch. When I went back to school again, they all wanted to hold my hand.

When they were Country School Students and Teachers, perhaps Mona Breckner and Clare Wivell had a desktop that looked something like this. What treasures these pages held!

Clare Bakke Wivell

Clare Bakke Wivell is the daughter of Norwegian immigrants who settled in central Minnesota near Lake Mille Lacs. Clare was born in 1896, one of five children. Clare is a unique educational historian whose expertise is the log cabin school in the forested area south of Lake Mille Lacs at the turn of the century. Clare completed teachers training at McIntosh High School.

When her grandson Scott and I interviewed her, we did not realize that this one hundred-year-old queen of the one-room rural schools would focus her story on a detailed journey through the first few grades of her grammar school years.

O Pioneers

I was born a few miles north of Isle, but at that time there was no Isle at all because it was all woods. Our schoolhouse was built of logs, about three miles from our house. At first there were no roads, just the school built in the woods, no road or anything. Later we had the roads built by the lumber companies. They were full of rocks and mud puddles and roots. Later the state made one straight road east and west. Then they built a new school located on that road. Then we were only two miles from school.

Because the area was unsettled or new country, the school was not built until 1905, when Clare was nine and her brother Arldt was seven. As a result, both began first grade at the same time. When her grandson asked her to tell about her grade school years, our history lesson began. When Clare described that magic moment almost ninety years ago, her eyes lit up and her voice was filled with awe and wonder. We were suddenly right there as the teacher gave them their first books—one for Arldt and one for Clare.

My First Book

The teacher, a young girl from Stillwater, on the first day handed each of us a first-grade reader. Oooooooooh, boy, new books with pictures in them! Were we interested! We wanted to learn something about the people who were in those pictures. We thought we could read it so we took our books home. We studied together and memorized words. We studied the first page until we knew every single word that was on that page.

Then the next day we carried the books back to school, of course, but the teacher didn't pay any attention to us. She had us busy because we were looking at our books. That evening we took our books home again, and we studied until we knew every word on the second page. We kept that up and we learned the words as we went along. After only a week and a half we knew a lot of the pages.

Then one day my brother raised his hand and asked, "Teacher, please may I read?" She hadn't paid any attention to us except to give us the books. So Arldt stood up near his desk and he started on the first page. He read and he read, turned pages, turned pages. At first the children were watching. Pretty soon they were all laughing aloud because he had read so many pages.

Then she said, "That will be enough for today. But you may read again another time." But that other time never came because after three weeks, the weather became rainy, and we couldn't walk in the rain and the mud. We stayed home, but we had the books with us. So we still went on reading and studying at home. It went that way the rest of the year. So three weeks was all the schooling we had, but we knew the whole first-year reader.

Second Grade
In 1906, the second year, the teacher gave us each a second-grade reader. Well, that was just as interesting. So we started the same thing. This new teacher didn't pay any more attention to us than the first-grade teacher had. She never called on us to read aloud in class. It was just Arldt, I, and the two books. We learned everything in those books. That was all the schooling we had the first two years—only the books.

All the rest of the grades were the same. We missed a lot of school because of the snow. They didn't keep the roads plowed during those days (1907–1913). Besides that, many people had tonsillitis—aching and pus and the tonsils would open up. We stayed home part of the time also because we had tonsillitis and the measles.

Pocketknives and Library Books
The boys were anxious about getting their pocketknives, the ones where the blade closes in the handle. My brother and all the boys were so proud when they got their knives.

You know what I mean? And when they got 'em, boy, they played all those games with the knives, but I can't remember the names of any those games. Then they carved their initials everywhere, even in many trees! Oh, yes, they carved some initials in the desks, too, but they were careful to put them in a place where it didn't show. They had their names carved everywhere, it seemed.

And in my home school the boys made their own skis and brought them to school, and all the children—well, not the girls—compared their skis; that was a big subject!

While the boys were doing that, we girls were reading. I read many library books. There was one book, *The Girl of '76*. There was an apostrophe. It meant 1776, but the 17 was left out. Well, I didn't understand that was the year. I thought it was her age. And I thought it wouldn't be interesting to read about a girl who was seventy-six years old. Later I found out it referred to politics in our country.

Clare told that story with a deadpan look. Then she broke the unflappable teacher mask and laughed with gusto. I got the impression she had told that story more than once.

What Did You Learn in School Today?
When her grandson asked her what they had taught her in normal school, she shrugged her shoulders, paused a moment, and then became Scott's teacher, not his grandmother.

Teacher Clare Wivell may have had the same books that lined Verna Ziegenhagen's desk: a copy of the state curriculum, McGuffey's Eclectic Reader, her book on effective teaching techniques and other worn favorites.

They taught us how to ask questions. I remember one thing they said: "How did Minneapolis become a great center for flour?"

She looked at her grandson, who assumed she was just giving an example, but then she asked the question more emphatically, playing the role of the teacher.

"How did Minneapolis become a great center for making flour?"

Her grandson looked like a seventh grader suddenly awakened from a wonderful daydream. He pulled back, cocked his head, and said, "You're asking me?"

She knew her art. She just waited.

"Well," he said, "because it was located on the river, and ahhhhh...."

He paused a bit too long for the teacher, who waved her index finger the way teachers do. Then with great emphasis and years of practice, she filled in the missing information when a student falters with the fatal "and ahhhhh."

"It was located in great fields, where farmers raised great fields of grain. That's the kind of question we were taught in normal school."

Clare's Schools

Then Clare listed the schools at which she had taught: Osclun Community School, Hillman, Cloverdale. There were others but she could not remember them. The stories about her teaching experiences seem to have faded with time, or perhaps they were just waiting for another day.

1917

In 1917, World War I touched all corners of America. Four million recruitment posters appeared showing a stern Uncle Sam pointing his finger and exclaiming, "I Want You!" In April the United States declared war on Germany, and the Conscription Act was passed in May. Unrestricted U-boat attacks began. Americans sang "Over There" and "You're in the Army Now." In Washington women marched in support of an amendment for women's suffrage. David Sarnoff marketed a single radio box. V.I. Lenin led the Bolshevik revolution in Petrograd. T. S. Eliot wrote "The Love Song of J. Alfred Prufrock." Mona Breckner completed her normal training and began teaching in Goodhue County.

Mona Breckner

Mona Breckner's father was born on the Isle of Man. He worked as a ship's galley boy and came to the United States in 1858, settling in Goodhue County. Mona was born on November 25, 1895. From 1900 to 1907 she attended District 108 in Cherry Grove Township near Kenyon in Goodhue County.

Mona Breckner, grade one, is first on the left.

The Fainting

During the winter term the older boys who had not completed the eighth grade came to school and that was the most problematic time for the teacher. They didn't have much of a feeling for education.

They were there to have a good time. There might have been as many as twelve or fourteen boys. There were always discipline problems. There was one boy who was such a troublemaker and the teacher had such a hard time with him. He used to torment the children on the playground during the recess and noon periods. She got pretty upset.

She was a big person and well trained. She was not afraid to try to talk sense into this kid. Well, he was a smart aleck, a bully, and he had all the kids scared to death because he really manhandled them.

Once she caught him and called him into the schoolroom and had a bout with him. I think he attacked her because he was a big, strong guy. When we came in at the end of the noon recess, she had fainted. She was lying on the floor, and he had run out the back door and disappeared in the group of school kids. He didn't leave the grounds, but he was frightened. I don't think he touched her. I think she got upset and couldn't handle him in conversation, and she knew she couldn't think of handling him any other way.

Apparently he backed her into a corner. She had fainted before in certain circumstances. Anyway, she was lying on the floor when we came in. I sent one of the little guys back to the house where she was boarding and asked to have the man come immediately. I didn't know what to do, but we did pull her out from behind the door because she was kinda jammed back there. We knew he backed her into the corner and intimidated her. He certainly had her buffaloed.

The man came and excused the school and took her home. He was not a member of the school board, but he reported immediately to my father, who was the chairman.

They expelled the boy and told him if he ever raised any objection, they would bring him into court for attacking the teacher.   **c. 1907, District 108**

In the spring of 1917, Mona completed her teachers training, and in the fall she was hired for her first teaching assignment in the Foss District of Holden Township.

We Never Quit
At the close of that school year, we were preparing for the state examinations for the seventh and eighth

Mona Breckner, c. 1917

graders to be eligible for admission to high school. There were four or five candidates, and this one young boy, Norman, wanted to take the history examination. Norman was sure he could pass, so he tried. When the examination hour was over, Norman came to my desk with his papers. I asked him how he did. He frowned and said that he was stumped by one question. It asked what the capital initials A.E.F. stood for, relating to World War I. I asked him what he thought they meant.

He thought and thought, and finally he said he guessed they meant "Americans Everlastingly Fight."

When I told him they stood for American Expeditionary Forces, he responded, "I never *heard* of that name."   **1917, Foss District, Goodhue County**

Mona's father bought a farm near Hallock and her brothers went there to farm the land. Mona went north to be with them during the winter, teach during the school year, and help them in the summer months.

A Steed Indeed
During the fall and spring, I drove a pony out to the school because they had a barn. During the winter I lived in town. I had a pony that wasn't too dependable, an exotic kind of a guy, and he just wanted to have his own way about a lot of things. I was careful about not getting him excited. Otherwise he was a pretty good guy.

I drove the last mile to the school. It was a highway that was fenced in on both sides. It was such a narrow roadway. I had a little trouble if I met anybody, especially if the weather wasn't so good.

I saw something ahead was moving and the horse saw it too. His ears perked up and he began to prance. I thought, "I don't know what I'm going to get into here, but something's up there ahead. It was a flock of five or six hundred sheep being moved from one pasture to another. They filled the road. Here was my exotic steed, standing on his hind legs, looking this thing over.

I thought, "I'm not going to get down. I'm going to hang on, and I'm going to talk to him a bit and tell him, 'Steady, steady.' Sure enough, we met that flock head-on. I've never seen so many sheep piled on top of each other in one horde. They belonged to James J. Hill, the railroad tycoon, who had bought lots of land up there. They were moving his sheep from one of his farms to another.

I stopped the horse and the sheep piled around us. There were black sheep running on top of the rest. The horse just accepted it. When they went past, he just picked up and we went on our way to school. It was just one of the things you had to be ready for on a common school day.
     1919–1920, near Hallock, Kittson County

I asked Mona why she became a crusader for the welfare of others, especially children.

My father came to Castle Rock in 1858. He made a deal with the judge of probate to help Scandinavian newcomers. He bought twenty to thirty eighty-acre parcels and signed them over to immigrants for no interest, the farm to be paid for when possible. Many exchanged labor for land and many times he simply gave the farms away when they couldn't pay. My father taught me compassion.

Mona became the district representative for the State Children's Bureau and the executive secretary of Child Welfare. Later she became supervisor of Minnesota's Emergency Relief Administration. Eleanor Roosevelt selected her to coordinate Minnesota's efforts in the Matanuska Project in Alaska. In 1942 Mona became a representative of the League of Nations and was assigned to China.

1918
Lillian Treptow Thisius taught during historic times. During her first year came the armistice ending World War I. Approximately a week before Lillian stepped into her second school, women's suffrage became law when Tennessee ratified the Nineteenth Amendment. That fall women helped elect Warren Harding to the Presidency. That year the first Miss America beauty queen was crowned in Atlantic City. F. Scott Fitzgerald, twenty-three, published *This Side of Paradise*, and Sinclair Lewis wrote his famous satire of small-town life, *Main Street*.

Lillian Treptow Thisius
Lillian was born in 1896 on a farm northwest of Wells in Faribault County. She took her teachers training during her senior year and completed her certification in the spring of 1918.

A Teaching Family
There were nine children in our family, six girls and three boys. Five of us girls were teachers. My dad took some of us to our boarding houses on Sunday night because he couldn't get us to all the different schools the next morning. All the money that we earned we gave to our parents to buy shoes and pay dentist bills for the rest of the family. We were happy to be able to do that.

The Facts of Life
In my first year I was so surprised to find that in the spring and fall the parents kept the big children out of school to work in the fields, the girls as well as the boys. The eighth graders weren't in school, so obviously they were not able take their state board examinations.

Consequently, they couldn't go on to high school. I worried so much about these students and worked so hard helping them catch up that I weighed only 109 pounds at the end of the school year. I was totally exhausted by spring.

We felt sorry for the children, but we never asked the parents about this. We just hoped the children would come. You didn't boss the parents. But many of these children who just went through the eighth grade became great farmers. They had learned to read and write.

When Johnny Came Marching Home
I was teaching at District 40, the Pink School, on Nov. 11, 1918, the day World War I ended. One of the school board members came from Wells to tell me that school was dismissed because the war was over. The people where I boarded came with a horse and buggy to get me and we all went into town to celebrate. Bells were ringing, the siren was blowing, and people in the streets were clapping. The next day we talked about what the end of the war would mean when all the boys came home. That was good!

We all rejoiced to hear the news. There was a letting down, too, from the heights to which they had attained. There was now a silence in place of the bugle call to duty, a duty to which their spirits had become attuned. Our boys had served, had lived, and had given. I knew one young man as a dear friend who died overseas in the war. His memory is very dear to me.

The Pink School near Wells where Lillian Thisius received the news that World War I had ended.

Chapter 6

The Initiation

Rural Teachers Wanted

"Local school boards are looking for seventeen-year-old to twenty-year-old graduates of nine-month normal training to teach in isolated one-room schools. No married teachers need apply. Salary will be negotiated as low as we can possibly get it. No fringe benefits.

"Finding room and board is teachers' responsibility. We suggest you bring warm winter wear and a hearty constitution as nearest boarding possibility is one mile from school. No guarantees are provided that people boarding teachers are not eccentric. Board is not guaranteed. Beds free of crawly creepy things are also not guaranteed. On occasion snow or sand may blow through window casings. Heat and hot water may be found in kitchen. Private bathing will be done in living room before family awakens.

"Teachers are responsible for chopping wood and carrying coal into school, hauling water from nearby farm if the well malfunctions, starting stove, and banking stove at night.

"Teachers should sharpen skills for hunting small game such as mice and other rodents. Teachers should be prepared for all kinds of devious student behavior. They must possess the skills to discipline students who are a year or two older than they are."

Country School Teachers signed their contract enthusiastically. But sitting on the elevated chair behind the teacher's desk was not the same as sitting in the shiny student desks!

The Banquet

Years later when the country schools had been consolidated, the Country School Teachers held a great banquet to celebrate their careers. Because the teachers are generous and forgiving, they invited the Great Gods of Country School Teaching, who returned their RSVPs with gusto.

As the teachers reminisced about those "good old days," the gods, who had also aged considerably, leaned back in their solid-gold swivel chairs and grinned. Some could not contain themselves and roared. They rubbed their hands, smiled, and congratulated themselves on the devious ways they had initiated the young idealists. They toasted their devious deeds.

"Oh, you wonderful teachers. You were so inexperienced, so naive. You thought you had seen it all, but didn't we have some surprises for you? In your wildest imagination, you couldn't possibly have predicted what awaited you in those little buildings. We concocted a marvelous initiation stew. What a feast! We dished it out and you ate it with gusto," the gods exclaimed. "Now let the banquet begin. Refresh our memories."

Ninety-three year old Clara Rybak took the last sip from her coffee and began the story fest.

In the Beginning

I didn't have any training. I graduated from Jordan High School in June of 1921 and I had no intentions of going into teaching. A friend of mine had a sister who taught in a rural school. She said, "You have to go to Shakopee to take a test and then they'll certify you." That's all there was to it. I had never been in a country school in my life and I had no training.

We took the bus because cars weren't very popular at that time. But there was a bus from Mankato to Minneapolis that stopped at Jordan and Shakopee. We went to the courthouse and we took the test. I passed and my friend didn't. Well, I had a certificate. Then I had to show my state board exam results. If you had an A+ in anything, you got a special certificate.

Now I had the certificate but I didn't know what to do with it. Suddenly, all these school boards came to visit me and I had a choice of several jobs. I decided on Helena, which is half way between New Prague and Jordan, about four miles by railroad.

I thought, "I've got a certificate. I might as well use it." But I had no training whatsoever. My father thought I should get some training, so I went to Mankato and took two courses, but I took the wrong classes. I took nothing that pertained to teaching in a rural school, so the classes weren't any use at all.

I went out to Helena to look at the school. The school board told me there would be about twelve students. I was supposed to order school supplies. I looked around and instead of buying what I needed for the students, I decided the school needed a clock. We needed it because the students should know how to tell time; also, I got a few books.

Then I went to the State Institute that fall and bought a hectograph, which was made of steel and used a jelly-like substance. I wrote my seat work and put them on top of that jelly and I could run off about a dozen copies. That's the way I prepared for the next day. **Clara Rybak taught at Helena near Jordan from 1921 to 1922 in Scott County.**

First Snow

I was eighteen when I taught at my first school. The older boys had to stay home to work in the fields. A month or so later, on the morning of the first snow, I looked up and the hall was full of men. I went out to ring the bell, and I saw all those men. I thought they were school board officials from another school coming to hire me. I walked in and they all followed me. They were my pupils.

Mildred Dahl, 1922, Redwood County: Mildred taught in the rural schools for over twenty years.

Muck!

I was eighteen in the fall of 1923, just barely old enough to get a teaching certificate with one year of teachers training. I signed a contract to teach in a one-room school with forty boys and girls from grades one through eight.

After finding a place to live and with only a vague idea of what lay ahead, I visited the school to plan my first day. It was a bright, sunny day and the building had been scrubbed clean. Everything looked so good. The school was spotless.

Unfortunately, the next day it rained. The road was red clay, the kind that gets very sticky when wet. Also, the road was being rebuilt so it was mud from fence to fence. All forty of the youngsters tramped through that mud and tracked it into the classroom.

To clean the room at the end of the day, I used a shovel, which was much more effective than a broom. That first day I decided someone else could have the ten dollars a month which I would have received for doing the janitor work.

When I walked home that night, my feet felt as if I were walking on snowshoes. The only alternative was walking through the cow pasture. Though raised on a farm, I had never quite gotten over my fear of cows. But I decided to risk the cows rather than walk through the mud again.

Florence Carlson, 1923

Snobbery

We rural teachers were looked down upon by the teachers who taught in town. Apparently they thought we didn't have enough sense to attend college longer and become a teacher in a school that had more equipment, more students, and all the rest of what they thought was necessary.

That's the way I felt. Everybody seemed to think that the town teachers were quite a bit better. We had many subtle reminders. At Balaton we had a weekly newspaper, and when I was going to Mankato State Teachers College for summer school, I went back and forth by train. There were other girls from the same town going home too, but they were taking classes for town teaching. The editor put in the paper all the names of the people who came home, but we country school teachers were not on that list. Some of those gals who taught in rural schools spent their money on fur coats and fancy clothes, and it didn't do any good. They were still considered rural school teachers.

Lillian Livingston, 1921 to 1926, Lyon County

Two for School and School for Two

My first job was in a new school near Nowthen. For the first month or so I had only two children. One father whose two children should have been coming there said I was too young, so he let his children walk by my school and over to the next district. I was nineteen. But the next year he sent them.

Laurena Hanks, 1925, District 38, Hanks School, Anoka County

Enough!

After having taught in three country schools, I went to Mankato to get certified to teach in the junior high. I had good cooperation from the country school students, but I considered my time wasted with all the nitty-gritty manual labor: carrying in the coal, carrying out the ashes, sweeping out the mud and dirt before I could go home, and then retracing my path home in the dark for two miles. I was tired of chopping wood and trying to start fires with little or no paper, corn cobs, or kerosene. I never had time to sit down and study lessons for the next day. The only illumination was daylight or kerosene bracket lamps with reflectors. There weren't even enough books for me to keep a set at home for studying.   **Mabel Luing, 1925, Nobles County**

The gods started clanking their spoons on their cups, yelling, "Good show. We showed you who sits on top of the schoolhouse bell. More cake! More of tales of woe!" Helen Merville eyed the gods coolly and spoke with polished dignity.

Dining on Sleep

For years the teacher had roomed at a nice farm across the road from the school, but the wife had

Helen Merville

died during the winter. The farmer had hired a housekeeper who stayed there. Of course it would have been scandalous for a teacher to stay there. But they didn't want the teacher anyway because they were courting. I could understand that. Why would he want a teacher around? They got married, and then they kept a teacher again.

That meant I had to stay at a farm a great distance from the school. They were as backward and lazy as anybody could be. The only heating came from a coal heater in the dining room and the kitchen range. I had no heat whatsoever in my room on the second floor because they always closed the door at the bottom of the stairs. On bitterly cold mornings the edge of my quilt next to the wall had a glimmer of frost. I got sick and the doctor said no more sleeping in an unheated room. The family said they would work out something. They surely did. When I came back from school, they had moved my bed downstairs to the living room. There was a large arch between the living room and the dining room. I found out fast what it meant to have no privacy.

Even after all these years I still harbor a grudge, remembering how I had to start for school on stormy, cold, dark mornings and the farmer and his brother sat at the table, leisurely having their "umpteenth" cup of coffee, never offering to hitch up the cutter and give me a ride. They had no dairy cows so they just sat around all day. **Helen Merville, 1927, near Godahl, Albin Township, Brown County**

A Sick Tale

Several men working at the place where I was boarding helped with the milking and cheese making. One of these men bet that he could swallow a mouse, so they set out mouse traps.

That day I had the stomach flu, so they took me down from the upstairs bedroom to the master bedroom that opened to the kitchen.

The men caught a mouse. That evening when they were done with their chores in the barn, this guy swallowed that mouse. I had been vomiting all day. I shouldn't have looked, but I was curious. When I peered out of that bedroom, I saw the tail of that mouse slide down the man's throat. Then I really got sick.   **Lempi Keto, 1928, on the Iron Range**

A Nice School for All

My school was located right next to Highway 169 near Belle Plaine. The bad part of it was we couldn't keep the door locked. Every time we locked it, someone broke the lock, so we decided not to lock it. If someone wanted to, they just walked right in. There were many things taken from the school. We couldn't leave any personal belongings there—pen, ink, or books. It was scary teaching there, just thirty feet off the highway. I don't know who did the stealing. People from miles away, maybe. Perhaps some local people.

One morning there was a man leaning up against the entry, smoking a cigarette, a transient. I was very leery and waited. I turned around and walked back part way to where I was staying. Finally he took off down the road in the other direction. I was very scared. **Elizabeth Brown O'Connell, 1928–1930, District 38, Blakeley School, Scott County**

That Took the Cake!

I had a large, poor family. One of their little boys broke a window. The clerk told me if one of the youngsters broke a window, either the child or the parents had to replace it. The teacher was supposed to send the notice home. So I did, but I got a pretty rough one back. His mother said she thought I was pretty bold to ask her to pay for a window when they couldn't afford windows for their own house. She was very bitter and certainly was not going to replace the window. I told the clerk, and the school board replaced the window. After I had received the letter, the boy got really sassy. He thought his mother was right behind him. We were selecting songs and he waved his hand. He was in the front row. I chose somebody else, not because of the problem but because it wasn't his turn. He said, "You always take somebody else besides me."

I said, "No, I don't."

He yelled, "You do, too!" And that was it. He had sassed me too often. I wouldn't take anymore, so I slapped him.

He cried, "I'm going to tell my mother!"

"You do that," I said.

The next morning when he came back and I asked him, "Did you tell your mother that you got slapped yesterday for being sassy?"

"Yes," he said.

"What did she say?"

She said, "Good for her!" On my birthday his mother sent me a decorated cake. **Mary Elliot Mahoney, 1929, District 8, Larson School, Wright County**

Surprise
My first day was frightening. There were twenty children. They were big boys, very big boys, much more experienced in the ways of the world than I was. I thought, "I'm not going to like this at all."

One of the boys said to another in Czech, "Boy, does she think she's smart!" That really set me off. I spoke fluent Czech, so I said, "Yes, and because I am, you're going to sit at this desk and I'm going to sit at that one." Well, that gave me the courage I needed. The boy decided I was smarter than he was and we got along fine.   **Bea Slavik, c. 1930**

Onley Turner Bridges skipped classes in elementary school and high school. When she completed her brief teachers training program, she became a licensed teacher. In 1928–1929, she began her teaching career at Oak Point School near Lancaster in Kittson County.

What Love Had to Do with It
I had forty-five pupils, all eight grades, and I was still only seventeen. The boys in the eighth grade were the same age I was but much bigger. I told

Onley Bridges

them, "I do not intend to spend any of our time with discipline problems."

The first day one of the boys came in during recess. He was a big kid, as big as my dad, and he said, "If you have any trouble with these kids, why just send them to me and I'll take care of them." They had had a big problem the year before. The teacher was fired. She was blamed for an accident that happened on the playground.

A few years after I had quit teaching, I was at a dance and one of my former pupils came and asked me to dance. We were dancing away, and we started talking about some of the things that happened, and I said, "Well, I thought I was so lucky to get by with all those kids and not have any discipline problems." He had been in the fifth grade when I was teaching, and he said, "Well, of course, you know all the boys in the eighth grade were in love with you." **Onley Turner Bridges, 1930, Willow Creek School 95J, Lake of the Woods County**

T. Everett Helmsletter from the Baudette area was an eighth-grade student at Willow School in 1930 when Onley Turner arrived to restore order to the school.

Simply Marvelous!
In my last year in that school with Onley Turner as my teacher, I recall her taking care of approximately forty kids, and it boggles my mind. Well, she dealt with it. She was seventeen, tiny, and in order to give herself a little more stature, she wore spike heels. On one occasion some of the kids who were as old and much larger disputed the position she had taken. She stamped her little foot in exasperation and said, "You think I don't know!" That incident passed and that apparently dealt with it.

Here were these big boys and here was this marvelous girl. Really, she was no more than a girl, and most of us were infatuated with her and that helped keep things under control.

At the end of the term, she tried to take the best possible care of that eighth-grade class in the hopes that everyone would pass. In that last month she gave that class really special attention. We all passed!

In 1904, Viola Loftness O'Day's father, Andrew Loftness, donated one acre of land in Excel Township, Marshall County, for use "as long as it was for school purposes." Then with the help of a hired man, Viola's father built the school. It opened in 1910 and became known as the Loftness School, District 133.

Viola Loftness O'Day and her sister Bernice began the first grade in 1917 with their two older brothers and a sister. Viola and Bernice graduated in 1925. Thirteen years later Viola returned to teach at the Loftness School. She signed her contract for eighty dollars a month. Other teachers had their salaries lowered to as much as forty-five dollars per month during the Depression, but Viola's salary never changed.

Call Me "Miss"

I had attended grade school with Martin Clifford, Alfin Jorde, and Edson Hillyer. They couldn't see why they had to call me "Miss Loftness" when they knew I was just Viola. Then it seemed important. Now I think I'd agree with them.

Viola's grade school class at District. 133, 1919: Viola is fifth from the left, the blond head in the center.

Crack Up

Teaching in the home school where I had attended class only five years earlier had its problems. I worked in the summer for at least two weeks before school opened, getting the school ready. The school board had installed a brown-jacketed heating stove

Viola O'Day and Max, 1930

and twenty-five nice new single desks to replace the double desks. I appreciated the desks—at least I didn't have to sandpaper off my initials in the old ones. However, the books were another matter. It seemed putting names and initials in books was permitted, and I must have made the most of it. I spent much of those two weeks erasing my name. But the first day I felt ready—blackboards filled with work, books arranged by classes—everything ready. I'd even drawn on the blackboard a peaceful September calendar with drooping colored sunflowers. The forenoon was fine. I had a full morning of classes, but right after lunch, Nels M. Engen, the county superintendent, walked in, sat in a back desk, and made himself comfortable. (I'd heard of such things happening!) He took his notes and gazed around. Then suddenly he got up, gathered his papers, and came up to the front of the room, and said, "Is this your first day?"

I said, "Yes, this is my first day!" With that he was gone. He never expressed any opinion about my teaching. He didn't help me a bit.

It was a very windy day, and I was getting so tired. After the last recess, I helped the little first graders onto the porch, fighting the wind. I slammed shut the outside door and set off the crockery drinking fountain, perched on its spindly-legged metal supports. It tottered, swayed, and crashed to the floor. I was so tired, but as I kicked the pieces under the sink. I laughed as I thought of the children hurrying home to say, "Teacher broke the fountain!" That night when I took a piece of chalk to cross out Day One on the calendar, I contemplated whether my teaching career should end with just one day.
Viola Loftness O'Day

Marvel Shaughenessy Rice and my mother, Fran Moore, were best friends at Belle Plaine High School. In 1932 Marvel taught at the Kerry Lake School in Sibley County. She was hesitant about telling her story. Marvel knew how the gods would react. *To Court* was a favorite phrase of the gods.

A New Paint Job

One of the families in my school was quite large. They had a sixth grader who was cute as the dickens but a bit of a trouble-

Marvel Shaughenessy Rice

maker. During the first year I taught I was going with a boy in town who ran a chicken hatchery. My student was in town one day with some other boys. The snow was fresh and they made some heavy snowballs. Well, they opened the door of the hatchery and threw those snowballs in. Of course they could have broken many of the eggs in the hatchery.

The guy I was going with and two other guys were helping him paint a boat in the back of the hatchery. They grabbed the kid when he threw the snowball, took him into the back room, pulled down his pants, dipped the brush into the paint, and swiped him a few times across the rear end. The boy's

parents then sued the guys for painting their son's rear end. One day my three friends came out to school before noon and said they had a subpoena that required me to testify that this kid had missed school and had nightmares from the guys painting his rear end. I was very surprised and upset.

I was so green. I said, "I can't go. I've got all these kids here." So what did I do? I sent all the kids home. They went home and told their parents that three boys came to school and the teacher went off with them. Imagine what they thought!

We didn't have television in those days to show us how court proceedings went. The attorney said, "Answer yes or no." I wanted to explain that this kid always had perfect attendance, but he did leave one afternoon for a short time. "Answer yes or no." That's all I was allowed to say. My, gosh, it was awful!

The judge threw out the case.

The gods jumped up, pounded each other on the backs, mocked their victims and yelled, "That was Ho Ho, the God of Trickery's idea. Marvel, we turned your boyfriend into a cheeky artist." They screamed for more cake and more of their villainous tales. Vera Flategraff stood, folded her hands, and glared at them over her glasses.

Statues in the Closet

At age nineteen, I began my teaching career at a small school near Remer, sixty miles from my home. My folks brought me to a very nice boarding place and then took me down the hill to the little school. When I opened the closet doors, expecting to find books, I found Catholic statues and altar cloths. In those days the spirit of ecumenism had not developed. I was frightened and began to cry, insisting I couldn't stay. My dad took me by the shoulders and gave me a little shake. He told me that I was to teach there, go to church services, and that I would get along fine, which is what happened.

Vera Flategraff, 1932, unorganized Tabique, Cass County: Vera taught in Cass County, Beltrami County, and at the White Earth Indian Reservation at Ponsford in Becker County. Vera taught in public schools for another twenty-three years.

Manual Reading

I had a sixteen-year-old student and I was eighteen. He had his own Model A coupe that he drove to school so he could get home faster to help with the farm work. How he hated school!

He had reading difficulties. Nothing had worked. He hated everything about reading and didn't want to try to learn. So I taught him how to read by using the operator's manual for his Allis Chalmers tractor. His family had an Allis and so did we. I gathered up all the Allis Chalmers material we had at home, and that's what I used to teach him to read. We took the tractor apart. This was something he was interested in. We used pictures to explain things when we went through the manual rather than read about every part. I told him the parts of the tractor, and then I showed him the word in the manual. I showed him where to look in the book when the tractor needed service. In the end, I gave him the manual to keep.

He read because he was interested in that tractor. He remembered many of the words. I don't know if it was the position of the words in the book or if he remembered them from sight.

Even though I was eighteen and he was sixteen, I think he respected me because I was a neighbor girl and his family respected my family. He's a very successful farmer now.

Geraldine Massmann, 1933, District 43, Indian Grove, Lincoln County: Geraldine taught for thirty-eight years.

The gods stopped chewing. They wrinkled their foreheads and looked puzzled. They didn't like stories in which Country School Teachers thwarted the gods' plans. They booed and hissed, but Geraldine just grinned defiantly. She had her cake and was going to eat it, too.

Esther Meline was next and her hands trembled a bit as she stood to face the gods.

Two Little Words

I had a first grader who always kept busy. He never got into any mischief. One afternoon he said, "Miss Anderson." I was busy and didn't answer him. Soon came a loud shout, "MISS ANDERSON, I swept the hall. Ain't you going to say, 'Thank you'?"

That day a first grader taught me something I have used all my life: "Thank you" is easy to say.

Esther Anderson Meline, 1933, District 33, Wright County

A Unique Painting

I had an embarrassing moment the first year I taught school. I was only eighteen years old, and I had just taught for a couple weeks when the county superintendent came unexpectedly to visit me. Generally, I would have had all my work planned, but the night before I decided to make my room look nice, so I put up new curtains and did some painting. I even painted the visitor's chair.

When Mrs. Sohl came in, I forgot that I had done any painting and I asked her to sit down on the visitor's chair. She did and everything went well. I

complimented myself that everything had gone so smoothly. The lessons were good and the kids were on their best behavior.

When she went up to look at the globe, the kids started giggling and laughing. "What could the reason for that be?" I wondered. Then I noticed her

coat all splattered with green paint from the visitor's chair.

That was my worst moment, but I went over and I put my arms around her and said, "I'm sorry." But she was so nice about it.

She said, "Don't worry about it." I went to see her on Saturday to see the coat after she had it dry cleaned. I offered to pay, but she would not let me. She was just as nice as could be. She always remembered that incident, and we laughed about it. Actually I didn't laugh much but she did.

Edith Larson creates a new style!

Edith Larson, 1931–1933, District 14 North, Mille Lacs County

What's a Dollar Worth?

My teachers training teacher took me out in the country for a job interview and said, "Now don't tell them you are from Williams because we are in Roseau County. They will only hire teachers from this county."

I got the job, which was four miles out of Warroad. I received fifty dollars, but it wasn't a check, just a piece of paper. The person who cashed these warrants took two dollars and fifty cents, so I ended up with forty-seven dollars and fifty cents.

The school board treasurer had lost a son and he had to pay for the funeral, so he stole all the money. The school board didn't have any money to pay the teachers. I had taught all the way to Christmas, and all I had were these pieces of paper. I had to quit because I couldn't afford it. But early in January the government took over and the board called me back. They paid me to the end of the year. However, they didn't pay me cash for what I had earned already. I gave those warrants to my dad who paid the grocery bill. **Mae Wilson, 1933–1934, Algoma School, Roseau County**

Wanda Krousey taught in the country schools of Todd County for six years and Morrison County for fourteen years.

The gods leaned forward and listened attentively. They knew there was nothing like an irate father to make a first-year teacher quiver. They thought they had softened the feminine Country School Teachers' hearts so that no tiny eighteen-year-old was a match for a ranting, raving man. However, Wanda was not flustered a bit.

Facing Truth

This man and his wife had a large family, so they had hired a girl to help with the household. The girl was single and the neighborhood gossip had it that the father liked to take the girl to dances while his wife stayed home with the babies.

One day a seventh grader made a comment as to what went on between this man and this girl while he was escorting her to the neighborhood dance. The man's children went home and reported what had been said. The next morning "Daddy" brought his children to school, grabbed my seventh grader, punched him in the face, and bloodied his nose. I said, "Take your complaints to the school board."

He was arrested and had to pay a fine of fifty dollars, and in those days fifty dollars was quite a fine. The school board member who came to get firsthand information about the incident said that he thought the boy hadn't said anything that wasn't the truth. Believe it or not, we got to be friends when he could no longer bring his troubles to school.

Wanda Krousey, 1934, District 134, Todd County

A Snake Charmer

A week prior to starting my assignment at Greenfield School, I received a telephone call from the county superintendent. He wanted to talk to me about the school to which I had been assigned. I thought this was very unusual.

He told me that the teacher who had taught there the year before had had a bad, bad year. Every weekend the students shot out the school and toilet windows. The teacher was afraid to be at the school by herself. I learned that all this devastation to the school and the students' constant harassment caused the teacher to end up in the Fergus Falls Insane Asylum where she died. I resolved those kids weren't going to put me in any asylum!

On Tuesday morning before school when I opened the drawer to get the student register, I found a small snake. I picked him up and twisted his tail around my hand. I said, "Brownie, you and I are going to have fun today." Then I put the snake back in the desk drawer.

At nine o'clock I rang the bell. No one budged. I very politely told them it would be a good idea if they came in because I was as close to the county superintendent as the telephone.

I went back, but they didn't follow me. I rang the bell again. This time they came in very cautiously. I introduced myself, wrote my name on the board, and asked them to stand when I read their names out of the register. When I pulled the drawer open, they ran outside. They knew that snake was in there and they thought they would scare me.

I wound the snake around my wrist again and walked outside. I said, "Boys and girls, I'm not threatening you when I say the superintendent should be told what's happening, but if you cooperate, he doesn't have to know."

Then I told them about my beliefs and I also told them that Brownie was going to live with us. "Would you like to learn more about him?" I asked.

The entire morning of that first day we studied about Brownie. Some students looked up information in the encyclopedia, some built a cage, some captured flies for food, some picked grass and got water.

I dismissed them about eleven o'clock. About a half hour later my landlady came and told me I would be having a lot of company that afternoon. All the grandparents, aunts, uncles, and parents of the kids had called and wanted to know who this "snake charmer" was. At one o'clock forty people gathered in the school. I brought out Brownie, introduced him and told them that, yes, we had learned all about our friend. They were delighted. They said it was the first time their children had come home from school eager to go back.

Celia Johnson Wiedenhoeft, 1934, Greenfield School, Itasca County: Celia taught at District 1, Greenfield, Hansen Lake, Gratten, and Wendigo in Itasca County. Celia taught for forty-two years.

Dressed to Kill

On the first day of school I came all dressed up and wearing my spike heels. The twenty-five children had been in to take a look at their new teacher and gone out to play. Before school started, there was a great commotion behind the school. Some of the girls rushed in to tell me the boys were fighting. I tripped out in my high heels to find two of the biggest boys going at it. I never said a word. I grabbed them and said, "If you are going to fight, I'm sending you home. There'll be no fighting in this school!" That was the first and last fight.

Pearl Jacobson Hanse, 1934, District 45, Huntley School, Stevens County

The gods squirmed nervously. First a rookie teacher solved the old snake gambit and then someone dressed for the prom stopped two ruffians from doing their duty as troublemakers. "That's enough of those fairy tales! You're makin' us look bad." Hazel Amlie smiled as she rose.

Getting the Ax

It was my first year of teaching and the time came to fire up the stove for the first time. I had never

Hazel Amlie, c.1935

seen coal in chunks that were so large. They were fourteen inches by fourteen inches. I didn't know what to do with them or how to get them into the stove. I decided to use the ax to chop the chunks into pieces. The chopping wasn't very good for the ax and I never did break up any of the coal chunks. Worst of all, I was black from the coal dust and the chips. Then I decided I had better chop the coal after school. The next day my brother came and broke the coal with the blunt side of the ax. I told the school board I wouldn't come back if I had that kind of coal. I got briquettes the next year.

Hazel Amlie, 1935, District 2, Pope County

Phyllis Van Buren Rupp, who had never attended a rural school, got a job in a prairie school between Breckenridge and Fergus Falls in Wilkin County. Phyllis' stomach became queasy as she looked at the smirking gods.

Blowing in the Wind

My first day at school was just horrible. I was so upset. I'm a little subject to migraine headaches, and of course, I got one that day. I was feeling so ill I had to leave the children in the school and go outside to throw up. The wind was blowing so hard across that prairie it just blew the vomit out of sight. There wasn't any sign of it anywhere. On the prairie at mid-day the wind is just fierce.

I let the children go home a little bit early. I had no idea what I was doing or if I was doing it exactly right. The children could sense I wasn't well. They were so kind and helpful. I didn't know if I was going to be able to stick it out. But the children, especially the two older boys at whose home I stayed, knew how things should go, and they helped me from then on.

That winter was the coldest ever in that part of the state. My dad brought us out from Fergus Falls one Monday morning and the thermometer outside the school read forty-two below zero; in the school it was forty below. The two eighth graders, who lived where I boarded, saw smoke coming from the chimney. They came to school but they shouldn't have. The older brother had such a poor little coat. At one time it had a sheepskin collar, but all the fur was worn off and the leather around the neck froze his chin and neck. Their older brother had a new Ford V-8 and he came over in the afternoon and got his brothers and me. I was paid forty-five dollars a month for eight months. **Phyllis Rupp, 1935–1936, District 82, Nilsen Township, Wilkin County**

Nausea Migraine split the silence with his laughter. A churlish pair of gods, Revulsion and Blustery Cold, winked at each other as Gail Palmer stood to describe her year in Lyon County.

Split Schedule

District 2 was a very unusual district. It was five and a half miles from the north end to the south end. The Yellow Medicine River ran through the middle. On the north end they had a school and on the south end they had another school. For four months of the year, I taught in the South End School and the kids would then take their books home. When school resumed after Christmas, we went to the North End School. Therefore, everyone did not have to travel the long distance all year.

This was an Icelandic community. During January, a woman was hired to teach the students catechism and religion. They took time out of the school year for religious education. I did not teach during that month. There certainly was no separation of church and state in that school

Gail Palmer, 1935, Lyon County

Boarding Life

Because I was part of the family, I was expected to take part in all the activities. I was expected to go to the Icelandic church. The sermon was in Icelandic, and I didn't understand any of it. I just sat and looked at the beautiful stained glass windows  and hummed when they sang the hymns.

The landlady was crippled and had to take care of the grandfather and her large family. She did the best she could. But one thing that bothered me no end were the flies. In the fall they were so thick. There were no screens on the windows.

Gail Palmer.

Each morning up went the windows and the flies swarmed in. They fell into the gravy and the mashed potatoes. It was ugly but I knew I had to eat it because there was no other place to go to get food.

In the winter the house was very cold. They burned green cottonwood that just sputtered and putzed along. There were no storm windows. When it got to be forty-three below, it was mighty cold upstairs. I slept with one of the girls. In the morning we built a little paper fire in the range, wrapped the stove lids in paper, and took them into bed. That meant we had to get up first to get the lids back before the others woke up.

Gail Palmer taught for forty-one years, fifteen years in the country schools in Lyon and Blue Earth Counties.

Traveling Con Artist rubbed his hands and salivated when he met naive innocents like Lorraine Steussy. Beginning teachers were his primary prey. He knew that when the Class of 1939 spoke, Hannah Sanders would also have to describe how she was duped. Did the wolf in sheep's clothing catch Lorraine Steussy?

Flimflammed

One night just at closing, a man walked into the school. He was little, wild-eyed fellow. Maybe he hadn't shaved for a while. He wanted to sell magazines. He wanted me to hurry up and subscribe to this magazine. I was in the process of helping the kids. I didn't know how to get rid of him before I let the kids out. He was near the telephone and I was far away from it. "I don't have a bank account," I said, "and I don't have any money."

He said, "You could write a check on the Kasson bank, and then you could put some money in the bank." I postdated a check three months for the magazine to get him out. Finally he left. Then I regretted writing the check. I went to the bank and told them what I had done. That man had gone downtown in West Concord and cashed the check right away. Those people didn't know me, and they didn't look at the date. However, the bank said that I didn't have to pay it. **Lorraine Steussy, 1936, West Concord, Dodge County**

Big Money

I began teaching in 1936 for forty-five dollars a month. The women in town said, "I don't know why they pay those teachers so much money. We'll go out and work for—" and then they'd name a figure of less than forty-five dollars. I wouldn't say these women were hostile, but they didn't think the teachers should be getting that much money. They didn't think it was a big problem to get someone to come out and teach for that little. I heard this second hand, but I heard it from enough rural teachers to know that it was true. We teachers were familiar with this attitude. That was when salaries were at the bottom. People were hard up, so they would have been happy to teach for forty dollars.

Lorraine Steussy, 1936, West Concord, Dodge County

In 1936, Laurabelle Martin taught in the Bechyn School in Renville County. The goddesses were particularly upset about Laurabelle's disciplinary prowess.

A Rocky Start

Many people in the community were Bohemian. There were twenty-four students in all eight grades, seventeen Catholics and seven Protestants. One noon hour I heard a lot of yelling and arguing so I went outside to check. They were throwing rocks at each other. The Catholics were on one side of the building and the Protestants were on the other side. Some students were peeking around the corner of the building with rocks in their hands ready to fight in what looked like a religious war. Immediately I had them come in and go to work. They learned if they couldn't play peacefully, there would be no noon hour.

Laurabelle Martin taught for ten years in the rural schools and another eighteen years in the Wabasso public school system.

Myrtle Burman Carson attended two grade schools in Aitkin County: District 76, Lakeside School, and Malmo School. She began her teaching career at age twenty in the Broselle School in Aitkin County from 1934 to 1936. From 1937 to 1939 she taught in the Dahl School near Cokato in Wright County.

Myrtle Carson, 1934

Wow!

We knew nothing about our students when I went out to do my practice teaching. One of the boys had an artificial eye. The first day he went out into the cloakroom. Then he took out his eye and washed it in the washbasin. That shocked me. It was very scary because I knew nothing about it.

1933, Aitkin County

When Myrtle Carson was twenty years old in her first year of teaching, she experienced a challenge that tested her courage, compassion, and teaching philosophy. Family life suddenly became intertwined with her teaching obligation to care for all children with equal love.

Integrity

There was a family who moved in whose father was a heavy drinker. He had attacked other people with knives during ice harvest time. My folks had a resort and my dad put up a lot of ice. We had a country store, too. This man wanted more credit for groceries and so he went to talk to my dad about it. He went to the ice house. He had been drinking. Dad said, "You know you have a pretty big bill. I don't know if I can let you have any more credit."

The man got angry and picked up a big ice shovel that had a sharp edge and swung up at dad. Dad stepped up close to the man and the man cut the heel off Dad's boot.

The word got around that he had threatened dad, so the neighbors who had also had incidents with the man convinced Dad to take him to court. The man was sent to Stillwater. The man's wife had a knack of quoting scripture that could condemn anyone to hell for putting him in jail. She wrote many letters like that to my dad.

At that time of the trial, they were living about four miles from us in another school district. In the fall I found out they were moving into my school district, and I thought, "Oh, what am I going to do?" I was very scared. I thought I would have to be very careful and just handle the crisis when the time came. I was only twenty then.

They had four children. One of the boys was in second grade and he was very naughty. On the way home the other kids punished him. Finally the mother came to me and said, "The kids are being mean to my boy." I was really shaking, but I tried to be as calm as I could. I just tried to do my duty and do what was right. I had to be fair to all the kids.

I said, "Maybe it's because he's mean to the kids in school." I told her how he punched them with his pencil and other very aggravating things he did. She never bothered me again. I never realized I had the courage to act. I just did what I could at the time, and I think that God was always there to help me do what was right.

After the man got out of Stillwater, he came to my dad and asked if he could pay off his bill. Then he went to work for my dad at the resort.

I have a cousin who is blind and the girl that comes to take her shopping and take her around is the daughter of the man who attacked my father.

Myrtle Carson, 1935, Broselle School, Aitkin County: Myrtle taught for twenty years, four in the country schools.

Wanna Trade?

When I first went to the school to meet the people with whom I was going to stay, the man said, "I'll build your fires in the morning if you help my wife with the dishes at night." That sounded like a wonderful arrangement. I had no idea about how to build a fire. He got up at six o'clock every morning and built the fire. The school was warm when I arrived. All I had to do was help with the dishes for four people at night. That was a great trade-off. When I was at the college taking courses, I didn't think about building fires. And they certainly didn't have a training stove! **Edith Clafton 1938–1940, Arbo School, District 318, Itasca County**

Veronica Blees Smith had a reputation for diving into her work. When she said, "Fire up," the gods cringed. She was also known for giving the gods the "slip." Veronica stood before the gods, grinned, blushed, and began her tales.

Safe at First
Twenty children, all eight grades, a one-room school and a brand-new teacher. Mix them all together that September day in 1938 and you would have found one scared bunch. For some reason I don't remember much about that first day. After school I was feeling very inadequate and I wondered how I would continue to cope. A car stopped outside. I looked out and to my great joy, there was a classmate who also had just finished her first teaching day. She was the most welcome sight! With a big howl, I dashed down the steps, missed the last one, and landed spread-eagled beside her feet, blubbering. **Veronica Blees Smith**

Veronica Blees Smith, 1938

Skirting the Issue
My boarding house was a mile from school. Snow pants were very new then and I appreciated them for my walk. I kept a skirt or two at school, but the previous Friday I had taken them to my parents to wash. On Monday I put on the snow pants and headed for school. When I removed the snow pants, wow, no skirt, just a slip! The school was very warm because the neighbor man had started the stove on Sunday night. I wore a summer coat under my winter coat that morning, so I wore that summer coat all day long. I told the students I felt cold. There was no way I could turn the furnace down because the students needed to keep warm.

The spring sun shone brightly through the windows. I was so hot. I didn't have any trouble stripping down the minute the students left. I locked the door, whipped off my coat and did the sweeping and cleaning in my slip. I never knew if the students guessed I was not wearing a skirt. **Veronica Blees Smith taught in District 7, Stevens County, from 1938 to 1939. Veronica taught for twenty-one years.**

The Big Fire
It was my first year of teaching. The school building was a two-story structure with a stage and a hall upstairs. We were preparing for the Halloween program when one of the boys raised his hand and said there was smoke in the corner behind me. I had made a fire in the stove upstairs. I sent him to the neighbors for water. They lived quite a distance from school. They called on the party line and all the people rushed to the school to put out the fire. But it was no use. The school burned, but we were able to save many of the books and supplies as well as the potbellied stove since the fire started in the second story.

The school had just finished burning when the fire inspector came on his yearly inspection. He concluded there was a crack in the chimney, so I was vindicated. **Fern Breckheimer McCormack, 1939, West School, Pine County**

Fern's story sent the gods into an absolute tizzy! One romped around, pretending she was Fern, shrieking hysterically. Others babbled like "rubber neckers" on the party line, but most mocked the teachers. They had waited all night for "the day Fern had a hot time at the old school" story. "Now that was an initiation! What a hot time in the old school tonight!" they yelled.

Norwegian Wood
I stayed at a place that was two and a half miles from school. After the first lasting snowfall, a school board member who lived across the road where I stayed came with a pair of Norwegian skis. These were plain wood, never waxed, with leather straps for my feet. His only comment was, "You could save about a mile if you ski cross country."

I accepted the challenge—too young to know better—thinking the time saved would be most worthwhile. I had no poles, no ski boots, just "get up and go." I found the ski trek not bad at all; in fact it was fun. This was in the rolling hill country and the hills were not too high. The last hill coming home which was at the end of the tour was the steepest. My landladies wondered if I would make it standing up or not. Sometimes I didn't.

I found out most of my students also skied to school. It was quite a scene with our skis poked into the snow up against the school. We combined our morning recess, our noon hour, and our afternoon recesses and skied on a nearby hill. That was fun!

Dorothy Carey, 1938–1941, Clay County

Lip Sync

I was not quite nineteen when I began teaching. Two boys struck fear in me. One towered above me and I thought, "Oh, dear, how will I ever handle those boys? What if they are as mean as the nasty

Edith Ailie, 1940

boys were at my own school?" I had memories of the bully at Little Swan. I stood five feet, two inches tall and one of these guys was at least six feet tall, going on fifteen years old. But they were nice kids. However, their dad was on my school board, and he was a tyrant. They had a younger

sister in the second grade. She had a monotone voice and sang loud. I was putting on the Christmas program, and so I told her to sing real softly, just barely whisper. The next day the father brought the girl to school, walked in, and yelled, "How come my daughter can't sing out loud?" He was intimidating and angry! I hemmed and hawed. I don't know what I said but somehow I smoothed it over.

Edith Ailie, 1940, District 55, Meeker County

From 1939 to 1942, Hannah Sanders taught at District 82, Wayside School, in Pope County. When Hannah stood up to tell her story, the gods sat smugly, looked at each other, rolled their eyes, and grinned. Traveling Con Artist could read the anxiety in Hannah's face. All the gods thought Hannah's initiation was one of Traveling's most devious accomplishments. How he relished this!

Skinned

Teachers many times fell prey to agents and salesmen because they felt the teachers had money. In the first year I taught, I made $71.50 a month. One day when the kids were in class, there was a

Hannah Sanders

rap at the door. I opened the door and here was this man who had this great big box with furs in it. I didn't know if he had stolen them or what. He opened that box and threw around all those fur coats, and I had a bunch of kids in the room. He wanted to sell me a coat. He told me that so-and-so down the road had

bought one. That coat cost me $55. That was one of the biggest mistakes I ever made in my life. It was nothing but rabbit fur. That salesman went right down the road from one school to another.

Hannah purchased her coat on November. 3, 1939. She told the treasurer to make the final payment. Hannah got a bit of revenge: Note: Fur (rabbit) Coat Salesman.

Hannah Sanders also taught in Swift and Kandiyohi Counties, but she never bought another rabbit fur coat. After buying a pig-in-a-poke, Hannah earned the reputation among her students as "She who cannot be tricked."

Silence. Not one guffaw from the gods. Silently, they reached under their chairs and pulled out their rabbit fur coats. Pandemonium!

Dirty Sheets

My school was located midway between Sacred Heart and Renville. When I arrived in the fall of 1942, the building was new because the old schoolhouse had burned down the previous year. The new school was a good-sized building with two chemical toilets, an oil-burning furnace, no running water, and a library with no books. For the children's recreational reading, I ordered boxes of books from the Traveling Library.

There were twenty-five students in eight grades. For each of the classes there was just one set of textbooks. Reference books, other than five dictionaries, were nonexistent. The people had built a new building but couldn't afford more than the basic supplies.

I have many negative feelings about my one year in that country school. I roomed in a three-generation home. I went home on the weekends, but during the week I stayed in the daughter's room. She taught in another rural school. When she came home for the weekends, she got the clean sheets and I got to use them when I came back. She gave me a tiny space in the wardrobe and a corner of one drawer. My other personal space was my suitcase.

We had been told to expect friendliness and help in the rural schools. No one, not even the school board members, ever came to visit the school or offer me any help. As far as all the invitations for meals, etc., they were nonexistent, except for one first grader's birthday party. All this for $720 a year. There was no chance of my returning for another year like that.

Annette Gimmestad Potter, 1942, a rural school between Sacred Heart and Renville in Renville County

Feudin', a Fussin' and a Fightin'

I had sent out resumes to different schools. These school board members came to our normal training teacher and said they were looking for a teacher. Later I found out why they had come there. In that school they had had a lot of trouble. It was difficult for them to get a teacher because of all that trouble. I didn't know anything about it.

So I took the job. I heard rumors about the school after I had signed the contract. Several people said, "Oh, you don't want to go out there. They've had a lot of trouble. There's a lot of feuding going on."

That's exactly what it was—a feud between two families that was carried into the schools. I certainly didn't know what I was getting into. On top of not having much experience, I had an enrollment of twenty-one kids, all grades, and this feud going on.

Who knew what the feud was about? It was a family that—well, it was their thing; they just liked feuding. It was like the Hatfields and the McCoys in the Ozarks, and I didn't know anything, just the rumors I had heard. I found out in a hurry.

One of the families had a boy, a seventh grader named Francy, and the other family had three boys—an eighth grader, a seventh grader, and a younger one. I began to see that there wasn't anything that Francy could say or do that was right. The other boys, Max and Harold, were always putting him down.

As time went on, this conflict began to escalate. I went out with the kids at every recess and every noon to keep tabs on them and keep them from fighting. But one day when I was especially busy, I couldn't go out. The kids were playing ante-over the schoolhouse. It sounded as if they were getting along all right. I rang the bell and the kids ran in.

I could tell as soon as they came in that something had happened. The younger ones all had these frightened looks on their faces, and they all rushed to their desks and sat down and looked at me as if they were wondering, "What is she going to do?"

And then Harold and Max ran in. They looked as happy as the cat that swallowed the canary. They sat down all breathless and red in the face. Then they looked at me. Francy wasn't there. Pretty soon I heard him. The air was blue out there. He was cursing and swearing. He came storming in—black eyes and bloody nose. He was a mess.

Harold and Max had waited until they were alone with Francy on one side of the schoolhouse and then they beat him up.

I kept my cool. I washed him up and calmed him down. Then we went back to our classes. I kept the three of them in during the next recess and visited with them. I don't know where I got the idea because I had no experience with this kind of thing, but I got a piece of paper and I drew up a contract. "Whatever your problems are, you don't bring them to school." In the contract I said, "If you do, I'll have to take you to the school board." They signed the contract and that was the end of it.

At the beginning of the year on the first day of school, Harold and Max's father had come to school. He was an old German farmer. He said, "You see to it my boys behave. If they don't, give them a lickin' and when they get home, they'll get another." So I knew I would have no problem with them because I had his support. But the other family was a different story. According to Francy's mom, he could do no wrong, and I was not to punish him.

Another time during class those three got into it. Francy had looked cross-eyed at Harold or something, and Harold punched him. To keep them apart, I had to call on my seventh grader, who was twelve years old and weighed 175 pounds, to help me part them and restore order.

Francy's mom heard about this and said that what I had done was wrong. She marched to school one day with her knitting. She sat in the back and watched me teach. It

Madame De Farge

reminded me of *A Tale of Two Cities* and Madame DeFarge, who knitted the names of those people that were to be beheaded. Obviously, she made me nervous. After school she told me that some people were not cut out to be teachers, and I was one of them. That was my first and only year of teaching, but that was enough. I couldn't take another year like that. I grew up fast that year, but it was a good experience. I got married that spring.

Gertrude Weiss, 1941, Maple Grove School, Leader, Cass County

The Walk
On the first day I was going to impress my students so I wore high heels and nylons. The day went fine. I started walking the two miles to the farm where I was living. I stepped in a gopher hole and broke off the heel of my shoe. I couldn't walk two miles like that so I took off both shoes. I also took off my nylons because they were so precious at that time. I walked those two miles in my bare feet.

Julie Johnson, 1945, Lac Qui Parle County

Burp!
My father went with me the first morning I had to start a fire in the potbellied stove. He thought he had done a good job. Not too long after all the boys and girls were assembled, the stove belched and all the pipes came tumbling down into the classroom. We had to send the children home. One of the board members' wives helped me the rest of the day clean the soot from that lovely, clean room.

Donna Poppe Nibbe, 1947, District 20, Stevens County

With that final story and the image of soot covering Donna's sparkling school, the gods broke out in thunderous applause, not for the teachers but for the creative ways they had found to initiate so many novices from 1921 to 1947. They congratulated each other, knowing there were hundreds of teachers not able to attend this banquet who had also experienced their cunning.

The gods were a bit uneasy about the teachers who had thwarted their attempts to make that first year miserable, but they quickly forgot those heroic exploits.

Thanking the teachers for a memorable evening, the gods filled their pockets with whatever goodies were left on the table. They even took the flower centerpieces. Then they walked out the door, split into two lines, and headed for home.

Dwelling Place of the Devious Gods of Initiation
The gods don't really dwell here. This outhouse is part of the famous Pink School located east of Wells. Legend has it that the gods tricked the people into thinking they had enough red paint for the school. When they discovered the gods had tricked them, they had to add white paint to the red. The result was a pink school. But this may be just the gods' version.

Chapter 7

Impish Imagination
and Mischief Maker

As I traveled from one corner of the state to the other and talked with Country School Students, I wondered if students in the north woods were different from students on the western plains. Would students who cut timber in the forests be like students who tilled the soil and harvested the crops?

The only thing I know for certain is that some Country School Students in all parts of the state hung around with two nasty companions—Impish Imagination and his buddy Mischief Maker. Those rascals were constantly whispering in Country School Students' ears. Impish Imagination and Mischief Maker delighted in persuading Country School Students to skip class, smoke a corn silk cigarette, and with lots of conniving, to plague Country School Teachers. Now when Country School Students sit around and pour themselves a mug of concentrated Nostalgia Juice, they just gotta tell those stories 'cuz there's a lot a braggin' that's gotta be done, ya know.

Those pesky guys, Mischief Maker and Impish Imagination, get rambunctious bein' jailed in Country School Students' minds year after year. They keep a scratchin' and a clawin' at Country School Students' Conscience to let 'em escape now and then. An' if they get a whiff of Nostalgia Juice, hold the reins of the buggy tightly 'cuz they're gonna take you for a ride.

Well, the following folks got nippin' on the Nostalgia Juice, and you know what happened: Mischief Maker and Impish Imagination showed up and stories from four different decades slipped out past Conscience.

Dick Branvold, age 92, grew up in Goodhue County; Signe Eklund, age 85, grew up in Norman County; Winnie Dunn, age 83, and her brother Dale, age 74, attended school in Otter Tail County; and Gordon Ostby, the youngest at age 66, followed Mischief's calling in Swift County.

Dick Branvold
Dick Branvold was born in 1905. He attended District 61 West in Wanamingo Township, Goodhue County, from 1911 to 1920. Dick is one hundred percent Norwegian and proud to tell it.

No English Here
We were seven first graders and we were all Norwegian. Nobody could speak English. The teacher had a reading book with a picture of an animal, and she asked the first one of us to tell what it was, but he didn't know. He knew, but he didn't know how to say *rabbit* in English. She kept on. When she came to me, I said *hara,* the Norwegian word. Well, the next kid did the same—stuck his head out and said *hara.* The teacher laughed because she was Norwegian, too.

Blowing Smoke
In the fall we picked up and dried out clover blossoms and rolled them into cigarettes—rolled the paper around them and smoked them like cigars. Everything burned. We used newspaper. It burned fast but we got a little smoke out of it. Later we smoked grape vines. They were hollow on the inside. We started one end on fire and sucked smoke through that. It was real strong smoke. Later we chewed tobacco and smoked cigarettes. Once one of the guys smoked a cigar in the school and the teacher wanted to know who was smoking. We said it was a guy who smoked a cigar and drove by the school. I don't think she believed that.

A Running Start
We had to stay after school once in a while as punishment, but we had that figured out. If a kid went the same direction I went, he'd take my clothes so then I could come running out the door after school, sneak out. I didn't have to stop to take my jacket. The teacher just stood and hollered. You could hear her for miles. She was mad. Once Norman had to stay after. The teacher watched him so he couldn't run out. But the next day he ducked down under the seats and slid on the floor until he got to the door, and then he ran out. That was the end of that.

Mischief Maker taught Richard more devious things than sprinting out of school and avoiding the teacher's efforts to control him.

More Trouble

We picked on the girls when they had to go to the relief station. There were holes in the back walls. We had sticks stuck in there. We poked them. The minister's sons started that a few years earlier. We got heck for that, too.

Impish Imagination and Mischief Maker sat at Dick's feet, reminding him of his unusual business enterprise. They also convinced him to 'fess up about his liquid lunch. They refused to allow him to forget that he owed much of his entertainment to them.

More Than One Way to Skin a Cat

There were a lot a skunks. On the way to school I set traps. I had a 22-rifle at that time so I could shoot the skunks, but once I had to kill it with a stick and I got sprayed. Come in the schoolhouse, sat down, and the teacher told me to go home.

I skinned them, put the skin on stretchers, and shipped them to the Percy Fur Company in St. Louis, Missouri. I got three or four dollars for the ones that had stripes from the head back, a dollar and a half for the two stripes.

I skinned a cat once—one that had died. Like the skunks, you had to pull off the tail bone. You couldn't tear the tail off. Then you wouldn't get anything. So when I tried that on the cat, I pulled the tail right off. So I sewed it back on. I think I got a dollar and a half. It was a big cat.

Wildlife

When I started school, it was wild country. I was fourteen and I remember seeing a timber wolf on my way to school. He didn't come too close. He circled away and then he sat down and howled.

Lunch Hour Brew

We skipped school. We'd tell the teacher we were going over to the neighbors during the noon hour. A farmer had a hired man from the cities, a bachelor who lived in an empty house.

We knew he made home brew so we'd sneak over there and get some. We didn't drink too much, just a nip or two at lunchtime. Our parents never knew. When the teacher asked where we were, one of the kids told her where we were and what we were doing. She never bothered us though.

(Signe) Viola Eklund

Viola Eklund attended the one-room school in Spring Creek Township, Norman County, from 1918 to 1926. Viola recalls walking one and one-half miles to school. She feared the wolves. One very cold winter she saw them almost every morning.

Viola enjoys telling stories about her rural school. She remembers the good times playing tic-tac-toe on the board in front of the class with the boy who was her deskmate, playing games in the hay meadow across from the school, and learning to square dance and polka on the lumpy entryway to the school.

Viola also remembers a few events which were not quite so pleasant.

Vaccination Time!

In second grade the older boys decided to vaccinate us as that was really going to happen. They took metal pencil tops and heated them and burned us on our arms. I had a scar for years. Our sixteen-year-old teacher told us not to be such big babies.

I Have To...!

We had three teachers during the 1919–1920 school year. One was a sixteen-year-old girl and one was an old man. I was dared by my friend and seat

Viola (Signe) right holds her sister Olga's hand so she can't run away. Viola is developing "the look" needed for good discipline.

partner to stand on top of my desk the first day Mr. L. taught. I had to take her up on that! "Little girl, please sit down," was his remark. I am sure I expected to be spanked. He would not allow us to go out to the outhouse during school and I *had* to go. I was very mad at him and I decided to go to the outhouse.

He stopped me by the door. I said, "I *have* to go!" Then I wet my pants right there.

Saved by the Bell!

When I was in second grade, two older boys held me between them and took me to the church and laid me down on the entry floor and told me to say my prayers as they were going to kill me. I was so scared. They took out their knives and talked about how they would do it. In the end they decided to wait another day for it was time to start school.

Ugh!

Sometimes four or six of us carried water from the farm about a quarter of a mile from the school. The well for the school had a dead gopher in it so we couldn't drink that water.

A Bell of a Surprise

The last teacher had no control. When she got provoked, she grabbed the bell on her desk and rang it to beat the band. One day one of the boys gathered a whole handful of rabbit pellets from around the school, the church, and the barn. He put them under the teacher's bell. I guess you know what rolled all over! The poor teacher usually cried, but when she was irate, she tore that bell to pieces!

Bam!

One day the boys filled a half-gallon pail with water and wired the lid on tight. Then they threw it into the stove. What a blast there was! The clay (or plasticine) balls were peppered all over the walls and the blackboard.

Nuts to You

The school was so old they built a new one-room school on the other side of the church. Then we got a man teacher. We were used to double desks, but then we got single desks. He played with us and we had a self-governing association. We each had our jobs. He could go outside to smoke and not one thing was bad.

We once had our parents buy bags of peanuts, and on a Friday afternoon we really peppered him. But he returned that one on us at a later date. A friend of mine and I were both "in love" with him.

Heavenly Guidance

One of my friends used to stay overnight with me. When my friend was twelve, her mother died. A month after her mother had died, my friend again stayed overnight. Rather than go to school with the other kids, we went ourselves. It was such a beautiful spring day so we fooled around on our way to school. We decided to play hooky, but my friend was afraid to skip because she thought her mom would see her from heaven so we went to school.

Signe Viola Eklund, 1918–1926, Spring Creek Township, "New Holland," later called Columbia District 35 South, Norman County

Done by Dunn

For seventeen consecutive years, children of the Dunn family attended District 174, Girard Township, in Otter Tail County. The last to attend were Winifred (Dunn) Chesborough and her brother Dale D. Dunn.

Winnie Dunn followed her older brother and sister to District 174, attending the country school near Henning from 1920–1928.

Down and Out

I was six years old in 1920 when I started school. That year I had a teacher that did not like me. I was shy and inarticulate and a slow thinker. My older sister told me what to do and I did it. One day the teacher sent us first graders to do some work on the blackboard. I did not perform as the teacher wished. She made me stay at the blackboard until I fainted. I didn't learn much that first year.

The Old Ball Game

One year the school board hired a teacher who had just married and moved into the neighborhood. Her husband drove her to school in their open Model T Ford. But she was always the last person to arrive. There were several big boys in the school who threw erasers and chalk around the room and did as they pleased. One day they hung a ball on the end of a wire from the ceiling. The wire had been there to hold up the stove pipes. When they hit that ball, it swung across the room and smacked us on the head. None of us behaved. We learned nothing so the board asked her to resign at Christmas.

The Union Forever

One family put their underwear on in the fall and didn't remove it until spring. We changed clothes each week. We bathed each week in a tin tub. My two sisters and I bathed in the same water because we had to carry it a long distance.

And our clothes were clean, too. I hated those long union suits that buttoned all the way down the front. Mine had a drop seat with three buttons, but I could never reach that middle one. I did like the cozy, clean feeling when I put a clean suit on.

I hated the garter belt that was supposed to hold up my black cotton stockings. I folded the bottom cuffs of the union suit and pulled those black stockings over them, making sure they did not lump up under the stockings. All us kids wore our union suits to bed because the rooms were cold and the fire went out at night. Each day the legs of my underwear stretched out and became more difficult to hide beneath the stockings. One day during recess, I was in the middle of our circle game. Suddenly the kids all laughed at me. I didn't understand why they were laughing until I felt my stocking slide down below the underwear. Then I felt the cold hit my legs.

What's that draft?

Winnie Dunn's younger brother Dale continued the family traditions in Otter Tail County from 1929 to 1937.

Ungrateful

I guess we were pretty mean, mischievous or both. One time when I was in about the fifth grade on Halloween, when we got to school, the teacher had the doors locked and would not let us in. The shades on the windows were pulled down, too. Smoke was coming out of the chimney, so we knew the teacher was there.

A man doing field work next to the school told us to put a board over the chimney. That would smoke her out. Some of the older boys, bigger than me, climbed up on the wood shed, then onto the roof, and put a board on top of the chimney. Sure enough! The teacher came out real quick. The smoke billowed out the door and windows. We all acted like we could not get up there to take the board off. Finally someone climbed up on the wood shed and pushed the board off. Would you believe that nice teacher had bought a whole bunch of stuff to decorate the school: orange and back crepe paper pumpkins, and witches. She had been working hard to decorate the school room for us. After school that evening she gave us a nice party with favors, candy and the works, even though we had smoked her out. I do not think any of us even thanked her for the nice party.

Organ Music

One time I found an old mouth organ. I took it apart. Inside a mouth organ there are plate-like things with little tongues on them that make the musical sound when you play it. I took one of these plates and stuck it up on one of the window frames outside the school. When the wind blew, one loud musical sound hummed throughout the school. The sound nearly drove the teacher crazy, but the kids didn't seem to mind it at all. No one but me knew where the noise was coming from or what was causing it. I finally showed the teacher my handiwork after a few days. Then we took it down.

That Little Stinker!

My dad always had sulphur around to make salve or something for the livestock. When I put the sulphur on the hot stove, it made a fine stink. I usually did this at the start of recess or just before noon. We then went out to play. By the time we came back in, the teacher had most of the windows open to air the place out. It took several hours to get rid of the smell completely. I don't think the teacher ever knew I was the one who did it.

A+ in Following Directions

We had this small six-year-old boy in school. He did whatever the bigger boys told him to do and it got him into a lot of trouble. Whenever he got in trouble for listening to the older boys, the teacher made him sit under her desk where she kept her rainy-day rubbers. One day the big boys told this kid, "The next time the teacher puts you under her desk, pee in her rubbers." But the next time he got into trouble, the teacher sat him on a stool at the end of her desk instead of putting him under it. The teacher went to the back of the room to write something on the blackboard. While she was doing this, the boy did exactly what the older boys had told him to do. He took the rubbers out from under her desk and peed in them in front of all the students.

Gordon Ostby

For eight years Mischief Maker and Impish Imagination ceased their wandering. They found a home on the Ostby farm. Little Gordy Ostby was just the kind of kid they were looking for, and Gordy was looking for buddies.

Gordon Ostby attended District 67, located three miles north of Benson in Swift County. From the years 1937 to 1945 Gordon and his buddies created their own fun. Sometimes they were the victims of fun by others, such as the time he and four others were locked in the outhouse. According to Gordon, "Trouble was about the only kind of entertainment we could get."

A Live One

One winter morning we were cleaning out the stove, helping the teacher. We took out all the coals from the day before, but we missed one piece of coal that was still live. Then we put in the new coal. I threw on the kerosene, and BAM, the thing exploded. It blew off the door and the steel jacket.

Scrubbin'

At the time I was in the first grade. On Halloween night ten of us guys went to the school, but at first we couldn't get in. We had a box of empty whiskey bottles. We crawled through a little window in the coal bin and then went into the school. We lined up all the whiskey bottles in the front of the room and wrote very dirty words on the blackboard. Someone must have seen us and told the teacher. The next day we had to get down on our hands and knees and scrub the whole floor. Next we had to scrub the blackboards. Then we had to scrub the whole outhouse; that was the worst!

That's Shocking!

We used to cut across our neighbor's field on our way to school. One of my friends was very pokey. He was always way behind. Our neighbor had an electric fence. One day it was raining. We all joined hands and grabbed the electric fence. Then we saw the neighbor's calf. Two guys grabbed the calf and we told Pokey to grab its tail so he held on tight to the tail. We let go of each other's hands and you could see the spark jump down the line between our fingers. Pokey on the end got the worst of it. The shock knocked him right down to the ground.

A Whole Lotta Shakin' Goin On

One day we were sitting in school, studying and reading. It was pretty quiet. All of a sudden, BONK—something crashed into the side of the school. The whole place shook. Again—BONK and the whole place just rattled. That was the day the neighbor's bull came to school. He backed up a bit and smashed into the side of the school! BONK. We all started laughin' but the teacher didn't think it was very funny.

Some of us went out and whistled for the neighbor's dog. It chased the bull away. The teacher asked whose bull it was, but the boy whose dad owned the farm about a half mile from the school wasn't in school that day. It was their bull.

I Can Fly!

Our neighbor had a cutter, and he took about fifteen of us to school in the winter. Caesar was a smart aleck who constantly bragged, "I can do anything." We got tired of hearing that, so we decided to do something about it. We decided we'd fix 'im.

We tied a scoop shovel to the end of the cutter and dared him to ride the shovel. He stood on the scoop and held onto the handle. "You can't do anything with me," he bragged. The driver "spooked" the horses by snapping them with the whip. They turned a sharp corner and threw Caesar over a barbed wire fence into the next field. Our sides hurt from laughing so much.

When the Nostalgia Juice ran out, Mischief Maker and Impish Imagination decided it was time for them to hit the road and find some other Country School Students who needed to tell their little secrets. Hundreds of gallons of Nostalgia Juice were cooling throughout the state.

Chapter 8

Oh, They Could Tell a Story!

Although Nettie Wait was born in Yellow Medicine County and Malinda Heaney was born in Freeborn County, their paths followed a similar course. In many ways they represent the lives of most Country School Teachers. Born on farms, they toiled with demanding chores, but at the same time they began their search for learning. They attended country school, high school, and normal school before setting out on their teaching careers. And, like other Country School Teachers who felt their dedication and contributions had been forgotten, they loved to tell their stories.

Nettie Pedersen Wait

When Nettie Wait's former students talk about her, their eyes brighten, their voices soften, and they nod with reverence paid to one who taught with her heart and soul.

Nettie went to country school near Clarkfield. She attended Luther Normal School in Madison from 1914–1918 and began her teaching career in Leeds, North Dakota. She returned to teach in Porter, near Granite Falls.

Perhaps Nettie was such a success as a country school teacher because she had experienced eight years of nasty weather, interesting teachers, and academic achievement.

People described Nettie as "a fireball," "a no nonsense disciplinarian," "creative," "a gifted writer and storyteller," and "a terrific athlete and a wonderful shortstop."

When I walked into Nettie's home on the corner of 5th Avenue in Granite Falls, I knew she was well prepared for our interview. Her stories, which she had written for her writers' group, were stacked neatly on the dining room table.

She read a few, but when she set down the papers and told them from her heart, I felt as if I were walking to school with her and her family, sitting around the stove warming my feet, and facing my students on that nervous first day of teaching.

Walkin' on Water

Going to the country school was really a rugged experience. We had to walk against the northwest wind a mile and a half if we cut across the fields. When we did drive when the weather was bad, it wasn't that comfortable because we had an open sleigh and it was that much farther than when we walked. It was very cold.

Nettie Pedersen Wait, front row, far right, in the dark dress, was in the first grade in 1910.

South of schoolhouse there was a slough which we had to cross. In the spring or in the fall when it was thawing, if we happened to fall, we stayed wet all day. But we had my mother's long woolen stockings, which she had knitted, and we also wore long underwear. We didn't dry out very fast.

If we happened to fall as we were crossing that slough—we always tried to jump from one knob to the other—then we just stayed wet, but it didn't seem to affect us any. I don't remember that any of us got sick from it.

One day my younger brother walked across the fields, the creek, and the slough. He stopped at the door during school hours and said, "I ran all the way over here." Well, all the kids laughed and laughed at that. The teacher asked him where he had walked to get so muddy and wet. "Well," he said, "I walked on the ground and looked at the creek," which wasn't quite true. My big brother had to take him home.

Pain

When the teacher saw that we were very cold and crying, she took off our shoes and stockings and washed our feet in cold water. I remember how awfully cold that water was. She rubbed our feet with a coarse towel and that helped.

We had a boy who had polio when he was a baby. He couldn't walk except with crutches. He was very heavy, too, but he was a very good sport. He never complained. One day it was awfully cold. We were sitting around the stove trying to get our feet warm by putting them on the stove's jacket.

Suddenly this boy cried. A hush fell over the whole school room. We had never seen him cry. We certainly knew it was cold when he cried. He must have been about thirteen or fourteen years old at that time. He had to endure the pain from the cold.

There wasn't much the teacher could do for him because he couldn't lift his feet up on the jacket of the stove the way the rest of us could because he wore those heavy braces. I'll never forget the hush that fell over the school when he cried.

Normal School

Nettie Pedersen Wait was the salutatorian of the 1918 senior class at Lutheran Normal School. Her speech in May, 1918, is filled with youthful idealism about teaching, but the reality of the horrors of World War I tempers the joy of graduation and the thrill of beginning a teaching career.

Nettie Pedersen, first person in back row left, celebrates graduation from Lutheran Normal School with the class of 1918.

Nettie's Graduation Address

"We have offered to assume the responsibility of helping to make our nation in the future, not a great nation, because it is great and has been so, but to make it greater, and this we shall do by making the children entrusted to our care great citizens, great statesmen, great soldiers, and great patriots. No, we shall not make them so, but we shall give them the first strong impressions, and if these take root in their hearts, there is little fear for their manhood."

from ***The Normal School Echo***

Boarding Home Dilemma: To Tickle or Not to Tickle

I boarded with Mr. and Mrs. Anderson, Alvida, a senior in high school, and their sons Carl and Leonard. Years ago the houses were not built with privacy in mind. Mr. and Mrs. Anderson occupied the bedroom downstairs, and the boys in a bedroom of which the stairs were a part. To reach Alvida's and my room, we had to go through the boys' room.

One night the renter shared Carl's bed. He was just recovering from a bout with the flu. He was in bed when Alvida went upstairs. She called

Nettie Pedersen Wait, c. 1919

to me, "Nettie, come up here." I flew up the stairs two steps at a time, so I nearly caught Carl in a state of undress. He sprinted into bed as fast as he could.

Oh, how Alvida laughed! She was lying on the bed on her back ha-ha-ha-ing. I tickled her ribs a little, which made her guffaw all the more, and she didn't stop.

Soon we realized this was not funny. It was frightening! Mrs. Anderson came upstairs. We lifted Alvida to her feet, but she kept on laughing. The renter put on some clothes and came to our aid. Her mother alternately scolded and cajoled her, but nothing helped. We had to be careful not to say anything that was the least bit humorous.

Finally her hysteria began to subside. It had been a whole hour since Carl's bedtime acrobatics. Too much laughter is not good medicine, and I never tickled anyone again.

Peeved

Teachers often had a hard time getting to school on time. I stayed at a place where they never got around to having supper before nine o'clock at night. Since I'd only had sandwiches for lunch, I was almost starved by nine o'clock.

One time I was so peeved about that I went to bed without any supper. Well, they brought me supper, and the next day we had supper at a decent time. But the day after that it was the same old story. And it was awfully hard to get them up in time for breakfast so I could get to school and fire up the furnace to make it warm for the kids.

For that reason many a teacher moved from place to place rather than put up with those conditions. It was more often the boarding place than the students that decided whether you'd teach at the same school another year.

Initiation

When I began teaching, there were two boys about eleven and nine who didn't come to school the first week. I couldn't imagine why they had to stay home and work because they were so small. But they came at noon and teased the little folks, and the little folks were bothered by it. So I went out and got after them.

It happened that that family didn't believe in discipline. They thought, "Let the children do what they will." So the kids and some grown-ups hollered at me as I went by in the evening. It was very humiliating. That happened many nights. Sometimes I hated it so badly that I stayed until it was dark so they couldn't see when I went home.

They learned to like me and then they quit tormenting me.

Writing Assignment

Nettie believed in developing strong writing skills and had her own definite ideas about what was important in composition. She required her students to know grammar and mechanics, but for Nettie the heart of composition was good content. She made some interesting discoveries when she read her students' papers.

Where There's Smoke?

I had two eighth-grade boys who were potential writers. Neither of them had much understanding of punctuation. A period here and there would do, but to publishers that is a minor matter, I believe. Good content is what counts.

For composition one dry fall day I asked them to write a story about a fire. One looked at the other, whose face had turned red as a lobster. I had no idea why. One wrote a story that he invented; there wasn't much to it. The other one decided to tell the truth about an embarrassing event.

Nettie in the early 1920s

A little west of the schoolhouse a tiny brook flowed amidst the tall weeds. One of the boys related in his story that just beyond the stream, the boys decided to set fire to the stubble, let it burn about a yard wide, and then put it out. As soon as the match was struck, the fire raced across the field. The boys ran home to tell their dads to come and fight the fire. It was a long way—one and a half miles.

I boarded at the boy's home so when I left for the day, I crossed the scorched area, but thought nothing of it. At that time it was common practice to burn the stubble. I thought the farmer had set the fire to clear the stubble.

Oh, it could have been such a catastrophe! The next day as I crossed the well bridge over the stream, I noticed in that some places the tops of the weeds on the opposite side were charred. If that fire had really taken hold and gone on the other side, a set of brand-new farm buildings would have gone up in smoke. So would the lately built schoolhouse.

I learned about the boys' misadventure from this English lesson. I respected the boys' parents for not telling me, but I'm sure all felt better when we could discuss it freely. The boys didn't mean any harm and no harm came, but it certainly could have.

Ouch!

I told the children to write a story entitled "How I Earned Some Money and How I Spent it Wisely." What they earned they spent for things for school. They could get a lot of school materials at that time for even a dime or a nickel. They could buy a thick pencil tablet for a nickel. One girl got a dime for helping a lady carry her packages and a puppy. Another boy got a quarter for catching a couple of roosters for his mother.

One little stinker said, "One time my dad said he'd give me three dollars if I'd split up a pile of wood. When I was almost through, I cut my toe, so I spent my three dollars doctoring up my toe."

All-Star

As a child Nettie was known for her athletic skills, especially in baseball. As a teacher she helped her students excel in athletics as well as the classroom. One of her students who played on her team said, "When we had competition among the schools on play day, our team was prepared far better than any other school and we always won." He said, "She could catch a ball as fast as any boy could throw it!"

When I asked her if this was true, she said, "Yes, I was quite a ball player. I had fun with the kids. We were a very athletic family, and all the time when we went to country school we played ball. I was the only girl left who stuck with the team, and if I had quit, we wouldn't have had enough to play baseball. So I played ball. I think I was shortstop."

How d' You Do?

Jim Lecy, who was a student in Nettie's school, speaks about Nettie in superlatives. "She was the best. Once we had a program and she wrote the lyrics for a song about us that had everybody laughing. She was a very creative teacher."

> How d' you do everybody,
> How d' you do? (repeat)
> We sent out the invitations,
> So you'd hear our recitations
> And attempts at imitations,
> How d' you do?
> Chorus: How d' you do, How d' you do
> How d' you doodle doodle doodle do?

> Please forgive our little errors
> As we're all beset by terrors.
> How d' you doodle doodle doodle do?
> II
> How d' you do, Billy,
> How d' you do?
> How's the temperature up there?
> Is it cold or is it fair?
> Is it hard to split the air?
> How d' you do?
> When she wants to stroke your hair,
> Does she get up on a chair?
>
> III
> How d' you do, Andy,
> How d' you do?
> So you're sporting a sedan
> Are you proud of your tin can?
> T'aint the car, it's the man.
> If your fliver gives you bother,
> Get by parcel post another,
> How d' you do?

Requiem

Nettie Wait was born on May 1, 1899. She died on January 27, 1996, a few months after our meeting. Nettie was a country school teacher for eleven years. Her love of children and passion for teaching enriched the lives of her students. We are all richer for the gift of her stories.

Malinda Wacholz Heaney

With an hour to spare before an afternoon interview, I walked into 801 Luther Place in Albert Lea and asked the activities director if she knew any residents who would be interested in sharing some of their tales about going to country schools. Without a moment's hesitation, she said, "Malinda Heaney and Helen Mattick." They are always telling us about those schools. (Helen's stories are in Chapter 9.) Some

Malinda Heaney

people think that stories have lives of their own, that they find their listeners. Perhaps that "inner life" guided me to Malinda Heaney.

Malinda Wacholz attended Cloverdale School, District 87, in Freeborn County. She taught at Sunny Brook School, District 118, Kiester Township, Faribault County, from 1924 to 1926. From 1926 to 1928, she taught in Freeborn County at her home school, Cloverdale.

Word Lover

I have many wonderful memories of the years spent in our country school. My earliest discovery was that the words on the blackboard were not the same. Each one was different, and I had to learn the difference. I was in love by words.

I remember how delighted I was to learn the big word *beautiful*. When I got home that night, I searched the newspaper for *beautiful*, hoping to find it and read it to the family.

It wasn't anywhere, so I underlined all the little words that I did know which appeared on the front page, especially *the*. My parents firmly scolded me when they picked up the paper that evening and found it all marked up.   **c. 1911**

Deadly Spelldown

We had a list of 1,000 spelling words which we studied for the annual spelling contest. All five of us at home were studying the same list. When we were milking, we spelled the first 100 words without anyone pronouncing them. The first word on the list was *amputation*.

I still remember the word I missed as a fifth grader at a local contest at Sharps Corner School which eliminated me from further contests. The word was *deceased*.

The teacher who pronounced the word had a very definite lisp. When she said the word, it sounded as if it had a *th* in it so I spelled *detheathed*. If you missed the word, you couldn't enter again.

We loved the competition! How we loved those spelling contests with other schools! We had school yells, and we stood together and shouted them as our horse-drawn sled was pulled into the school yard.

When you're up, you're up.	'V-I-C-T-O-R-Y
When you're down, you're down.	Strawberry shortcake, Are we winners?
When you're up against 87 You're upside down!	Well, I guess. 87-87-yes-yes-yes!

Spelling chants, c. 1914

Side by Side

A very early exposure to the life of a rural school teacher greatly influenced me to become a teacher. My home school, District 87, was located on my father's farm. Our house was small and our family large, but teachers all chose to stay there because it was so close to the school.

They didn't mind sharing a bedroom with my two sisters and me, and the teacher had to sleep with one of us. In a large room serving as a kitchen, sewing, and dining room was a table large enough to seat twelve people. Each evening after supper, the table was cleared, and one half reserved for the teacher and her books and papers. The other half was where we kids did our homework. Before I had homework, I was allowed to sit at the table and color or look at a book as long as I was quiet.

A Great Day

On my tenth birthday several neighborhood girls came to help me celebrate. I was jumping from the hay mow to a hayrack, half filled with hay. I missed the rack and fell on the concrete floor. I didn't break any bones, but I couldn't walk for a year. Since I couldn't attend school, many of my schoolmates and neighbor kids spent time with me playing school. That fall I spent six weeks in the hospital as the doctor's "guinea pig." Again I missed six weeks of school, but finally I returned home, walking on crutches.

The following spring I returned to school. That was a great day in my life because I realized how much I had missed it. Although I had missed so many months, I had kept up on my work. The teacher gave me my assignments and was always there to help me with any questions I had.

April 22, 1915, to fall, 1916

They shall have music to light up their lives.

What a Gift!

My grandparents lived in a small house on our farm. They had a beautiful organ, which my grandpa played. How wonderful it was to hear that music! On many summer evenings when their windows were open, my sister and I stood outside their home and listened as my grandpa played and my grandma sang. When I was nine my grandpa died and we inherited his organ. What a happy day it was when they moved their organ into our house!

All of our teachers could play, and we gathered around the organ and sang. I realized then that if I were going to become a teacher, I must learn how to play. The closest music teacher lived twenty miles away, so I decided to teach myself. I used a book called *How to Learn to Play*. I became so engrossed in reading the notes that I forgot to work the pedals. But I finally learned. After I became a teacher, I was very thankful for the hours I had spent because music became a very important part of my teaching.

Malinda has recently completed her autobiography. Many of the following school stories appear in the first section of her book.

Although Malinda had decided in first grade that she was going to become a teacher, she nearly changed her mind when nurse Belle Thompson entered her life. Nurse Thompson's heroics, facing disease and the threat to her own life, almost swayed Malinda to become a nurse.

Dark, Gloomy Days

In the spring of 1918, when I was thirteen, I wavered a bit in my lifelong ambition to become a teacher. The Spanish influenza epidemic hit our neighborhood. Many families were struck with the illness. In my family George, Billy, Walt, Elmer, Martha, Huldina, Dena and my mother were stricken at the same time. The doctor sent nurse Belle Thompson to care for my mother. Miss Thompson spent six weeks caring for her. I was very fortunate not to get sick and so happy to have the nurse come and take over.

Those were dark, gloomy days, and they were repeated in many families. My sister Martha, Harry Pfanning, and I were in a school play. We got together on a Saturday to practice. We walked home, and as we parted, Harry said, "Now don't get sick!" By Monday Harry was dead. No doctor was able to reach him. We never gave the play.   **1918**

Many Country School Teachers traveled a challenging journey in teachers training before earning their certificates. They encountered demanding teachers, undesirable living conditions, and hours of studying. Malinda's most difficult trial was finding a position. She traveled through the labyrinth of administrative bungling before finally finding a school with an opening.

All's Well That Ends Well!

Albert Lea, Austin, Wells, and Blue Earth all offered programs in teachers training. Wells had a limit of twelve and the rest had a limit of sixteen. On Labor Day of 1923, I went to enroll. One of my former teachers found me lodging and a job, working for her neighbor, Madame Bessenson, a music teacher. My mother and brother George took me and my little trunk to Albert Lea. I was very nervous about working for someone with the title of "Madame," but she was very nice.

On the way to the school, I discovered the quota had been filled. The superintendent called Austin: quota filled. Mankato had an opening, but I had to be there the next day. But first I had to go back to Alden to get my transcript from the high school. Early the next morning mother, my brother George, and I headed for Mankato Teachers College.

Mother suggested we stop and check at Wells. The quota was filled, but the superintendent suggested we wait until the 9 a.m. deadline to see if there were any last minute cancellations. One girl failed to show. Since I had the highest scholastic record of those waiting, I was accepted. I found a place to work for room and board. Mother and George left for home.

The next day I had attended one class when I was called to the superintendent's office. There I met the very angry father of the student who had forfeited her place. The father argued that farm chores had caused them to be late and demanded I give up my place which rightfully belonged to his daughter. The superintendent said the position was legally mine. Then the father became even more irate, demanding, and insulting.

I decided remaining in Wells under those circumstances would be very difficult. But what could I do? I didn't want to lose a year of school! Mother and George had left. Then I thought of Blue Earth. We called and discovered the only boy in class had canceled that day, and if I could be in Blue Earth by 6 p.m., the place was mine.

I turned to the crabby father and told him that if he would take me to Blue Earth and get me there by 6 p.m., I would give up my place to his daughter. I packed and we headed for Blue Earth. The ride was unforgettable. I tried to be friendly and carry on a conversation, but both father and daughter were uncooperative. The father grumbled constantly about the long drive and said he should be home doing chores. He wasn't in the mood for talking.

When I arrived at the school at 5:45 p.m., Miss Marian Drake, my new instructor, was waiting for me and gave me three addresses for places to stay. The nearest was Sixth Street. My unwilling chauffeur took me to the corner of Sixth, stopped at the curb, and unloaded my belongings. He announced that this was as far as he was going. He said he had fulfilled his agreement. But before he drove off, he reached in his pocket and pulled out a ten dollar bill, and said, "That should take care of you until you find help."

I gazed at the disappearing car, feeling lonely and deserted. I found a place to stay, roomed with two other teaching candidates, and began my teachers training in the fall of 1924.

A Sad Day

Esther was one of my roommates. She was our best, but most extravagant, cook. Since her sister was paying her way through school, she always had money. She would shop after school, come home, lock the kitchen door, and prepare supper. The meal was never served until 7:30 or 8:00, and by this time my other roommate and I were famished, but we were never allowed in the kitchen.

Esther was very attractive and had many dates. Unfortunately, her social life came before her studies. She neglected her work and fell behind on special projects. Then she had to stay up all night to catch up, but she couldn't catch up.

One day the state inspector came and asked to see our many projects. He questioned us on our projects and work. Esther had not finished her work and was unable to answer his questions. As a result, she was asked to quit normal training. What a sad day for us when her parents came to move her! We had grown to love each other and she was part of our family.

My Hope Chest

During my first year of teaching I stayed with Mr. and Mrs. Lou Hintz. Mrs. Hintz was shocked to learn that I hadn't prepared a "hope chest." It was customary for every young woman to embroider and crochet linens and doilies for her first home. I knew how to do the work, but I hadn't had the time to prepare this dowry. Emma would not accept my

Malinda Wacholz Heaney, right, and a colleague, dress in turn-of-the-century formal wear for a school event.

excuses that I was too busy with school work. One Saturday she went into town and bought material for me to work on. When I saw what she had purchased, I was astonished. She had bought a dresser scarf, a three-piece buffet set, a luncheon cloth, four napkins, and some fine material for embroidering pillow cases. She gave me the thread and loaned me the hoops and needle. As soon as supper was over, I was expected to sew with her. I realized I had better stay in school until supper time, do my correcting, and plan for the next day because there was no escaping the needle work after supper. Sometimes I did my schoolwork upstairs following the handiwork sessions.

After recalling a disagreement with her father about scratching problems in the barn woodwork and teaching the livestock, (Chapter 3), Malinda explained her philosophy of teaching and why she moved her first school to the maple grove.

When I Can Make the Rules

I found the trees and bushes were a more receptive audience. They at least nodded their heads if there was a gentle breeze.

If the trees in that maple grove could speak, they could reveal a lot of my feelings and frustrations as a child. They were my refuge when I was sad or happy, and especially when I had been unjustly punished with a spanking. I vowed if I ever became a teacher or had a family, I would never, never spank my children. I vowed I would always tell them in advance everything they couldn't and shouldn't do, and then there would never be a reason to spank them.

Malinda Wacholz's teaching career ended in 1928 when she became Mrs. Bob Heaney.

Chapter 9

Spare the Rod?

Dear Diary,

    I'm three weeks into the school term. If things don't get better, one of these mornings I'm going to pack up my clothes during the night, get up extra early, and take off for parts unknown. I'm going crazy. Most of my students are wonderful, polite and well mannered. But I swear some of them were raised by pirates and others by untamed ruffians.

I Got the Low-Down Disciplinary Blues

They taught the latest school techniques,
To tame the savage beasts,
Radical theories so unique,
An educator's feast.

Throughout the years their arsenal sprouted
With ways to stem the tide.
New psychology they touted,
And spewed it out with pride.

I signed the line at seventeen,
So lucky, I believed.
I want to rant and rave and scream
For being so naive.

My theory class, all fluff and bluster
On hooligan control,
Never dealt with bully "Buster"
Or how to keep my soul.

My churlish rogues can spit and swear
And act the playground scourge,
Dunk in ink the pigtailed hair,
'till I want to sing their dirge.

Then they steal some snoose and stick it
Twixt their lips and gums,
Swallowin' juice until they're sick,
They make the outhouse run.

My wretched little knaves can spit
That juice before it dribbles.
Then scoundrels to the playgrounds flit
To tease the girls to nibble.

Billy climbed the school bell tower,
Then couldn't get back down.
Sam fell out of the cottonwood tree,
Six stitches in his crown.

One day my tires lost their air,
Quite a mystery.
My imps said, "Teacher, have no care.
We'll pump them for a fee."

These guys have cigs and love to smoke 'em.
Of course, they're going to fail,
Maybe the sheriff would play a joke
And cart them off to jail.   -TM

    As you can see, Diary, the barbaric ne'er-do-wells have driven me to the brink of desperation. Well, tomorrow's another day. I've packed the wooden ruler used by my mother and grand-mother when they taught. They named it "Old Knuckle Rapper."

    And I have another surprise for the children tomorrow. I've invited the fathers of the trouble-makers to visit class and bring with them their favorite "Discipline Makers." Or, who knows, maybe I'll just head for San Jose and take a dip in the ocean!

    Just picked up my mail. Got a letter from Helen Mattick, a teacher friend. Things look brighter. Wow! I think I've found a mentor!

Helen Mattick
Helen Mattick began teaching in 1926. She taught in the following rural schools in Freeborn County for twenty-three years: Hollendale, Opdahl, Lerdal, and Conger.

Here Comes the Old Bear!

I was known for strict discipline. On the last day that I was teaching in the Lerdal School, the superintendent came and asked me if I would be available

to finish a school in Moscow Township. I asked him what the problem was. He said, "Well, they threw the teacher out bodily and the kids are uncontrollable. Would you like to take them?" Well, with my disposition, I said that I would try. I met with the school board on a Saturday and they told me what an awful mess the school was in. There were thirty-five kids, many quite big. They said, "You can do anything you want with them. We'll stand behind you; only one thing: you cannot kill 'em."

On Monday morning I rang the bell, and they flocked in like you have never seen. They almost ran

Helen Mattick, 1926

over me. I stood in the front and they started throwing books. I don't think they intended to hit me; they just wanted to scare me. I never moved an inch. Finally that got tiresome, so they settled down.

I told them what they had to do. However, they just snickered or laughed, so at the end of the day I said, "I'm going to send all you home tonight, but tomorrow I'm going to have a paper on my desk with the number of minutes you have disturbed me. You are to report this to your parents. You will make this time up after school. Bring your lunch because it might be late."

They went home laughing and snickering again. They came back the next day, and several of the big boys thought they would get me. One boy crawled in the window, and I took him by the nape of the

neck and pushed him out and told him to come in the door. Another one decided to crawl under the seats and tickle all the girls' legs. Well, the girls were really mad. I watched him do it until he was all the way up to the front. When he got to the front, he crawled out from under the row of desks. I grabbed him by the nape of the neck and pushed him down under the desks. I said, "Now that's the way you came up here and that's the way you are going to go back. Girls, everyone of you can kick him in the rear as he goes by." Well, that settled that. But that wasn't the end of it.

The boys went to the toilet and being kinda proud or something, they decided they would see who could wet the ceiling. I went out there right when this was going on. Of course they were embarrassed. I said, "All right, now you go up to the school and get a broom and a pail of water and wash all this." They complained that the water was running down their arms. I said, "I can't help that. That's your problem. You just wash that." I never had that problem again.

When it came time to go home, I kept those that had to stay. The others made up their time and left, but I still had four big boys sitting there. I lit the lamps. I reminded them I had the school board behind me and they had better just sit until their time was up. I ate my supper while they watched me eat. About seven o'clock four fathers came to the school. They stood in the entry way and said, "Now listen! This is enough! We want our kids home!"

I said, "Don't you dare step over that threshold. These kids are going to sit out their time. That was the agreement. That's what I told them to tell you. So don't step over that threshold." Then I said, and I wouldn't dare say this now, but I said, "If I were a parent, I'd be ashamed to be a father of a kid who acted like this."

They walked out and waited outside. When those boys went out, I don't know when I have ever heard kids get a thrashing like those four boys got. From that night on they were the best kids in the school.

The Loving Bear

The parents of those four boys who had given me so much trouble came when they found out their sons were supposed to graduate from eighth grade, but there was little chance that they could pass the state boards. I said to them, "OK, I will sit as long as they want to sit after school and help them with the stuff I know they have to have to graduate. I sat every night with them until 6:30, giving them time and instruction. They all graduated. To me, that was a great success because they became one of the best groups of kids I ever had.

After completing her career as a Country School Teacher, Helen Mattick taught in the Hopkins school system for twenty years.

Vi Fleischer completed her teachers training in 1928. She signed a contract to teach in a country school west of Dumont in Traverse County for ninety dollars a month. In her first difficult disciplinary situation, she forgot a principle she had learned in her training classes.

Flag Pole Blues

When I came to school, I knew someone had been in the building. But I didn't look around too much. The building was quite new and the carpenters came

Viola Fleischer, age18, 1928

out once in awhile, but I didn't think anything about that. When I looked around I noticed that some of the health posters the county nurse had given us had been marked up and defaced. Someone had drawn cigars, mustaches, and beards on the faces. When the youngsters came to school, I asked who had done the decorating. They were quite flabbergasted. No one answered. They all looked at each other, and I didn't know just exactly what I should do because I didn't know who to blame. But I knew someone was guilty.

The day went by and nobody admitted anything, so the next day when they came to school, I had another idea. All the person had to do was write on a piece of paper "I did it." I received no papers at all. Then one little boy came in and said, "Who fixed the flag pole?"

I said, "What's the matter with the flag pole?"

"Well, when we took the flag down yesterday, the rope was broken and it's fixed today." Then I knew that Alfred, the carpenter, who did the pole climbing, had fixed the pole. All of a sudden it dawned on me. It was Alfred who had been in the school and decorated the pictures. I was so embarrassed that I didn't dare tell the youngsters I knew who did it. Maybe they figured it out, but I never admitted I knew. I was very careful after that before I accused someone of doing something naughty.

Vi Fleischer taught in the rural schools of Traverse County for seven years.

Alice M. Reiners completed her teachers training at Mankato State College in 1929. She taught six years in rural school District 60 in Nobles County.

Unthinkable!

I had so much trouble with the B. family. The father was American and his wife was German. He met her as a soldier during World War I. I had many problems with Mrs. B. One of her boys was in trouble constantly. The children were nervous and high strung. The kids came home with tales about other children that weren't true. My mother heard Mrs. B. and another German lady, Mrs. L., talking on the telephone. Mrs. B. thought it was terrible if I disciplined her children. My mother knew what had happened at school before I got home.

Mrs. B. couldn't tell a straight story about her children, and the other lady had a boy who was just as much of a problem case as Mrs. B.'s two boys. Sometimes those two women even fought among themselves.

One morning Mrs. L. was at school when I got there. She said that she was going to kill one of Mrs. B.'s kids. I said, "No! Mrs. L., you don't touch any of these children here." The kids walked up the steps and she finally got in her car and drove away. They tried to be neighborly, but it wouldn't last.

One day one of the B. boys wet a little boy in the outhouse from top to bottom. The other boys told me. I slapped the B. boy across his fingers hard with a ruler. I tried to shame him because I felt so bad for the other boy. So the B.s tried to get rid of me because I'd whipped their son. What the mother should have done was talk to him and explain to him. I told the older sister why I did it. But Mrs. B. thought it was always somebody else's fault.

When she couldn't come to school because she was pregnant, she sent her husband. Poor Mr. B. I felt sorry for him married to her. He was quite timid and very polite. He'd just say, "Mrs. B. sent me down. I had to come down and talk to you." I could get along with him but not his wife.

Alice Reiners, 1930–1936, District 60, Nobles County: Alice also taught twenty years in public schools.

In 1933, Margaret McDougall taught District 104 students in Becker County.

Son of a Gun!

One October morning a board member who had a first grader in my school came very early. He said he wanted to talk to all of us. First, he told me that one of the boys had brought a gun to school and hid it under his coat. I was unaware of this. The man was concerned the other children might want to handle the gun. Next, he asked the boy why he had brought his gun to school. The boy explained that he liked to hunt rabbits. The board member explained why he should leave his gun at home and told him never to bring it again. I thanked him for giving the students a lesson on gun safety. No one ever brought a gun to school again.

Margaret McDougall taught for thirty-eight years, sixteen in the rural schools of Becker and Otter Tail Counties.

Anita Schrupp graduated from La Crosse Teachers College in 1935. Anita rode her horse to District 36 in Houston County, galloping to solve those first-year disciplinary problems.

Forbidden Fruit

I was eighteen and my oldest student was sixteen. I soon found out he smoked cigarettes. I told him I would appreciate it if he would stop. He said he couldn't. It was a habit and he had been doing it for years. I consulted the county superintendent who said the boy couldn't smoke on the school grounds or in the presence of any students.

One day the school board president's son brought a bottle of wine to school. I saw it in his pocket before school started. At recess time I told him what I had seen. He said, "Don't tell my paw."

I said, "OK, take the bottle to the outhouse, empty it, and bring it in, and I don't want any more trouble from you." He became an ideal student.

Anita Schrupp, 1937

From 1942 to 1943, Esther Norhar Babiracki taught in the country school in Beaver Bay.

Call Me Feisty

I had been teaching in Beaver Bay a week when I received a threatening letter from the superintendent that said, "You have been sent to a school with severe discipline problems. If you don't keep these kids under control, people in the community will tattle on you." It was so threatening and it frightened me to death. As a result I became a very strict teacher. I used every ounce of my energy to keep the kids under control. I used severe discipline.

Two weeks later, there was a knock on the door. There stood a large man, smoking a cigar. He was the chairman of the school board. He said, "I want to watch you teach." I kept on going.

Finally, he asked me to talk with him out in the hall. He said, "My fifth-grade daughter is scared to come to school. She said that if you smiled, your face would crack. She is scared because you're too strict."

Well, I just about died. His daughter was such a sweet little thing and the best student I had. He went on and on. I asked him what he wanted me to do, and then I told him about the letter.

He said, "Don't pay any attention to the superintendent. Listen to the people in the community. We're the ones who count."

I said, "What am I going to do here? I'm between the devil and the deep blue sea." Then he started to leave. He was so big and I was so little, but I stood in front of the door with my hands out, blocking him, and said, "You can't go until you tell me what to do."

"I don't know anything about teaching," he said, and he left. He backed off and was polite to me for the rest of the year.

When I got back home, I called the superintendent and told him I wanted to quit. He came with the county nurse the next day. I told him I was quitting. "Oh, don't," he said. "If you get criticized by that man, it means you are the best teacher in Lake County. You can have any school in Two Harbors."

I told the superintendent, "That city isn't big enough for that man and me." I was pretty cocky.

I eased up, but I did quit at the end of that year.

The following year Esther Babiracki left Lake County and taught in Cromwell in Carlton County.

In 1945, Laurabelle Martin began her teaching career in District 15 in Renville County.

Foiled

After the first two weeks, everything in the District 15 school was going well, except for one fourth-grade student who hadn't completed many assignments. I reminded him, "Your mother sent you to school to work and learn something. You must work and study like the rest of the students."

Gordon still wouldn't apply himself. He had a brother in the sixth grade and another in the second grade who were excellent students.

One day, after I had reminded Gordon to get his books out and go to work, he just sat and looked at me. I walked down the aisle and took him by the arm and walked him into the hall. I picked up a slat from a peach crate, swatted him on the seat three or four times and told him when he had stopped crying to come in, sit down, and go to work.

I closed the door and went on with the class work. It wasn't too long before we heard the door squeak. Gordon took a few steps to his seat, sat down, and went to work.

I really didn't give this much thought because Gordon was as busy as the other students. Their mother zoomed up to the school as usual the next morning. I heard the car doors slam and it dawned on me that I would be getting a sermon from her for paddling her son.

To my surprise, I heard the car buzz away from the building. The older brother walked up to my desk and said, "My mom said that you did the right thing, spanking Gordon. He did the same thing last year with the other teacher. She couldn't make him work so he got to go to the Danube school. He thought he could go to Danube again if he didn't do his work."

Laurabelle Martin taught eleven years in the rural schools of Renville County. She then taught in Wabasso from 1963 to 1981.

Ailie Kinnunen began teaching in 1925 and taught for eighteen years in the rural schools of St. Louis, Cook, and Carlton Counties.

A Deadly Lunch

At first the children brought their lunches to school. Then the board gave me permission to buy the groceries and hire a cook to make the meals because we had so many poor children who didn't have food to bring from home. We were also given surplus food. Once we were given a five-pound package of cheese. Toward noon time one of the boys "took" that block of cheese and a gang of the boys went up to the cemetery and ate that cheese. That was a great treat for them. That afternoon

Ailie Kinnunen, c. 1928,

the supervisors came in to check on my lunch program. I was really embarrassed. I reported what had happened, but they weren't too concerned. They just said, "Let it slide."

Ailie Kinnunen, 1945, St. Louis County

The following story is unlike the other stories in this chapter because it is told by a student.

A Parable

The teacher put all our names on the board at the beginning of the year and wrote "100" under each. This meant each one of us was starting with a perfect score in deportment. If we did something wrong, the teacher deducted points. The teacher wouldn't say anything. She'd just walk to the board, erase the 100, and write in 99 or whatever number of points she wanted to write. If we dropped below 75, that meant we failed deportment for the year.

One of the guys was kinda wise. He liked to talk to other kids, and he had this smirk, a grin that really irritated the teachers. On the first day he was talking and the teacher erased the 100 under his name and wrote 99. He said something like, "What's that for?"

Then the teacher erased the 99 and wrote in 98, no words, just a quick erasing and a reduced number. Then the kid said something like, "What did I do?" The teacher erased the number and reduced the number five or ten points. This continued until he had dropped below 75! That meant he failed deportment for the year and the first day wasn't over. Then the teacher slapped him again.

This went on all year. While he was in that school, he had two teachers and they slapped him repeatedly throughout the year. They slapped him so many times at one sitting that his face was just white from being hit. His face was red but it was white where they had slapped him so often. We could see their finger marks on his skin.

The rest of us just had to sit there and watch it. The kid just continued to sass back. We didn't tell our folks. Our parents were strict Germans and they would probably have said, "He had it coming!" I guess we just accepted this as discipline back then.

But nobody ever won. **St. Benedict, Scott County**

In 1951, Charles T. Steenblock taught in District 106 in Mower County. Charles developed a unique philosophy of discipline.

Havin' Fun

I found that it helped discipline if I kept a kid after school. November was always a good time for that because it got dark so early. The students thought it was later than it was. If I did school work or read, the kid could still outlast me. If they had to work, I had to work, too.

So I played solitaire. I hated cards, but I played solitaire because that really infuriated them. They associated card playing with having fun. But if I were reading or doing school work, they didn't feel I was ignoring them. They figured they could out wait me on that. But if I were playing cards, they figured I could go on having fun all night.

Charles T. Steenblock, 1951

Dear Diary, I've tried all the tactics used by these teachers. I started lifting weights but I'm still having problems. I screamed today! No success!

In 1962, Hazel Peschel taught in the Hellerman School in Stearns County.

The Sprinter

The Hellerman School lost the teacher they had had for over thirty years. Her sister tried to take her place, but she didn't have any discipline. The kids were uncontrollable, so the board came looking for me. I had recently undergone surgery and weighed only 110 pounds. When I walked into the board meeting, they looked at me and said, "Do you think you can handle eight grades and thirty-seven kids?"

I said that I would give it a try. They asked me to come at 10:00 the next morning, so they would have time to dismiss the teacher. I arrived and began to teach. About an hour later a fifth-grade boy asked if he could go to the bathroom. I excused him and went on with my class. I thought nothing of it.

When he came back in, he opened the hall window and jumped out. I had been told that he did things like that. Well, I ran out of that room as fast as I could. When I caught him, I brought him in, laid him over the kindergarten table, and paddled him in front of the rest of the students, not to hurt him but to embarrass him. It did the trick. He never *Hazel Peschel, age 20, 1939* tried anything like that again, and I had eight good years there until the school closed in 1970.

Hazel Peschel, 1962, Hellerman School, Stearns County: Hazel Peschel taught for fifteen years in the rural schools of Todd, Meeker, Cook, and Stearns Counties.

Dear Diary,

What a wonderful view of the ocean! What a relief to escape from all those nasty discipline problems! The gulls catch the gentle breeze and float into the sky. I think I saw Jonathan Seagull yesterday. I love sprinting into the water and diving into one of those huge waves. The cold salt water washes away all those bad memories. This is paradise. But the summer is almost over, and I'm going back to my remote little school surrounded by the giant trees of Cook County. I know I grumble a lot, but I miss those children. Sometimes I have problems, but they don't seem so overwhelming as I lie here in the sun reading One Hundred Ways to Better Discipline Without Losing Your Sanity.

Things will go better this year. I'm taking a pre-school workshop from Helen Mattick, Hazel Peschel, and Charles Steenblock.

Gotta go. Time for my ten-mile run before my hour of weightlifting. See you in September.

Chapter 10

They Roared in the '20s

Most of the teachers in this chapter are in their 90s. They began their teaching careers when they were teenagers and taught through the "Roaring '20s." However, the images most people associate with this era were quite foreign to the strict religious doctrines of the Norwegians around Granite Falls, the German Lutherans in the New Ulm area, or the Dutch Reform Church around Edgerton.

People on the farms of Freeborn, Chippewa, Beltrami, and Wadena Counties seldom dressed in flapper chemises or tuxedos, danced the Charleston, or poured alcohol from silver flasks. Typical farmhouses, barns, or country schools did not glitter from the lights of dazzling chandeliers or throb to the beat of ragtime.

A few adventurers did hear the "roaring" and their dancing spirits answered the call of the three-piece bands and the forbidden dance halls. However, the bright lights of Broadway and the Great White Way were a million miles from Lulu Rud's Cedardale School near the Rainy River.

Lu (Lulu) Rud
Lu Rud was born in Birchdale in 1898 and attended Indus School from 1904 to 1912.

Lulu Rud c. 1908

School Days
I went to a little school near Manitou Rapids with only six students. It was near the Manitou Rapids but now nothing is there. Our school was small with two rooms. Sometimes we had our classes outside. The little building we were in was turned into a schoolhouse. It used to be a bachelor's house, divided into two parts. When he was living there, he lived in one part and had his horses in the other. It had to be pretty well cleaned out before we used it for a school.

During recess we played games. Some we made up. One we called "toad in a hole." We dug a bunch of holes in a circle. Then we put a hole in the center. We tried to shoot stones into the center hole—toad in the hole.

Annie Just Disappeared
My oldest brother was a janitor for the school. Everyday the teacher asked what we wanted to sing for opening services. Every time the little Mason kids, Addison and Roy, popped up and said, "Little Annie Rooney." We got pretty tired of "Little Annie Rooney." So when my brother built the fire one morning, he sent "Little Annie Rooney" up the chimney. He put the music in the fire. We didn't sing "Annie Rooney" anymore. When the Mason kids asked for "Little Annie Rooney," she wasn't there; they looked but they couldn't find her. My brother never said anything about it. We knew where she went, but the teacher didn't.

Sioux Neighbors
The Sioux Indian reservation was right across the Rainy River from our school. In the winter the Indians came across to the American side to fish. They cut a hole in the ice and put down some branches and balsam boughs. They put a blanket on top of that and wrapped themselves up in another blanket and fished down that hole. This was approximately 1912.

The Indian children had their own school. We did go over and visit their school. It was a real treat. The reservation was right across from our house and my dad used to have the Indians come over and peel poles and posts for him. We did learn quite a few Indian words. The girls used to come over to our place and make out orders to Sears Roebuck, and then when the orders came, they'd come back and pick them up.

After graduation from Indus High School in 1918, Lu Rud attended three months of teachers training in Moorhead. In 1920, Lu signed a contract to teach at Cedarwood School, which was located seven miles from Frontier, twenty-two miles east of Baudette.

1920

When Lu Rud stepped on the boat to take her down the Rainy River, she had no idea that Antoine de Paris had created the mannish bob haircut for fashionable women or that school children in the cities could now buy a new choco-late-covered ice cream treat called the Good Humor Bar. Isolated in the north woods, Lu had no chance of reading two new controversial novels: *Main Street* by Sinclair Lewis and *This Side of Paradise* by F. Scott Fitzgerald. During her vacation breaks, Lu would have had to travel far to attend the opening of The Ziegfeld Follies or watch Douglas Fairbanks fly across the silver screen in *The Mark of Zorro*.

LuLu Rud takes the Rainy River boat to school.

Up the Lazy River

To get to the school, I had to go by boat. I traveled on the Rainy River in a gasoline launch that took mail the seven or eight miles from Indus to Baudette. It must have been three or four hours, though, because they had to stop at all the little mail places along the river. I rode down to farmer Seymor Lloyd's house. From there I went by wagon, seven miles back to Cedarwood School.

Batching It

I batched in the schoolhouse. I lived in there all winter long. It wasn't so bad. There were neighbors about a quarter of a mile, so I could go there any time I wanted to and visit. To pass the time in the winter when I was alone, I read most of the time. I didn't feel particularly lonely. One night it was a little bit scary because I heard some animal outside on the other side of the wall from where I was sleeping. The animal was snoring. I don't know yet whether it was a bear or what it was. I didn't get up to see. I always carried an Iver Johnson pistol. One time when I was out walking, I saw green eyes staring at me, and I shot at them. Whatever it was, probably a wolf, it disappeared into the woods.

Miss Lulu Rud, 1920–1921

The school had a boxwood heater, a long stove, something like a barrel with a flat top I could cook on. The only heat in the building was close to the stove. It was fairly warm in the school because there was always wood which I carried in. The county contracted for the wood and they had it delivered right next to the schoolhouse. I had to split it sometimes, which was a lot of work. I washed my clothes in a washtub. No running water. I brought the water in and heated it on the stove. There were outdoor toilets, and they had to be taken care of, too. Once in awhile I had to wash them down. Not in the winter time, though. I ate oatmeal every morning. I didn't plan my meals out before I went shopping. Usually I ate meat and potatoes and sometimes cake or doughnuts for a special treat.

The river was not open all winter. For seven straight months I stayed at the school all alone. There was a two-week break at Christmas time, but I stayed at the school. It was a fairly mild winter. The roads were usually open enough so I could get on the trails anyhow.

Social Life

The store was about seven miles away. I went once a week, usually on Saturday and stayed overnight with the Lloyd family. During the weekend, we visited quite a bit. They didn't play cards. My social life was mainly the seven-mile walk, buying my groceries, and visiting with the Lloyd family. They had two boys and a little girl, but there was nobody my own age around. Then I'd head off on Sunday morning for school. I carried my groceries for the week in my backsack.

Lu's road to Cedardale

Paid by Scrip

I was supposed to be paid sixty dollars a month. The county was broke at that time so we were paid in scrip, and I had to wait for my money until the county got rich enough to pay us. The grocery bills, and so on, I had to charge until I could get my checks. It was way towards spring before I got paid. I went most of the year being paid by scrip. I had no money. But the only place to spend money was the local grocery store because there wasn't any other entertainment. I signed for the groceries, and then I had to pay up in the spring. I don't know how the grocery store handled it. I didn't have any difficulty getting paid in the spring.

No visitors came! Lulu lived alone for seven months.

Alone

My family never came to visit me because it was too far for them to get in there. I didn't have too many books there and there was no place to get books, but I read quite a bit from what I had. There were always lessons to prepare for the next day and papers to correct.

I was never invited to my students' homes. That was the funny part. The Hartnows were the only ones that really had me come out to their place. I didn't visit too often. There were only two families, four children from one family and two from the other. They knew I was up there all alone. There was no local entertainment that I knew of. If they did have some, they didn't invite me.

I stayed at the school for seven straight months. I decided teaching was not the job for me. It kind of entered my head that I wasn't advancing my own knowledge with my teaching. I worked at the store in Indus, clerking for one summer. Then I met a guy and in 1922 we were married.

1921

Rudolph Valentino set hearts a flutter as *The Sheik,* and Charlie Chaplin broke those same hearts as *The Kid.* Coco Chanel introduced her perfume No. 5, and the Parker Pen Company sold "Big Red" for seven dollars. Country School Teachers sang "Ma, He's Makin' Eyes at Me" when a suitor came calling. Judge Landis barred Shoeless Joe Jackson and the infamous Chicago Eight from baseball for life. Johnson and Johnson gave Country School Teachers the healing gift of Band-Aids.

Gwen Dansuer Judge

Gwen Dansuer Judge began teaching in 1921 at the age of eighteen. She taught until 1925 in schools near Plainview in Wabasha County.

Something Up My Sleeve

In 1921, $100 a month was a lot of money. I was going with this man. The school board told me to come out because they wanted to talk to me. When I went in, my boyfriend said, "Don't you sign that contract." We were kind of planning on getting married.

I said "No, I won't sign the contract." Well, they offered me such a good salary that I didn't have the heart to turn it down. So I had the contract up my sleeve when I came out.

He said, "You did sign that contract, didn't you?"

I said, "Yes, I did." He was really mad at me but I told him,"You know, I couldn't turn it down." A few years later I didn't sign the contract. I married him instead.

To Sin or Not to Sin?

I used to love to dance, but my landlady said, "If you go to a dance, you will go straight to hell, so remember that." She was quite religious and when I came home late, she would be waiting for me the next afternoon when I got home from school. She would ask, "Did you go to a dance last night?" She always wanted to know everything.

I couldn't lie. I'd say, "Yeah, yeah, I did." I loved to dance. But she was nice to me. She tried to be a mother to me because I was quite young. I think she thought I needed a little guidance.

66

And she didn't want me to go out with men. Of course, I went out with men when I went dancing. Oh, boy, when I came home after I'd been to a dance with men, she lectured me. She told me I had sinned. Dancing and dating were wrong. Now that I'm older (ninety-four), I know she was just trying to guide me. But I just loved to dance, and if I had a chance to go to a dance, I went, sin or no sin.

Oh, My Darling!

I remember I always loved green and blue. Those were my favorite colors. In those days we didn't have a lot of clothes. We didn't have a lot of money to spend for clothes. The first year I taught, I bought clothes. I guess I spent everything I earned to get dressed up. I was all dressed in blue and green. Everything matched. All the old business men sat on their gossip benches, and when I walked by, they said, "Oh, here comes Darling Dansuer." They were shocked. They never called me Gwen. They always called me "Darling Dansuer." Believe me, I came home dressed up.

When Gwen's feet said, "We've got to dance," she connived and finagled ways to reach the music. Then she met herself in a revolving door.

Trapped

When my future husband came to see me, he always brought me flowers or candy or some gift. But this other fellow, oh, could he dance! But he was such a

Gwen Dansuer Judge began her career at age eighteen.

cheapskate. He never brought me anything. I couldn't stand him because he was so cheap, but, boy, could he dance. So I often went to dances with him without my future husband finding out. When my fiance couldn't go, I called the cheapskate.

My fiance called me on a night we had a date to go to a dance and he said, "I'm sorry, but I just can't come to pick you up tonight. I called to say "I'm sorry."

After I had talked to him, I thought I'd call this other guy because I wanted to go to that dance. I called and he came. He drove into the yard, and who drove in right behind him, my husband-to-be. I knew I was in real trouble. I knew that sooner or later I'd get into trouble because you can't pull those tricks. But I tried. I probably wasn't even twenty.

He knew I was cheating on him. He said, "You make up your mind and make it up fast. It's either him or me." So I got rid of the other guy. I told him to get lost.

I was brought up in a very strict home. I didn't have a lot of leeway. My dad was very strict. So when I got out on my own, I was going to see if I couldn't do things I never got to do at home. And I really did until he said, "Gwen, make up your mind right now."

Buddy, Better Get on Down the Line!

One family had four children, and they were all good workers except this one little girl. She was cuter than a bug, but lazy. I'd give her work and I'd say "Now, I want you to get this all done." I'd praise her and say, "You're a good worker and I know you'll have it all done. Then bring it up to my desk."

Well, she doodled on the paper instead of doing the work. And I could see this from my desk. I'd get so irritated. She wasn't doing any work. She had a little red velvet dress on and I went back and I didn't mean to, but I grabbed her by the shoulder. I was so mad at her. And I ripped her dress out of the shoulder seam.

Then her dad, a great big guy, came after school and knocked on the door. I opened the door and he said, "I'm going to clean your clock!"

I wasn't very big, but I said, "Now, just a minute. You're sending your children here for me to teach them. And if she doesn't learn anything, you wouldn't be very happy. Do you know that this little girl is lazy?" He agreed.

"I'm running this school," I said, "and if you don't like what I'm doing, there are two or three schools down the road. You just take your kids down there."

He was my best friend when he left. He wasn't going to haul those kids to another school. That girl studied from then on! He put a quick stop to the doodling. They baked me a cake for my birthday.

Lillian Livingston

Lillian Livingston, born in 1902, began school in 1909. Lillian's grandmother and mother made it perfectly clear as to what was socially acceptable and unacceptable behavior for a Scottish girl.

Not the Marrying Kind

I was nearly seven when I started school in District 18 in Lyon County. My sister, who was five and a half, went with me. We lived on Grandpa's farm. Mother had been the hired girl when she married Dad on Grandpa's farm. Grandma and Grandpa Livingston were still living on with us.

My sister and I played in the kitchen on cold winter days while mother and grandma worked around us. Grandma talked and talked and talked. Her main topic of conversation was marriage. She had the idea that a girl was no good at all unless she had her man by the time she was seventeen years old. Twenty-five, that was awfully late! You pitied

Lillian Livingston, 1921

her then. But she was absolutely a disgrace if she hadn't married by then. So we listened to that all the time.

My mother, I don't think you could call it racism, but she was definitely against certain people. Before my sister and I started school, she told us, "Well, there'll be one other family of white people besides yours that will be going to school there," and she told us who they were.

So we went to school, and I thought that those horrible people would be there. I decided not to pay any attention to them; they just were not nice people. But then I saw all these boys. Some of them

"This is where the evil Swedes and I went to school. My teacher finished only the eighth grade. I have no idea how I learned, but I could read fourth-grade material in the third grade."

were really nice fellows. But Mother was never going to have a son-in-law from that group. The ones that she disliked, the ones that she considered not acceptable families, well, they were the Swedes!

So that bothered me. Here were all of these boys and they were kinda nice, too, and if a person was going to pick out somebody to marry from that group, it would have to be a Swede. That would have been terrible and it just couldn't be!

Mother's attitude certainly affected me. One time something happened in the schoolroom. I can't remember what it was, but I got mad at the teacher. When we went out for recess, I was not very far out the front door and the door must have been open a crack because I said something about "that darn Swede teacher!" She heard what I had said and she looked out the door. I don't remember what happened after that, but I was flabbergasted.

Finance 101

I worked for the bank president for three years to pay for my room and board while I attended high school. He was so impressed with my diligence and academic achievement that he suggested a unique way for me to finance my education. He agreed to lend me money to use to get my certificate to teach in the rural schools. He arranged for me to get a life insurance policy made out to the bank which lent me $100 to attend summer school in order to teach. When I paid the bank, I got the policy, which helped me every step forward. I kept that policy up for years and years, and every time I wanted to go back to school for something, I borrowed from it. It was a very handy thing to have.

Bigotry 101

I went to Mankato State Teachers College. Actually, we weren't trained very well. However, the only incident I recall is the day one of the instructors in health class said, "Now if you ever become interested in some person from the South, watch out! There might be Negro blood there." He stressed that point. I don't know why. He must have had some reason, but he was very insistent that we know that. I was curious about why he was so insistent. I had never seen a black person. **Lillian taught in Lyon, Murray, and Nicollet Counties from 1921 to 1926.**

Teaching 101

In my first year of teaching, one of the older boys, who was about thirteen, got mad at me, but I don't remember why. On Friday night he said, "I'm not coming back here! I just am not coming back."

68

So I spent a worrisome weekend and I watched for him on Monday morning to see if he came. Well, when he came, he had a big bouquet of lilacs. I could hardly see him for the size of the lilac bouquet. I never heard anymore about why he was mad.

The boy who let the lilacs speak for him is standing next to Miss Livingston (top left), 1922, District 60, Lyon County.

Cold and Bored

Certain places housed the teacher year after year so it was expected that I stay at the same place. The place was so cold that I took my clothes to bed so I could get up and jump into them fast and run downstairs where there was a fire. There was no heat upstairs. Wind chills hadn't been invented yet, but chilblains had. Each day I woke in the cold, walked the half mile to school, fired up the stove at 7:30, and taught the full schedule. But what was worst of all was the boredom. There was nothing to do in the evenings. There was no radio. There wasn't anything to read, no paper, no magazines, no library books in the school, so I embroidered—stuff I never used, all perfectly useless, a waste of time.

1922–1923, District 110, Murray County
Lillian Livingston taught a total of forty-two years, five in the rural schools.

1924
Little Orphan Annie appears in the comics. Like Country School Teacher, Annie extols the values of rugged individualism. Kleenex Kerchiefs and Wheaties, "the Breakfast of Champions," appear on grocery shelves. Country School Students meet *Bambi* **for the first time. The year is the first for an around-the-world flight, Chrysler cars, the Winter Olympics, MGM, Columbia Pictures, IBM, Saks Fifth Avenue, and DDT. Americans elect President Coolidge. New Yorkers march in Macy's first parade, and Helen Arbes parades off to her first day of teaching, humming "When My Sugar Walks Down the Street."**

Helen Arbes
Helen Arbes grew up in Wadena, and in 1923 she completed the one-year teachers training course at age seventeen.

First Year at Blue Grass
My first year of teaching was 1924 in District 38 in Wadena County near Blue Grass. That school was a bleak place surrounded by a jack pine forest. The farmers cut the trees and took them into Menagha to be used for telephone poles. I was so isolated there. The school sat out in the woods with nothing but a country lane running by. I got eighty dollars a month for eight months. I lived in a farm

Helen Arbes, 1924 District 38, Fairview School, Verndale, Wadena County

house. These people were very quiet people and it wasn't a very good place for me to be, homesick and lonesome as I was. I had thirty-eight kids in that class from only six different families and three kids were retarded. I didn't know they were retarded. I just thought they were not very smart, but I did the best I could.

Little Red Riding Teacher
I took a path to school that went across a meadow, over a river, and through a woods rather than walk on the road because it was only about a mile. In the big woods the big timber wolves crossed my path. I saw their tracks when I walked through there. Later, some hunters from Wadena came and shot several of them.

The Sawmill Guys
In 1925, I went to a school nine miles out of Menagha. There were a couple fellows who had been dating the schoolteachers, and they competed to see who could take me back and forth from school to my boarding house. They worked at a sawmill across the way. Axel was the one I depended on because he had a little more money, and he was a little more responsible than Lawrence. Lawrence was handsome and I kinda liked him, too.

They watched to see when I would take the flag down at night. The flag hung out so they could see it from the road. Then they raced to see who would get there first to take me home. Once in awhile I got left because between my taking the flag down and taking it back into the school, they came by and thought I'd gone home, so I had to walk home.

One night Lawrence came over to pick me up and he said, "Oh, I feel so sorry for Axel. He had to go home sick. They think he has the flu." Lawrence then asked me to go to the movies in Menagha that night, and I said, "Sure."

We drove by Axel's house and felt so sorry for him because he was sick. We got to the movie in Menagha, which was nothing but a hall with a movie in it. We were sitting there enjoying ourselves. When we turned around, there was Axel, sitting three seats behind us. He never said a word. I didn't marry Lawrence, but Axel married the teacher who came after I left. **1925, District 19, near Menagha**

I think I'll act gruff and hassle that timid new teacher. Helen Arbes creates "The Legend of Billy Goat Gruff."

Stymied

I had a problem with a billy goat. There was a little footbridge from my boarding house to the other side of the river. This darn billy goat didn't like me. Every night when I came home from school, that billy goat waited for me on the bridge. He just stood there so I couldn't get by. Every day I had to call to my landlord to get the billy goat off. I suspect my my landlord wasn't happy with me.

First Woman Coach?

In 1927, I went for my second year of college at Moorhead. I took a course in coaching because it was the only course I could get to fill in my schedule. Coach Nipsick, who taught the class, was disgusted to have a woman in the class. Then I got a position in Dumont in Traverse County. We also had the first two years of high school, which

another woman taught. There were eight kids in those classes who wanted to play football, so I coached football for those eight kids. I designed the plays I had learned from Coach Nipsick. We had two pictures on the board like he did, but with no more than seven or eight boys, how do you play football? Nevertheless, those boys could still say they played football. **1927, Dumont, Traverse County**

1925

When Rose Tyrholm and Blanche Olson become Country School Teachers in 1925, John T. Scopes is convicted in the famous Monkey Trial for teaching evolution, Hitler publishes the first part of *Mein Kampf*, Pretty Boy Floyd terrorizes the Midwest, Ramon Navarro stars as *Ben Hur*, and Tallulah Bankhead shines in *Fallen Angels*. Forty thousand Ku Klux Klan members march in Washington, D.C. The Charelston becomes the rage, synthetic rubber is developed, the first issues of *Cosmopolitan* and *The New Yorker* hit the newsstands. Radio station MSM broadcasts Barn Dance, which will soon become the Grand Ole Opry. Americans are singing "Yes, Sir, That's My Baby" and "Sweet Georgia Brown."

Rose Tyrholm

Rose Tyrholm attended elementary school in District 50, Gordonsville School, in Freeborn County from 1913 to 1920.

Strength

We were taught by Miss Ione Flatt. One day someone knocked at the door and she answered it. I'd heard my grandma say that people could turn white as a ghost. Well, Miss Ione Elizabeth Flatt turned white as a ghost when she talked to that person, but she came right back in. She said "Now, children, where were we?" Then she conducted school serenely for the rest of the afternoon.

My father often picked us up because this gave him an excuse to stop in and gab with his pal Ross Buchanan. When I got to Ross and Mabel's house that night after school, Ross said, "What a tragedy! Miss Flatt's father was hit by a train and killed this afternoon." Those people had come to the door, and, I presume with less than the desirable amount of tact, had given her that message. Yet she remained the teacher. She didn't upset us children. I will never forget that day because she maintained such a calm atmosphere. No one was aware that tragedy had befallen her. She was so strong!

Loss

In 1918, when I was in fifth grade, Miss Ione Elizabeth Flatt gave up her position and went to Washington to do war work with Miss Pierce, another one of my teachers. We had a substitute who said, "Oh, you have such funny names here. Where did you get those names?" She acted so haughty and we were unaccustomed to that.

During that fall of 1918, the Spanish influenza burst on the scene, and our beloved Miss Pierce died in Washington, D. C. Our classroom windows on the east side faced the church and the windows on the west side faced the Rock Island Depot. When we heard the train whistle, the substitute teacher couldn't prevent us from flocking to the west windows. Miss Pierce was coming home.

We watched the unloading of the casket into a horse-drawn hearse. Then we followed right around, looking out the east window as the coffin was brought to the church. We were upset because we were not dismissed to go to Miss Pierce's funeral, but I don't think there was a dry eye in that room because she had been one of us.

Two weeks later they brought my Uncle Will's body from Camp Cody, New Mexico, where he had also died from the influenza. But this time I saw the funeral because we sat as a family. We sat in the church, waiting for that casket, but they couldn't bring it in because of the danger of the influenza.

When we left the church, we went down the road just a few miles to the cemetery. I had never seen grownups cry until that day when they lowered Uncle Will's body into the grave. It was one of the worst days of my life. My father didn't cry. He just moaned. Those two deaths in 1918 were terrible for me. I was going on twelve.

Rose taught at the following schools in Freeborn County: District 60, Westside Hollandale, Campbell, Mansfield, and Itasca.

Will You Be Kind Like Them?

The school wasn't ready to open on the Tuesday after Labor Day. They had just putzed along getting it built. There were two old Norwegian carpenters who didn't move very fast. I insisted they teach me how to putty the nail holes, and I puttied every nail hole in that schoolhouse. I was so impatient to get the building finished.

Many people came to talk to me while I was puttying. One lady said, "I have a daughter who will be in your eighth-grade class." Then she asked me if I knew my grandmother very well. My grandmother lived in Kansas City and only came for visits. I adored her. She was my role model. She had been a teacher, but I didn't know her that well.

This woman said, "I think the world of her. In 1898 I was just sixteen, fresh from Bohemia. I was staying with my brother. There was this handsome young boy who spoke Bohemian. I fell in love with him and sadly I became pregnant. My brother forced me out of the house. I was walking in the snow without boots or winter clothes, wishing that I could die.

"Along came your grandfather Bragg in his cutter. He pulled up and said, 'You shouldn't be out here. Get in the cutter.' But I was afraid. I couldn't speak English. I thought perhaps he was going to take me away or kill me. But he tucked the robe around my knees and went right on around the corner up to his house. He just drove right up to the door and called out to your grandmother, and she came and got me.

"She took me in and fed me along with the family, and they made me comfortable. Somehow I managed to communicate my problem to your grandmother. First your grandfather got my young man, and then he got the minister. We had a wedding right there in your grandpa and grandma's house. Your grandma played the organ and sang a hymn. She said I was properly married before I had the baby."

She said, "I have always felt that if God and church was any better than your grandfather and grandmother, they'd have to prove it to me."

She told me this story while I puttied, talking even after it had grown dark. I think she wanted me to know her story and to know what kind of people my grandparents were. I think she hoped I would be that kind of person for her daughter Eleanor.

1925, District 60, Freeborn County
Rose Tyrholm left teaching after the 1925 school year, but she returned in 1945 and taught at the following Freeborn County schools: Westside, Hollandale, Campbell, and Mansfield.

Blanche Quist Olson

Blanche Quist Olson was born in 1906. From 1912 to 1920, she attended elementary school in District 36, which is located between Blue Earth and Delavan.

During those years she had many teachers, some who ruled with a hose and some who taught with a gentle touch. Blanche's grade school years were filled with many experiences which helped form her ideas about what teaching should be and what it should not be.

Miss Molasses

We didn't get to go to town very often with a team of horses. One time I had to have new shoes, so dad took me along when he went to the creamery. When I came back, my teacher was so mad. She said, "I taught those people long division while you were gone. You can just stand up to the board till you figure out how to do it." I thought that I'd be there six weeks trying to figure out how to do it. How would I know unless I knew how to start?

Then she said, "Get busy and do something."

I said, "I don't know what to do. How can I do it when I don't know what to do?" She had a big ruler, one of those kind you used to stamp letters. She cracked me across the face. I let fly with my book. I didn't hit her. I missed her, unfortunately.

I went to my seat and gritted my teeth. I said, "I'm going to tell my dad, and he's on the school board." She pulled on me but I hung on to the desk. She didn't teach me much. She spent so much time filing her fingernails that she hardly had time to teach school.

The next night she had a date with a guy who was working at our place. Boy, she was all molasses. The next day she had to make up to me.

1912–1913

Miss Hose

We had some boys who were nasty. I can remember them getting punished. The teacher had a big piece of hose, and she'd whale the daylights out of them. I cried when they got hurt because I figured she was doing a lot of damage to those kids.

She was a nice teacher, but if we did something wrong, we really got it. My brother got into quite a bit of trouble, so I had to do the crying for him. One time she sent the boys to get water. They had to haul it a quarter of a mile across the field because we didn't have a well. Next she chased the rest of us outdoors on that really cold, raw day, and she locked the door. We all had to go outside, little kids and all, so she could have her dinner in peace. Those little kids cried because it was so cold. When the boys got back with the water, she wouldn't let them in, so one of the boys swore at her.

She whaled the tar out of him. She hit him wherever she could reach him because he was trying to get away from her. She was just laying it on. He had a nosebleed and I don't know what all. I never forgot it. I thought it was just awful. But I never liked the bird. He was mean to us girls.

Later that day his dad came down to my dad, who was on the school board, and the boy's dad complained that she beat his son up pretty good. Dad said, "Well, they go to school to learn, and if they don't behave, then somebody has to pay for it."

The boy's dad had had a few drinks and by the time he left, he said, "Ya, that's true. I'm going home, get a whip, and send it down to the teacher so she has a good whip." **c. 1915**

Blanche completed her teachers training in 1926. Like many country school teachers, she remembers her students as if they were sitting in front of her today. One after another, her stories about her students dramatize the life and emotions of Country School Teacher. Blanche taught in Faribault, Freeborn, and Waseca Counties.

Blanche's first teaching job was unique. She signed up to teach in the Jones School near Winnebago. But in 1927, the school had only two students. When Blanche said she wouldn't stay to teach only two students, the board insisted on keeping the school open, so Blanche resigned and moved on to District 112 near Bass Lake, also in Faribault County.

Part 1: Tommy

The school I taught in south of Blue Earth was a toughie. Oh, man, they had a terrible time out there. The first day I came, the students said, "The last teacher we had here we cut the running board on her car and carved it all up with our knives."

I said, "Don't anybody touch my car because they always go to jail if they do." They didn't say anymore about that.

Then they said, "She sometimes got mad and jumped up and down and pulled her own hair."

"Well, I may pull hair but it won't be mine," I said, and, "I'm not gonna jump up and down."

They were just terrible, and they swore like pirates. One day Tommy cut loose with some cussing. I can't remember what he said, but I said, "Well, Tommy, looks like you're in trouble. You better stay and we'll talk about it after school."

After school he said, "Would you like me to wash the boards for you? I better clean the erasers too." I thought he'd go right out the door. But no, he cleaned the erasers, and then he sat down and said, "Anything else you want me to do?"

"No," I said, "I guess that's about it."

"Well, if you're going to punish me, you better do it because otherwise dad will whale me when I get home."

"No," I said, "I don't think I'll bother. I don't think you're worth it. If this is the way I'll have to deal with you this year, I don't think it's worth it." The kid cried, and I never had a speck of trouble from him. Whenever I wanted something done, Tommy was right there to help me. I bet if I'd have whipped him or even touched him, I would have been in trouble.

Part 2: Tommy's Home
Tommy came from a big family, and they had a terrible time. One time my car wouldn't start, and I had to walk down to their place and call. They had straw on the floor for the kids to sleep on. They had no upstairs. There were so many of them they didn't have beds. I stood there making my call from the wall phone. When I got back to the car, I felt a bedbug crawl up my leg. They went home for dinner every day, and I swear they had onions and bread every day. They had to eat something.

Part 3: Tommy's Brother
Tommy had a brother in the second grade who swore like a pirate. On the first day of school I gave him some problems—some had plus and some had minus. He paid no attention to the directions and added them all and forgot completely about the subtraction problems. "Oh, my, Richard," I said, "it's too bad you did those all the same. You didn't even look at those signs. Some were plus and some were minus."

"Well, goddam you!" he hollered. "I worked them and I ain't doin' them again!"

"Oh, yes, you are!" I said. Well, he did them over. Cussed like a pirate! But those kids couldn't help swearing. Their parents swore all the time.

Part 4: Tommy Returns
About eighteen or twenty years later I went to a dance out at Walnut Lake, which is south of Easton. This big, tall guy in a navy uniform came up and asked me to dance. It was my Tommy
1929–1930, Faribault County

Sausage Anyone?
The women from the State Department used to come out and visit. We never knew when they were going to rap on the door, but they usually came out in March. The Mothers Club had made some curtains, but nobody wanted them. I didn't want them, but the women put them over the bottom half of the windows so the kids couldn't look outside. One of these ladies from the State Department came in and looked at those curtains. "Well," she exclaimed, "this looks like a Polish meat market!"
1938–1939, Freeborn County

1926
Country School Teachers' looks change with the perfection of the permanent wave method, which makes "permanent" the fashionable hairstyle. Romantics sing "Baby Face" and "Gimme' a Little Kiss, Will Ya, Huh?" Movies get sound. Slide fasteners are named "zippers." Country School Students will read *Winnie-the-Pooh* and try to model their lives on *The Little Engine That Could*. Gertrude Stein hears a garage foreman say to his employee, who is working on her car, "You are a lost generation!" Henry Ford's workers will now work eight hours a day and five days a week. First-year teacher Myrtle Olson Russell, like most teachers to follow her, will discover her work days are ten and twelve hours long.

Myrtle Olson Russell
Myrtle Olson Russell attended Pine Lake School, District 27, near Cambridge. She had several wonderful teachers who inspired her to become a teacher. However, not every teacher won her love and affection.

The Kiss

I never missed a spelling word, but the day I did, I had to stay after school. We had to stay and write every word we missed fifty times. Some of the students did a lot of writing on the board.

I had two and a half miles to walk home, and I didn't want to walk home alone so I passed a note to my neighbor to tell her to wait. Because I got caught passing the note, I had to go up to the board and write my word fifty times. Then when I was ready to go, the teacher called me up to her desk. I was close to tears, and I guess she felt sorry for me. So she took me on her lap and kissed me. I hated that. She made me hate her. I could never like that teacher afterward. I felt she just added insult to injury. It was so embarrassing.   **c. 1915**

Myrtle, far right, operated on this 1920 photograph.

The Mad Hatter

My neighbor man bought this funny-looking lady's hat with a low crown and a ribbon in the back. He walked by wearing that. Mother laughed at him so he decided to give it to me. I hated that hat. I didn't want to wear it, but mother made me wear it. She said, "Because he gave it to you and you walk past his place every morning to school, you better wear it so he can see it." That's why I cut the hat out of this picture, so nobody else could see that crazy hat.

c. 1920, grade six

Myrtle Olson Russell completed teachers training in 1926 and began teaching that fall in District 20, Cedar Creek, Isanti County. With several years off to raise her children, she returned to the country schools in 1938.

A Cat's Life

I had a boy who came fresh from Sweden, and he didn't know a word of English. Fortunately, I knew Swedish. One day when he was frustrated with English, he said, "Jag onskar jag vore en kat sa at jag behovde inte ga pa skolan." (I wish I was a cat so I wouldn't have to go to school.)   **1928**

"A Rose by Any Other Name"

I was always a strict disciplinarian. Every spring we had a cleaning day. Of course on the day we were going to rake the lawn, they thought that I wouldn't discipline so much.

I was raking and one of the boys next to me thought, "Here's my chance now to do something I wouldn't get away with otherwise." So under his breath I heard him say, "Myrtle has a turtle in her girdle." I kept on raking as if I had never heard it. That frustrated him more than anything.

1940–1942, Grandy School, District 47

Ghoul-ash

We had a bachelor janitor who was quite a character. Sometimes he would warm up the leftovers from noon, hot dishes and hot lunches, and treat us with them after school. We looked forward to those treats and appreciated his kindness. We found out later our treat was what he had saved from what the children had left on their dishes.

1942–44 Stanchfield School

Myrtle Russell taught from 1926 to 1938 , took a few years off and returned in 1940 and retired in 1954.

1928

In 1928, Marie Smilanich, Emma Grunke Ortenblad, and Lillian Anderson step in front of Country School Students for the first time. Other famous people who make their debut this year include Amos 'n' Andy, Lawrence Welk, the Mills brothers, and Mickey Mouse in *Steamboat Willy*. Americans elect Herbert Hoover President. CBS and the National Council of Christians and Jews are founded. Bad liquor claims the lives of 1,565 people, and 75,000 imbibers are arrested. Penicillin launches an antibiotic revolution. Country School Students cheer when bubble gum is perfected. Rice Krispies and Peter Pan Peanut Butter appear on grocery shelves. *The House at Pooh Corner* is added to the school library.

Mildred Eldred Smilanich
Marie attended District 1, Cunningham School, Itasca County, from 1914 to 1921.

The Cunningham School, 1914, Itasca County: Marie Eldred is seated second from the right in the front row.

All Shook Up

There were only five students in my grade. It was just like being tutored. When I completed the second grade, my reading was very good and I knew all the multiplication tables so they skipped me into fourth grade. I missed all the information about fractions. When I was in the sixth grade, I had a teacher who literally shook me up because I did not have my assignment finished. Instead of teaching me the fractions, she shook me as if that would help me learn. When I brought my work up for her to check, she just gave me a good shaking. She wasn't one of the teachers who advanced me so she didn't understand that I had been advanced and missed the work.

My father helped in the evenings, but I was afraid of him. He said, "Well, what's two thirds by three fourths? That's no problem. You just multiply the numerators and the denominators." He didn't show me. I didn't know what a numerator was. It was a foreign language. The next day I would bring my work up to her and receive my daily shaking. In my first year I had to teach math with the teacher's manual. That's how I learned math.

Don't Mess with Me!

The second year that teacher was there, I sat behind Chester. I decided to tease him. I had a pin that I had stuck in the end of my pencil and I pressed it up through the seat and poked him. He jumped and yelled, "Marie punched me with a pin!"

The teacher hit me all over my shoulders and arms. My younger sister said, "I remember that. You didn't cry and looked at her with blazing eyes and refused to cry."

The teacher had married and went less than a half mile home for dinner. Her husband, a carpenter, fixed the noon meal, so she left us alone to eat. So I went outside and knocked Chester down. I pounded him and said, "If you tell on me, you're gonna get more tomorrow." Well, he didn't tell on me again. I was bigger than he was.

The War Is Over!

I remember the day World War I ended. I was in the fourth grade. My oldest sister lived about a block from the school. Everything was quiet, and all of a sudden the teacher saw her waving. The teacher knew it was an emergency, so she opened the window to see what my sister wanted. My sister yelled, "The war is over! The war is over!" That was such wonderful news because my brother was in the army. It was very thrilling!

The teacher whirled and whirled around the room so happy the war was over. Then she went to the piano and played "When Johnny Comes Marching Home," "Keep the Home Fires Burning" and all the other patriotic songs she had taught us. That was really quite a jubilant moment as we all sang along.   1918

Marie Eldred Smilanich graduated from Bemidji Teachers College in December 1927.

Marie Eldred began teaching in 1928 in Beltrami County. In January she took the place of a young man who had taught at the school for three years and who had accepted another job. Replacing this popular teacher was a difficult task. That year she discovered a unique method for curing laryngitis. She also met Warren, that one special student a teacher never forgets.

Busybody

One of the first things my landlady told me was that my skirts were too short. "You're a lady teacher, and you must wear long skirts." Well, the style was to wear skirts above the knees and I had just come from college where we wore those short skirts. But I did try to conform to what she wanted.

Quack! Quack!

I got a very bad siege of laryngitis during the middle of the winter. The landlord, who was on the school board, told me to take a day or two off to get over my laryngitis. I went to bed that night. I was almost asleep when the door opened, and he and his wife came in, carrying the lamp. They had a bottle of kerosene and a feather. They were going to dip the feather into the kerosene and swab my throat to cure my laryngitis. I said, "Oh, no!"

"Yes, this will help," they said. It's a clean feather. We washed it."

But I refused to let them swab my throat with the kerosene. They must have thought I was a terribly stubborn teacher. Somehow I survived the rest of that year, but I didn't go back.

Puppy Love

There were only five students in that school. One spring day my sister and her friend came out to watch me teach. They sat in the back. I was not as self-conscious about my teaching anymore. My sister, who was a commercial artist, drew little smiling puppies on the blackboard behind her. I was laughing and trying to teach school. While this was going on the superintendent walked in to supervise me. That really shook me up. However, I don't think she saw the puppies.

After teaching in Grand Rapids, Marie returned to the country school and taught from 1944 to 1946 in District 1, Bergville School, near Northome.

Doctor Vernon

One day a first grader and a second grader were being very mischievous while I was teaching the upper grade social studies. At recess I said, "Donny and Vernon, I want you to stay in. I have something to talk about. You know I am so proud of your reading. You are doing such a good job. Donny, isn't Vernon reading well?" He was the first grader.

"Yes," said Donny.

"And, Vernon, don't you like Donny's reading?"

"Yes," he said.

I said, "Well, you know the reason you are reading so well is that I'm taking a little bit of time from the upper grade kids so you can learn more. What did you do today but sit back here today like two little sillies and interrupt everyone. It isn't easy for me to teach if someone is being silly. So what do you think you should do about it?"

Donny, the second grader, said, "I think we should cooperate."

"I'm glad you said that, Donny, and let's shake on that and remember to be quiet when we are having our classes. How about you, Vernon?"

He looked frantically around and said, "I'm going to operate, too."

They did "operate" better from then on.

Warren

I had two orphan brothers in the Bergville School. Years later the younger brother called to tell me that his brother Warren was dying of Lou Gehrig's disease. He said, "I was reading to him, and I said I was a lousy reader. Warren said, 'Well, you certainly can't read like Mrs. Smilanich. She's the best teacher I ever had. I'd sure like to see her again.'"

His brother called me and asked if I would come to Park Rapids to read to Warren. My daughter drove me up from Minneapolis. I visited with Warren for half an hour. We talked about the days at Bergville School, and I asked him if he remembered the spitball party.

"No," he said.

"Well, you probably weren't in on it because you were studying all the time. Out of the corner of my eye, I saw all those spitballs shooting across the room. I didn't say anything then. At recess I said, 'I want everyone who has been shooting spitballs to stay in during recess. You know who you are.' Four with big smiles came swaggering up to the desk."

"I know you like to make spitballs," I said, "so we're going to have a spitball party." I put a jar in the middle of the table and cut paper up into little inch squares and told them to fill the jar.

They said, "Well, Kip was doing it too, and he didn't stay in."

"Well, he's missing the fun, isn't he?"

One of the fellows said, "Can I have a drink? I don't have any spit."

"Well, that's the fun of it," I said, "to see how many spitballs you can make without spit."

One of the other boys said, "I'll never, never make another spitball again."

We were kind of joking about it. Then I said, "Now go and take care of Kip." Kip was usually very dressed up and very clean. When he came in, he looked as if they had rolled him in the mud. I didn't say a word to Kip. The fellows took care of him. I was very sweet about the whole thing. It was a party and we were having a good time.

Now here was this brilliant boy, lying there, so crippled with disease that all he could move were his eyes. He looked up at me and said, "You didn't catch me." I couldn't tell from his eyes if he was kidding me or not. Just five days later he asked his family to remove the life supports so he could die in peace. Later on his brother also contracted Lou Gehrig's disease and died.

Marie later taught in the Department of Special Education in the Minneapolis school system and at Kenny Institute from 1948 to 1958.

Lillian Peterson Ehlers
Lillian Ehlers attended District 29 in Pope County. From 1928 to 1929, she taught in Swift County. From 1941 to 1957, she taught in the rural schools in Stevens County.

"Them Bones, Them Bones, Them Dry Bones"

There were times at school when we were able to correlate subjects so that all the pupils in the grades would be involved in the project at their own grade level. We were studying the bones of the body, and as a culminating activity, we decided to make a replica of a skeleton. We used an old basketball for the skull, sticks for the

Lillian Peterson Ehlers, 1928

bones in the legs and arms, and curved barrel staves for ribs, etc. Then we hung this so-called "skeleton" up on a bracket. Little by little, the names of these bones became familiar to all the grades at school. They learned them by repeating them over and over.

We played kittenball when weather permitted. During ball games, I often heard someone holler, "I broke my ulna," or "I bumped my cranium," "Someone kicked my tibia," and "I broke my clavicle." They used the scientific names until they sounded like doctors. By the time the kittenball season was over, they had mastered the names of the major bones in the body. This made the lower grades feel very grownup.

Toro! Toro!
One cold morning I wrapped a bright red blanket around me for the walk to school. As I was trudging along, I had to pass a big cattle feeding lot. I did not know then cattle don't like red! Across the feeding lot charged the whole herd, bellowing and pawing, wondering what that huge, bright red monstrosity was. They probably thought, "We must get rid of that phenomenon." The stampede commenced! I was frightened, to say the least! But as they neared the fence, they gave up the attack.

An Ugly Surprise
Driving out to school on a beautiful fall morning, I looked forward to finishing a number of projects. It didn't turn out that way! The schoolhouse had been broken into by some pheasant hunters. The place was an absolute mess. My desk and books were covered with pheasant feathers, blood and guts! The stench of the spoiled meat reeked throughout the room. I found the remains of more pheasants tossed into the stove. What a terrible mess that was!

First, I got a good fire burning and disposed of the garbage. Then I noticed they had written "Thank you for the candy bars we found in your desk" across the board.

I needed soap and water to clean up the mess. As I went into the kitchenette to get it, I found that the intruders had used our wash basin as a fry pan. The place was a terrible mess! They had fried their pheasants on the electric hot plate. The scorched meat in the greasy pan was quite a sight. Needless to say, the children and I spent most of that day cleaning the school.

A Close Call

A snowstorm blew up from the northeast, a real whiteout. With no telephone there was no communication. Parents, however, started coming for their children. All of these families lived in the opposite direction from where I had to go, but they all asked me to come home with them. I didn't want to leave because there was no way I could let my family know. It would only worry them if I didn't show up. I didn't dare stay by myself in that building. Therefore, I hurriedly put on my coat, cap, scarf, and boots, and started out. My coat just covered my knees and my boots came to my ankles.

I started north to reach my destination, about a mile and a half away. I had only gone a short way, and I was so tired because that northwest wind pulled the air right out of my lungs.

I became so exhausted that my only refuge seemed to be to lie down in the snow and relax. Oh, that felt so good! But my better judgment said, "Get up. Get going or you'll die in this storm."

I started out again. I couldn't face the icy wind any longer so I turned and walked backwards. The backs of my legs from the tip of my short coat to the top of my short boots grew colder and colder. With every step I took I could feel my legs freezing.

In the whiteout everything looked alike, and, unfortunately, I got lost. When I got my bearings, I realized I had gone beyond our turnoff. Finally I made it. As I opened up the door and the room temperature hit, I lost consciousness and collapsed.

When I came to, I saw that my family had gone to the well and gotten two five-gallon cans of cold, cold water. I was sitting by the stove with a leg in each can, thawing out. That was the remedy in those days. I was put to bed, but I was so bitterly cold they couldn't find enough blankets to keep me from shivering. There was no way to contact a doctor.

My legs soon swelled up like balloons. They were as red as fire, and they really burned. I wasn't even able to have a sheet touch them. The next day the storm subsided, and a neighbor took me fourteen miles in a horse drawn bobsled to the doctor. I am so thankful the doctor saved me from having to have both legs amputated.

Lillian Ehlers taught one year in Swift County, 1928 to 1929. She returned to teaching in the country schools of Stevens County from 1941 to 1957. She taught in the Morris public school system from 1958 to 1970.

Emma Grunke Ortenblad

I arrived in Kerkovan forty-five minutes early for my 8:30 a.m. interview with Emma. When I called, she said, "Oh, that's no problem. Come over right now. I just finished baking cinnamon rolls and the coffee is ready." What a way to begin a long day of interviewing! Emma Grunke's childhood experiences at District 51 were filled with lessons about gymnastics, chicanery, and hygiene.

A Short Year

I started school in 1912. We went until February when the school burned. In the spring Mother thought we should be in school, so we drove three or four miles in a horse and buggy. The roads were so muddy. We went two weeks and then she gave up. We stayed home until October when the new school was ready. We missed from February until the end of the school year and then September into October. That first year I was in a world of my own. I was too young to start school. The teacher sat me on her lap and put my brother and sister at her side. I was not ready for school, but Mother had three more at home so she was glad to get rid of three of them. The teacher was very good to me.

Unlucky Rabbit Feet

Some of the boys caught rabbits, which they ate in their homes. One day they brought the rabbit feet to school. At recess they offered these rabbit feet as prizes to us girls if we would stand on our heads. Of course, we didn't do it. One of the girls was a bit retarded, and they kinda went after her, but she knew enough not to listen to them. In those days girls wore dresses, no slacks or jeans. They were hoping we would stand on our heads and then our dresses would fall down. Nobody wanted their rabbit feet that bad.   c. 1916

Not My Favorite

We had a teacher I was scared of. She often reminded us that "Cleanliness is next to godliness." We had health inspection nearly every day. "Wash your hands and faces and come to school cleanly dressed," she said. That was good advice, but then we noticed a spot on the side of her face. We counted each day the dirt was there. It was there three or four days, so we knew she hadn't washed her face. That was a secret we enjoyed.

She certainly wasn't my favorite. I sat in a desk by the wall vent where cold air came from the unheated library. I got chilblains on my feet. I suffered in silence with frozen cold feet because I was too scared to close the vent. As we recited our lessons, she tatted lace. She hit some of the kids across the head when they couldn't do the work right. When she told us go to the blackboard to work, I got nauseous. Then she took me out to the porch for some fresh air. She never punished me, but I was so scared that it affected my vision and I often got faint.   **c. 1916**

Emma Grunke, teachers training class of 1928

Emma Grunke began teaching in the fall of 1928. In the third week, Emma's mother died during surgery. "Life had to go on, and I tried not to put my feelings on to those children." Emma taught school in District 90 and District 10 in Chippewa County.

What Goes Up
I had let the beginners practice writing on the blackboard. They were having fun writing and drawing because writing with chalk was new to them. I had a room full of other students, and I was working with them. Then one of these beginner girls stuck a piece of chalk up her nose. As the chalk got moist, it swelled bigger and bigger. I had to get the chalk out before she went home. I pushed down on her nose, trying to work the chalk out slowly. We finally got it out—and no tears.   **1928, District 90**

Suffer the Little Children
The family I stayed with during my first year had three little children. There was friction between the parents, who finally got divorced. On my birthday my boyfriend had given me a present. My landlady went into my room and opened the package. Then she said something to me about the gift, and I said, "How did you like it?" She got terribly mad because I knew she had opened it. That Christmas I gave her little girl a doll and I gave her two boys gifts as well.

They had to give back their gifts!

When the parents were divorced, I moved to a different place. Later these kids came with tears in their eyes. The girl gave me the doll and the boys brought their gifts back. Their mother made them return my gifts. She was so vicious. It hurt me that this lady was so unreasonable. She wanted to hurt me because I loved the children and they liked me. The little girl cried when she had to give up the doll. She was so heartbroken. What a terrible way to treat one's children!

1928, District 90, Chippewa County

Lillian Anderson Hanson
Lillian Hanson was born in 1901 and attended District 120, Sunberg School, Beltrami County.

Please Excuse Lillian Because...
I didn't start school until I was seven because there were wolves nearby and my mother wouldn't let me go. Obviously, we were afraid. I missed forty days that year, but I still completed two grades. In June, 1917, I was promoted to the third grade. I finished with some high school classes in 1923.

Trauma

Lillian Hanson

I never got into trouble, but one day our teacher was reading *Uncle Tom's Cabin* after the noon hour. There was a funny incident in the story. My friend, who sat across the aisle from me, looked at me and grinned, and I looked at her and grinned. The teacher thought I was making fun of him. He marched down the aisle and grabbed me by the arm. He squeezed my arm and said, "Don't you ever do that again!" I was mortified to death because I hadn't done anything. That incident bothered me all the years I went to high school. I felt he treated me unjustly and embarrassed me. But I was mad at myself for looking across the aisle. Later he became the superintendent of the school I was teaching in. One day I told him what I thought of him. He said, "Oh, Lillian, I never got after you." But that incident bothered me for years until I told him about it and finally got it off my chest. It was a traumatic thing. And I liked that teacher so much. He did a lot for me, but that incident bothered me for years.

Wham!

There were forty kids in my school with a lot of big boys. We had a lady teacher. One day when she walked down the aisle checking papers, one of the boys stuck his foot out and tripped her. In a flash she grabbed a book and whammed him on top of the head. She practically drove his head between his shoulders. I'll tell you she never had any trouble with that kid or anyone else.

1921, District 120, Sunberg School, Beltrami County

In the spring of 1928, Lillian Hanson did her practice teaching in Beltrami County.

Lunch Guests

I did my practice teaching at a little country school near a railroad siding called Scribner. The teacher who taught in the school and I were invited to eat dinner with a Russian family that had eleven kids. For dinner we had potatoes and fried pork belly. The house had split doors; you could open the top or bottom half. Well, the chickens walked in and out while we ate our dinner. The floor was dirt.

In the fall of 1928, Lillian Hanson began her teaching career in Malcolm School near Grygla in Beltrami County.

True Love

About a week before school was to start, a forest fire destroyed the school. It was a hot fall day. Early in the day my cousin and I had driven the horse and buggy to Four Town with the cream. Then we stopped where I boarded and visited with them. At that time everyone was alerted about the fire. We tore home those four miles to my house. We were so worried because it was dry and the fire was headed toward our place. The fire just rolled through the tops of the tall pine trees. Several homes were

destroyed and two people died. The place where I had boarded burned down and all the animals were burned.

The fire was then about three miles from our house. We would have been killed if the wind had not shifted. We closed all the windows, but ashes from the fire sifted into everything. We even found them in the clothes trunk. The force of the wind blew them everywhere.

In the meantime, one of the Finnish girls that I had in Malcolm School had a calf that had won a prize at the fair. She was so afraid that her farm and animals would burn that she led her calf six miles to our place as the fire burned on each side of the road. You should have seen that kid when she arrived. She was the worst looking mess you ever saw.

She was going to save that calf, but the irony was that her farm didn't burn. Somehow the fire went around her farm. But she didn't know that would happen. She thought every thing would burn, and she was going to save that calf. It took us all afternoon to clean her up. Her hair was just a mass of cinders and debris. She was a wreck. She was completely worn out, but she saved her calf.

1931, Malcolm School, Beltrami County

Lillian (back row, second from right) keeps an eye on the class. They knew if she saw RED that meant TROUBLE.

Red

My first year was traumatic. I was just eighteen. The teacher from the year before let the kids do anything—throw matches, jump out the window and all kinds of things so I was really set up. I had eight big eighth graders, mostly boys. The first day this kid who was sitting in the back started to whistle. You talk about seeing red. I've heard of it. Well, I saw red! It's a fact. I can't remember what I said, but I really gave him hell. I never had any trouble after that.

During the 1934–1935 school year, Lillian taught at the Aure School in Beltrami County. Lillian's landlady taught her a new art form—trickery. What a deal! Room, board, and chicanery!

The Great Bamboozler

Hazel, my landlady at Aure, was really fun. She was always playing jokes on people. She had three brothers who had taught her how to spit, and she could spit "dead eye." She was married to a World War I veteran who was an invalid, so she did all the work. She was always playing tricks so he became suspicious of everything she did. Once she cleaned the coffeepot by putting ashes in it and boiling the water. Her husband drank some and accused her of doing it on purpose.

She hired a man to work on the barn. Now this fellow was always teasing us. He slept downstairs so one night we worked a thick cord through the wall and attached a big blanket pin to his covers. In the middle of the night, we heaved up the blankets off him. We also tied the pickles together with a fine thread. He took one and it slid out of his fingers back onto the tray.

My landlady was very poor and had very little furniture. She had some old chairs with the bottoms worn out. She put pillows on them. We put a real stiff hair brush in the pillow of his chair. He simply could not figure out why he had such a hard time sitting in that chair. He never did figure it out.

Because he was always playing tricks on us, one night the landlady took the flour sifter and sifted flour on every step going up the stairs. Then we knew if he was spying on us.

One time we had a few boys over to play cards. A friend of mine had brought back a cotton ball from down South.

We told them we had planted the cotton seeds in a container. She cut the bottom out and put an atomizer in there. Every time they came they asked if the cotton had started to grow.

In the spring she planted the first dandelion that came up in the container. That night she said, "Yes, the cotton has finally come up."

"That looks like a dandelion," they said.

"Well, just smell it," she said and squirted them with the atomizer when they did.

We had no other entertainment. We had to use our imaginations to make things lively.

Hattie Hallaway was born in 1909. Her father came from Switzerland and her mother from Holland. After high school she began teachers training by borrowing twenty dollars a month from her sister to pay for her room and board in Wheaton. Hattie taught in the rural school of Stevens County from 1929 to 1935.

My Inspiration

When I was in high school at Chokio, I asked to leave the room to go to the lavatory, but I stood outside Mrs. Lundberg's door. She had the third grade. I listened to how she taught. She was bubbling and laughing and having such a good time teaching. I didn't see that humor and bubbling personality in my teachers. I said, "That's my goal. I want to be a teacher like Mrs. Lundberg." After my mother was through visiting my teacher, she visited Mrs. Lundberg. Mrs. Lundberg said, "I think Hattie should be a teacher. If she wants to go to Wheaton for teachers training, she can stay at our house for twenty dollars a month." She lived up to her promise and I lived up to mine. I became a teacher.

Mama Says

I couldn't get a school near my home in Chokio because they wanted experienced teachers. The first school I went to was south of Alberta. This fellow came out of the house, and he said, "Well, a lot of our teachers get married."

My mother said, "Then she can't stay. She's not going to get married. She's going to teach school."

My mother was twenty-seven when she got married and she had ten children in thirteen years. So she was very much against us even having a steady boyfriend because she didn't want me to get married and have as hard a life as she had. She cleaned for rich people. But she wanted her kids to have an education so if something happened to our husbands, we could make a living, which is the way it turned out.

He said, "That's fine with me." I took the job. I got ninety dollars a month and paid twenty dollars for board and room. I paid my sister twenty dollars each month. I bought my mother her first washing machine and paid sixteen dollars a month on that. I had about ten dollars left at the end of the month.

Hattie taught until 1935. In 1952 she renewed her teaching certificate and taught until 1972.

Chapter 11

Echoes from the Heart

Mining stories buried deep in the heart is an emotional journey. Sometimes Country School Teachers sat up straight, and their faces glowed as they recalled wonderful memories. They virtually sang those stories and their eyes glistened as the melodies floated around them. Often, however, burrowing deeply into hidden recesses, giving up beat-skipping tales, or peeling back a scar to free a buried pain played echoes from the heart.

Many times during our story-telling sessions, Country School Teachers hesitated, stopped in mid-sentence, and jerked up their heads. They gripped the chair or clasped their hands tightly as though they were about to pray. Their eyes widened and their mouths slackened just a bit. They had just mined a story from the heart. Then they often hesitated, weighing whether they should share their story with a stranger, whether they could bear the pain of the telling.

Often we cried together, and I understood why Country School Teacher often said at the end of the story, "I had forgotten about that. I never thought I would tell that story to anyone."

Fatherly Love

My father worried about me walking the four miles to school. He was afraid there might be some vagabonds along the way so he rented a piece of land where he cut wood. On Monday mornings he walked with me to Helena. He walked me there, cut wood, and then went home. He did that every Monday morning for the whole year. When the weather and roads were good, he took me out by car, but the roads were a problem in the winter and you couldn't drive. I stayed at the Helena Store during the week and then on Friday night I flagged the train and took it to Jordan for twenty-five cents. **Clara Rybak, 1921–1922, Helena, Scott County**

Pathos

All the children had been given toothbrushes and paste—I think it was from Colgate. One day little Adolph, a second grader, did not raise his hand when I asked if the they had brushed their teeth that day. "No," he said, "but my mother used my toothbrush to scrub her elbows." **Martha Carlson Peterson, c. 1927, District 96, Kandiyohi County**

When They Said "Overalls," They Meant It!

It was a cold March, but the river had thawed out a

Olga Peterson, age 19

bit. One of the families came early every day so naturally I had to be there at 7:30 so they could get in. One day this little fellow in the second or third grade came in and his worn overalls were frozen stiff. "Oh, what happened?" I asked.

"I fell into the river. I went through the ice." Now they lived very close to the river, and he could have gone home, but he came to school instead. I said, "Well, you know, we're here with just your brothers and sisters. I think I'll just take those overalls off you and dry them over the stove and wrap you up in my coat.

"Yea, you can do that," he said.

I took his overalls off and he didn't have a stitch of underwear on, not a single stitch. But that didn't bother him a bit! I wrapped him in my coat and we dried his overalls. Here it was March and it was freezing! I suppose he couldn't find his underwear, if he had any. Imagine how cold he was, walking a mile in those stiff overalls! **Olga Peterson, 1932, Happy Hollow School, Clearwater County: Olga completed eighth grade at the age of twelve and high school at age sixteen.**

The Gift

My teacher, Janet Harkin, taught my second grade class. She never married and spent her adult life teaching in rural schools. From the perspective of my eight years, she appeared very old—rather grandmotherly in character—but in fact, she may not have been much over forty. At the close of that school term, there occurred an incident which I will never forget.

Mysteriously, a large shipping carton appeared at the school and during the final hours of the last day, Miss Harkin opened it and handed each of us a book. At that time I could read quite well and the printed word entranced me with its marvelous tales of people and places. To have a book of my own left me ecstatic. Mine was *The Tale of Frisky Squirrel*. I still have that book and I dug it out to see if Miss Harkin might have inscribed her name in it but not so. On the fly leaf was written simply: For Master Everett Helmstetter.

Presumably all of the books were so inscribed so each kid would get an appropriate book—no small task considering there were some thirty-eight of us. As usual our plodding minds come to the recognition and appreciation appallingly late.

Everett E. Helmstetter, 1928, Willow Creek School, District 95J, near Roosevelt

In 1933 at the age of twenty, Ordella Walseth Lecy began her teaching career. For most teachers, students, parents, and everyone in the surrounding area, the educational and social highlight of the year was the Christmas program.

Most Country School Teachers tell about their programs with pride and joy. That night the students could show off their declamation and musical accomplishments.

Lanterns were hung for light, candles lit up the tree, and students waited for the presents stacked under the tree. Parents, grandparents, aunts, uncles, and especially Ordella's students looked forward to the annual celebration.

Ordella, c. 1933

He Didn't Hold It Against Me

We started preparing for our Christmas party in November. We had a beautiful Christmas tree with candles on it. The room was full of parents. You could just feel they were enjoying the program. The last thing the students were going to do was exchange gifts, and that's when the tragedy occurred. The oldest boy, who was eighteen, was playing Santa Claus. As he reached under the tree for a present, he got too near a candle and the cotton trim on his costume caught on fire. The tree was very dry and it burst into fire and he got burned. One of the fathers wore a mink coat and wrapped the boy in that and rushed him to the hospital. I don't even know how the people got the tree out.

It spoiled the whole program. When I had Christmas vacation, that tragedy bothered me so much. I felt so terrible about it because a reporter wrote the story for the newspaper and the article haunted me.

I felt the fire was my fault. Everybody was having such a good time, and the boy was having fun playing Santa Claus. He was such a nice boy. He was burned some in the face, but he didn't have any scars. He came back to school, and he didn't seem to have any ill feeling. He didn't hold anything against me. The fire was just an accident.

I didn't have a Christmas program the next year. I've had the same guilt feeling every year at Christmas time for these past sixty-five years. I was just sick. I guess tree fires happened in other schools, but I shouldn't have put candles on the tree. I had such a special feeling for those kids and that boy. He died in the Navy.

In 1933, Ordella Walseth Lecy taught two miles west and a half mile north of Echo in District 8 in Yellow Medicine County.

Annabelle

In 1934 when I arrived for my second year at District 2, the chairman of the board informed me that the mother of some of my students had passed

Gail Palmer, 1989

away. She had left behind her husband and four children. The youngest, Annabelle, was a year and a half old. The father asked the school board if Annabelle could come to school with the boys if they took care of her.

I asked the board what they thought about that plan. They said, "It's not up to us. It comes down to whether you are willing to let her come. You already have twenty-eight kids in the school."

The board chairman said, "We've thought about the boys taking turns taking care of her, but it seems a shame they would have to lose their education because of Annabelle. They might not keep up."

I said, "Well, why don't we try it." I'll never forget that first day. Annabelle came down the road with her three brothers, carrying her little Karo lunch bucket in one hand and her rag doll in the other. She was going to school and she was happy.

The community was very closely united. I think the parents had talked over the situation with their children because when she arrived at the school, the children all gathered around her and said, "Come on. Let's do this or that." They were so kind to her.

She was as happy as a lark and all the other kids were so excited about having her in the school. They said, "We'll help! We'll help!" The girls said, "If she needs to go to the outhouse, we'll take her."

When she got tired of sitting with one of us, she went to sit with someone else. She was far too tiny to reach the top of the desk, so we placed the thick unabridged dictionary under her to boost her high enough. When she moved from one person to another, the kids just moved the dictionary.

She loved reading most of all. When I had class for the first graders, she always sat on my lap. She listened to what we read and pointed at the pictures and told us what the picture was all about.

The next year her father asked if she could come again. I said, "School wouldn't be school without Annabelle." I stayed there for three more years. When I left, Annabelle was four and a half. She could read, draw and color, write and name the letters and numerals, and sing all the songs.

She had had twenty-nine teachers. How much richer our lives were for having Annabelle in class with us! Many of the students did not have brothers or sisters. They treated her as their sister. If we played ball, they didn't wait until the end to choose her. They chose her early in the game. She worked like a trooper for her team. If she touched the ball, they yelled for her to run to first base. They always let her get there. Her presence carried over to the parents. I'm certain the children went home and told what they had done for Annabelle. When Annabelle had a birthday, it was a riot. Everyone had a little cake or gift. They really fussed over her.

I think the brothers did not suffer the pain of losing their mother quite so much when they saw all the children caring for their sister.

Gail Palmer, 1934, District 2, Lyon County: Gail taught for forty-one years, fifteen in the rural schools of Lyon and Blue Earth Counties.

He Blinked First

When I came to the school, I was told about a boy who had a reputation as a troublemaker. On the first day I stepped out on the playground for recess and he was swearing like the dickens. Before I thought, I said, "Laverne, go in and take your seat!"

Then I remembered that in teachers training the instructors had told us emphatically, "Don't give an order unless you are sure you can carry it out!" There was no way could I make that boy go in and take his seat if he didn't want to. He was thirteen or fourteen and bigger than I.

He looked at me and I looked at him. But he blinked first. He went in and took his seat. I thought, "Oh, never again! I'll try to remember what I just learned."

I went in and talked to him. I didn't scold him. I appealed to him, saying, "Laverne, you are the oldest boy in the school, and whatever you do, the little kids will imitate. You know that we can't have those little boys swearing like that."

After that I never had a discipline problem in that school. If someone got out of hand, Laverne settled it for me. He had no difficulty handling the troublemakers. He was just that kind of boy.

Laverne and I stayed friends. The last time I talked to him was in 1941, just before the attack on Pearl Harbor. He had already enlisted and was leaving in a few days. That boy with only an eighth-grade education was made a bombardier. His plane was shot down and nobody ever found it. That hurt me and of course it hurt his parents. They never got any word but "missing in action."

In 1933 Margaret Lybeck taught at Bush Valley School, located in the center of a triangle between Houston, La Crescent, and Hokah in Houston County.

An Honor

The lady who was our first-grade teacher in 1931 was only twenty. Before she passed away in 1993, she had asked to have the six of us who were in the first grade to be her pallbearers. She kept track of us over the years. If our names were in the paper, she would send it to us. We had a nice relationship over all those years.

Most of us stayed around Iona, so she always knew how we were doing. She had relatives, but she asked us to be the pallbearers. It was an honor.

Vincent Crowley, 1930–1938, Kronberg School, Murray County

The Best of Times, the Worst of Times

I had a boy in class whose mother had died. His parents had lived in northern Minnesota in the wilderness. When the mother died, the father had to leave the kids with anyone who could take them. He came to this area to find work. He found work on a farm and later married the farmer's daughter. She was slightly handicapped.

Then he sent for his oldest boy, who was fifteen, so he had to go to school. He was a very disruptive boy, very angry at the world. He took his knife and carved into anything. He gashed into the walls, desks, whatever. At Christmas time I gave him a new knife. He said, "That's the nicest thing anyone ever did for me." Then he quit that destructive carving.

If he had to stay after school—he usually didn't get his work done during school, and I couldn't just let it go so I made him stay and hand in something—he would break into the schoolhouse at night and throw stuff around.

I knew he didn't have money because his father was not very good to him so I hired him for fifty cents a week to help me. He was very faithful. He carried coal and emptied ashes, all for fifty cents a week. He was very good about everything, except his studies. I still had to keep pushing him on that.

Later I heard he shot at his father and was put on probation and had a very rough time after that. The last I heard he was in jail in the Dakotas for robbing a filling station. He didn't have much of a chance. I think probably those months he was in school might have been his best time.

Virginia Rue Carrigan, 1935, Jackson County: Virginia taught seven years in Jackson County rural schools.

In 1935, few Country School Teachers included sex education in their curriculum. When Celia Wiedenhoeft was hired, her board challenged her to solve the school's most difficult problem.

The Facts of Life

I was called by the superintendent to deal with another problem much more serious than breaking windows. The children in this new school walked to and from school, pretending they were adults. Some children were sexually abusing others. Some were having sexual intercourse. I was supposed to straighten out these problems. I was twenty-two years old and single. I wasn't qualified to do this task. When the superintendent explained the problem, I said, "You are going to help me. Tuesday morning I want a lawyer, my supervisor, the county nurse, the entire school board, and you to be present. I want you people to get together right now to decide what you are going to say to the parents. Letters must go out to all of them and they must be there for that first morning instead of the children. This is not something for the teacher to handle."

I got my wish. When the problem was presented to the parents—many knew about the sexual activity but had done nothing—I got full cooperation. I told the superintendent that if the county provided funding to transport the children, we could take away this opportunity for them to have sex on the way to and from school. They bought two buses. From that time on we had no problems. On the first day of school, I did not talk about this problem because it had been taken care of at home. Having the meeting with the parents solved the problem.

Celia Wiedenhoeft, 1935, Hansen Lake School, Itasca County

Revenge

The first year I taught, I had a boy who was mentally handicapped. He was sixteen years old and taller than I was. His father, who was also mentally handicapped, said that if I would let the boy come to school until he was sixteen, that's all he wanted. The boy's uncle was on the school board that hired me. He knew I would help his nephew.

The teacher before me had a very difficult time controlling him. I was very fearful of having him in class because he was very destructive. He had broken a door and a window. Every time we did some activity, he was a hindrance.

I began by treating him with kindness. I showed him I cared. He chomped his food and drank his sauce off the cover of his lunch pail. First, I taught him good manners. I told him if he wanted to come to reading class, he had to learn to eat properly. When I taught the children about brushing their teeth, he said, "I don't have a toothbrush." I gave him one. I never thought of his brother at home. He and my student used the same toothbrush, so I bought another one. I even shared my lunch with him. His mother didn't know how to pack a lunch. She made a raisin sauce, thick with corn syrup.

When I came back to school after Halloween, I discovered that someone had destroyed all the children's unit projects, including their butterfly and bug collections. The children's drawings were torn apart. However, nothing of mine was ruined. On my desk was a paper. He couldn't write his name, but he had scribbled on it so I knew he had been there. I knew he had done it, but I couldn't understand why.

I drove to his uncle's place and told him what had happened. I said, "Have you told him not to come to school now that he's sixteen?" Later I learned that the school board had informed the boy that he didn't need to attend school anymore because he had turned sixteen and wrecking the school was his revenge. The next morning the boy came with his father and begged me to keep his son in class. The father said, "He has learned so much. Will you keep him?" That was so traumatic, so heart-rending.

What was sad was that school had really changed him. He hauled in all my coal and all my water; anything I wanted, he did. But there had to be an end to the problems. I couldn't teach the other children. It was such a difficult situation.

From 1936 to 1938 Ruth Domingo taught in District 29, Reimers School, Stevens County. Ruth taught for twenty-five years, eight in the rural schools.

Help from My Friend
I taught at the White Earth Indian Reservation. Their previous teacher had literally been driven out by her students. So I was trying to keep a fairly tight rein on those same students. I had kept a boy and a fourteen-year-old fourth-grade girl in for half of the hour-long noon. When the girl walked past me at the door, she called me a name, which no one called me without retribution. With no connection between my brain and my hand, the latter slapped her face.

The next afternoon her mother visited our classroom with her darling baby in a beautifully beaded carrier. She told me to do anything I needed to do to make her daughter behave. However, there was a lucky break for me as she had formerly told another teacher that she was there to beat me up. This teacher talked her out of it by doing lots of commenting about her baby and the beautiful beading—a lucky break for me. **Name withheld, 1936**

When the Wheaton Normal School wouldn't accept Pearl Jacobson Hanse because she was only sixteen, she interned for a year in the School of Life. She met Death the night she was on duty when the woman she was caring for died. She met Life as she administered chloroform to her cousin while the doctor delivered her child. Wheaton decided she had matured and accepted her the next year when she was seventeen.

She Touched Me
I had a little girl who had epilepsy, and she couldn't learn. Her mother told me that before the school year began. The other children were very considerate, but when we played ball and other games, she wasn't able to play. I tried to create a sense of self-worth in that girl by having her sit next to me. I had her do things like pound erasers and ask someone to come in from outside, little things. I don't know if she felt good about herself, but her mother felt good about how she was doing. She never said how she felt, but she always wanted to be right next to me and touch me, which wasn't always the best for the rest of the children, but they were used to it. I think my strength was that I loved them. **Pearl Hanse**

Concern
In one of the schools, the little boys about ten and nine worked in the fields while school was going on. Their fields came right up to the schoolhouse. That was really bad for me. I felt they should be in school and that they should not be out there doing manual labor with those huge tractors when they were so little. But I never dared say anything to the father or mother. When the boys came back to school, I said, "I saw you out in the field. I sure was worried about you." They would just grin.

Pearl Jacobson Hanse, 1937, District 20, Horton Township, Stevens County: After four years in the rural schools, Pearl taught for seventeen years in Morris.

One day the county superintendent came to tell Wanda Krousey that a boy from a correctional institution would be enrolling in her school. The superintendent assured her that if the boy caused any trouble, he would send him back to the institution. The boy was fortunate because his new teacher was an adventurer who knew how to explore her students' hearts. Wanda helped him find a few treasures.

Ed

The boy came from a broken family and was staying with his aunt and uncle. He would be sixteen in March and only planned to go to school until then. I tried to interest him in staying in school to graduate, but his interest wasn't there. I found that he liked to read, so I told him that if he got his assignments in on time, he was free to read library books. I felt that he would be learning by reading, and he liked to do that. We had no problems. He did his school work and then he spent his time reading.

The kids always enjoyed throwing rocks at the bell in the tower. They liked to hear that pinging sound. I told them I didn't think throwing rocks at the bell was good for the bell. I told them I didn't want it to happen again, and the next time anyone threw rocks at the bell, they would lose their play time and have to stay inside

I was putting work on the board one noon when I heard a "ping" and then many other "pings." I stepped outside and reminded the students that those who had thrown rocks would have to give up their noon hour. Not a soul moved. They just looked at me. After a few moments Ed stepped forward and said that he had thrown rocks so he would go in. When Ed came forward, so did the other guilty parties. I wonder where he is today? **Wanda Krousey, District 60, Morrison County: Wanda taught for thirty-seven years, twenty in Todd and Morrison counties.**

I Didn't Know

There was a family of three young boys. One was in the first grade. Their mother had left them so they lived with their father. They moved a shack in, and it had a stove and a table and beds, and that was about all. They moved from one location to another, wherever the wood was available. Those children came to school every day it was possible. They were clean, and they tried to learn, but they had problems, so very many difficulties.

Blanche and student, 1937

I would think that I had accomplished something that day, and the next day they would come back but they forgot what they had learned. I know today what the problem was. I didn't at that time, and it's one of the things that I regret. They were hungry. Those children were really malnourished. They weren't getting the food that they needed. They couldn't remember things. **Blanche MacAllister Swift, 1937–1939, Pine Valley School, Cass County**

Where Is Childhood?

Children in that area were shy, and many of them came from very poor families. One family had four girls in the school. They all came down with trench mouth. I discovered they had one toothbrush between them, and they were all using that one. I did buy them toothbrushes, but that was too late. The first-grade class had one boy who was missing all his teeth. Another one stuttered, and the other one had white hair. I said they looked like three little old men because they looked so old.

Leona M. Kelly began her teaching career in 1938 in District 87 in Lac Qui Parle County where both her father and an older sister had begun their careers. She then taught in Yellow Medicine and Cottonwood Counties.

Please Come with Me

The father of one of the first graders had come from either Ireland or Scotland. He was big burly guy, who told me he wanted to visit the school. I told him to come. He came one afternoon and sat and visited with the kids. All of a sudden he burst into song. He sang "Little Red Wagon," and he sang it beautifully. The kids were enthralled. They were so impressed, but his little boy was so embarrassed. A few days later, the boy's father died. The mother called me and said, "Could you please come with us to the mortuary? Billy doesn't want to go unless his teacher goes with him."

Allie Riehle

I thought, "What can I do?" But I went. I met them in the entryway and I sat and visited with Billy for a while. I told him how proud I was that his father had come and that I was sure both he and his father were proud of his singing because we all enjoyed it. He really brightened up. We walked into the mortuary and he was just fine.

Allie Riehle, 1938, Blackie School, Itasca County: For twenty years Allie's rural students at Blackie, Wawing, Wendigo, and Cohasset "called her name and she came."

The Child Knows

I had one little boy who was a great comfort to me. Some feuding among the farmers happened in the district, and it spilled over into the school. It involved quite a few families. But this boy didn't care what the trouble was. He was very even tempered, always cheerful, always joking. When they played a game, he didn't play to win. He played for the fun of it. He was only a third grader, but he knew there was trouble in the school. He knew after I had been there two or three years that it was getting to me. When he finished his work, he went into the library to read. When he found something nice, he brought it up to me and let me read it to myself. I finally left the school, but I remember that little boy. He died when he was about twenty-three. That hurt me because I remembered how nice he was.

Florence Orlusky, c. 1937, Jackson County

Compulsion

We had a little boy who was in the first grade. He had diabetes and struggled with it all the time. The

Edith Salvervold

children were all aware of it and were very kind to him. They tried not to flaunt their cookies and their pies. But during the second year sweets suddenly began to disappear from their lunch pails, and we couldn't figure out why. The kids all went out and played at lunch time, but this little fellow was so starved for something sweet that somehow he got back into the room and took things from the lunch pails. Only the sweet things had vanished.

The children showed such compassion when they discovered what had happened. I talked to him privately. The children were so kind and understanding. For them it was a wonderful learning experience. They understood why he was so driven.

Edith Salvervold, 1939, Buzzle School, Beltrami County

As I interviewed Marge Abbot in her kitchen in Brainerd, she occasionally glanced at a four-by four-inch photograph behind me. Nineteen-year-old Marge Abbott and her twenty-one-year-old sister Iola looked down at us, reminding Marge of her first years of teaching. Marge Abbott's kindness, love, and compassion radiate from that young face. She told her extraordinary stories as if we all practiced such love for one another in our daily lives.

Iola and Marge—the teaching Gray sisters

Bless the Innocent

When I was teaching in the Nokay Lake School, the parents asked the new teachers out for supper in the evening. I was told to be leery about this one particular family, but I couldn't tell them "no" when they asked me to come for supper. I went. I was quite surprised to see a home like that. The kitchen floor was dirt and a little stream ran through the kitchen from one side of the house to the other.

I thought, "Do I really want to eat here?" But I ate, and as I was eating, I could see little beady eyes here and there. I thought, "Ah, ha, the kids weren't telling me any stories; it was the truth!" The boy and girl would come to school and tell about how the rats bit them at night. When I saw the eyes here and there, I thought, "Yes, they were telling the truth because there were rats in the house." But I tried to be as nice as I could and get some food down. It wasn't extra clean, but I did stay there and eat supper, hoping I wouldn't be asked back there again. It was a trying experience.

When the children came to school the next morning, they wanted to know if I had enjoyed myself. I said, "Oh, yes!" The little girl got so excited because I said I liked being at their home. Apparently they didn't have many people come there. She was so excited that she wet her pants. I didn't know what to do so I put her over the big register in the floor.

That was the biggest mistake I ever made. It smelled up the whole schoolhouse. We had to hurry and open the doors and windows.

This family was really a backwoodsy family. The children and the mother would come to school on this old, white, bony horse. The gals would get one dress dirty and put another one on top. When that one was dirty, they put another one on top of that. They would be wearing three or four dresses at once. I tried to talk to the daughter and tell her you don't do that. When the one is dirty, you put on a clean one. But mother did that, and, therefore, so did the daughter. **Marge Gray Abbott, 1939–1942, Nokay Lake School, Crow Wing County**

Better Than Drippings

In those days the children didn't have very good lunch pails, just old syrup pails that mothers packed. Their sandwiches didn't have meat, just bread and lard, just the drippings from the bacon. I decided the seventh- and eighth-grade girls should learn a little bit of cooking.

We had a three-burner kerosene stove and I asked the parents if they would send some vegetables once in a while or some rice from which we would make vegetable soup. Other days we would make Spanish rice.

I volunteer at the state hospital and I met one of the students who was in my class at that time. He said, "You know, Miss Gray, I have never forgotten the Spanish rice we had in our school." I said, "Verl, that was many years ago. That must have been fifty years ago when you were just a little guy."

And he said, "Oh, but that tasted so good. I've thought so many times that if I could just have a dish of Spanish rice that you had made." I made a batch of Spanish rice and took it into him, and he was so tickled because it hit the spot. It was the same thing he had remembered. **Marge Gray Abbott**

Missionary Zeal

There was a family whose home life was not very good. I brought the children home with me. I took turns. I did this a couple times a week for the whole year. There were about four or five children in one family. The parents liked it. They thought it was great. They weren't as bright as some parents. They just had more and more children. They liked my taking the youngsters and doing these things for them. You couldn't get away with that nowadays, but in those days you could.

When they were at my house, they had good manners. I could see their little eyes just a-shining. They really enjoyed coming to my house. Of course, they had a good meal. Their little tummies were full before they went to bed.

Then they'd have their baths and that was, I think, one of the most thrilling things in their lives, to get into the tub and have that bath because at home they had just a pump outside. They had to haul in their water.

At home one youngster got out of the tub and another one got right in for as long as it took for all of them to bathe. At my home they had a bath in the regular tub in the bathroom. Then I put the youngsters to bed. They had a good clean bed to sleep in.

I also made clothes for these children. I made dresses for them out of flour sacks and they were so proud of them. The flour sacks or feed sacks were pretty, flowered ones in those days. I sewed some things for the boy, too. Somebody had given me an old wool coat, and I ripped that up and I made pants for him. I made lots of mittens for the family out of that old wool coat.

One of those boys became a professor at the University of Minnesota. I saw him a while ago at the mall. I wouldn't have known him, but he walked up to me and asked me if I was Miss Gray. Then he said, "If it hadn't been for you, Miss Gray, I don't think I would have ever gone on to high school and college and become the professor I am today." He talked about things that I did for him and what I had done for his family.

I did this because I'm that sort of a person. When I find that a youngster should have help, I go ahead and do it. I've done it for a long time. Mom always said that if she could not find me, she'd look for a group of youngsters and I'd be in the middle of them. I was always with kids.

I've always taken people under my wing, and I guess I won't get over that. I've been out at the state hospital working with the youngsters there for seventeen years.

Margaret (Marge) Gray Abbott taught in the following rural schools in Crow Wing County from 1936 to 1949: Lake Edward, Nokay Lake, Esden, and East Oak Lawn.

Ethel Bengston Hjelle taught in District 45 between Willmar and Pennock from 1937 to 1939 and in Sunburg from 1939 to 1942.

A Warm Hearth

In my first year of teaching, I stayed in a log house just across the road from the school. Many mornings when I woke up, there was snow on the window sills. The water in the pitcher was frozen. But the farmer's wife would always be pounding on the door, "Here is the hot water, Ethel." She was a lovely person. She was so kind. She came over to the school many nights because she had made some rolls and coffee for me. Her husband was a great violinist. Every night after supper he played. The grandmother lived there, too, and when I came home, she would be rocking and singing. It was a wonderful atmosphere. **1937, District 45, Kandiyohi County**

Ethel Bengston Hjelle, c. 1939

Sitting Down on the Job

One time we were talking about skiing, and I said I enjoyed it. So the boys decided they were going to test me one day. They said, "Well, we have a long noon hour, Miss Bengston. Can we go skiing in the hills. They are not far from school." I thought about it for a minute and then I said, "Sure, that will be fun." I could tell before we left the boys were itching to do something. At noon I had to bundle up all the first and second-graders and then off to the hill we went. I noticed the boys were awfully excited to get to that hill for some reason. When I got out to the hill, one of the first-grade boys came to me and whispered, "Miss Bengston, when you get to the bottom of the hill, sit down."

A first-grade guardian ski angel

They had made a jump for me on the bottom. I went down and things went beautifully. I reached the bottom easily. They were all waiting for me to hit the jump. Then to their surprise, I sat down and sailed over the jump. "Wow!" they said. I can still hear it today. They thought I was just wonderful.

Well, I was raised on the farm with five brothers so I knew how to ski, and thanks to that little first grader for telling me about the jump, I had no trouble. **In 1939, Ethel had forty-eight students in the Sunburg School.**

Hank Lankow was the school clerk of court. When Joyce Chatwood interviewed for her first job at the Lankow School, one of Hank's first questions was, "How much do you want?"

"All I can get," said Joyce. She agreed to the previous teacher's salary of $125 and the interview was soon over. Later Hank became Uncle Hank when Joyce married his nephew LeRoy.

The Poor Reader and His Filthy Books

We were required to spend one dollar per person on library books each year. That fall we learned that Cadmus books had bought the rights to books with expired copyrights and printed them on inexpensive paper with colorful hard covers. The books sold for $.99 or less; primary books often were only $.29. The clerk of the school board told us to spend fifty dollars, which bought a lot of books! How we all poured over the catalogs, with each pupil indicating his preferences!

One student cast a shadow over the dream, however. She reminded us that a local bachelor always took home some of our library books. If the children were outside playing and saw him walking toward the school, they said, "Here comes Newton for some more books." He never knocked. He just walked in whistling or grumbling. He often said hello to the children, but that was about it. He took the books he wanted and never checked them out.

The students didn't want these new books ruined! We solved the problem by making a special bookcase out of an orange crate that we covered. We put a skirt in front to conceal the books. The bookcase had a place of honor in the main room. When Newton came for books, we did not say anything about the new books! He always brought the books back filthy and smelly. This man was positively the dirtiest person I have ever met. His house was open to cows, sheep and chickens. One person peered into the house when the man was gone and saw a part of a watermelon on the table. He could tell which meal was which by how dark it was from all the fly specks.

When the man got sick, the hospital would not admit him until he was taken to the jail and cleaned up. When he died, he had been living in his old car because he would not pay the price of renting a room. He was a college graduate. When he died, he was worth about a half million dollars. The last time he came he said, "It's getting too hard to see." By this time he had read all the books in our library.

Joyce Chatwood Lankow, 1944, Wilkin County

In the class of 1944, there were no Lankow children in Joyce Lankow's Lankow School.

Dime, Dime, Who's Got the Dime?

We were also encouraged to enroll all the students in the Junior Red Cross program. The usual contribution was ten cents per student, and with one hundred percent enrollment, we were entitled to put up a window sticker. When the packet arrived, the students lined up with their dimes—except for the eighth-grade boy. I praised them, mentioning that John was the only one left that had not contributed.

I had seen him hold back as his three brothers presented their dimes. He quickly informed me he had paid. I pretended to look for it on the desk, then said it probably was under a paper. I would put in the dime, so we could have one hundred percent participation. He knew I was covering up for him. I had his loyalty the rest of his time as my student. He knew that I was someone he could trust. Years later he and his wife named their baby after me.

Joyce Lankow, 1944, Lankow School

Killing the Spirit

I had a little girl in third grade whose mother was Native American. She had married a poor specimen of a man, a drunkard. My heart still aches for that little girl. Her mother stoically took all sorts of abuse. One time her husband deliberately tripped her in front of a car as she crossed the street. She was probably eight months pregnant.

The little girl had about two miles to walk home from school, much of it parallel to a pasture. One day she came back to school, afraid to go further because the bull was trying to get at her through the fence. Just then the father charged into the school, bellowing at her for not coming home. I tried to explain what the problem was, but he just yelled that she was expected to come right home after school. I had no car, but I would have walked her home if he had not come. I probably would have been as terrified as she was. The town hurt for that little girl and her mother.

Joyce Lankow, 1945, Umland School, Grant County

No Refrigerator

I had a little girl in school whose father raised mink. He bought meat for the mink to eat. He had a refrigerator in which he kept the meat. This little girl became very thin. However, they had no refrigerator in the house for themselves. The father was very strict. When I told them that I thought the girl was ill, they finally took her to the doctor. It was a long time before she came back to school. She was undernourished. **Florence Hartwig, 1946, Dodge County: Florence completed high school in 1919. She taught in the "town school" from 1921 to 1925, married, and began her rural teaching career in 1943 and taught there until 1949.**

My Honor Student

In my first and only year of rural school teaching, I had twenty-five students in all eight grades. At the end of the year twenty-two of twenty-three students passed the State Board examination. The only failure was an eighth-grade boy named Wesley, who had no intention of going to college.

However, this boy who couldn't pass the exams did the most wonderful, unexpected thing the day the county superintendent visited us. While the children were outside for recess, she criticized my methods and she criticized the manners of all my children—which I could not understand.

Apparently some of these supposedly "ill-mannered" children were listening outside and they didn't like what she said about their teacher because later, Wesley, who sat in the far corner of the room, made a trip to the wastebasket. Well, Wesely took the long way which led him in front of the superintendent where he pointedly said, "Excuse me." He did the same on his return trip. I could have hugged him, but he was taller than I, and I don't think he'd have appreciated it!

In 1942, Annette Gimmstad Potter taught at a country school located between Sacred Heart and Renville.

No Halloween Joke

During the afternoon recess I sent the children outdoors while I prepared for the Halloween party. I closed the shades and hid the peanuts around the room. I was so busy preparing I wasn't aware of the problem outside until I returned to the place where I stayed. The mother of the three students informed me that all her girls talked about after school was that some of the boys were threatening to castrate a second-grade boy. No doubt they only meant to scare him and the girls, but I was happy that nothing happened. No one had told me about it during or after the party because I had told them all to stay out of the school while I prepared the party. The next day I cleared up the problem with some of those older boys. **Margaret Brunn Roel, 1941, District 68, Benton County**

This Isn't in My Contract!

One little first-grade boy dirtied in his pants every single day for a week or so. He gave me such grief. Every day I had to change his pants. His dad sent a clean outfit with him every day because he knew what was going on. His mother had to leave the family for mental health reasons and this was a traumatic experience for the boy.

That's probably what was causing his problems. I just cleaned him up and we went on. It didn't seem to affect the boy. He didn't seem to pay too much attention to what was happening. He didn't seem to want to make it out to the toilet.

Beatrice Scharf, c. 1945, Itasca County

The Love Sweater

A boy came out to stay with one of the families in our district. His mother had killed—I don't know how many of her kids—two or three. They figured she had done away with her husband also. The boy was a real moody kid. You can understand why.

One time we were getting ready for Christmas, making gifts for the children's parents. The boy just sat there with a belligerent look on his face. I said, "Well, aren't you going to make something for your mother?"

He said, "You know where my mother is?"

I said, "Yes, she's in prison. She did something wrong. She is paying for her crime. But she is still your mother. You should still love her."

He looked at me kinda funny, and then he went ahead and made something. That night when we had our Christmas program, the boy came wearing a new handknit, yellow sweater, trimmed with maroon. I said, "Oh my, that's a pretty sweater! Where did you get it?"

He said just as proud as could be, "My mother made it." **Blanche Olson, 1945–1946**

Here's Anna

On the first day of school, this mother brought her little girl to school. I can still see her. Right in front of the little girl and everybody else, her mother said in a loud voice, "Here's Anna. She ain't too good at learnin' but you do what you can for her." They had convinced her that she was dumb. I wondered what her life was like at home.

I thought, "Oh, how damaging! How rude to say that in front of the little girl." She looked so depressed. I worked so hard to build up her self-esteem. I said something positive to that girl every morning when she came to school.

I tried to be positive every day about what she had done. If she wore a dress that wasn't all that pretty, I'd find something nice to say. I also had to be very positive about her lessons. It meant a lot to her to do well. I put her good papers up for the other children to see, even if they weren't the best. I went out of my way to build her self-esteem. We worked together, played together, and cried together.

Just to get a smile from her was hard. To get her to speak, to say "good morning" was like pulling teeth. She and another little girl started first grade the same year. The other little girl did a better job of getting her to speak than I did, but I kind of pushed the other little girl to do a lot of talking. It helped to get someone her size and age to talk to her.

Geraldine Massmann, c. 1949, Lincoln County

My Leather Coin Purse

This family went out chopping wood one weekend. Somebody needed an ax so the farm hand threw the ax to the father just as the boy darted out. The ax hit the boy in the back.

He was a patient at Children's Hospital for quite some time, but unfortunately he died. I think he was nine or ten. All the students and I were honorary pallbearers. That was so sad. I still have the coin purse that he made for me when he was in the hospital. The children there made things out of leather. I think he made a coin purse for everybody in the school. We didn't talk about his death much in school because the children and their parents talked about it at home. It seemed that the farm families were so close in those days and they talked about everything. They were very strong people, and we were a family in the school also.

Gladys Schmitt, 1936

My husband and I were running our service station when this boy was killed. I was teaching, of course, and we were building our house at the same time. One day the boy's parents came to the station and asked my husband what I needed, what they could get me for a Christmas present. My husband told them that I didn't have a hand mixer, so that's what they gave me for Christmas.

Gladys Schmitt, District 53, Brown County

The Apology

A homeless man lived in a boarding house on the south edge of town. He didn't bother anyone. Then one sunny fall day the boys ran up to me and said, "Miss Norby, Bozo is laying in the playground, rolling his eyes and shaking all over. He can't talk! He can't even get up!"

I raced out to view the situation. What a sad sight! I tried to talk to him, but he couldn't answer me. He had been drinking so much that he was having seizures. I sent the little ones to play on the other side of the building. Then I sent the two boys to tell the blacksmith who got some other men to help remove him from the school grounds. One man

under each arm, they carried him off, his feet and head dangling. They carried him to his old brooder house shack near the railroad tracks. Then I explained to the students that the man had a serious illness due to his excessive use of alcohol.

A few days later after school, there was a knock at the door, the inside door. He walked right in. I stepped into the entry to talk to him because I didn't know what to expect. He apologized for wandering into the school premises and exposing the students to such a scene. He said something like, "I'm here to apologize for what happened. It certainly was not the thing to do. Guess I got mixed up in my directions.

Anna Norby Johnsrud

But I promise it will never happen again. It was not good for the children to see a drunk like me."

I accepted his apology, and he promised it would never happen again. He left town before the next school term began. **Anna Norby Johnsrud, c. 1951, Farwell School, Pope County**

My Aunt Marietta Sharkey and I always found time at every family gathering to share teaching stories. Her face mirrored her feelings as she told the following stories of anger, frustration, and compassion. She recalled in detail events that had happened fifty years ago.

Many teachers said, "We were family. There was no intolerance." However, sometimes the dark side of human nature found its way into the lives of Country School Students.

She's Different

We were all out for recess, all grades, one through six. On the north side of the driveway there were trees; otherwise it was an open area. I had a group over there that was playing kittenball, and I noticed that three of the boys were missing. I told the kids to keep playing, and I went down to check on those three boys. They had taken one of the third grade girls and they were hanging her. They had a rope around her neck; she actually had a rope burn. Well, God, I just went into an absolute tizzy. I marched the three of them right into the school, and I called one of the school board members. I said, "I don't care what you are doing. This is very crucial; you have to come right now." He never asked what the problem was. He came right away. I had him come into my room where I had the three boys

Marietta Sharkey

and the little girl who was the victim. She still had the red marks on her neck to prove it wasn't a story I had concocted. He suggested we call the parents of the three boys and meet with them after school. This was at the last recess so there was only an hour of school left.

When the parents came, it was interesting to see how they reacted. The mother of the first boy was a dear, dear lady and her kids were always sparkling clean. She said, "My goodness, we eat together, we pray together, and I try my very best to see that they are raised right." She was so ashamed of what her son had done.

The mother of the second boy was irate. "What have you done to my child? My child wouldn't do anything like that. You're accusing him of something he wouldn't do. Son, were you part of this situation?"

"Yes, I was," he said, and she has hated me ever since he said those words.

The father of the third boy said that he was going to make sausage out of his son. He was going to crucify him and kill him and everything else.

It certainly was a lesson in how three parents handled the situation. What a typical situation that we find in education today—parents think their children can do no wrong! Oh, I was frightened!

The mother of the first boy asked her son whose idea this was and where they ever got this idea. It was the oldest boy's idea (a sixth grader) that they hang this little girl because she was different from everybody else. She had a handicapped mother, and she came from one of the poorer families in the district—so hang her. It was one of the low points of my life. I felt like an absolute failure after that. As hard as you try.... **Marietta Sharkey**

Sometimes the dark side lived in the parents.

Win One, Lose One

Two sisters were being raised by their grandparents, who were very, very poor. I was preparing a Christmas program and I was going to use my daughters' dance costumes. One of those little girls was going to wear one of the little knit tutus. A couple of girls went into the bathroom to fit on these things, and one came out and whispered to me that one of the sisters didn't have any underwear pants and she didn't want to come out.

I went home that night and stopped at the clothing store. I bought half a dozen pairs of underwear pants. I put them in a bag that looked like it didn't come from a store and sent it home with her that night. There were so many poor little kids that were suffering.

But here is another story that has a completely different twist. Every day this boy came to class in tattered clothing. I bought a pair of shoes, a pair of stockings, and a little pants with an elastic waist band. Then I took some of my boys' shirts, and I sent him home nicely dressed.

He came back the next day dressed again in tatters, not in the clothes I had sent home. His parents expected me to redress him and send more clothes home. I learned a sad lesson: you can't help people that don't want to help themselves. **Marietta Sharkey**

Humiliation

These people had six or seven boys, and the youngest one was quite slow. One day he came to school without underwear and his pants were torn. X. was the teacher. He went to the office and called home and said to the father, "I'd like to have you bring some good clothing for your child. He has no underwear on and his pants are ripped and the other students are ridiculing him."

The father came to the school with the underwear pants in his hand, opened the door, walked right in, and threw it at his son right in front of all those other classmates. Then he said, "Tomorrow morning put your underpants on at home!"

Now wasn't that a horrendous thing to do? That was over forty years ago, but every time I see that man, my skin just prickles. I wonder how anyone could be so inhumane as to do that to your own child, for god's sake. **Marietta Sharkey**

And a Child Shall Lead Her

I had a girl in the second grade who never talked. All of her written work was perfect, so I knew she listened and was very bright. When she entered the third grade, her dad and I decided she would need to speak or he would take her to a specialist. Her dad was on the school board. The girls' mother was ill, so her two aunts took care of her.

I decided to take my preschool daughter out to visit the girl and her aunts. The little girls went out into the garden. When my daughter asked her some questions, this girl who never talked answered her.

I had a little talk with the girl the next day and told her what a beautiful voice she had. For a few days I asked her questions in class that she could answer with one word. It worked. How happy we all were when she recited "Why Do Bells for Christmas Ring?" in the Christmas program!

Mildred Kilen, c. 1953, District 70, Jackson County: In addition to teaching twenty-two years in rural schools, Mildred taught twelve years in the Lakefield public school system.

During the 1957–1958 school year, Mary Lou Erickson taught in the Union School in Meeker County. Because of the pain in their lives, some of Mary Lou's students had not yet learned to "fly."

Chasing a Dream

Bobby was the spokesman for the group. He came to me on a cold, snowy, blustery day in March, but there was just a hint of spring in the air. "Mrs. Erickson, is it OK if we make some kites?"

My instant answer was, "Yes, if you make good kites, ones that will fly, not just kites to spend time on." His shy smile told me that he understood the message he must relay to the others.

Bobby was the second child in a family of five boys whose father was verbally abusive. His mother worked incessantly to keep the family fed, clothed, and together. Her main concerns were not for the four boys in school but for her son Mike, who remained at home with cerebral palsy. The four boys in school carried a sense of shame as well as love for their brother. I knew if these kites were made at home, their brother Mike would then be able to share in the excitement. Three weeks later when there was a sunny hint of spring in the air, Bobby announced, "They're ready!" At first I was puzzled, but then I remembered our bargain.

Much to my surprise the other children became involved. On the designated day the four brothers, two members of another family, and three more from a third family were ready to fly their kites.

Mary Lou Erickson

They had made their kites from wrapping paper, newspaper, and tissue paper. They were held together by paste and tape. They were crude, yet beautiful. They had created their kites by using whatever materials were available. The balls of string were made of twine and grocery string. They had tied them all together and wound it into a ball.

The spring day was bright with sunshine and a bit of wintry chill still in the air. The sky was blue and gusts of wind waited to carry the kites skyward.

The boys made simple rules for the launching: everyone gets three tries and everyone runs as far as the driveway by the plowed field. I don't remember whose kite flew the highest or stayed up the longest. I only remember the anticipation and excitement, the girls yelling, the boys hollering at their kites and at each other, the cheering and laughing, and the look of satisfaction in their eyes as they chased their dreams at the ends of those strings.

When Christmas came that year, their mother sent a note and asked me to stop there on my way home from school. She had a Christmas present—a blood sausage she had made that day. However, we just couldn't eat it. We were not used to eating blood sausage, and I thought, "Oh, I wish they had it because they needed the food and I knew they loved it so much." **Mary Lou Erickson, 1957–1958, District 3, Union School, Meeker County**

Chapter 12

Romancin' the School Marm

The Suitor's Song

The schoolmarm's new at District Four,
Looks like someone I'd adore.
She cuts her hair in a New York bob,
Like to marry a girl with a job.

The last four left my heart so torn,
I wandered aimlessly forlorn.
Wore my plaid, Brylcreamed my hair,
One date later they didn't care.

Took the first one to my poker game,
Guys all said, "What a real hot dame!"
Took the second to the picture show,
Askin' mom really dulled the glow.

The third was a beauty, looked so fine,
Took her to the fair to judge the swine.
The next one dated with alarm,
Loved the city and not the farm.

Found a princess in number four,
Had the blue eyes I adore.
Took her home to meet my folks,
Brothers regaled her with dirty jokes.

Things will change this time, you'll see.
I hardly know it's the same old me.
Got some lessons on etiquette,
Her heart's a beatin' now, I bet.

I cleaned and polished the Model T.
Next to me she sat with glee!
Took her dancin', bought her a rose,
She's got that look, think I'll propose.

Bought a ring, walked down the aisle,
Friends believe she's changed my style.
I found a gem at District Four!
My heart's not achin' any more.   -TM

A Rocky Romance

I had dated my husband-to-be for many years. Then he went into the Navy. One day here came a brother

Ruthe wasn't impressed by rock tossing.

of one of my kids to pick him up from school. The man carried two small rocks. Over and over he threw the two rocks into the air. He caught them and then threw them again. Throw, catch. Throw, catch. I think he was nervous. He just kept juggling the rocks. I tried to be very busy. I didn't want any part of it. But this went on, day after day after day, wasting my time. Finally I had to tell him. He would have liked to date me, but he never got around to asking me. He just kept juggling those two rocks. **Ruthe Dahlseng taught seven years in the schools of Pope County.**

The Crooner

I hadn't been in the district very long before they began telling me about eligible bachelors that were always after the schoolteachers. I was just amused. I went out with this one fellow a few times in his old Ford and rattled around. I had a friend I visited on weekends, and we usually went cross-country

Gladys Sutherland, 1948

skiing. She had a friend she wanted me to meet, but he was really her friend. Well, the people where I was boarding began to gossip about me. Then I told them I was going out with this guy and that guy. Instead of the gossip making me more careful and making me think I shouldn't go out or I shouldn't do this because they were talking, it made me do just the opposite. One day this new guy and I were driving along, and I saw behind me the lady who did all the talking. I thought, "Well, I'm going to show her." So I reached over, put my arm around the guy, and pulled him real close so they could see. I'll tell you we both laughed our heads off. But he eventually married someone else.

There was another fellow in Springbrook. The people told me that I was number seventeen in his pursuit of a schoolmarm. I never was interested in him, but he came quite often. He liked to sing "Moonlight and Roses."

It didn't make any difference where we were, he'd start singing "Moooooooooooooonlight and rooooooses," and I'd laugh. I couldn't stop. He would be sitting on the davenport and he'd begin to sing. He didn't need any music for encouragement. Usually the man and woman I boarded with would be in the room with us, too.

Sometimes he took me to the movies and he'd sing in the car. I tried not to laugh, but I always knew I was number seventeen. He had gone to all the teachers when they came up there to teach.

I had met someone in my first year of teaching, so I wasn't interested in him or anyone else. However, I wasn't engaged so I ran to dances. I loved to "kick up my heels." **Gladys Sutherland, 1925–1926, District 22: Gladys taught for a total of five years in three Kittson County rural schools. Not one of her classes was taught in the moonlight.**

Come Early

When I was nineteen, I started teachers training at Glenwood. A girl who worked in a restaurant there had asked a guy to take her to Starbuck to a dance. She said, "If you and Louise, a girlfriend, can come down here, you can come with us." So I went. Here came Ted in his Ford coupe and we went to Starbuck, but there wasn't any dance. So he took us out to eat.

Ella B. Olson, c. 1926

When we went home, she stayed with me. I thought I'd encourage Louise, so I said, "He looks like a nice guy. Why don't you go for him?"

She said, "I think I will."

On Sunday we walked downtown. When I saw Ted, I said, "I changed my mind. This one's for me."

When we walked up to Ted, he said, "I'd like to take you to the show tonight."

I said, "Well, I have dates for 7:30 and 8:00, but if you come at 7:00, I'll go with you." We were married six months later. **Ella B. Olson, 1926: Ella taught for twenty years, four in rural Pope, Douglas, and Otter Tail Counties.**

Opportunity's Knocking and Knocking

Rural teachers were often selected by the local swain to accompany them to the basket socials, school programs, and whatever excitement the community offered. Early in my first year of teaching, my fourth-grade twin girls stayed for a little while after school and seemed eager to talk about something.

They whispered and giggled a bit and then one of the little girls blurted out, "Our brother Harold always dates the schoolteacher!" With that bold statement, they snickered and left. Later I learned that this had been the procedure, but as I was already "spoken for," I missed the opportunity.

Martha Carlson Peterson, c. 1927, District 96, Kandiyohi County

Mopping Up

A young fellow from a family I called the "Birth of a Nation Family" because they had so many children wanted to take me to a movie in Hibbing. I took the eighth grader who lived where I boarded along with us. The guy couldn't even find the movie. He didn't know where he was. Finally he found the theater. He walked right in ahead of the rest of us, no manners at all. When we came back, he wanted to stop the car. I said, "No, I want to go right home." I was glad I took the eighth grader along because that gave him

"I'm going to mop that man right out of my hair."

no opportunity at all to get too chummy. It was quite an experience. But that wasn't the end of it. I had stayed after school alone one night to mop the floor. He wanted to give me a ride home. I took the mop with me to the door and said, "No, thank you, I'm not through with my floor." That was the end of it.

Lily Johnson, 1927–1928, District 1, O'Leary Lake School, Itasca County

Getting Tough

You could put a line right down the road, Germans on one side, Norwegians on the other side. This German father had three handsome kids. Now, it never failed that he would stop to pick up his kids when he knew darn well they had gone home. Every kid walked in those days, and so did his. I was very uneasy. For a long time I did my work as fast as I could and got out of there before he came. I was scared to death of him. One day I said to myself, "Why be scared of him?" I told him, "If you ever stop again after school is out and your kids have left, I'll report you to the school board." He never stopped again. **Helen Merville, 1930–1931, District 54, Brown County**

They Really Gave a Hoot!

While I was teaching at Haupt School, I met Mitchell, who was a teacher at Bergville. He took the bus to a point headed toward my school, and I walked down the railroad tracks to meet him. During these Friday night walks toward Mitchell, the train went by about 4:30 p.m., and the engineers would signal to him, toot the horn, and point back to indicate I was on my way because they realized we were going to meet. This happened almost every Friday. The same engineers were on the train every time and they knew what was happening and they hooted that horn. We met right at that crossing.

The hooting and whatever else happened at the railroad crossing came to an abrupt end when Marie's husband-to-be was transferred to another school.

When Mitchell was transferred to another school, I was quite disappointed. I had to stay at the Haupt School, so I went to the superintendent and asked for a transfer closer to Mitchell. He told me to stay there but to keep everything ready.

One day the children were having their recess when the door opened. In came the superintendent with another teacher. He said, "This will be your replacement." The children gathered around him and said in chorus, "Ah, go on!"

Before he came to the school, he had told the people I stayed with that this was going to be the new teacher. They said, "Ah, go on!"

I was transferred to Grand Rapids and Mitchell and I were soon married. **During the 1929–1930 school year, Marie Eldred Smilanich taught in District 1 at the Haupt School in Itasca County.**

Just a Friendly Wave? Ya, Sure, You Betcha!

I always walked across the field to get to the school. Right across from my school was a farm place. The house and my schoolhouse were opposite each other. I had a seventh-grade boy and a plump little fifth-grade girl from that house. Every day after I had climbed over the

There he is again. I better wave to be polite.

fence, the farmer would be out there and he would wave at me. Well, having his two kids in school, I wanted to show respect so I waved back. A couple

The real Mildred Kilen!

months went by and pretty soon his wife came to the school, and she really read the riot act to me. She said, "What do you mean by waving at my husband every morning, you red-headed flirt?" She was really upset. I was taken aback. I didn't know what to think. I hurried home after she bawled me out and told the people I stayed with. I felt so bad, but the man at whose home I boarded was on the school board, and he laughed and laughed. He thought it was so funny. After that when I walked by, I always turned my head. I didn't know if the farmer was out in the yard or not, but his wife claimed that whenever he saw me coming, he quickly got up from the table or anything he was doing, and got out there so he could wave at me. Wasn't that ridiculous? **Mildred Kilen, 1933–1935, District 58, Odin School, near Mountain Lake, Cottonwood County. Mildred taught for twenty-two years in the rural school of Cottonwood and Jackson counties.**

Healing the Sick

My boyfriend thought it would be such a nice thing to come over to the school and surprise me. He and a friend came near dismissal time. My boyfriend sent his friend in, and he said, "There's somebody out here who's sick. Do you have a drink of water?"

I said "yes" and gave him a dipper of water. Then I noticed who was out there. Of course the kids were very curious. "Who was it? Who was out there, Miss Picha? Who was it that was sick?"

I said, "I don't really know." You didn't talk about your boyfriends in those days. However, these students were used to the teacher's boyfriend coming to school. The boyfriend of the teacher who had been there the year before was the mailman, and he stopped every day. So I guess they expected something like that when I came. When you're teaching in the country like that, everybody knows what you're doing.

Ida Welter, 1932–1933, District 52, Scott County

Food for the Goddess

I went to teach at Stingy Lake. I was the only single woman in the whole community. The whole county was filled with married women who had come there as single women to teach school. In addition, I had a radio. If the guys took their car batteries out, they could hook them up and play my radio. My future husband and his four brothers all came to where I was staying to play the radio. The brothers were all single and very eligible.

One night Abe would bring a piece of venison. The next night Harry, my future husband, would bring me some fish, flour, or bread. He was a better cook than I ever was. Each night they would bring me something, but only Harry was really interested so I married him. **Margaret Pickering, 1933–1934, Stingy Lake, Itasca County**

Hanky-Panky

When I was in the first grade, our teacher came to school drunk. I don't remember it, but my sister told me about it. We must have played all day long. When we got tired of playing, we all went home. The parents all asked why we were home, and we told them that our teacher was drunk and asleep at her desk. My mother was on the school board and there was another tee-totaler on the board. Well, they went to the school and canceled her contract and fired her right then and there.

My eighth-grade teacher had her boyfriend come and they'd go down into the basement. Then

I hope those kids are behaving!

we'd go outside and look through the window 'cuz we knew hanky-panky was going on down there. They were just huggin' and a kissin' to beat the band. We stood outside watching and giggling. He'd come to school during the school hours and she'd suddenly have to go down and check the furnace. **Florence Maas, 1934–1942, District 93, Rice County**

What can a lady do when teachers training says you can't say "no"? What can she do when her suitor just sits and stares?

The Quiet Man

There were many young bachelors, but the hardest part was that I wasn't interested in any of them. I'm very tall and there were a lot of "shorties" that wanted to go out. There were dances. The people I lived with always went and I did, too. I never lacked for a partner, but it was impossible to turn anybody down or to be choosy. I couldn't offend anybody. The music consisted of a piano and a fiddle player. It wasn't too fancy a deal, but it was something to do. A couple of fellows drove down to my home during the summer to see if I would go out with them. One time mother and I were sitting on our front porch and this young man came in and sat

Alice Hande: Maybe the guy in the car talks!

down. I don't know if he was too bashful to ask me to go with him or what, but he and my mother and I sat there for two hours. I didn't dare ask him to leave. I don't think he knew how to approach the situation. I was so afraid my mother would leave, but she didn't. He finally left. He had a friend waiting in the car all that time. I never could figure out what was going on. We never went on a date that was any more romantic than that. **Evelyn Ogrosky Hande, 1935, Witoka School, Winona County**

Peppermint Romance

Every time I went to a different school there was always an eligible bachelor trying to date me. The people I lived with tried to introduce them to me. They'd want to come over and play cards, but I knew they were trying to romance me. This one old fossil came all the time. I didn't know how old he was, but he was *old*. Every time he came he brought peppermint schnapps. He had a little bottle with a few inches of schnapps in it. If there is anything I can't stand, it's schnapps. I could expect him about once a week, but I never did drink his schnapps. When I quit teaching at that school, he quit coming.

Name withheld, 1937–1938, Waseca County

A Smelly Matchmaker

One of my friends was teaching and a skunk got under her school. She didn't know what to do, so one of the girls ran home and got her uncle. She ended up marrying him.

Doris Erdahl, c. 1938, Stevens County

Roller-skating Romance

I had two older girls as students, and I took them roller-skating. I took them home after school and picked them up to go to Austin. We had a crush on the neighbor boy who was about eighteen. The girls liked him but he liked me. They got jealous if he skated with me more than he did with them. It was comical. Nothing ever came of it.

Bertha Everson, 1940, District 50, Mower County

Froggie Knew

On the last day of school, we had the Finishing Program. Ruth Piepenburg, our teacher, was leaving our school that May. As part of our program we sang, "Froggie went a courtin', and he did ride, mmmmmmm. Froggie went a courtin' and he did ride, mmmmmmm." We all wondered if we sang that song because Ruth, who was being courted, was leaving to be married. **Donna Poppe Nibbe, 1940, District 41, Sunnyside School, Stevens County. Ruth Piepenburg Domingo, whose stories appear in this book, did marry and returned to teaching in 1958.**

Parking Fees

We had a granary on the vacant place, our other farm. There was just a machine shed and a granary there. It was on a bare 160 acres. And we had to go over there and load oats for feed grinding. Anyway, the place just grew up with weeds. But all of a sudden here are these two paths going in there, car wheels, so my brother and I didn't think much about it, but somebody just went around and parked on the back side of that granary. So one day we took an old coffee can over there and we hung it on the post and we put "Parking 5 cents an hour." By golly, we came back the next day, and here we had a nickel. Three different times we got nickels. Finally it leaked out that it was our teacher, but we did not know if it was H. and L. or S. and L. at that time. None of them were married. To this day they will deny it. H. says it was S., and S. says it was H. They didn't stop going there but they did stop paying.

Allan Angelstad, student, 1943, District 51, near Kenyon, Goodhue County

He Could Take It!

It was wartime. This man had told his son, who was home on a furlough from the Army, that there were some teachers and he should meet one. "There is a really cute one," he said. I was engaged to someone else, and I think this guy knew about it. He had to think about it. Should he come and visit? He did come, and then my friend Lila took him most of the evening! She had me make the lunch and she sat with him in the living room. The two of us wanted to meet each other, but she just took over.

Well, then I got brave. I said as he was leaving, "Say, I want to walk out with you." If I hadn't been a little aggressive, he would have disappeared out of my life. Then we got acquainted. We had coffee together and then we walked out and sat in his car for about a half hour. We couldn't stay in the car too long because it was a cold winter.

We didn't see each other again because then the war broke out and he had to go overseas. He was gone for five years and I didn't see him. All that time we wrote letters to each other. I still have them, but I can't look at them, now that he's gone.

I told my mother, "This is love at first sight. I'm gonna marry Art."

The guy I was engaged to was overseas also. I wrote to him, too. When they came back, I told the other guy I was marrying Art. I had to wait until the war was over. I figured Art would have been most hurt if I hadn't accepted him as my husband. I sent the ring back to the guy I was engaged to and told him I was marrying Art. I figured he could take it.

1941, A Heart Throb from the Iron Range

Spying
One evening the teacher's boyfriend came to pick her up. All of us boys had climbed up in the trees and sat in the branches, waiting to see what we would see. First, she came out. Then he came out and locked the door. Then he started kissin' her.

Of course we started hollerin' and screamin' and yellin,' "Hurry up! More! Kiss her again! Give it to her!" We really got punished for that.

Gordon Ostby, grade seven or eight, c. 1943, District 67, Swift County: Gordon and his buddies were infamous for making their own entertainment, including spying and tormenting their teacher's courting ritual.

Cupid
Next to the school there was a fellow who was working in the field. He was always close to the school building after the kids left. One night I heard someone pumping the pump, getting a drink of water. The next night the same thing happened. Then again on the third night I heard the pumping. Finally he got brave enough to come into the school to get acquainted. He was a cousin of someone I had gone to school with. He asked me for a date, and I said, "There's no harm in this," but I wanted to make sure we didn't go someplace where I would be seen by anyone else, so we went to Benson.

Nothing ever came of that. But there is more to this story. Audrey, one of my students, was always talking about her older brother, who was in the Army. I think she was interested in having me meet

him, so she talked about him. The second year I was there he was discharged in November.

Audrey came to school all excited because her brother was home from the service. She said, "We always bring our Christmas tree for the program. We'll bring it."

I certainly hope this teacher is as pretty and nice as my sister says she is. This could be very embarrassing.

The next morning someone stood in the door, holding a Christmas tree. It was her brother. He came to the program that night. He very conveniently helped me clean up after everyone had gone. Then he saw me home. It was love at first sight.

Laverna Birkland, 1948, District 54, Kandiyohi County

High Apple Pie in the Sky Hopes!
I was eighteen when I began teaching. In one of the classes I had a sixth-grade boy. Once I had to slap him on the hands, the only student I had to punish that way in my five years of teaching. I never had to punish him again, and he was the first student to give me a gift at our picnic, which was also the last day for our school and all the other rural schools in the county. That spring we consolidated with the nearest town and the school was closed.

At that time I was going with a handsome Irish guy who came to the school now and then to see me. Years later, after I had married my Irish visitor, I attended a celebration of some

Merlin Moore c. 1943: "She's my wild Irish rose!"

kind, where we met this student and his wife. We stopped to visit, and I introduced my husband to him, mentioning that this man had been a student in my country school. He grabbed my husband's hand to shake it and said, "At one time I hated your goddamn guts!"

My husband, looking very surprised, said, "Why did you hate my guts?"

"I had such a crush on Miss O'Malley," he said, "and when you stopped at school one day, I knew I no longer had a chance in hell!"

We all laughed, and my husband said, "You were only a kid at that time."

"I know I was only a kid, but I had big ideas."

Eveleyn O'Malley Moore, 1943–1944, District 21, Le Sueur County: The man who stopped at the school and won the heart of Miss O'Malley is my uncle, Merlin Moore.

There were many rules the country teachers had to follow, but the most inviolable rule of all was that married women could not teach. No one ever really gave a satisfactory explanation as to why married women couldn't teach children, but stories abound about women who postponed engagement and marriage to teach. Others, like Doris Callahan, found ways to escape the commandments handed down from Mount Education Department.

Let Me Check My Drawers!

I practice taught for this woman who was getting married, and that's why I got the school. That was in 1944. If you were engaged or married, you were fired, so that's what happened to the teacher. My husband-to-be was going into the service and wanted me to marry him. He asked me several times. I said, "No, I'm going to teach school, and I can't be engaged or I'll lose my job."

That didn't seem to make a difference to him because one night he slipped a ring on my finger anyway. So I kept it, but I always carried it in my coin purse. I took it to school every day. I knew if the word got out, even in the middle of the year, I'd get let out because you had to be single.

He wanted to marry me. He wanted to leave his Oldsmobile to me. Oh, he tried to talk me into marrying him. He said that if he got killed, I would get ten thousand dollars for insurance and everything. I said, "Nope, I didn't want that." I had heard of someone that had been two-timed, and I didn't want

to be two-timed. I was this innocent little girl of nineteen, but I wasn't stupid.

Then one day my future sister-in-law stopped by after school was dismissed. I didn't have the ring on. I met her at the door, and I made an excuse to get up to my desk and put on the ring. I took it off when she left. I taught there three years while he was overseas. I don't know if anybody else taught while engaged. **Doris Callahan, 1946, Oakland School, Freeborn County**

Doris Callahan played Hide the Ring!

The Trickster

I had a coal furnace in my first school. To get to the furnace, I had to open a trap door next to my desk and go down to the cellar. About the time it got cold enough for me to need the furnace, I was going steady with Earl.

On Sunday nights after he had taken me home, he would stop at the school to start the fire. He had to wait for the kindling to get burning hot enough before he added the coal. Then he had to wait until he could shut down the damper before he could go home. While he waited, he was always up to something, writing notes or doing something. Usually he sat at my desk and wrote me a letter. Then he tucked it under my blotter. This may sound ridiculous since he had just left me a few minutes earlier, but I did look forward to reading it in the morning. We were busy preparing for the annual Christmas program. In the back there was a table full of clothes the children had brought for their costumes. One morning I unlocked the school door and there sat a man in the back of the room. I screamed.

"Marion, when I look at you, I'm absolutely speechless."

I thought it was a man. Well, it certainly looked like a man. But it was some of Earl's work. While he waited to complete his furnace duties, Earl had stuffed a coverall full of clothes making it look like a man. He set it in a desk and propped a hat on its head. Sitting there with its arms bent at the elbows and its head tilted a little to the right, it looked so real. Of course, I could only see it from the back, so I couldn't tell who or what it was. But he certainly looked like a man. It really scared me!

Later that winter we had a snowstorm on a Sunday night. I was rooming with a school board member who had two children in my school. That morning he took me and the children to school so he could check the furnace.

As we walked into the room, I saw it! Earl had written on the board in big letters, I LOVE YOU! I LOVE YOU! I was shocked and embarrassed. I grabbed an eraser and began erasing. Of course, the board member and his girls told everyone in the district about it.

Earl and I were engaged in April 1947. When I came to school wearing my diamond, I wondered how long it would take before the students noticed it. It wasn't long. I looked up after helping some primary children and every face was beaming.

Marion Larson, 1947, District 70, Kandiyohi County

Pumpkin Head Love

One of my students, who is now my niece, wanted me to draw a picture of her uncle, who was living at their house. I had never met him and I had no idea what he looked like. It was near Halloween so I drew a picture of a little man who had a pumpkin head. She took it home and showed it to her uncle. The next day she came back with a picture that was a little worse. Underneath the picture her uncle had written "Teachers' heads are more like pumpkins."

Shortly after that he came to see who had drawn his picture. At that time I lived in Coleraine and rode the bus to school. One night he came and offered me a ride home. From that time on I didn't ride the bus. Finally we were married.

Beatrice Scharf, 1953, Balsam School, Itasca County

"Hey, there, Pumpkin Head, what say you and I get mushy and teach those kids that pie aren't square?" (apologies to all geometry teachers!)

Chapter 13

You've Got to Laugh A Little

The Teachers' Salvation

I woke this morning an' checked my vanity.
Will this be the day I lose my sanity?
The weather's bad; the kids are lazy.
The fire won't start; I'm going crazy.

My whole world's crumblin', falling apart.
Don't know where I'll end or start.
Each day I think it couldn't get worse.
Should've listened to mom, been a nurse.

Billy fell down in a pile of manure,
Stunk up the school like a putrid sewer.
Mary vomited from eating her paste,
Said it smelled good, she liked the taste.

The boys are smokin' and learning to chew.
Sally tore her dress, just brand new.
The mice each night on the books do feed.
Pretty soon they'll all be able to read.

Salamanders are movin', so are the snakes.
How much more of this can I take?
Johnny gave Eddie a bloody nose.
Mom will be in today, I suppose.

My car won't start, the landlady's cruel,
Feeds me nothing but water and gruel.
It's blisterin' hot or ice cold freezin'.
I'm sweatin', shakin', tremblin', or sneezin'.

An eighth grader says he's in love with me.
At sunrise tomorrow, I'm gonna' flee.
But Eddie'd be walkin' and wave a toad.
I'd lose my mind and run off the road.

I'm gonna giggle, hoot, cackle, and crow,
No matter how awful things may go.
I'm gonna laugh, find the side that's sunny.
I burned the school? Isn't that funny!   -TM

Sometimes when historic events are set to music, students learn their lessons quickly. Nora Hendrickson remembered this ditty she had learned as a young girl in grade school over seventy years earlier.

Canning the Kaiser
Oh, Bill, Oh, Bill,
We're on the job today!
Oh, Bill, Oh, Bill,
We'll seal you so you'll stay!
We'll put you up with ginger,
In the good old Yankee way,
While we are canning the Kaiser!
Nora Hendrickson, c. 1920, Freeborn County

No Work Today!
Many of the children were old enough that they could have stayed at home. Some came but they didn't do much work. Before they came to school, the students did all the chores and all the work at home. One day Lester was leaning back in his desk with his arms folded. I walked by and said, "Lester, what are you going to do today?"

"I'm gonna do nothin'! Gonna do nothin!"

"Well, why did you come to school?" I asked.

"I just came to school to rest!" he said.
Mildred Dahl, c. 1922

The Same Way
One day I came to school and the kids were all excited because Wilfred Gerkin had crawled up in the bell tower. They all said, "How is he gonna get down?"

I said, "He'll get down the same way he got up there." Well, he got down. He was just experimenting. He was full of the dickens. Later I married his brother. **Edna Erickson Gerkin, c. 1924, Isanti County**

She Sees All, Knows All, Draws All!
One Sunday morning two young men came to the teacherage and asked my friend Helen and me if we would like to go skiing behind their car. We said that we would like to try it. They were careful and no one got hurt, but it really was crazy. I never told my folks. On Monday in drawing class Helen asked the children to draw what they had seen over the weekend. After school she brought three drawings into my room—pictures of someone riding on skis

behind a car. Of course, they never found out who was behind that car. **Alice Ekroot, 1926, Makinen School, St. Louis County**

Fleeced-Feathered Friends

Alice Ekroot, c. 1926

We were going to have a fair. The students brought things from their gardens and other things from home. At noon the father of one of my pupils came to see the fair. He asked me, "Where are my chickens?" I had no idea what he was talking about. He had sent two of his prize chickens with the bus driver to be entered in the fair. Apparently he didn't tell the bus driver the chickens were to be entered in the fair.

I said, "Chickens? I haven't seen any chickens."

Well, the women at the Arnold Presbyterian Church were preparing a chicken dinner for that evening. The bus driver had taken the chickens to the church instead of the school fair. The women dressed and cooked them.

All five teachers at the fair had tickets for the chicken dinner. It was funny but it was also sad. The owner of the prize chickens was furious and rightfully so. It caused quite a commotion in the community. **Alice Jederberg Ekroot, c. 1927, Arnold School, St. Louis County: Alice taught in the rural schools of St. Louis County from 1925–1938.**

Myrtle Russell, age 19

The Plural of Mouse

In 1928, if children had not graduated from eighth grade and did not intend to attend high school, they had to attend at least thirty days or until the day they turned sixteen. Gustave had stayed out of school for two weeks to pick potatoes. I dreaded that first day that big Gustave must come for his compulsory thirty days. How mistaken I was! It was Gustave who helped the first graders and settled arguments. As far

as eighth-grade grammar was concerned, he just didn't have it. When I asked him for the plural of mouse, his answer was "rats."

Myrtle O. Russell, 1928, District 27, Isanti County: Myrtle taught for more than thirteen years in the Isanti County schools.

Too Late

The trustees didn't really care about the school or keep it up. There were no blackboards, just boards on the wall, common boards that were painted black. Of course, the chalk showed up, but they were hard to clean. They always had that gray look. Just about the time the school board members got slate boards, the state closed the school.

Elizabeth Brown O'Connell, 1927–1928 District 30, Kilkenny, Le Sueur County

Needled

The school had no basement and the floor was always so cold that I developed chilblains. An old Norwegian lady who lived in the neighborhood told me she had a good remedy from the old country. She took a piece of cardboard and stuck a darning needle half way through it. Then she held the end of the cardboard and tapped the bottom of my feet in dozens of places with the tip of the needle. It worked. **Helen Merville, 1927, Brown County**

Anyone who goes mining for country school stories can find a bonanza with Bea Slavik. She is the Queen of Storytellers in the New Prague area.

A Small One

At the Christmas party my mother thought we should have a Santa Claus. She had a friend who had a Santa costume, and she said, "I'll have her come out there and she can give each person a present." But, my, she was a tiny lady. One of the kids said, "Such a small Santa Claus!"

Bea Slavik, 1930, Le Sueur County

A Short Week

I taught at Lanesburg. It was a country school, but it was a Lutheran school. I was the only Catholic in the school except for one little girl. Their teacher got scarlet fever. I was at home just playing bridge. When they asked me to replace the teacher, I said, "No, I don't want to teach." But they were desperate for a teacher. They needed me.

Finally Reverend Martins asked me, and I said "yes," but I told him I could never be there on Wednesday afternoons. Under no circumstance would I teach on Wednesdays.

Now imagine that. He knew as well as anyone else that was my bridge club afternoon. That wonderful, staunch, non-card playing man said, "I will teach religion that afternoon and your husband can come and get you. Then you can go." I taught four and a half days a week. He knew exactly what I would do. He knew I was addicted to bridge and would never give it up. **Bea Slavik, District 61, Lanesburg School, Le Sueur County**

Make Mine Thin
One morning I was at the hotel and this man was there with his mother for breakfast. He was my student at Lanesburg and now he's a professor at a Lutheran college in New Ulm. I said, "I bet you don't remember me."

"Oh, yes, I do," he said.

"And I remember you and those flat sandwiches, the ones you made so thin," I said.

"What do you mean?"

"Your mom used to send sandwiches in your lunch. I caught you putting your sandwich on the seat and putting a geography book over it and sitting on it because you liked your sandwiches real flat. You said you liked them better than the fat ones."

"I don't remember that," he said.

"Well, I've had over one thousand students and that made a big impression on me because I never would have eaten a flat sandwich."

Bea Slavik, District 61, Lanesburg School

A Goober Shower
I liked to reward the students for good behavior, so every once in a while I would have a peanut shower. All those who had behaved well could participate and usually they all took part. They all stayed in their desks and I threw peanuts all over the room. When I said, "Ready go," they could gather as many peanuts as they could. Anything that fell on their desks was theirs. It was pandemonium, but they all had fun. **Florence Lind Janike, 1931–1938, District. 112, Fahen Township, Roseau County: I met Florence at the Old Timers' Picnic south of Roosevelt in the Beltrami State Forest. Relatives of the first settlers gather there each year to celebrate their heritage.**

Stripper
It was September and I had over twenty kids in the school. One day it was just plain hot. In those days teachers had to dress up. We wore a dress, long hose and girdles. I could hardly wait 'til those kids left so I could take my girdle off. As soon as they got out of the building, I slipped off my girdle and laid it on the desk. Then I went out to the biffy.

"Ahh, How was your day Miss Sontag? Nice weather!"

When I came in, here was this young man sitting at my desk. He was a young, unmarried neighbor who had come in to visit with me. And there was my girdle laying on the desk! I simply tried to ignore it and so did he. We went right on with our visit. **Doris Sontag, c. 1930, Blackduck Area School, Cass County**

Run, Spot, Run!
We were reading the story of Dick and Jane and Spot and how they had built a sand castle. Well, Spot tore down the sand castle. The three of us were sitting and talking about the story, and I said, "Oh, what in the world is Spot going to do?"

"Run like hell!" said one of the little boys.

Olga Peterson, 1932, Birchwood School, near Mineral Center, Cook County

This Too Shall Pass
In my first year of teaching, I had a kid who swallowed his pencil. Those were the Depression days. People didn't have money so you would wear the pencils down until they were about two inches long. And there you'd sit with that pencil and think and put it in your mouth. That day all the hands shot up. "Billy swallowed his pencil!" And was he bawling!

What were we going to do? Once my sister had accidentally swallowed a tack and mother called the doctor. He told her to feed my sister dry bread and the tack would pass on through.

So I had all the kids open their dinner pails and haul out all the little bread crusts. They had plenty because in those days the kids didn't eat the crusts because they were usually as hard as bricks. We fed him dry bread. Things turned out just fine. A couple days later his parents reported that he was all right. He stayed home for a few days but he was just fine as nature took its course. **Hildred Oliver, 1932, District 63, Nobles County: Hildred taught in Nobles and Murray counties for nine years.**

Hydrologists

It was a very rainy day and there was a lot of rain standing on the ground also. It had stopped raining and at recess time I looked out the window and the boys were just working away out there on something. I went out to see what it was they were doing. They were working like troopers. They were digging a ditch trying to run that water into the girls' toilet. I said, "You can close that up in a hurry." **Veronica Hergott, 1943, Denzer School, Le Sueur County**

Poet Laureate

I assigned my fifth graders to write a poem. So this boy turned in his poem about Arlene, a first grader, and based it on "Mary Had a Little Lamb." He was a little rascal, but he was a lovable rascal.

> Arlene had a chew of gum.
> She chewed it long and slow,
> And every place that Arlene went,
> The gum was sure to go.
> She carried it to school one day,
> Which was against the rules.
> The teacher took it away from her
> And chewed it after school.

Margaret Lybeck, 1933, Bush Valley School, Houston County

The Mimicker

One winter day I decided to wear my special red wool turtleneck sweater. I didn't wear that sweater very often. That day I decided to wear red fingernail polish to match my sweater. I didn't wear nail polish very often either. Not many people wore nail polish. That was a very poor farming area. Most families were barely making a living. Farm wives especially wouldn't have had time to baby themselves with nail polish. I'm not sure exactly what was so special about the day. I think it may have been Christmas time. That polish was not like today's polish. It took a long time to dry and it didn't last long. The next day I was mimicked by Dorothy, a fourth grader. She had used red food coloring for her nail polish. Dorothy came from a family of all brothers so she was especially tuned in to any feminine examples. She was so proud of herself when she arrived with her red "fingernail polish."

Esther Nordland Lickteig

Dorothy, the Queen of the Red Fingernails, is second from the left: 1933, Magnuson School.

I didn't tell Dorothy that I noticed her special nails. I didn't want to embarrass her. I'll always remember her red food-colored fingernail polish. **Esther Nordland Lickteig, 1934, Magnuson School, Freeborn County: Esther, born in 1901, taught in four Freeborn County schools from 1930 to 1936.**

Don't Touch the Charmin!

My older sister Sigrid Sandi taught at Steelsville, near Dassel, in 1933 during the Depression. In her first year she was told to order enough toilet tissue for the year. She had no idea how much she needed and she evidently ordered plenty because it was still stacked up on a shelf in the storage room when she left three or four years later.

Grace Swanson, 1933–1934

Unflappable

During all my years of teaching in the country schools, the toilets were outside. I had one little girl in first grade who always wore denim coveralls with the buttoned flap across the back.

When she had to leave the room to go to the toilet, she always came up to the front of the room and waited for me to help her. Then I unbuttoned the flap, and she held it up as she walked back the length of the room to the outside door.

When she came back in, she walked up to the front of the room, holding the back flap up, and I buttoned her up and sent her back to her seat.

Wanda Krousey, 1934, District 149, Todd County

Love on the Rocks

My students all knew that I was dating Edwin Sharkey. There was a kid named D., who was a bad, bad, bad kid. Whenever anything  came up that had the name Ed or Edwin in it, he would pick it right up and make some smart comment. His brother M. used to make the fire every morning, so I had a nice warm building when I arrived. One day D. went into the basement with M. and wrote "Ed Sharkey" on every one of the bricks in the chimney. I'm sure there were hundreds of bricks with Ed's name on each one as far up as the little runt could reach. I made D. wash every single one with soap and water, but that was time away from school upstairs, so the punishment didn't bother him.

Marietta Sharkey, 1936, St. Thomas, Le Sueur County

Lucyle Tabbert used the "write on the board" punishment until she met Mr. Literal.

A Boy of Few Words

This little boy was naughty on the school ground, so I told him to stay after school. I had written a sentence on the board: I will be more careful when I play. (100 times) So he wrote on the board: I will play more carefully. (100 times) Then he left.

Lucyle Schmalz Tabbert, 1936, District 56, Long Lake School, Cottonwood County

The Grocery Bear

There were three girls from one family going to  school. Their father had gone to town and gotten some groceries. Then he stopped at the school on the way back. He wanted to know if he could borrow his girls to chase a bear through the woods. What really happened was that he had a bunch of groceries. He had to walk back home and he needed help in carrying the sack of flour and other staples.

Blanche Swift, c. 1936

So I excused the girls and they helped their dad carry the groceries home. **Blanche MacAllister Swift, 1935–1937, Unorganized Klat School, Cass County**

The Runaround

On the last Friday of each month, I was given my $50 paycheck. I took it to the little village of Clitheral to cash. Since there was no bank, I went to the general store. They told me they did not have that much money in the till. They gave me $15 and a check for $35. Next I went to the restaurant. They gave me $15 and a check for $20. Then I went to the garage, and they cashed the check for the remaining $20. I did that with every check for that entire year, and sometimes I had to go to four businesses to get all my money. **Winifred Dunn Chesborough, 1936, District 53, Otter Tail County**

Half and Half

I taught half a year to finish out a term another teacher had not been able to complete. My room at the place where I stayed was a little part of the main room of the house and was separated with great big curtains. My room was very small. We had no electricity at that time, so it was dark and very difficult to see. When I got to school, I discovered I had one shoe of one pair on and one shoe of another pair. I was trying to keep my feet under the desk so the kids wouldn't notice. In the middle of the morning, here comes the man where I boarded. He carried two shoes. He held them up in front of me and said, "Which one do you want to wear, Vera?"

Vera Flategraff, 1936, west of Blackduck, Beltrami County. Vera taught at the following country schools for

108

seven years: Cass, Beltrami, and the White Earth Indian Reservation in Becker County. Vera taught for another twenty-three years in public schools.

Singin' and a Scratchin'

Santa, the main character in the Christmas operetta, came down with chickenpox. There was no one who could be a stand-in. There were too many parts, too much talking, so no one had learned all the lines. We told the nurse about our dilemma.

She said, "He's exposed everyone already. He might as well go on." So Santa scratched and wiggled all through the program.

Mary, a first grader, was to sing "Away in the Manger" at the Christmas program. She got up, so proud of herself, and all the while she was turning and turning the hem of her dress.

Up and up it went until her lace-trimmed panties were visible. Everyone was chuckling. Everybody laughed and scratched through the entire program. **Louise Gruska, 1936, Cedar Valley 1, near Floodwood, St. Louis County**

What could better satisfy the appetite of a hungry story miner than meeting Esther Norhar and Lempi Keto at Louise Gruska's house in Virginia for a good round of stories followed by a delicious lunch?

Finnish Notes

Saturday night was sauna night. My landlady, her four-year-old son, and I packed our sauna bag with towels and clean clothes. It was lovely walking across the snowy fields to the neighbor's sauna. After everyone was steamed, scrubbed, and rinsed, we had coffee together and good cardamom biscuits were served. Then I played Finnish hymns on an old organ. This puzzled some of the neighbors so much that one of them sent a letter to the Duluth paper asking how was it possible that a teacher who was not Finnish and knew very little Finnish could play Finnish music! The editor explained that music was a universal language. The notes were the same in any country. **Louise Gruska, 1936, Cedar Valley 1, near Floodwood, St. Louis County**

Does Heat Rise?

The county superintendent stopped in one cold, wintry day. She noticed they had their boots on. She asked where the thermometer was. I showed her. She said it should be closer to the floor. It didn't make the room any warmer. **Anita Schrupp, 1937, District 36, Houston County**

He Didn't Show

We always had a program for Columbus Day. One of the girls went home and told her mother, "We had our program for Columbus. We drew the three ships on the board. Mary sang and Billy read and I recited my poem." The mother said, "Well, what did Columbus do?"

"Columbus," she said, "he wasn't there!"
Doris Erdahl, c. 1937, Stevens County

Gelled Belles

In 1937 and 1938 when I was teaching in St. Thomas, we didn't have the luxury of having setting gels. Dad used to raise flax. My sister Dorothy and I would go out to the granary and bring in half a cup of flax, throw it in a kettle, and put in a couple cups of water and boil it. That made this gooey, messy stuff like the gels today. Dorothy used the gel to set the girls' hair in those tight waves for the Christmas program. Their hair got stiff as a board. Those girls were so proud of those waves. They could put their hands up there and those waves wouldn't move. I had twenty-eight girls in the school and she set every one. Then around the edge of the hair after she had set the waves in the back, she put in pin curls. She had about a thousand setting pins. Those girls thought they had died and gone to heaven.

Marietta Sharkey, 1937, St. Thomas, Le Sueur County

Do As I Say, Not as I Do

My brother claims this story is true. My dad, who was the teacher, chewed Copenhagen from the time

William Herzog

he was ten until he died at age eighty-four. The boys in school at that time all chewed from about the time they were about ten or twelve. They also chewed in school, too. They just swallowed the juice. Dad didn't approve of the boys' chewing. He could tell if they had Copenhagen in their pockets because he could see the outline of the round cans in their back pockets. Then he'd confiscate the snuff. That's what kept my dad in tobacco all those years. **Bill Herzog speaking about his father William Herzog, who taught in District 22, St. Joseph, Scott County in 1937**

A Giggle Miracle

Once I combined all eight grades for a language lesson. As the class moved into the usual semicircle in front of the room, Fred moved his chair back. When he sat down, he almost missed the chair. He looked up and said, "Oh, oh, that was almost the end of Freddy!" A few students got the giggles. Soon the giggling spread until we were all laughing so hard. Then an amazing thing happened. One of the students who stuttered became so relaxed because of the laughter that he read aloud without stuttering. The words flowed so easily. That day I learned the value of laughter. **Veronica Blees Smith, 1939, District 7, Stevens County**

Estelle Grinde began teaching in 1930. She taught in the rural schools of Pennington, Marshall, and Roseau Counties for eleven years.

The Good Life

One noon hour the superintendent and teachers training instructor came to visit. They also brought an educator from Washington, D.C., who was there to inspect country schools. She wanted to see what life was like in a school like ours. They came at noon, and the boys went out to play. But the girls were curious about this company and even more curious about this woman who stared at them. The visitors walked around inspecting everything. All the girls lined up on one side of the room.

"I love this country air!"

The lady from Washington wore pincher glasses on a long chain. She looked over the top of her pinchers and said, "My, such healthy-looking children." Then she exclaimed, "My, aren't they fine! I suppose country life is so invigorating!"

A few days later it was raining so hard the children couldn't play outside. One fifth-grade girl said, "We can't go outside, so let's play school. We'll be those people who came to visit school. You be the superintendent; you be the teachers training teacher, and I'll be that lady from Washington, D.C."

Then she made some pincher glasses out of clay and stuck them on her nose. She said in a voice mocking the woman, "My, such healthy-looking children. My, aren't they fine. But I suppose the country life is so invig.... What was that word Miss Hanson?"

"Invigorating," I said.

"What's it mean?"

I said, "It's when you feel real sharp. Your blood is tingling. On a cold winter morning you feel ambitious to go right to work."

One January morning it was about thirty-five below. My student walked into the school. Her eyelids were all frosted. Her frosted scarf was wound around her head. "Good morning, Miss Hanson," she said. "Isn't the country life invigorating this morning?" **Estelle Grinde, 1939, Roseau County**

Estelle Grinde's wonderful sense of humor helped her survive the nerve-racking visit from the Washington dignitaries. Perhaps nothing tested Estelle's ability to laugh at the world more than "life with Albert."

Albert

Albert was a very bright kid with a wonderful imagination. But he was full of mischief. In the fall we banked the school with straw bales to keep it insulated during the winter. The parents had also made a toboggan slide, which they also banked up with straw. The students always arrived before I did. One morning when I arrived, they shouted, "Miss Hanson, you came just in time to see Albert go through fire." Albert had put a flax straw bale at the end of the slide and he was going to go down the slide and go through fire. He had seen something like that at the fair.

I said, "Albert, that straw bale is so close to the school that you could burn the school down."

"Oh, I never thought of that," he said.

I had him sit right in front of me. I couldn't look at him without laughing because I knew there was so much going on in that mind. One day I rang the bell and he leapfrogged all the way from the back to the front. I said, "Albert, go back and come in the right way."

"Ya," he said, "I can do that, too." I had to turn my back because I always broke out laughing.

Estelle Grinde, 1939, Roseau County

Home

Once a mother brought her family over to see me in my home. She said, "My little boy thinks you live in the schoolhouse, so I wanted to bring him over and show him that you have a home of your own."

Leona M. Kelly, c. 1939, Lac Qui Parle County

Joy Ride

One day Johnny, who was eight years old, decided at recess that he was going to go home to get his bicycle. His home was at least four miles away and it was a hot, hot day. When the kids came in from recess, I asked where Johnny was and the kids said, "Oh, he went home to get his bicycle."

I knew he couldn't make it, so I put two older girls in charge and went to find him in my car. He could have gone down the road to the left or the right. I started down the road and a farmer working in his field told me he hadn't come that way. I went back the other way, and I found him about three miles from the school. His nose was bleeding and he was crying. He was a terrible mess so I hugged him. I knew he was just misguided and didn't know how far it was to his home. I asked him what he wanted to do—go home or back to school. He wanted to go home, so I took him there and explained to his grandma what had happened. When I got back to school, the youngsters were fine, but the two girls came up to me and said quite seriously, "You had a telephone call."

"Who was it?" I asked.

"We don't know," one of the girls said, "and we didn't want to tell them that Johnny had run away from school so we told them you just took the car and went for a ride." Oh, my gosh! I thought it was the county superintendent, but it wasn't. It was a lady, telling me she had seen little Johnny walking down the road. I couldn't get over it. They said I just went for a ride during school!

Mae Wilson, Carp School, Lake of the Woods County. Mae taught for forty-one years, and twenty of her twenty-one years teaching in the country schools were spent in Lake of the Woods County.

Allie Riehle and a teacher's friends: paste, glue, construction paper, and a vivid imagination.

Where Does It Go?

We had a unit about evaporation. We left some snow on the counter and when we came back on Monday it was gone. I washed the board and asked, "What happened to the water? When your mother washes your clothes, she hangs them outside. Why do they dry?" We went through all these examples and lessons, but I never heard them use the word *evaporate*. Then one day we were lining up to wash our hands. One of the young boys came up to me and tugged on my sleeve and said, "Mrs. Riehle, come here quick!" I asked him what had happened.

"Well," he said, "someone wet all over in the bathroom. Should we wipe it up with a towel or should we let it evaporate?" At least he used the word correctly.

Allie Dalbacka Riehle taught in the following rural schools of Itasca County for twenty years: Blackie, Wawing, Wendigo, and Cohasset.

See the red truck. Why is it at Allie's school?

Run, Dick, Run

During the first year I taught, the man who lived across the road built the fires each morning. One

Allie signed her first contract in 1938.

very cold morning he was a little too enthusiastic. By the time I arrived, I could see smoke billowing out of the attic so I called the fire department. The day before I had written my lesson for that day. On the board I had written, "Run, Dick, run. I see red. Can you see red?" When I went back in after

the firemen had left, I noticed they had embellished my story. They had written, "Run, Dick, run. The schoolhouse is on fire."

Allie Riehle, 1938, Blackie School, Itasca County

The Unmentionable

Warren used to come to school early, leave his books and lunch, and go to check his traps. His trap line was just past the Schmitt place where I boarded. One morning on his arrival, I said, "Warren, would you take this note to Mrs. Schmitt, and she will give you something to bring back?" I needed a dust rag, and she was always willing to supply one. When he returned and all the other children were gathered round and school was about to start, I said, "Warren, did Mrs. Schmitt give you something for me?"

"Ye---ee---ss," he slowly replied, looking embarrassed.

"Where is it?" I asked.

"Out in the hall," he said, again looking uncomfortable and embarrassed.

As I headed for the hall, one of the children asked, "What did she give you, Warren?"

"Oh something the teacher forgot to wear this morning, I guess," he replied.

What was in the sack? A torn, beat-up, white cotton petticoat! **Edith Salvevold, c. 1940, Riverside School, Beltrami County: Edith taught for thirty-two years.**

Secret Santa

At the annual Christmas program I had one of the school board members play Santa. He was out in the woodshed where my husband dressed him so no one would know who Santa was. I had a gunnysack full of gifts—one for each student as well as a gift for each school board member and Santa, too. I had a box of cigars wrapped for each one.

Well, I forgot the packages in Santa's bag. He came in hollering "Ho, ho, ho." He was busy reading the names and handing out the presents.

When he got down to the bottom of the bag, he found the presents for the school board members, and he passed them out. When he got to the last name, he called out, "Pete K.? Pete K.? Oh, that's me!" Everybody clapped and yelled because they all knew who Santa Claus was that year.

Lola Prigge, 1940s, District 21, Brown County

He Could Sling it!

I was teaching in a school twenty miles east of Hinkley. I had hired a boy who lived near the school to build the fires during the winter. I had to walk quite a distance, so I wore snow boots to school and left my shoes in the school.

When I arrived one morning, the boy said there was still fire in the stove when he came to make it. Someone had stayed in the school overnight and fed the fire. But my shoes were missing! Later someone told me of seeing a slingshot made from my shoes.

Fern Breckheimer McCormack, 1940, Ogema Township, Pine County

The Threat

Leona Simonson, 1944, Meeker County

I had a first-grade boy who could not learn to count to five. No matter how much I tried with various objects, he could not count to five. One day I said to him, "Tomorrow you are going to count to five or that little red comb that's in your pocket is going to be mine." The next day he came to school without the red comb.

A Tough Day

One lovely spring day we went on a field trip. On the way home a little first grader said, "I'm tard an firsty and I'm hot. I'm dis bout everfing." **Theodora Holden, 1940, Moose Lake School, Carlton County**

The Rule: No smoking allowed in the school or on school property. But what happens when the students give you a free afternoon? In 1943, Florence Hartwig had a surprise visitor.

Caught in the Act!

One day in May there was a Market Day in town and the big event of the day was a free movie for

Ah, the refreshing pause!

everyone at 2 p.m. All the children wanted to see the movie and had talked to their parents who agreed to pick them up at 1:30. The kids just told me about it that morning. We skipped recess and had all our classes done when their parents came to pick them up. After they had all left, I kicked off my shoes, lit a cigarette, and decided to catch up on a little paper correcting. I was busy when I heard the door open. I looked up and there stood the county superintendent, who had come for a visit.

I put out my cigarette and explained why I had no pupils in attendance. We spent a pleasant hour discussing the children's work and plans for the rest of the school year. No one mentioned the cigarette.

Florence Hartwig taught at District 72, Buck School, Dodge County from 1943 to 1944.

Paste Jar Revenge

After a bitterly cold weekend, I arrived at District 79 to find the thermometer registering twenty below. It took a while to get that old coal furnace heating. In checking the damage, I found our large glass paste jar was frozen solid with the jar still attached to the paste but broken in many places. Laurence, a sixth grader, volunteered to take the jar to the garbage.

He must have slipped and cut the inside of his hand. While I was washing off the cut, he saw the

blood and he fainted into my arms, but he immediately recovered from the shock. As I bandaged the injury, Clifford, who was in the fourth grade, watched us with eyes and mouth wide open. He looked terrified.

Leone Brown Hedlund, far right, first row, 1944, teachers training class

When Clifford wrote the story of the accident for our school newsletter, he wrote, "I thought Laurence had died!"

Leone Hedlund, c. 1945, District 58, Kandiyohi County

Birth Control

One day one of the little Norwegian boys in my class said, "Oh, Miss Solem, come quick to the window. My mama and papa are going home with a new baby."

Well, in those days if you were going to have a baby in the Shevlin area, you went to Mrs. Anderson, the midwife, and you stayed there until the delivery. If it was winter you went early, because you might not make it if you had to take a sleigh ride that far. When the sleigh went by, the student said, "Miss Solem, would you like to have a baby?"

"Yes," I said, "someday I hope that I will get married and have a family."

Then he said, "If you want one, you yust go work for Mrs. Anderson for two weeks. You'll get one." **Vi Solem, Solway, Beltrami County**

Wiggles

Little Jackie had brilliant red hair, freckles, and a sweet little face to go with them. During a class with another grade, there was a ripple of giggles in the room. I glanced up and all were busy studying. A few minutes later they giggled again. Still nothing was evident. By timing the space between the interruptions, I glanced up just in time to see Jackie wiggling his ears. Wiggling was an understatement. He wiggled his whole ear! When I caught him performing, he got a worried look on his face. I praised him for what he could do and asked him to come to the front and teach us all how to do it. No one else could master it, so he was a celebrity.

Joyce Lankow, 1945, Wendell School, Grant County

This Way or That Way

Joyce Lankow, c. 1945

At that time, people who were left-handed were often forced to use their right hand to eat or write. However, one first-grade boy was truly ambidextrous. When he wrote on the blackboard with the second graders, he used his right hand. In play and working at his desk, he often switched to the left. There was no consistency as to which hand the boy would use to put on his overshoes or mittens. He could put on either first, one time using one hand, the next time the other. In games he led with one foot on one occasion, the other, the next time. Once I placed two colors on the desk, each pointing outward. He took one in each hand, wrote his name from the center out with a perfect mirror image.

Joyce Lankow, 1944, Lankow School, Wilkin County

It Can't Get Any Worse!

My worst day at school was in October of 1958. In the morning a first grader vomited all over my beautiful, full-circle, quilted skirt. Neither her parents nor I had a phone, so I washed my skirt in cold water while I was wearing it. Then I cleaned up his mess. At noon I usually burned the junk before we played ball. It was obviously too windy to burn because the fire got away from me. The kids and I put out the fire, but it got very close to the schoolhouse. I always played ball with the students at noon. I told my students that the rest of the day couldn't get worse as I pitched the first ball. Wham! My six-foot-tall eighth grader smashed the ball through the church window across the road. In the afternoon the first grader got sick again. She stood too close and at the worst possible moment, she vomited all over my skirt again. **Myrtiss Weckwerth, 1958, St. John's Lutheran School, Yellow Medicine County**

This Little Piggy Went to ....

My tiny school was located in the middle of nowhere. I had six students, but only four of them came every day. One late fall afternoon I was in the school, correcting papers after all the students had gone. I heard this noise in

"Come children. Let's visit Miss Johnson. Maybe she'll read "Three Little Pigs."

the hall. Some walking, walking, thumping, thumping. "Who's out there?" I asked. No one answered. More walking, walking, thumping, thumping! "Who's out there?" I asked again. I was getting a little afraid, being out there all alone. It wasn't dark, but there was no one else even close by. I didn't know what to do.

Finally I decided to go out there and find out what was going on. I shook the knob and opened the door. There, crawling under the extra seats, was a mother sow and her six little pigs. They had crossed from the neighbor's farm to my school. They must have liked the cool floor and thought it was their barn.

So I chased the sow and her piglets back to the neighbor lady's place. Imagine! Here comes the schoolmarm, chasing those pigs. It was the biggest news around. It even made the newspaper!

Julie Johnson, 1945, Lac Qui Parle County. Julie told me this story at the Kandiyohi County Fair.

Lord Sandwich

We always said a prayer for lunch. We had a prayer that we had memorized, but once in a while a child would ask, "Can I say the prayer?" They didn't have to pray, but praying was permissible so we always did it. The prayer we were saying was, "By His hand we all are fed. Give us, Lord, our daily bread." Well, this little boy was saying something that didn't sound just right so I went up close to him and listened. He was saying, "By His sandwich we all are fed. Give us, Lord, our daily bread." I thought, "How appropriate because we were all eating sandwiches." I never said a word to him about changing his prayer. **Ardus Wangen, c. 1950, Mower County**

I Saw the Teacher....

Three of the boys in my class had seen their mother's boyfriend kill their mother. Their father then bundled them up and took them to their grandpa and grandma for the year. Their grandparents lived just across the field from the school, which sat high on a hill. Of course, the grandparents spent much of the day watching what happened at the school. I'm certain they were under a lot of stress because of what had happened.

One night after school the boys asked if they could stay to help me clean. I said, "Sure." They got to playing. I was getting things ready for the next day, and they were having the best time. One of the girls who had stayed to help me was chasing them around the school yard with a broom.

Soon a pickup came into the driveway and their grandpa got out. He was so angry. I don't know if I've ever seen anyone so angry. He had been watching from his home. He thought I was chasing those boys of his with a broom. It took a lot of talking on our part to convince him that I wasn't beating them, that they were just playing. **Mary Lou Wilson Erickson, 1957, Union School, Meeker County**

The Gatherer

Every night after school we swept the floor. We used that reddish-colored sweeping compound. Jimmy was absolutely intrigued with that compound. He used to gather it while we were all involved in the sweeping. A country school is a closely knit community. Often after school I stopped at Proc's Store to get what I needed at home. Many times I would meet a mom or dad of one of my students. One night I met Jimmy's mother at Proc's, and she said to me, "Mary Lou, would you ask Jimmy to stop bringing that sweeping compound home with him? Every night he comes home with his pockets stuffed with that

Jimmy the Gatherer keeps an eye on the clock. "School's nearly over. Time for pocket stuffing! I love that greasy kids' stuff!"

stuff and it's got a smell to it and it's got an oil in it and it gets on my hands. Would you ask him not to bring it? I've talked to him, but it doesn't do any good. He still fills his pockets with it every day."

Then I remembered there was usually compound sprinkled on the floor around Jimmy's desk. The next day I had a little conversation with Jimmy about the compound, and he stopped scooping it into his pockets while we were sweeping.

Mary Lou Wilson Erickson, 1958, District 74, Hilltop School, Meeker County

Hazel Peschel began teaching in the rural schools in 1939. She taught in Todd, Meeker, and Stearns Counties for fifteen years.

Ha! Tricked Ya!

The board members always sat on the stage for the Christmas program. Rosanne, the daughter of one of the board members, and I dreamed up something a little special for our last program before the school year closed.

She had a candy store at the side of the stage and several little children came up and bought candy. Then I asked the three board members to go up on the stage. They looked at me and each other with a "What's going on here?" look, but they went. Then Roseann closed the curtain.

Another little boy came up and asked for some candy. Roseann opened the curtain and said, "I'm sorry, little boy, but all we have left are these three big suckers!"

The audience clapped and laughed so much that the board members decided everything was okay.

Hazel Peschel, 1970, Hellerman School, Stearns County

Chapter 14

Mr. Country School Teacher

In the graduation photographs of Country School Teachers, usually one or two men stand conspicuously among their female classmates. Their collars are tightly buttoned and their suits have probably been purchased for this special occasion. Like the young women in the photographs, they are about seventeen or eighteen years old. Many have become teachers because jobs are difficult to find. The nine-month normal training is relatively inexpensive, and they can soon be earning a living.

Many of these men tell stories about being recruited by school boards that were in need of someone with "firm discipline." Often the children in their schools had gained infamous notoriety for tormenting previous teachers, damaging school property, and "raising hell." The school boards often hired "iron-handed discipline," which was sometimes more important to the board than the teacher's academic excellence.

When Mr. Country School Teacher married and had children, he often left teaching and sought higher paying jobs. War and the Great Depression drove men from the classroom after one or two years. But many stayed and, like their counterparts, the irrepressible schoolmarms, they changed the lives of Country School Students.

Frank V. Heck

Frank V. Heck taught in Brown County, Jim Pearson taught in Benton and Mille Lacs Counties, Burton Kreitlow spent two years teaching in Wright County, L .E. Anderson taught in Mille Lacs County, and Dale Wright's country school teaching was split between Wadena and Otter Tail Counties.

When I was welcomed into Frank Heck's apartment to mine his stories, I knew at a glance that "Here is a vibrant man." Tucked into every nook and cranny, papers, books, and pictures tell the tale of his life story. Wherever I turned, I found music, music, music—instruments, sheet music, records—the passion of this Leader of the Band. Frank's eyes sparkle, and a hint of a German accent flavors each tale.

Frank V. Heck was born in 1907 in New Ulm. He began his teaching career in 1928 in Brown County, where he taught in districts 70, 5, and 4 until 1939. From 1939 to 1941 he taught in District 157 in Blue Earth County near Welsh.

Frank V. Heck c. 1930

Trial Number One

I made several trips during the summer to examine my first school. One day a respected farmer, who had seventeen children, and a young lady were cleaning the school. As I neared the door I heard the man say to his helper in German, "Who is coming now?"

"Oh, that is the schoolteacher who will be here this year," she replied.

"A man teacher? I think our school board would have more sense than to hire a man for a woman's job. That fellow really should be doing some useful task."

Frank won the respect of the doubting father with his wit, dedication, talent, and personality—qualities which would win the admiration of students, parents, teachers, and administrators for the next fifty years.

When the man who thought teaching was a woman's job realized I could speak German, he said, "Since you can speak, read, and write German, then you should teach a half hour of German each day."

I said, "Well, how many children do you have?" and the man said, "Seventeen."

"And how many farms do you have?" I asked.

"One," he said.

"You can only leave one on the farm. The rest will have to find work in town. And what language do you think they will need to know? When the children in this district come to school, most of them cannot speak a word of English, and they need to know English if they are to succeed in their business or work. I think it is good for people to speak two languages, but in America, English is the language of business." I taught German a half an hour after school closed at night, but I didn't get any takers. They were all anxious to go home.

1928, District 5, Cottonwood Township, Brown County

Another Opening, Another Show
Curtain 1

Frank's Christmas programs reveal that he was teacher, showman, and entrepreneur. Frank convinced the school board to hold the annual program in the Searles Church Hall, charge admission, and use the money to buy books and supplies. The board argued that this had never been tried and was unusual for the traditional Christmas program but Frank won their approval.

Reserved tickets were sold for fifty cents. All seats were sold out for the Friday, Saturday, and Sunday performances. The shows and an additional basket social netted the school $178.38, which bought many books and supplies.

The Christmas program was a vaudeville extravaganza. Between acts there were skits and playlets. Of course there were Christmas carols. The program even had an orchestra, a group of Frank's musician friends from New Ulm. The program was just like the musical *Oklahoma*.

The Topsies from Topsy-Turvey Land with masks on the backs of their heads and skin-colored cloth with a colored hair line to cover their faces did a precisely performed drill which gave the impression that every action was backward.

Another Opening, Another Show
Curtain 2

When I came back after Christmas vacation and met with the school board as to how the money was to be spent, they proudly showed me a planetarium they had purchased with the Christmas money from a fast-talking salesman. It was a mechanical toy to show the rotation of the earth.

I said, "Oh, no, boys, I want to spend that money, and you're going to let me spend it. I can show the same thing with a flashlight, an orange, and a grape. Remember, I was supposed to have the right to decide what to buy. Here are the forms from two publishers for the books and supplies we need. You will write the checks for these because you cannot go back on your word."

They said, "Don't you know we can fire you?"

I said, "You can fire me at the end of the year but just get me the books."

The board members broke out laughing and told me to order the materials.

In 1931, Frank met with the board members from District 70 and asked for a salary of $105. It was the Depression and other schools were paying $75 per month. But the board felt they needed a strong teacher. They talked to each other in German and said they would offer him $75, but if he wouldn't accept it by Monday, they would offer him the $105 he requested. Of course Frank spoke German and he went home knowing he would have what he requested on Monday morning.

Later at a board meeting, one of the members said something in German. Since it was something I was concerned about, I answered them in German.

One of the board members said, "Frank, when we hired you, did you know that we would meet your request if you didn't accept the lower offer?" I said "yes" and we had a good laugh about that.

1931, District 70, Brown County

Perhaps the board was willing to pay Frank $105 per month to acquire a strong teacher because the year before the students had made life so miserable that three teachers had left the school. However, Frank was an experienced Country School Teacher, and he carefully planned his tactics, using psychology and a unique approach to discipline to impress his students.

Meet My Friend

On the first day of school, I rang the bell and nobody came in. "Well," I thought, "I'll just play this real cool. I'll sit down at my desk and hold a book and make believe I'm reading and wait until the kids come in." Finally after about fifteen minutes, they came trickling in, wondering why I didn't scold them. I read a while after they were all in.

Then I said, "Now, boy and girls, I'm going to tell you something. I heard that you were tough, but I am tougher than the whole bunch of you put together." Then I took out a hose, and I said, "This is Lucifer, and do you know where Lucifer lives? He lives down here in my desk drawer. He's my assistant and if any of you don't behave, you'll get it. That's all there is to it."

"Now go outside and when I ring the bell, you have five minutes to get into your seats and to get organized. Your books will be in your hands and you'll be studying. No fooling around. And if you want to try me out, you try me out today." I had no problems after that.

That spring I was sitting outside eating lunch with the kids, and I said, "Now, boys and girls, what did you do with the teachers that you had to have three different teachers?"

They said, "We don't want to tell you. We've got too nice a school now."   **1931, District 70**

One of Frank's most effective teaching techniques was playing ball with the students.

The Trickster

I still get company from my students. At a school reunion some of the students said, "When we went out to play for recess, you pitched for both sides. You were kind of a smart cookie, weren't ya? You kept the score pretty even, kept it interesting. You were quite a stinker, but we liked it." I pitched in such a way that the score always remained pretty close. I pitched hard to the seventh and eighth graders.

Then he said, "And some days when it was real interesting, you said to us, 'If you work real hard when we get back to school, we can have the recess last a little bit longer.' Then you went into the school and set the clock back fifteen minutes so in case the superintendent came, you could say, 'Well, it's recess time.'"   **1931, District 70, Brown County**

Frank Heck, Mr. Country School Teacher, was also Mr. Music. In 1934 he started a children's band made up of Country School Students. Frank began conducting the New Ulm Civic Orchestra as a young man and led the group for many decades.

In 1943, Frank became county superintendent for Brown County, a position he held until 1953. From 1954 until 1973 he served as principal in the New Ulm schools. He continued working part-time as a reading consultant. Mr. Frank Heck was an educator for fifty years.

Harry Tordsen

Harry Tordsen was born in 1909, the seventeenth child in a family of eighteen. His dad was married twice. When his father's first wife died, Harry's mother raised the first nine children plus her own nine. No one dreamed of going to college.

Harry attended Lakefield High School. During the district basketball tournament, the coach from St. Cloud State Teachers College refereed the tournament. He was impressed with Harry's play and asked him to attend St. Cloud. According to Harry, "He was thinking about basketball, not my vocation." Harry attended St. Cloud and played basketball for four years and football for two years.

He completed his college degree with majors in geography, manual arts, and coaching. Harry was certified to teach secondary education, but he was not certified to teach in the country schools. He had none of the preparation required for normal school certification.

We'll Never Tell

Jobs were really hard to get because there were so many teachers. I couldn't get a job for one year. I had a chance to go to Warroad, but my parents wanted me to stay at home. I signed a contract at Round Lake in 1933. The board members came to me and told me they needed someone to discipline those tough kids. I wasn't qualified to teach rural schools but Round Lake had had so much trouble with the students. Teachers refused to stay. Some of them resigned during the year. Only the board members and I knew I wasn't certified. The board members kept it so secret that even the county superintendent didn't know.

Parental Support

The boys did whatever they wanted to do. They had broken sixty some windows the year before, so the board wanted a man teacher, qualified or not. On the first day I told the students, "You are not going to behave the way you did last year, and if you don't behave, I will kick you right out the door. You're out! I don't want you!" In those days you didn't have any trouble getting cooperation from the parents.

One boy wouldn't behave, so I just said, "Get out! I don't want you. Go on home!" He didn't like it but he left. I knew what was going to happen.

The father brought him back and said, "What seems to be the problem?" I told him.

The father took his son outside. I didn't see what happened, but he tossed him back into the school, tossed him right into the door in the hallway. I could hear him hit—thud! There wasn't a peep in the school. His father said, "If he doesn't behave now, send him back home." He was the best student I ever had.

Crunch!

On the first day of school, everyone was there early in the morning, waiting for the new teacher, trying to get acquainted. There were four boys who were as tall as I was and one was taller. Of course they wanted to show off before the girls about what they'd like to do.

I started teaching them football during recess and the noon hour. "Have any of you ever played football?" I asked them.

"No," they said, but one of the boys had seen it. Of course, I had played halfback for St. Cloud, but they didn't know that. I didn't tell them we could have played touch. I wanted us to play tackle.

I said, "OK, I'll show you how to play. You're all big boys and the girls can play too if they want to." We lined up on two sides. I only had a few students on my side, and they were the little ones and the girls.

The bigger ones, the tough seventh and eighth graders who caused all the trouble and broke all the windows, were on the other side. They were the ones I wanted to show who was going to be boss.

I lined them up and one of the big boys carried the ball. Bam! I tackled him really hard. Then another one of the big boys carried the ball. Bam! Again I tackled him as hard as I could. They backed off as soon as they were tackled pretty rough. Soon nobody wanted to be the ball carrier.

Normal Training Lesson Number 1: Establish Discipline. Use creative techniques to "Show them who's the boss!"

After I had tackled those big boys two or three times, they decided that football wasn't the game they wanted to play. It was just too rough.

However, they discovered how tough I could be. They knew who was in charge. There were no broken windows that year.

1933, District 119, Meyer School, near Round Lake, Jackson County: Harry Tordsen taught from 1933 to 1938. During the 1938 school year, he joined the Jackson County Sheriff's Department. In 1943 he was elected sheriff and served in that position until he retired in 1970.

Jim Pearson

To folks around Foreston, Cambridge, and Milaca, the name Jim Pearson is as familiar as the names of their own relatives. Jim takes them on wonderful journeys back to the days of their youth. He paints word pictures that capture time. His "Reflections" in the Mille Lacs County Times are filled with wry humor and gentle satire.

Jim Pearson went to Wildwood School in Benton County from 1921 to 1928. In 1934, he began

teaching at McKinley School, in District 43 in Benton County. He then taught in Mille Lacs and Benton Counties. He completed his seventeen-year career as a Country School Teacher by returning to his first school, McKinley, District 43. All his life, Jim has had a passion for nature and birds. Perhaps it all began one sunny spring morning as he set off for Wildwood School and his great adventure.

Jim Pearson c. 1939

A Kindred Spirit

When spring arrived in 1923, I was in the third grade. One morning when I was schoolward bound, I walked slowly down a country road, enveloped by the joyful music of birds. I reveled in their music and identified the different singers.

And then, rolling across the greening countryside, I heard one of the most unique spring sounds, the "booming" of the "prairie chickens," the pinnated grouse. I stopped and listened in fascination, wondering just how the sounds were made. I paused opposite the stone fence which stretched away from me, separating our farm from the neighbor's. I thought if I crawled along behind that stone fence, I'd get close enough to see them because they put on quite a show. And what a show it was!

Jim, c. 1925

But ahead was the school and the bell waiting for nine o'clock. But it got the best of me. Again the "booming" rolled across the countryside like a siren's song, beckoning me. I crawled behind the stone fence and raised my head between two stones, near enough to watch. Then the school bell rang. But it was too late. Nothing could move me from that spot with all the wonderful "booming."

I peeked over the fence. There they were! On a small, raised clearing, two males strutted and postured in their courtship display. The sun glistened on the two orange sacs under the feathered pinnates along their throats. The sacs ballooned and then "boom!" "boom!" The hens were all around them.

My folks kept this one place. There were some blueberries in there that my mother wanted and my dad would never mow it so the prairie chickens could live there.

The school bell jarred me back to reality and, of course, I was late. When I came walking into the school, there were forty-two student eyes looking at me and Miss Mary Martin's eyes were staring at me also. I spent the whole day miserable because I knew what I was going to get for my "hooky" tardiness. My schoolmate taunted me with, "Boy, are you going to get it!"

My brothers and sister hurried home to tattle-tale to Pa and Ma. My parents respected Miss Martin so much that any punishment meted out by her would be matched at home—with interest!

After school she called me up. I stood there before the desk. There was no use lying. I had to tell her the truth. Well, she got interested and asked me all about those prairie chickens. Instead of finding an unfeeling judge, I found a kindred spirit. Finally, she wrote out a note, sealed it, and sent me home. Then she said, "Good night. I'll see you tomorrow, ON TIME!" There were Ma and Pa waiting for me in the kitchen. I knew my brothers and sister had already tattled. So I knew I was in for it. I gave them the note and took my books and tin dinner pail into the other room. I came back to get my "medicine." Ma and Pa were silent,

Jim and a prairie chicken

just looking out the window over at that meadow. They were staring out at those ten acres they had set aside for the blueberries and prairie chickens. Ma lightly brushed my hair and turned to check the oven in the old kitchen range.

Well, I did get my lesson on the value of school time, but I didn't get my trip to the woodshed. The kids were all waiting behind the door, thinking that I would. All I got was that lecture. To this day I would like to know what she told them in that note.

The next morning, the first thing Miss Martin did was tell the big boys, "Open the windows. Now be quiet! Silence! Listen intently for spring sounds." But two of us were waiting for something special. Rolling across the countryside came the "booming" of the prairie chickens. We could hear them. Then she had me tell about the "booming."

A week later a magnificent bird book appeared on the library table. Only Miss Martin could have talked the school board into spending money for such a book. I got to take it home for the weekend after my sister had made a brown paper jacket.

1923, Lincoln School, Benton County

Jim believed the annual Christmas program was a great chance to teach not only the language arts and music but also something that kids could do for their community. Jim knew this program was the highlight of the year for both his students and their parents. It was a time for him to find special gifts as well as give them.

A Natural

I had a boy in the eighth grade and everybody looked down on him. He was morose and withdrawn. He thought, "People don't expect me to be anything so I won't." Teachers had passed him on because he couldn't do anything. He had gotten an attitude that he wasn't as good as the rest of them. When the Christmas program came, I thought about the boy and the role of Scrooge in *The Christmas Carol*. I thought, "He is Scrooge."

I gave him the part. I've heard John Barrymore and the greatest ones play that part, but Frank was as great. He raged, "Bah, humbug," and he told the people off, and sent off the little kids at the door, and all that. He played the role to perfection.

The crowd couldn't believe it. They just sat enthralled. It was something to admire. After that there was a transformation in that boy. The people respected him. I didn't know he had it in him. The kids respected him. That was his hidden talent. That program opened a whole new world for him in that community. Later he wasn't under that constant tension in which he thought he was being put down all the time. **c. 1955, Estes Brook School, Mille Lacs County**

O Holy Night

A first-grade girl from a sheltered home came to my class. Her parents had never let her be out and she was so withdrawn. I couldn't get her out of it. I was at my wit's end.

At the Christmas program we always had the Bethlehem scene. We needed a doll for the baby Jesus. Out of the corner of my eye, I saw her hand come up. Her eyes—I caught something there. The good Lord was telling me, "Here's your chance." And so I said to her that she should bring her doll.

And it turned out that this was her life at home. She had these dolls and put such big store by them. She brought that doll. It was a beautiful little thing. She had the clothes she had made for it. The other kids all admired it. It set her up. Then I thought she should play Mary, too, since it was her doll. She played Mary and that was the opening for her.

This withdrawn girl went to high school. I got an invitation to come to the class play. She was the lead part. Later on she went to the state declamatory contest, this withdrawn girl who couldn't even play. I set a lot of store by Christmas programs.

1949–1956, Estes-Brooke School, Mille Lacs County

Burt Kreitlow

Burt Kreitlow's home is tucked into the rocky banks of Lake Superior. His home is filled with stories that lie stacked and scattered about. Burt's stories also float throughout his house, reminiscing in every nook and cranny. When he told these favorite anecdotes from his grade school days and teaching career, the new stories struggled to find a bit of space. Burton W. Kreitlow attended Highland School in Wright County from 1922 through 1929.

Burt and his brother, 1937

Nothing sparks memories of "the good old days" like a trip back to the place where it all happened. One early evening while passing Highland School, Burt stopped for a moment to reminisce.

Speaking My Pieces

There was enough daylight left for a look at the old school, so I drove the half mile to where it stood. I stopped the car and just looked. This time the memories of my first Christmas program at that school flowed around me. It may have been because the only building still there was the school. It had changed, made over into a family home, but I saw it as the Highland School. Tears came to my eyes.

My first Christmas program in that building flashed before me. The year, 1921. There were no kindergartens in those days. Each Christmas the teacher invited all four-, five-, and six-year-olds not in school to learn a "piece" for the program. The unwritten pressures of the neighborhood meant that all complied. The mothers of every four-, five-, and six-year-old made certain their children took part in the program. Since I was now four years old and had already experienced the ordeal, having been in last year's church program, I was anxious to take part. I knew how to make people listen.

I learned a rather long piece about Santa; of course I believed in Santa. I had heard him on our house roof the year before and was already trying to figure out how to catch a glimpse of him this Christmas eve.

Ma had me practice my piece many times before the program night. During the same period I was learning to say "Humpty Dumpty" in Swedish. Each evening after supper I would stand in the living room and speak my "piece" loudly enough for Ma and Pa to hear in the kitchen. That was going to help me be a preacher some day.

The night of the program came. We bundled up in the sleigh, and with all the other neighbors we descended on the schoolhouse. It was packed, a stage in front of the room, a curtain that the big kids pulled and a teacher standing to the side announcing the numbers.

After two of the lower grade classes finished their songs, playlets and "pieces," it was time for us. One of the older students pushed me to center stage behind the curtain. I didn't understand that at all. Then the curtain opened. I was stunned. There was Ma in the second row. After the teacher announced that Burt would now speak his piece, I stood twisting my shirt until it came out of my pants. I tried to tuck it back in. At first there was silence from the audience. I looked around and saw Ma mouthing something. I couldn't tell what she meant, so in my loudest voice I asked, "Which one shall I say?"

"Santa Claus," she replied. I began.

> "Santa will come to my house.
> The reindeer bring him there.
> He will leave me toys and candy.
> 'Cause I've been very, very good."

By this time I was on a roll, my voice getting louder and louder. I saw the people standing around the big, jacketed, wood-burning stove with smiles on their faces. I continued without a pause through the final line,

"And we all love dear Santa."

Ma looked pleased. I wasn't sure what to do next, but being on a roll, I looked at Ma and said, "I'll do my other one now." And I went right into "Humpty Dumpty," supposedly in Swedish. No one ever told me about my accent but something brought the house down. I didn't know what to call it, but it must have been "star quality."

As I sat looking at that old school, my Humpty Dumpty piece came back to me. I am sure it came in the same dialect and broken Swedish with which I delivered it at age four.

> "Lilla Trilla sot betalkin
> Lilla trilla, trillla near
> Ingort mann, evort lan
> Lilla trilla yelp becon."

Like other country school kids, Burt and his buddies hunted gophers. However, they gave the ritual a unique twist.

Charge!

We always prepared a pail of water before school. We had a teacher without discipline for one year. We watched in the schoolyard, and if one of us gave the signal "gopher," two boys ran for the well to get the pail of water. Those two ran right out of the school whenever the gopher showed up, anytime, out the door. Then we jumped out the window and got to the other end of his tunnel. Then the rest would come out more systematically and grab clubs and brooms. That poor teacher was beside herself. I think she followed a teacher that was so strict that if we did anything wrong, if you held your arm out over the side of the desk, she came with a ruler and with the cutting edge, she hit our hands. She was a devil. I remember that because I was hit a few times, but she would hit anyone. We behaved out of fear. After she left, we ran wild for a year. Out the door after those gophers! **Burt Kreitlow, c.1924**

Safe at School

We had one family that lived near school that had eleven or thirteen kids. They were pretty vigorously disciplined at home. One of the kids got sent home for something mean, nasty, or dirty that he had done. Well, he went home.

The next thing we saw was this poor kid running down the road. His dad was running behind him with a black snake, those long whips used for horses. We could hear the cracks through the open window when that thing was snapping.

The kid finally got into the school, basically for protection. Then we could hear the teacher and his father yelling at each other out in the hall afterwards. He was yelling louder than she was. I don't think that teacher ever sent any of those kids home again. When they were sent home, they "got it."

My Reading Jacket

I read everything. On Saturdays I took a load of grain five miles with a team of horses into town to get it ground. While I was waiting at Moore's Mill for the grinding, I went to the public library. After prohibition ended, the public library was in one half of the building and the liquor store in the other half.

I could not take books out of the public library because we lived in the country. So I would read for the two hours I waited for the feed. Then I put the books back and hauled the feed home. They didn't want me there because the country people didn't pay for the library. Politics. But they didn't kick me out. They were embarrassed that this kid full of feed came in. I never worried about what people thought of me and my jacket covered with feed. I read almost everything. I liked adventure—Jack London, James Oliver Kerwood, and many others.

Burt taught at District 58, Walker School, in Wright County from 1935 to 1937.

Pugilistic Pedagogy

I wanted to stay at home to teach. If the school was more than ten miles away, I wouldn't take it unless they paid through the nose, which none of them would. I finally got one for forty-five a month, but it was a challenge.

This was the school of a bunch of seventh and eighth graders who had to stay until they were sixteen. They were all fifteen that year. That board was looking for the biggest, most vicious-looking teacher they could find. On the last day of school the year before, those kids chased the teacher with baseball bats and brooms and everything else a quarter of a mile down the road into a school board member's home. If they had caught her, they would have beaten her. They were vicious!

I took the job and the first thing I ordered was boxing gloves. That was the first order they filled—before the order for books. I knew nothing about boxing, but I knew something about boys as they get into pre-adolescence and adolescence. They were a vigorous group. What little we learned about boxing we picked up from some information that came with the gloves, nothing serious. With the boxing gloves and reasonable control, we had a lot of fun. We also got basketball backboards put up. Ultimately, we challenged the town school. That physical activity cleared up all the discipline trouble. I had absolutely no discipline problems.

The Christmas party was going to be at one of the parent's houses. My student came up to me and said, "Why don't you box with my brother Bud?"

I said, "Fine, we'll box. We're not going to fight. That's fine."

Everything was cleared out of the kitchen, except the good old country stove. I'm sure Bud was waiting for the right time. We had played around for a couple three-minute rounds. It was fun. Well, when I was backed up right next to the stove, Bud started one right at the floor, caught me on the jaw, lifted me up, and sat me right on the stove.

That was a great thing for the kids to see. It had nothing to do with discipline. It had a lot to do with fun and a hot seat. That was the end of my boxing career, but I think Bud knew what he was doing.

1935–1937, District 58, Walker School, Wright County

Normal school training advice to all teachers: Always maintain a sense of humor when things get "too hot to handle!"

Burt Kreitlow has an M.A. in Education and a Ph.D. in Education and Rural Sociology. He has worked in education for sixty-two years as a college teacher and professional consultant. Burt has published several books and is in the process of publishing another. Each year former college students gather with Burt for a seminar and storytelling.

L.E. (Laurel) Anderson

L. E. Anderson, 1937

L.E. Anderson completed high school at Upsala in 1934. He then attended St. Cloud State, where he lived in the basement of a funeral home and worked for a local doctor for twenty-five cents an hour. But he had no intention of being a mortician or performing surgery. He was twenty years old when he signed his teaching contract in 1937 to teach in District 15 North in Mille Lacs County.

Heavyweight

I graduated from St. Cloud in November of 1936 during the depths of the Depression. To my surprise I received a call from Mrs. Sophie Soule, county superintendent in Milaca. She asked me if I was interested in a "problem school" located in Opstead in the extreme northern edge of the county. Of course I was! I was so desperate to find a job I was interested in anything available.

The school board had terminated the tenure of the teacher because she was unable to cope with the disciplinary problems that had grown increasingly more serious. For this reason they decided to hire a man. It sounded as if they needed someone who was physically qualified, so in my application, I emphasized my physical attributes to the near exclusion of my scholastic qualifications, which were nothing to be proud of. I must admit that I exaggerated my size (190 pounds), but I did not feel guilty because I weighed nearly that when wearing an overcoat and my four-buckle shoes.

I met Mrs. Soule in Milaca and we drove to the Opstead Community Hall for the interview. The board immediately offered me the job at sixty-five dollars a month, the salary they had paid the fired teacher, but I held out for seventy dollars. Finally they grudgingly gave in. I was so elated at having a job that the long trip home passed in no time.

The Milk Run Blues

I had no car, there was no bus service, and the nearest railroad station was six miles from my home. So with my cardboard suitcase in hand I left home at 4 a.m. and walked the six miles to the station. I boarded the train on that bleak winter morning and hours later arrived in Isle in a swirling blizzard as the short winter day drew to a close.

The depot agent told me that if I hurried, the milk truck might give me a ride to the school. It was depressing, but somehow I found the milk truck as darkness fell. I resumed my journey in the back of a covered truck loaded with empty milk cans that bounced around as that cumbersome vehicle labored over the snow-covered road. After many miles we reached the Kalberg home, where I lived while I taught in the Opstead school.

The Trouble Maker

On the first day, the entry and the school were filled to overflowing. The larger boys congregated in the entry and eyed me with suspicion. The older girls huddled in a corner and emitted much giggling and laughter. However, not all the youngsters maintained their distance. A roly-poly third grader with beautiful brown eyes, a radiant smile, and glowing cheeks proudly called my attention to her new shoes that had been "ordered from the catalogue."

There before me sat the thirty-six youngsters who made up what had been described as the "problem school." Yet they appeared to be no different from any other group of youngsters.

But in a desk, isolated from the others, sat a frail, sallow stripling, who looked hungry and frightened. I learned that this fourth grader was a mischief maker who liked to bask in the center of attention, and what he lacked in size, he made up in initiative. He encouraged other boys to become mischievous while he went away unscathed.

Before my arrival someone had asked him what would happen with the new man teacher. "I'll shoot the S.O.B.," he said. So that's what I faced in handling "the trouble maker."

One wintry morning after it had snowed about a foot, "the trouble maker" and his brother came quite early and we were alone in the school. The "trouble maker" asked if he could go to the outhouse in the far corner of the schoolyard. I said "OK," and he went out, but he returned in record time. I asked him if he had gone all the way out to the toilet. He assured me he had so I went out to check. His tracks stopped just around the school corner by a yellow shaft where he had urinated.

L. E. Anderson's class at the Opstead School near Milaca. Which of the boys was his nemesis? Whose pants held the most dust and dirt?

When I returned, I asked him again if he had gone to the outhouse and he lied to me again. So I grabbed him and dragged him out to the woodshed where I gave him a good paddling. The dust flew from his corduroy pants. He never whimpered or shed a tear. He never told anyone I had paddled him. He was the only child I handled physically during the four years I taught.

He Scores!

Later I was beset by continuous contingents of mothers who visited the school, four or five at a time. They generally came in the afternoon, but occasionally a mother might come in the morning and stay all day to "better understand" what we were doing. Their visits gave me an opportunity to know them, but sometimes it made me tense and uneasy. They brought their knitting and sewing paraphernalia. These activities and their incessant visiting were a distraction for everyone.

However, their youngsters were better behaved and made a greater effort to do well, especially during their recitations.

Mrs. W. came to observe also. She had six children and a husband who was a half-pint, lazy, sociable man whom people took "rather lightly." Mrs. W. ruled the roost with an iron hand.

I'll call her son W. He was somewhat retarded and had a violent temper. For this reason the kids liked to pick on him. He did poorly in school. The only fact he never forgot was 1803, the date of the Louisiana Purchase.

One day when Mrs. W. was sitting among the other mothers, making me a nervous wreck, I asked all the other students for the date of the Louisiana Purchase. Nobody knew the answer. I called on W. and he shouted, "1803." Mrs. W. was quite pleased.

L.E. Anderson

The Intimidator

Finally spring came. One day during recess one of the boys told me there had been a fight behind the woodshed involving W., who had run home to inform his mother. After I had obtained the details from those involved in the fracas, I resumed classes. Looking back, I should have found out all the details, but being tired after a long day and being twenty years old, I didn't investigate.

On the way home I felt concerned about what W. had told his mother and what her reaction might be. I was uneasy because their farm was between the school and the farm where I was staying. It was necessary for me to walk by their house, which was located near the road.

When W.'s mother had visited the school, she seemed friendly, but I had observed her rugged physique. She impressed me as a person to be handled carefully. She looked obstinate and determined. She was a big woman and her two hundred pounds were well distributed over a compact frame. I had been warned by those who knew her that she was easily disturbed, and when she became angry, she was a veritable tigress. Those were my thoughts as I proceeded up the hill that hid their farm. I hoped I wouldn't be noticed.

Just below the top of the hill she stood waiting but she had seen me first. I would gladly have retreated quickly behind the hill and walked the four miles around the section to avoid her. W. had told her what had happened, but he had not given her the complete picture. This I found to be characteristic of the boys when reporting events in which they had been involved.

In simple language, "She gave me hell." She called me everything she could think of. I was in no position to defend myself so I could do nothing but stand and take her abuse. Certainly it was the low point of my rural school teaching.

That spring the board offered me a five-dollar raise, but I signed a contract to teach near my home. When Mrs. Soule came to visit the school and heard that I was leaving, she "worked me over," too, but nothing to compare with the thrashing that Mrs. W. had administered. **From 1939 to 1940, L.E. taught at District 114 in Stearns County. Then he taught three years at the Morris Agricultural School, twelve years at Kansas State University, and twenty years at the University of Missouri. "The four years I taught in those two country school were the most rewarding of my life."**

Dale Wright

Dale Wright attended country school at District 10 in Wadena County from 1924 to 1929. During much of that time the school bullies were a source of entertainment for the students as they devised ways to antagonize the man who was attempting to teach them. But they also tormented Dale.

Bullies

I went to a school that had thirty-five or forty kids. We had a man teacher who was a very nice person and, I think, a good teacher, but he was very poor on discipline. Some of the bigger kids really took advantage of him and played all kinds of tricks on him. One time they put some Limburger cheese on the stove. That stunk up the whole room. He drove his car to school and left it parked by the school-

house. They played all kinds of tricks on the car. They flattened the tires sometimes, which was mean; they gave him a bad time which he really didn't deserve. He would get mad and slam the books on the floor when they pulled these tricks. That just encouraged them. The kids took their lunches and ate them in the woods that surrounded the school. When the bell rang, they came back.

One day these guys made up a scheme and kept one of the younger kids out in the woods. They came in when the bell rang and told the teacher that Donny was lost. He dismissed the whole school to hunt for Donny. He wasn't found for a couple of hours. **1924–1925**

"Get It Going"

These older boys were bullies. I was kinda small for my age, and I got mad real easy so they enjoyed picking on me. One day I was fighting with one of them out on the schoolyard and the man teacher grabbed one of us in each hand and took us back to our seats for the rest of the noon hour. I was still mad so I got in one last lick. I reached clear across and got him one lick and didn't get any return because the other kid got jerked back.

Another time they were teasing me on the way home as we were walking past our farm. My dad was out near the road and I was crying and askin' him for help. He laughed and told me I would have to fight my own battles. I said, "I can't. They're bigger than I am."

"Well," he said, "you have to. If you have to use a club, get it going." The next time I got a board from the wood shed and went after them. I was never picked on after that. **1924–1925**

Dale Wright taught eight years in the rural schools.

Dale Wright completed teachers training at Staples during the 1935-1936 term. He taught in Wadena County, District 32, from 1936 to 1937 and in District 45 from 1937 to 1942. From 1943 to 1944, he taught in Otter Tail County, District 219, and returned to Wadena County, District 39, from 1944 to 1945.

The Diplomat

I chose District 45 because it was one of the larger schools and it had a reputation as being a hard school to manage. Consequently, it paid a little more. The reason it was considered hard to manage was that most of the families in that district were Finnish. Some of the beginners were unable to talk English when they came to school. They spoke Finnish at home all the time.

There was one family that was not Finnish. The father of this family caused all the trouble. He was always picking on the teachers and giving them a bad time because he thought the teachers were favoring the Finnish kids over his kids.

When I went to that school, I learned another lesson in dealing with people. Early on I made his acquaintance and got him to help me with things at school. In the fall we had a county-wide field day. I happened to be the chairman for the northern part of the county and I had to go up to Menahga, where the events were going to be held, and measure out the places for the races and jumps.

I made it a point to ask this man to help me. The day before the field events, we took the afternoon off and he went with me and spent the whole afternoon up there, working with me. Later in the year we had the basket social and I asked him to auction off the baskets. He was the King of the Walk that night. He never gave me any trouble. He thought I was the best teacher they ever had in District 45. I wasn't, but I learned how to handle him.

1937, District 45, Wadena County

Just Once

I had a big, burly, lazy eighth-grade boy. I had told him many times that when the bell rang, they were not to stop in the hall and get a drink because every kid in school would be lined up to get a drink. They were to get their drinks before the bell rang. He stopped and got a drink and then sat down. I ordered him to do something. I can't remember what it was,

but he openly defied me and said, "I won't do it." I took his glasses off, laid them on my desk and then I slapped him.

I didn't do any physical damage, but he acted like I did. He fell into the aisle and laid there, holding his jaw. I grabbed him by the shirt collar and dragged him into the hall and went about my business. A little later he came back in.

He had driven his car to school because he brought other kids with him. But that night they stayed at school and he went somewhere. He came back later and got the kids. Later the city electrician, who was working at the clerk of the school board's place, told me the boy had gone to the clerk. He went up to him and said, "Does that teacher have a right to take my glasses off?"

The board member said, "Sure, he's got to take them off if he wants to hit ya."

That was on Thursday and on Saturday his father drove in and challenged me. He wanted to know if I was so good at hitting kids would I want to hit their parents? I ordered him to leave my property, and I guess he felt it was safer to do that. He went to another board member to complain, and the board member said, "Well, if your son won't obey in our school, we'll have to send him to another school where he will." That was the only time I ever laid a hand on a kid.

Dale Wright, 1943–1944, District 219, Otter Tail County

Although fewer men became Country School Teachers than women, the lives of many Country School Students were influenced by their dedicated teaching.

Chapter 15

1930–1932

The Depression affects Country School Teachers as 1,300 banks close and four million Americans seek jobs. Teaching positions are treasured jobs despite reduced salaries. Blondie appears in the comics and Lowell Thomas reports the nightly news. Snickers candy bars, Hostess Twinkies, and sliced Wonder Bread appear but will be found in few Country School Students' lunch buckets. The Lone Ranger "Hi Ho Silvers" across radio waves, conquering evil, and Country School Teachers Ordella Arneson, Evelyn Nelson and Ruth Gould often feel like "lone rangers," fighting the battle to educate some of the 4.2 million illiterate Americans.

Ordella Arneson
Ordella Arneson attended grade school from 1916 to 1924 in Goodhue County.

I Love Mud
When my mother went to town, she looked for things on sale. She bought me a yellow coat, which had curly material and a black collar. I hated that coat with a vengeance. My dad thought that anything that was yellow was unpatriotic, like in the war, they called people yellow. When we walked to school, we walked along the edge of the road because of the mud. I had rubbers on. When I got about half way to school, I lost one of the rubbers. I tried to hop on one foot, but I fell flat on my face. The coat was completely covered with mud. I never had to wear that coat again and was I thankful.

Ordella attended Mankato State Teachers College from 1928 to 1930. She taught in District 48 in Rice County from 1930 to 1935.

The Band Played On
We had a little orchestra. The pupils brought old dish towels for their uniforms. I dyed them and sewed on red bands. We wore paper plates for hats. The instruments were called hum horns.

Ordella Arneson's band plays the Epsom fight song!

Epsom School Song
Epsom School, thy praise we're singing
We, thy children true,
While Zumbro Valley's ringing
Echo praise of you.
Chorus:
Children raising high their voices
Swell the chorus grand
Epsom School, our alma mater
Fairest in the land.
All the days we've spent together
Fondly we'll recall
Days of fair and cloudy weather,
Thou hast known them all.

I Felt like a Failure
We had a very poor family whose children went to my school. The father, who had epileptic seizures, wasn't able to do very much on his farm. The mother became a prostitute to make money. They had an old topless Model T Ford and their oldest boy took her different places in the woods where she met men. She had a very poor reputation.

This woman's sister died, but before she died, she gave her little girl to her sister, the prostitute. Many times they came to school with only bread with butter. It was really sad. The children were ragged and not very clean. They came to school barefooted as long as they could in the fall. This girl's clothes were unclean and ragged, so a few of the mothers got some money together and I took her to town and bought her a dress and underwear. She wore that dress every day for the rest of the year.

This little girl stayed in that home. I didn't know all the conditions at that time, but later on she wrote to me and told me she had to sleep with the boys. Then we heard stories.

They had a country telephone line and the neighbors would "rubber," listen in on the phone, and they often heard some man calling, making an appointment to meet the girl, who was getting to be twelve or thirteen. The stepmother let the girl become a prostitute just like her. It was a horrible situation.

This was reported to the county and the sheriff called me and asked if I would testify. He said, "Will you come or will I have to come and serve you papers?" I told him that I would come to the private hearing in the court house.

I had to testify about how the child dressed, the way she looked, that she was unclean, wore ragged clothes, and didn't have enough to eat.

I did not testify about the prostitution business, but you know how it is, everybody knew everybody, and others testified about how the men came to the home. Her father, who lived in Indiana, came and took her away from the only home she had ever known. As bad as things were, they were good to her in their way, especially one of the boys. But it seemed like a happy situation in Indiana.

The next year they all came from Indiana to appear before the judge. The step-aunt, the woman her father had married, had a daughter and these two girls were dressed alike. They came to my hometown and she seemed very happy. Then I didn't hear anything about her for many years.

Later on she came back here. By then she was old enough so she could read the court records. She told me her aunt had held her as a slave and that she had to wait on this cousin all the time.

She told me that I had put her into the hands of the devil because I had testified at the trial. Later in a letter she told me my testimony had also put her into the hands of witches. Eventually she spent several years in an institution in Chicago. I have not heard from her since.

I had to testify to the conditions I saw, but I felt I was a failure because I wasn't able to do anything for that girl.   **Ordella Arneson, c. 1933**

Like many other Country School Teachers, Ordella battled the weather to prevent it from stealing her life. History, as usual, has relegated these stories to its appendix.

Deep and White
The snow had begun in the gloaming
And busily all the night
Had been heaping field and highway
With a silence deep and white.

In the morning I was to experience the "deep and white." I had to drive five miles to the Epsom School. The family was dubious of my ability to drive in the snow, so I was thankful my oldest brother Henry offered to take me to school, as Highway 60 was a white expanse of glittering snow. If there were ditches, they were completely camouflaged with a white shroud.

Since it was early in the morning, there were no other tracks. Hank tried to keep the car in the middle of what he judged to be the road. Suddenly the front right wheel sank down into the deep snow in the ditch. He had misjudged and gone too close to the edge. The Ford listed dangerously, but the snow was packed so hard that we didn't tip over. The car just slowly and silently settled down for a "long winter's nap."

We were almost two miles from the schoolhouse, but if I cut through the fields and woods, it would be about a mile. So, abandoning my brother and the car, I started off through the fields. "This is exhilarating! I should do this more often," I thought.

The windblown banks were sculpted into fantastically grotesque figures. By then the sun shown brightly, making the snow glisten and sparkle with scintillating light. The clear air was invigorating.

I scurried down a hill. Suddenly I plunged shoulder deep into the soft snow of the ravine. In that sheltered spot the wind hadn't packed the snow, which was soft and feathery.

I tried to flounder ahead. My frantic efforts were fruitless because I couldn't touch the bottom. For a few moments I nearly panicked. Then I realized the "silence deep and white." I could see no habitation, and I knew no one could see me or hear if I called for help. I had visions of my frozen body being discovered when the snow melted in the spring.

It wasn't a formal, articulate prayer I uttered, but God provided the way of escape—not by way of a miracle but by my shopping bag. I had carried my papers and books in a large, black, oilcloth bag. I spread the bag out on the snow on my right side and slowly maneuvered myself upwards and sideways out of the seemingly bottomless pit onto solid ground. I didn't realize at the time that if I had placed the bag on my left side, I would have sunk deeper into the ravine.

I plodded toward the higher ground and watched for treacherously soft snow. As I plunged into the woods, walking became more and more difficult. Here the snow hadn't packed, so it was deep and heavy. However, the trees sheltered me from the icy blasts.

I feared I might lose my direction in the trackless wilderness. If I went straight south, the school was about a third of a mile, but if I went east, the forest extended for many miles. I checked the direction with the sun.

How welcome was the sight of the school when I came to the clearing! Thin wisps of smoke curled heavenward in the cold morning air. I breathed a sigh of thanks that my fire hadn't gone out during the night.

The fire I had banked the previous evening still glowed, the embers giving off feeble heat. After opening the drafts, shaking down the ashes, and placing some kindling on the hot coals, I soon had a merry fire going.

But, no students! A sister of the clerk had seen my car in the ditch, called her brother, and told him not to send his children to school. Other interested parents had "rubbered" on the telephone and they didn't send their children either. After eleven o'clock they began trooping in. The smoke billowing from the chimney had served as a signal to one mother that the teacher had finally made it to school. She telephoned the other parents, so the kids were cheated out of a holiday after all.

Ruth Gould

Ruth Gould attended Hillcrest and Bergville schools in Itasca County. After attending teachers training in Grand Rapids, she taught for ten years in Itasca County, including the Northwest, Horton, Hansen Lake and Suomi schools. Ruth taught for twenty-one more years in the public schools.

After attending country schools and growing up in the Grand Rapids area during the "golden days" of logging, Ruth knew the forest well. She knew how to cope with the unexpected.

Keeping "Cool"

In 1930, I was teaching in District 1 (318), the Northwest School near Northome. We began to

Ruth Gould, 1919

smell some smoke. The people burned wood a lot of the time, so we didn't pay too much attention to the smoke until it got so thick that we couldn't see the blackboard. Suddenly we realized we were surrounded by a slash-and-burn fire. I kept the children there because I didn't dare send them home. They had to walk and the fire was burning all around us. We didn't have telephones in the schools so I did what I had to do. The fire was circling us so there was no way we could leave. I didn't panic because when you grow up in this country, you anticipate such things and are ready for them. That part of the county was only open to homesteading in 1898 so the country was new. The big logging companies had cleared off the timber so the thrashings and stumps were what were burning. The dry grass was blazing all around us. But we knew what to do.

We grew up with events like that. I had no reason to think that that fire wasn't going to get us, so I had to take precautions for the sake of the children. You don't think, "We're doomed," when you are building up strength for children. You've got to be calm or they panic, too.

The oldest boy was in the sixth grade. We all went outside and he and I pumped water and soaked everything down around the school. Then the parents came to help and get the children. They brought gunnysacks and shovels and stopped the fire about half a block from the school.

My mother was coming to attend Ladies Aid about two or three miles from my school. Instead of going to Ladies Aid, we hauled fire fighters.

A Slashing Romance

In one district we had a superintendent of schools and two or three assistant supervisors. One day a new supervisor came and sat by the library. One of the eighth-grade boys decided he wanted a book while I was teaching first-grade reading. He went back to get a book, and I thought, "My he's been gone a long time." He was in the library, slashing books with his knife while the supervisor sat right there. I know the supervisor knew about it because I called him to look at all the slashed books. What a mess it was!

I could have used his help, but he just walked out. He never did a thing. He probably marked that against me. He was there to judge me as a teacher. I needed help from him but I didn't get it. He sat there and allowed the boy to cut up the books.

The boy had never been a problem. Some teachers thought it was a case of puppy love, and he thought the supervisor was my boyfriend. The boy was sixteen and I was nineteen. He might have resented my visitor and slashed the books in anger.

He was staying with his grandmother so I called her in. She said, "If that's what he's going to do, he can go out in the woods and cut pulp." And he did.

A Dear Deer

One of the girls had found a fawn and raised it. The fawn wandered down from the farm and came into the school. He walked up and down the aisles. It

never bothered me. It was good for the kids to learn to appreciate the deer that way. He wandered around and tasted books. He loved to nibble on the red penmanship books. He stayed about ten minutes and then went outside to eat. He was very *Ruth Gould's lunches are tasty!* tame and independent. Once late in the fall there was a snow fence at right angles to the school. The deer liked to stand there for protection from the wind. One day during hunting season, we looked out the window, and there was the fawn with about fifteen deer playing out there. The deer could wave their tails at the hunters who couldn't shoot them because the deer were inside the school yard. **Ruth Gould, c. 1933**

Evelyn Nelson

Evelyn began teaching in District 11, Upper Island School, in 1930. Included in her teaching career were six years at Tower Island School on the Prairie Island Indian Reservation and thirteen years at the country school in Welch. In 1963, the Welsh School, District 556, was the last country school still operating in Goodhue County.

Every teacher experiences a breaking-in period in which she discovers what her aim in teaching really is. Few discover this skill before walking into the classroom. Evelyn was one of the "lucky" few who learned she couldn't always hit the bulls-eye.

She's No Annie Oakley

I met my husband-to-be at the first school in which I taught. He had been doing some muskrat trapping and made enough money to buy a .22 rifle. I was interested in learning how to shoot also, so one Sunday afternoon we went up into the gravel pit and practiced shooting this rifle. When we got back to my boarding place, he suggested I practice shooting by the barn.

Evelyn Nelson and fiance, 1930

He put up a snoose box cover, and I shot it square in the middle. The following week the school board went to get the school's storm windows, which were stored in that barn. When I shot the snoose box, I shot through the top window panes of six of the eight windows. We had to replace all those panes. The following weekend my fiance and I puttied new window panes into the window frames. We also washed the windows and put them on.

Evelyn Nelson, 1930, District 119, Upper Island School

The Protector

I had a pair of twins in my reading class who sat in front of the room, and Helen, their older sister, sat in the back. Donald and Dorothy may have been twins, but they had two different personalities and abilities. Donald was a very slow reader, so Dorothy would whisper the words to Donald. "Donald," I said, "you can't have Dorothy read for you." Suddenly Helen, who had a terrible temper, took her inkwell out and threw it at me. It hit the slate blackboard behind me. I was aghast!

"Helen, what do you think you are doing?" I asked.

She said, "You don't have to scold my brother!" She just couldn't imagine that I should raise my voice to her favorite brother.

I said, "I'm trying to teach him to read and besides, I'm a friend of your mother and she told me to make you behave. So shall I tell her the story of the inkwell or what do you want to do?"

She became very frightened, but we patched everything up. However, everyone in the district soon heard the story. That was one of the first incidents that told me I had to find different teaching techniques for many of the children.

1930–1932, District 119, Upper Island School

Chewin' and Tattlin'

I had a sixth grader who liked to chew snoose. His parents gave it to him. He stuffed a wad into his mouth when he thought it was nearly time for recess. That way he would be able to spit once he got outside. But he didn't always make it. One day he put up his hand and asked, "May I go out to the toilet, Mrs. Nelson?" I gave him permission.

A couple of days later, well, you have a tattletale in every group, and the tattletale said, "Mrs. Nelson, are you aware that he chews snoose?" The next day when he asked for permission, I said, "no," and he had to swallow the snoose. As a result I had a sick student.

1932

District 7, Welch School: Evelyn Nelson taught in the rural schools of Goodhue County for thirty-four years.

Pearl Vitelli

Pearl Vitelli received her teaching certificate from Winona State in 1931. From 1931 to 1934 she taught at Homer and from 1934 to 1935 she taught in Minnesota City.

Pearl's initiation was almost standard fare for young female teachers.

That's a Lot of Bull—Snake

Out on the playgrounds we had a hill and woods behind us and the kids played there during their lunch period, especially if they had a whole hour. Two boys went up into the hill while the rest of us were playing around, and when the two boys came back, I noticed that they were ready to see what this city teacher was going to do and say. They just waited for my reaction. They had a fat bull snake, six feet long and as big around as my

Pearl Stienberg Vitelli, 1931

arm, hanging around their necks as they came down into the play area. I thought, "Oh, Pearl, be careful what you do here because it can be the beginning or the end depending on how you react to that snake."

So I steeled myself and went up to the boys and said, "Oh, what an interesting critter you have! What is it?" I never let on I was nervous. Well, they knew it was a bull snake, but what was it good for?

That they didn't know. They knew they just liked to catch and torment it. So I said to them, "Well, it's time for class now. Let's go in." All their fun had gone down the drain because that snake slithered down the culvert, across the highway, and down to the Mississippi River.

The next day I said to the boys, "I have been wondering about that snake of yours. Do you think we could find out if it's good for anything? It's an awfully big thing just to be laying around."

So I gave them as an assignment to look up the life of a bull snake. Before the week was over, every kid in that school knew all about bull snakes.

I was so glad I had steeled myself because I know very well had I not done it, I would have had muskrats, which were there in profusion, and other kinds of animals. But it was no fun teasing me so I escaped that. **Pearl Vitelli, 1934, Homer, Winona County**

The World in a Sandbox

I built this sandbox in the school and had it elevated. Usually the whole school had something going on in the sandbox. One project we had was the upper grades had to learn about Japan and so I used the sandbox as an art project, too. They shaped the topography of the islands in the sand and the little children added toothpick umbrellas. I found a way for every child in the school to be involved in what was going on in there. It became a community project because even parents came and contributed things to the sandbox.

The activities that took place in the sandbox were usually the students' ideas. It was a hands-on activity—using hands to create things. Once we studied the county of Winona and contoured the county. We had bluffs in the back of the school. We climbed up into these bluffs and came back with the vegetation.

Kids built a bluff in the sand and put in the trees just like it was behind the school. They put in dams and rivers. At the time Army engineers were talking about a nine-foot channel in the Mississippi River, so the kids built the dams and studied how the locks were going to work.

What I used the sandbox for was a chance to get up and move around to develop visual learning. We had maps, but they were flat. They didn't show the real world. The sandbox allowed us to see perspective and even change the landscape.

The Homer students slid down the school sidewalk.

That Guy's OK!

I'll never forget Elmer. Nobody ever mentioned to me that Elmer was mentally deficient. He was almost sixteen when I started teaching, but he always minded his own business. I decided Elmer couldn't just sit there like a wart. He didn't enjoy being with the upper grade kids, but he loved sitting in the row with the tiny children who were doing combinations of two and four. I always brought his chair and he sat in the circle with the little kids. He was perfectly happy to tell stories with the little kids in the primary grades.

I involved him in spelling and gave him a list. He practiced at the board because he was so big and needed that tactile motion. He practiced the words and wrote them on the board. No one cared a bit about what Elmer was doing.

Rather than give him a grade, I wrote OK at the top of his paper. One day I wrote it right after his name—"Elmer OK." Well into his maturity he called himself "Elmer OK." What a good education the kids got about someone who was different from them. They learned Elmer certainly was OK.

Pearl sat in her rocking chair when she told these stories. As she began this next story, her demeanor changed. The smile disappeared and she stared at me, weighing the power of each word, each heartfelt memory. She spoke with passion, cherishing each memory. And the more passionately she spoke, the faster she rocked that old chair.

The Prisoner

After I had been gone from Minnesota City for thirty-five years, I got an invitation in the mail to be the guest of honor at this seventh- and eighth-grade class reunion. When I got down there, the first question I asked was, "How on earth did you know how to find me?" By that time, of course my name had been changed to Pearl Vitelli. One boy said to me, "Did you forget how many times I mailed letters for you so it would get on the 4:00 bus?" At that time my husband and I were dating and this boy would see to it that the letter got to the bus on time.

But the interesting part of the story is that I had an evaluation of my teaching all rolled into one. One of the boys had been a prisoner of Japan during World War II. He said he nearly lost his mind because he was in solitary confinement. They wouldn't give him anything to read, nothing to do, and he never knew how he was ever going to survive the confinement.

He decided he had to try to re-live his life, so he lived it backwards until he came to the year he was an eighth grader in Minnesota City and he remembered me. One of my tricks at that time was to write—I had a book of proverbs that were rules to live by—and I used to put one on the board every Monday. I would leave it up there until Friday and then I would put a new one up.

At the end of the month I would give them extra credit for remembering those rules to live by as I had written them on the board the previous month and even months before that just to see how much attention they paid to these things that were all meant to teach a lesson. He remembered these and he recited many of them. I was absolutely flabbergasted because he remembered so many of them that I had long since forgotten.

Then he said, "Do you remember in mathematics you used to say, 'What do you know? What do you have to find?' and 'How are you going to do it?'" He said he remembered that was the way I taught math. I was just amazed at how much he remembered of the techniques I had used. He remembered how I had corrected his English papers and sent them back with corrections and pronunciation. He remembered how he had learned about colons and semicolons.

"You might think those little things from long ago weren't important," he said. "But when I had something to think about, when I thought about things that happened during that year you taught at Minnesota City, it kept me sane."

It was one of the most rewarding experiences I ever had because I realized I had taught a lot more than reading, writing, and arithmetic. He had settled in Seattle, Washington, but he said those memories of school and his time as a prisoner in Japan were so vivid that he had to share them with somebody.

He said, "That year was the fullest year of my life, that year in the eighth grade in your room."

On the word *room*, Pearl stopped rocking and said, "How's that for a teacher evaluation?"   **1935**

Pearl Vitelli finished her career at Grass Junior High from 1945 to 1973.

Mildred Mundale Blom

Mildred Blom began first grade in Rome Township, Faribault County in 1921, at the age of six. She began high school at the age of eleven and graduated when she was fifteen.

The "Sleeping Beauty" troupe goes on the road.

"The Play's the Thing"

We had a very creative teacher. We adapted the story of "The Sleeping Beauty" and wrote it into a play. Then we acted this play on the lawn of the neighboring farm. My mother made costumes. The boys were pages who had caps that had feathers.

Mildred Mundale, 1924–1925

Put Your Arms Around Me, Honey!

We had a small, snow-covered hill next to the school. Below the hill was a patch of ice. We sat on cardboard and slid down the hill and across the ice. The boys found a big piece of cardboard. They told us they wouldn't let us ride on it unless we put our arms around them and held on. We indignantly went to the teacher. She was really a feminist. We thought surely she would defend us, but she said, "If you want to ride, put your arms around them." So that's what we did.

Mildred Mundale, c. 1924

Too Young

I tried to enroll in the Blue Earth Normal School teachers training program in 1929 during the Depression, but they turned me down. They said I was too young. So we wrote to Mankato and tried to get into their one-year program because my folks thought that was all they could afford. I got a letter from President Cooper, who said they would be happy to enroll me in the two-year program, but they could not recommend me after only one year.

I was so afraid that I hardly ever answered in class. The other students were all two years older than I. We were studying *The Odyssey* in literature class. The teacher passed back our papers but she didn't hand me mine. Then she said, "Which one is Miss Mundale?" She didn't know my name because I hadn't answered in class. She said, "Oh, you have written this so beautifully!" I felt much better.

Home

I was so homesick while I was at Mankato. I thought the whole world was Norwegian with a few Germans thrown in. I had been used to my parents telling me what to do. They were too good to us.

I did not get home until November. Grace Armstrong (for whom Armstrong Hall is named) was a teacher at Mankato and she was from Bricelyn. Another woman from Bricelyn, Ora Kingsley, was attending school for some refresher courses. She told me I could ride home with them in her Model T. It was such a cold and rainy day that they bundled me up with blankets because I had to sit in the back seat. Grace drove and Ora sat next to her. As Grace drove, Ora read poetry, dramatically swinging her arms as she read. We barreled along about thirty-five miles an hour.

I will never forget how I felt as we pulled into our farm driveway. Even to this day, November days with bare trees and the dripping rain are just wonderful for me. I was home. I had been gone since September, a fifteen-year-old girl thrown into the whirlwind of college. As I went into our house, my two brothers and sister were so glad to see me, but I made short work of that and went right to the piano and played and played and played my heart out because I was so glad to be home.

Even today, sixty-six years later, on rainy, leaf-less November days, I can still feel how I felt that day because I was so green, so homesick. **1933–1934**

When Mildred was seventeen, she completed her courses at Mankato. Because she had a two-year certificate, she was qualified to teach in an accredited town school, but her applications were rejected because the school board members said she was too young and inexperienced, so she signed a contract to teach near Elmore.

That's No Bull

I had a first grader and his second-grade sister, who

Spring Cleaning, c. 1934

cut across fields to get to school. One day the boy's sister was sick, so she didn't come. As I was sitting at my desk after school working on some papers, I thought I could hear something in the back of the school, so I went out to check. Well, there was that poor little fellow, leaning against the building, crying as though his heart would break. Oh, he was upset!

"What's the matter?" I asked him.

"I have to go home and there's a bull in the next pasture. I'm afraid to walk through there."

"Well," I said, "I'll walk with you." So we climbed over fences and walked across fields to stay away from that bull. We could see him, but he never saw us. When the boy saw his dad plowing, he said, "I'm all right now." He ran on home and I went back to the school.

More Bull

I always stayed in school to work and prepare for the next day. When I walked home, I had to go past the farm that had that bull. Of course the boys would leave as soon as school was out and these little scamps would tease that bull.

One night when I went home, there was that bull standing right next to the fence, pawing, snorting, and making such a noise. There was just that little fence between us. The farm's driveway was not too far away, so I ran as fast as I could and

135

told them. They took me home. The next day that farmer sold the bull. I don't think it would have been so angry if the boys had not teased it. But the farmer sold it because it was too dangerous and he just would not have a bull like that.

Bull's Eye

One time one of the older boys brought a rifle to school. He set a tin can on a post and dared me to shoot it. And I did. I hit it, too. Then quite a few of the older boys brought their rifles, too, all daring me to shoot them. They just wanted to see if I could do it. Eventually I just quit shooting and they stopped bringing their rifles.

Mail Ordered!

Next to the school lived a young bachelor. Of course, the students always teased me about him. This bachelor's brother had gotten his wife through the mail. Since he had an extra name, he gave it to his younger bachelor brother. One day as I was sitting at my desk, the children came tearing in. "Miss Mundale, the bachelor just went by with a woman in his car. She was a lot prettier than you are!"

Another student said, "Oh, she wasn't pretty, but he did go by with a girl in his car." Well, anyway, he married the mail-order bride so I didn't get a chance at that bachelor. If you want the truth, go to a little child.

After "putting in her time," Mildred was hired by an accredited school, which meant she had finished the two-year teaching program. When she was nineteen, the school board members of her home school near Blue Earth hired her.

Back Work

Norma was quite a humorist, very witty. If a person who had been absent needed to make up work, I called it "back work." One time Norma handed in a paper. I asked, "Is that back work?" and she said, "No, that's head work."

Alice

A family from Appalachia came to work for one of the farmers in the area. They were quite under-privileged, but they had the most beautiful children. They had a sweet little girl who had the most beautiful blue eyes and dark hair. One day she came up to my desk, looked at me, and said, "I know your name. It's Mildred Miss Mundale." Then she looked at me again. "When I grow up, I want to be a teacher just like you." Again she looked at me. "When you was a child, was your name Alice?"

One day she was playing and she hurt herself. I didn't realize how badly she was injured, so I didn't send her home. The next day I found out she had broken her arm. I felt just terrible, so I bought her a doll and took it to her home. They were all so thrilled. The doll was such a great wonder for them.

Mildred Mundale Blom's class buttons up for recess frolic.

Spelling Counts

We studied a unit on farms, and one of the boys was giving his report about crops. "And then you go out and you calibrate." I couldn't figure out what he meant, so I looked at his older brother. "Oh, he means cultivate."

What Could be Worse Than This?

Once the boys went outside at recess, and when they came back, they were all soaking wet. I can't remember if they fell into the water accidentally or if they were playing in it, but they were cold and wet. Water dripped from them. I made them go downstairs, take off their clothes, and hang them by the furnace. Then I had them wear the girls' coats. They spent the rest of the day in those coats. Those poor young boys were terribly embarrassed, being virtually naked and having to wear the girls' coats. What could I do? I didn't dare send them home wet.

Monday's Sunday School Stories

Almost all the families in that area were very religious and went to church. But there was a family that did not go to church or attend any church functions. All the other kids would come to school and talk about Sunday school and the things they had done. They were at an age when this was very important.

Well, the little boy who didn't attend Sunday school naturally had nothing to say about that. One Monday morning he said to me, "Had a barn dance at our place on Saturday night. Steve got drunk. Ma kicked him out." That was his Sunday school story.

Here's What I Learned in School Today

When I started, I was just a young girl. It was difficult to adopt a professional attitude. I tried to act with dignity and separate myself from the children, to act as if I was their teacher and not their playmate. I used a different way of speaking and acting, the way I thought teachers should speak and act. Suddenly I had to be independent, resourceful, and creative. I learned I had within me the power to make do with what I had and to make something out of it. I was now responsible. **Mildred Mundale Blom**

Clara Jenkins

Clara Jenkins began teaching in 1931 in Morrison County. She also taught in Crow Wing County. Then in 1949, she moved to the Silverdale School in Koochiching County, where she taught for twenty years. Clara retired in 1971.

Clara Jenkins' kindergarten class and two of her fellow teachers in the St. Cloud teachers training program, 1930 to 1931. What game are they teaching the children?

Break In

The first year I taught I lived about two miles from Little Falls. A friend asked me to stay overnight.

Clara Jenkins, c. 1931

She picked me up after school. The next morning we packed lunches and headed for school. She dropped me off in front of my school. When I reached into my pocket, I didn't have my key. One of the windows was easy to open so I got two blocks of wood from the woodshed. I stood on those and crawled in. Luckily I had a Yale lock so I could unlock the door for the children. Picture what that must have looked like, crawling through that window with my legs sticking out. What a sight! That night I called my friend. The key had fallen out of my coat pocket in the bedroom. If any of the school board members would have come by and seen me crawling through the window, they would have wondered what I was doing. From then on I tied the key onto my dinner pail so I wouldn't lose it. **1933, Lennox School, Crow Wing County**

Bang!

In this same school I fired with coal. Of course, in the winter I tried to bank the fire so that in the morning there would be coals and I could get the school warmed up in a short time. One evening I threw in a bucket of coal and I covered up all the live coals. By the time that coal ignited, it blew up. It blew off the stove pipe and it shot soot all over the whole schoolhouse. I spent several hours sweeping up the soot. I finally did get it cleaned up so we were able to have school the next day.

1933, Lennox School, Crow Wing County

Good As New!

Our playground equipment was very, very limited. We had one kitten ball and a bat, a five-inch rubber ball, and a jump rope. One day one of the little girls took the rubber ball because she was going to be sure she had it to play with during that recess and she took it with her to the toilet in back of the schoolhouse. While she was in there, she bounced the ball. Well, you can guess what happened. The ball bounced down into the other hole. She came running in and you would have thought the end of the world had come. She said, "I lost the ball! It's down there! What'll I do now?"

I said, "Well, I guess we won't have a ball to play with if it's down there."

That night she went home and told her father. He went over with a flashlight and a rake and a hoe or something, and he fished the ball out of the toilet. She got it all washed up, and the next day she came back to school bringing the ball, as happy as she could be!   **1936–1937, Fort Ripley School**

A Hot Card Game

I was boarding with this older couple and every night we played hearts. The wife let her husband win just to be good to him or something. Well, in hearts that queen of spades is the one you don't want. I got caught with that queen. I don't know why I said it, but before we got done with the game, I said, "I was laying for you." She got so mad that she picked up the cards and threw them in the stove. I never played cards with them again. I expected my suitcase to be out in the snowbank the next day when I came from school.   **1937, Nokay Lake School**

Spit and Giggle

My best disciple was—well, take giggling. I'd say, "Now giggle until you're all done and there is nothing left to giggle at." At Nokay Lake School I had twelve boys and four girls, and there's nothing worse than boys that giggle. They'd look at each other and giggle over nothing. When they shot spitballs, I took my paper punch and punched all kinds of little circles on the floor and had them pick them up. That wasn't any fun. But no more spitballs!

Clara Jenkins taught for thirty-one years.

1932
President Roosevelt begins his fireside chats and assures Americans that "The only thing we have to fear is fear itself." CCC camps provide much needed jobs. *Newsweek* and *Esquire* appear in newsstands and Ritz crackers, Fritos, and Skippy peanut butter line grocery shelves. Laura Ingalls Wilder captures rural life in *The Little House in the Big Woods*. Revlon creates Tropic Sky nail polish to make Country School Teacher more beautiful, and Windex makes it easier for her to clean the school windows. Country School Students find two songs to explain their plight: "Say It Isn't So" and "Don't Blame Me."

Margaret Pickering

Margaret Pickering taught in the following Itasca County schools: McLeod, Stingy Lake, Birchwood, Hansen Lake, Balsam, and Warba.

Get a Job

Times were really hard in 1929 and 1930. I was in school in Bemidji. There were about ten of us in the class. Mr. Baker, the county superintendent, called us all out into the hall. He said, "I want to see all the girls from District 1," which became District 318—he knew us all from first grade on—and he hired every one of us right there. The other students couldn't get a job, and they were all crying. He just said, "As soon as you are through here, you have a job."

Never Been to Town

From 1934 to 1937, I taught at Birchwood School, which is located about six miles south of Calumet. The people were of Slavic origin. I had two children in the first grade who couldn't understand me and they were scared to death of me. One of the older kids helped them and told them what I was saying. They had never been away from home.

Some of the children who lived four or five miles from Calumet had never even been to Calumet. Their world was just their home. I had a car so I took some of them into Calumet and bought them ice-cream cones. I drove around the town, which wasn't much, and then I took them home. Some of them had never been in a car before. It was a crazy day, but the kids were really happy. Some of their parents did not have cars and the whole family was quite isolated.

"You're Goin' to Jail!"

I had this boy who was a real hellion come to my school. He wasn't supposed to come to my school. He was supposed to go to a school about four miles from my school. The teacher there was a big

Margaret Pickering, c. 1932

Irishman named Pat, who could control the kid. He manhandled the kid. So the kid just ran away and came to my school. The kid was in the fourth or fifth grade, not very big, but I couldn't do a thing with him. He wouldn't sit down or stand up when I told him to. He did as he pleased. Since he didn't like Pat, he had to walk the four miles to my school and he was always late. He was always bedeviling the other kids, who knew he didn't belong there with them. He kept everything in a riot, throwing books or hitting a kid or yelling so we didn't have to have school. He pinched other kids or sassed me back.

I called my supervisor in Grand Rapids and told him I didn't want the boy in my school, that he didn't belong there. So the supervisor came out and hauled him back to Pat. The next morning the boy was back in my school. This went on for a month. Every time Pat crossed him, the boy came back to my school. Each time someone came from Grand Rapids and hauled him back to Pat.

Finally his dad took him to the sheriff and said, "Here, you take care of him." So they put him in jail. I think he was about ten or twelve at the time. The sheriff was a huge man who wore a cowboy hat. He took the boy aside and talked to him and then he said to the father, "Well, he's your kid. You'll have to take care of him."

About a month later the sheriff walked into the school to see me. He didn't know the boy was there. That poor kid almost died. Well, the sheriff and I laughed and laughed. That kid was scared witless. The sheriff just said, "Well, Hi, J., how ya doin'?" Then he walked out. Finally the boy just dropped out in the seventh or eighth grade.

1932–1933, McLeod School, Itasca County

And the Chase Is On!

One day Jimmy was fooling around in class so I asked, "Jimmy, what are you doing?"

"I'm chasing a louse across my desk with my pencil."

My sister, who was teaching in the western part of the state and had a month's vacation, had come to visit me. She just about died. She got lousy and I didn't.

1932, Stingy Lake School, Itasca County

He Never Said a Word!

I had a student who was the most frustrating experience I ever had. W. was a very smart boy, but he never talked to anybody. He was in the seventh grade, a Finnish kid, and he never said a word. He was a very good student. If I asked him a question, some way or another one of the other boys would say, "Ya, W. said that that was right."

"How do you know?" I asked.

"We know he makes signs and we know what he means." But I couldn't tell he was making signs. I never figured it out.

They'd come in and say, "W. wants this or W. wants that."

I said, "You mean he said something?"

"No, but we knew," the kids said. But he never said a word. It was so frustrating because he was so bright.

I was boarding at a house and the landlady was Finnish. One day I forgot something, so I sent W. the few blocks to get. it. But he wouldn't speak to my landlady, even in Finnish. She was so angry because he wouldn't talk.

One of her sons asked him if he had seen the snowplow go by. Well, he had to answer that. Then she asked him why I had sent him. W. got furious. I suppose he was so embarrassed that he told her.

All the while I was his teacher he never spoke.

Now he is one of our best friends, and he talks and talks. He hasn't shut up yet.

1933, Stingy Lake School, Itasca County

Stuck on Me and the Pump

I had a first grader who was about half the size of the other first graders, about the size of a three-year-old child. He was a constant problem for me because he was so hyperactive. He had never seen silk stockings. I wore nylons, of course, and whenever we sat down to read or work together, he kept running his hands up and down my legs. His parents were very poor. He had older sisters, and this little guy was a tail-ender, cute as a bug's ear. But he was a little demon.

When my back was turned or when the big kids weren't watching, he'd run right out the front door. Finally I had to tie him to the seat with clothesline. I tied him up every morning and let him loose at recess and lunch. Our school was built right next to the scenic highway that goes to Bigfork. I couldn't let him get away from me. He ran right out the door, right onto the highway. To make it worse, there was a lake on the other side of the highway.

About the third or fourth day, he brought a knife and cut the clothesline. After that I got some braided clothesline that was very hard to cut. That poor little guy. After that I searched him for knives.

He couldn't say the first consonant of a word. One day he ran into the school and yelled, "Where's my ap and my oat?" On the playground those kids teased him, yelling "Where's my ap and my oat?"

He was a bright boy, but he was hyper, hyperactive, just uncontrollable. In the winter he put his tongue on the pump handle every chance he got. Anytime he got out of the schoolhouse, at recess or lunch, he stuck his tongue on that pump handle. I'd go out and pour some water on his tongue and get him loose. Sometimes the bigger kids would just grab a kettle of warm water off the stove and head out to the pump handle. Every time that kid turned around he had his tongue on that pump handle. I never thought of leaving him there because I didn't think he would have learned any lesson from that.

We didn't know about hyperactivity or enabling. None of us could bear to see the poor little kid sticking to the frozen pump handle.

I think he was such a bad little kid because he craved attention. He never left my side. He wanted to be right next to me. Even when I had him tied up, his desk was right next to me. He wanted to touch me. I'd say, "Now just sit down and go to work," and pretty soon he would reach over to touch me or run his hand down my nylons. He needed to be right next to me all the time. Unfortunately, when he was in the fourth grade, he and one of his friends drowned in the same lake he had tried to escape to so many times.   **1950, Balsam School, Itasca County**

Margaret Pickering taught for forty years, ten in the country schools.

Evelyn Olson Dorschner
Evelyn Olson Dorschner taught children in the rural schools of Steele and Rice Counties for thirty years. She had a Masters Degree in Fishing!

Dancing the Teacher
We had a teachers training teacher who had never been married. She was very stately and very much

Evelyn Olson Dorschner

down-to-business all the time, but we were quite young and loved to dance. Once we fooled her into going with us up to the golf course where there was a dance. Other people who had had her in classes said, "Don't tell me she went dancing with you because Lorena Vol would not do that!"

I said, "She did too. I even danced with her." She had never done that with any other class before. Maybe she danced with us because we acted closer to her.

She was very demanding and she was the boss, but we fooled around with her a little bit and petted her so she would do these things for us.

Kenyon, 1931–1932

Evelyn Dorschner feared what every teacher fears—students dropping out and students getting injured. However, she did not anticipate that both things could happen at the same time to the same person.

Rescued
One of the boys was quite small and he had trouble breathing. One day we had a blizzard and he had to go outside to the toilet. I kept thinking, "Well, now, he should be in here anytime." I was very foolish not to send someone bigger with him, but you can't think of everything at the time. I sent two of the eighth-grade boys out to find him. He had fallen into a big hole that the boys had dug and couldn't get out. He was having a heck of a time breathing. The two older boys pulled him out. We were so lucky that we found him.

1934, District 41, Steele County

The Rolling Stones

We moved from Rice County to Steele County. Now there was quite a difference between my age and the teacher who had retired the year I came. Of course the big boys were going to show the young teacher how they could intimidate me by rolling stones in through the door during recess.

I gave the problem quite a lot of thought and shed a number of tears before I decided to get tough. I kept the six culprits after school and showed them who was boss by taking them one at a time into the coal shed and using a strong hand on their bent-over derrieres. After that they respected my authority and became my best friends and they still are today. **c. 1952, District 49, Steele County**

Gone Fishin'

My husband was a trucker, and some days when he wasn't using his truck, I'd say to the children, "Let's get everything done now. Then I'll take the truck and we'll go fishing." I would never get by with that today. Parents would go crazy. Here I was with all those kids in the back end. My husband Archie helped fix fishing poles out of branches and hooks by bending pins. They dug their own worms. Sometimes we went ten miles to another creek.

Evelyn stands next to one of her husband's milk trucks. For ten years she and her husband Archie took students fishing.

Even after I stopped teaching at that school, the kids would come to me and say, "After school is out, could we have a picnic?" There is a little creek about halfway between Nearstrand and Kenyon. Here they would come on their bicycles, carrying their fishing poles, and we met there. They still thought it was fun, and by then they were all going to school in Faribault.

Evelyn Olson Dorschner had an extraordinary teaching career. She wrote the following: "The teacher every day was dressed/ In long skirt and white blouse./ She carried ashes from the stove/ Which often made a mess. Be happy that those days are gone/ but memories linger on."

Evelyn Dorschner taught for forty-one years. Thirty of those years were spent as Country School Teacher.

Teachers need imagination and inspiration from the Muses. Ida Picha Welter, age six, dresses to accept her gifts.

Ida Picha Welter

Ida Welter's teachers training instructor was "quite old fashioned." She tried to teach Ida how to sing. Ida admits, "I can't sing, but neither could my teacher. She was terrible."

It's Ugly

My teachers training teacher was no music teacher. She couldn't sing a note herself, and she was supposed to teach us how to sing. So she went down to the elementary school and got a grade school teacher who was very good in music to teach us how to teach music. The first thing she did was have us sing. When she got to me, she said, "You can't sing. Just don't say anything."

That kinda turned me off because after I went to college later, the instructors there said, "Better take music." Again the instructor said, "You can't sing!"

"Well, I know that," I said.

"No," he said, "what I meant was that your voice isn't beautiful. He had to say something, of course." I did get a C in the class, so I could teach. That was required, but I never did teach my kids how to sing. They knew how to sing much better than I did.

Ida Picha Welter completed her teachers training in 1932. In the fall of that year she began teaching in her home school in Scott County. In 1937 she substituted for her cousin in a school near Stewart. She returned to teaching in 1956 and taught until 1966.

Plowing Through Math

On my first day of school, the kids came and looked me over. I guess their parents had told them a few things. I had a student who was fourteen, only about two years younger than I. He didn't like to do his work. His mother had been a teacher in that school for several years. He thought, "I'll take my work home and mother can do it for me and Miss Picha won't know the difference."

I surmised that's what he was going to do, so I said, "Tom, you're going to have to stay after school and sit right here and finish this math."

"Oh, no," he said, "my dad is plowing and he needs me. Look right out the window. You can see him. I have to go over there and plow."

"You can do that when you finish your math."

"No, I have to go now," he insisted. I dismissed all the kids. Tom stayed sitting and did his math. He was bigger than I was so I don't know what I would have done with him if he would have tried to leave.

Years later I had his grandson in school. I asked the boy's mother what the grandfather had said. He said, "You behave yourself because that teacher expects it. I know she'll get it from you, and if you behave, you'll learn something."

Stubble Trouble

I had gone out to the school about two weeks before school started. I noticed the grounds of the school were full of weeds, so I stopped to talk to one of the board members. I told him I didn't think he wanted the kids running through those tall weeds. He said, "Oh, they should have been cut long ago," and so they cut them.

But they left this big stubble which was sharp and hard. Well, one of the kids fell on one of those stubble shoots and punctured his head. There was no telephone in the school so I told one of the kids to run to the neighbors and call the parents. They took her to the doctor right away.

She was OK, but the next day the school board was there with big rollers, the kind used to roll out roads, rolling down all the weeds, but that whole thing was really scary.

Tricky

The kids were on their way home after school, and one of them said, "Miss Picha, you have a flat tire on your car. Do you want somebody to come and help you with it?"

I said, "Well, if I do, I'll walk someplace and I'll tell them." Then the kids went home. Then this salesman came in. I don't even remember what he was selling, but he wanted me to buy it. I said, "Well, it's too bad because I don't think I can buy it. Will you do a favor for me?"

"Oh, sure, anything," he said.

"Would you fix my tire?" He did and I never saw the man again.

They Also Serve Who Only Stand and Wait

During the winter of 1937, I substituted for a week for my cousin who was teaching out on the prairie near Stewart. She was having some surgery and needed the time off. I stayed at the Zeman farm, about four or five blocks from the school. They took me in like I was one of them. But their house was not insulated. The wind just whizzed around. When I came downstairs to wash, the water was frozen in the wash bowl.

One time the weather was very bad but all the families brought their kids to school. Mr. Zeman started the stove. Of course, I didn't know the first thing about any of the kids. One of them stayed in back of the schoolroom all day. He never sat down in a desk. I took roll in the morning and he answered but he never sat.

The next day, the same thing. He always watched. When the wood got low, he brought in another load. When the water pail was empty, he got another pail, but he never sat down. He just stood there. My cousin told me not to worry. He was different and I just had to take him with a grain of salt, but it was unusual to have him standing there. At first it made me nervous but I got used to it.

One day I was teaching the curriculum and several parents walked into the school. I thought, "What in the heck are these people doing here?" Then one of them said, "Say, substitute teacher, don't you know that in winter we quit sooner?"

"No, I didn't," I said. "How soon do you quit?"

"Now!" they said, and the kids went home right then and there. The next day I knew better.

Ida Welter was a Country School Teacher for sixteen years.

Lillian D. Nelson

Lillian Nelson has lived in the Roseau area all her life. Her journey to become a Country School Teacher started in the early 1920s when she began grade school. Roseau winters are not kind.

Hi Ho, Hi Ho
Off to School We Go!

Students sometimes took horse-drawn toboggans to school. Lillian, front, with two neighbor girls and her niece, Helen Philips, is being pulled on one of these toboggans by their horse, Maud. The breezy ride required great balancing skills or else everyone fell off.

Lillian Nelson taught students in the rural schools for twelve years. She completed her teachers training program in 1931-1932 in Warroad. All her teaching was done in Roseau County where she taught at the following schools: District 25; America School, U18; Brandt School, District 3; and Falun School, District 36W.

Nosy 1

I'll never forget Loren, and I'm sure he'll never forget his science assignment—to collect nature specimens. He came to school on Monday morning with a huge wasp nest and a painful, swollen, red nose as a souvenir of the nest's final occupants.

Nosy 2

My first boarding place was really terrible because my landlady had no qualms about opening my mail. Fortunately, she had no one in school, but nevertheless, I moved to a more agreeable place.

Words, Words, Words!

I'll always remember the writing assignment I gave for the last week of school, which backfired from over-motivation. To inspire interest, I suggested topics such as "What I'd Do with $1,000,000," "When I played for the Chicago Black Hawks," "My Trip to the Top of Pike's Peak," and others. One of my pupils wrote forty pages. Others were not far behind. My last days of that year were very

occupied. One of those students published a story in *The Farmer* about how Paul Bunyan won a hockey game. She and her sister were honor students who later acquired doctorate degrees. There was ability and perseverance in many of those who attended the one-room schools.   **1932, District 25**

Which Way Is Up?

Albert and Bruno were the Katzenjammer Kids. Luckily, I met them later in my teaching career. Before school started, I was warned of previous discipline problems, so I was determined to keep a tight rein in force by announcing on the first day of school that any absences would have to be accompanied by written excuses.

However, I must not have made a great impression. Shortly after that Albert and Bruno were missing. No one knew where they had gone. They ran away and were gone for three days. They slept in haystacks and ate wieners. When questioned as to where they were headed, their reply was "Canada."

Lillian D. Nelson with primary students, 1932, Warroad teachers training

But when they were shown a map of North America, they had no idea where Canada was located. However, the episode must have been the necessary taming influence, as they suffered a lot of teasing. But they adjusted and became cooperative learners.

The Uninvited Guest

A fellow teacher and I were fortunate to have a town hall for our annual Christmas program. Everyone pitched in and decorated the hall as well as the huge native spruce tree. The two schools practiced marching in, singing their carols, giving plays and recitations, and marching out. All was ready for the big night. Then the day before the big program, most of my school came down with the measles, the end of everything for us! School closed for Christmas vacation. The other group gave their program as scheduled. Perhaps they blossomed later!

Lillian's students in the Brant School celebrate the end of state board examinations by going fishing.

Trust

From 1936 to 1939, I taught at Brant School under a most unusual contract. I wonder how many teachers taught with just a "gentleman's agreement." I had no written contract and no problems.

Horsin' Around

My first school, District 25 in Roseau County, was about four miles from my older sister's home so I went there for weekends. One Monday morning the roads were blocked by the previous day's snowstorm. So I donned a sheepskin coat, scarf, cap, and boots for a horseback ride on Molly to my boarding place. Molly was trained to return home when she was turned loose with the reins fastened to the saddle. However, that morning she refused to return until she had her breakfast in a nice warm barn.

I Choked

I drove a Model B Ford. To start it, I had to pull out the choke, providing an extra supply of gas. I left it out until the motor hummed steadily. Unfortunately, one day I was in a hurry to get home as the setting sun predicted the end of a chilly winter afternoon, and I had fourteen miles to go on icy roads. All went well until I arrived at the end of the road where it was necessary to make a forty-five-degree left turn onto another road. Obviously I was going too fast to control the car. I couldn't figure out why the car suddenly had a mind of its own.

By this time I was slowing down for the turn, but with the forgotten choke still out, I crossed the road and struck a pole supporting six mail boxes. I stopped right there! No damage was done to my car, but I had to suffer some good-natured ribbing from the owners who had to repair the mail boxes.

Making Hay!

Often a greater challenge than teaching was the problem of getting to school. When County Road 2 was constructed past our farm, I had definite problems. On one of my many back road routes I had to cross Hay Creek. Imagine my consternation when I discovered that most of the bridge was gone, and I would either have to cross on a few planks or drive several miles to get around it. With my heart in my throat, I chose the planks and gave a prayer of joyful thanksgiving when I crossed safely.

'Twas a Coal Day

Sometimes it got so cold that my car wouldn't start. One time when it was extremely cold, I set a pan of hot coals under my old Plymouth to warm it up. I was lucky it didn't catch on fire!

The Brandt School, District 3, near Roseau where Lillian taught from 1935 to 1939. She had thirty-seven students in grades one through eight.

Lillian D. Nelson's career as a Country School Teacher covered twelve years between 1932 and 1952, all in her beloved Roseau County.

Country School Marm rings the bell to begin a new day.

Chapter 16

Little Engines

In 1926 Walter Pippin wrote *The Little Engine That Could*. Overnight it became Country School Student's report card. The story of a train engine became an allegory for the American Way. Country School Teachers read the praises of the dedicated little engine. Country School Students knew the story by heart, and they could tell by the way Country School Teachers looked at them that they were indeed "Little Engines."

The message was obvious: If Country School Students threw enough coal into their engines, gripped the tracks of intellectual growth firmly enough, got a push now and then, they could climb over any Mountain of Ignorance and steam proudly down into the Valley of the Educated.

"I think I can-I think I can" earned a grade of C. "I know I can-I know I can" earned a B. "I can-I can" earned the mother-of-all-grades—A+.

The formula was simple: shovel in heaping scoops of effort-coal, heap on more determination-fuel, and pile on study-time. Then every engine would feel the euphoria of rushing down the far side of the mountain. If the engine faltered, Country School Teachers would find ways to help the Little Engines succeed. Something was defective in Little Engines who couldn't get past "I think I can" and "I know I can."

Some of the bright, shining engines steamed smoothly up and over the mountain. People cheered and the Little Engines swelled with pride. However, many chugged laboriously up the mountain, their pistons missing beats and their wheels slipping and spinning in frustration. Now and then they experienced the warm feelings of success. For some, no amount of effort or track-gripping could get them over the mountain. Sometimes Life pulled the tracks out from under these Little Engines. Some Country School Students have memories of sliding back down the tracks. Others recall the thrill of steaming downhill to a cheering crowd.

A Dilemma

I was the eldest in my family. I had five younger brothers. I was told by my parents to take care of my brothers. One day at school there was a fight out on the schoolyard. I went to see what was going on. My youngest brother was fighting with another boy. I jumped into the fray and broke up the fight by putting my arm around my brother. I pulled him into the school to tell the teacher.

Years later when he was telling his wife about the incident, he said, "Without a doubt, I was getting the worst of it, but I would rather have had my nose rubbed in the dirt than have my sister come to my aid. She shamed and humiliated me in front of all the kids." I have often thought about it all. What should I have done? He evidently resented me for a long time. I still don't know the answer.

Florence Hartwig, 1914–1916, Dodge County

Young Julius Schneider was one of many Country School Students who could never do anything "right." Julius now finds many of his country school experiences as topics for his poems.

from "The Left-Handed Man"
When I was born long years ago
Much to my folks' delight
They soon discovered their new son
Was left instead of right.

They would put me in a high chair
And hum a little tune
While I'd gobble up my corn mush
With my left hand on the spoon.

And when I was a youngster,
They sent me off to school,
For every boy must read and write
And know the golden rule.

We used to have a jolly time
When we went out to play.
But when the teacher called us in,
Things went the other way.

She came and stood beside me
With a pretty picture book
And placed it on my little desk,
So I could have a look.

But I couldn't turn the pages
Till I turned the book around
For the words were all wrote backwards
And the pictures upside down.

And each time I did my lesson,
I'd hear her stern command,
"My boy, you cannot write that way.
Please use your other hand."

So you see it wasn't easy
For a little lad like me.
Everything they did right-handed
Seemed as awkward as could be.

Julius Schneider, 1915–1923, District 70, Credit River School, Scott County

Hungry for English

One of the first days I went to school I couldn't understand English. My folks spoke Scandinavian at home and I couldn't understand the teacher so I started to cry. My sister asked me what was the matter. I didn't want to tell her I was so stupid I didn't understand the teacher so I told her I was hungry. The teacher said I could eat, but I wasn't hungry so I had a terrible time trying to eat.

Florence Linda Janike, c. 1919, District. 112, Fahen Township, Roseau County

Alone

I started school in Spring Valley, but I didn't pass because I was too bashful to answer questions. I knew the answers, so the teacher took me out in the hall and I answered every one. They didn't pass me in Spring Valley, but we moved to Fountain and they put me in third grade because I did know all the answers.

We had to go to Preston to high school. My dad took me out of eighth grade and put me in Preston, and my older sister who had graduated out of eighth grade was just ahead of me. I couldn't find my classes so I begged him to let me go back to Fountain and he did. My sister went one more day in Preston alone, and she came back with a complete nervous breakdown. She sat in my father's lap and hugged and kissed him. She had never done that before that day. She talked baby talk. In that high school she was alone. She just was never the same afterwards. My parents took her to the Rochester clinic and they put her on the sixth floor of St. Mary's, the psych ward. The doctors told my parents never to send her to high school again.

They never did, so I never went, either. There were so many more kids in Preston and she was alone in a strange place. I couldn't believe she was that bad when she came back that day. We didn't hardly know her. She stayed in St. Mary's for two weeks. She was better when she came out, but she was never just right again. It was different than country school where there were few kids.

Alice McNeil, 1919, Spring Valley, 1920–1928, Fountain, Fillmore County

English

I spoke German when I entered school at age five. I was the only student who couldn't speak English. I learned to speak English in two weeks after I entered school. My teacher could speak German and English. She said, "Sie den spatz." ("See that sparrow.") She had a great big bird chart. I loved birds and she had me reading in a month. Eight eighth-grade students also "took me under their wing" and helped me.

Ruth Domingo attended District 41, Sunnyside School, Stevens County, from 1921 to 1928.

I Can and I Will

District 105 was not always the most comfortable place even though I loved going to school. I never missed a day in spite of the problems. My family and my cousins were the only Swedish kids in the school. I can still remember the scathing tone of voice the other kids used when they said, "you dumb, white-headed Swede."

When I was seven and in the third grade, a new family moved into the district. The youngest of the four boys was in the third grade, and I thought it would be great not being the only person in my grade. However, instead of providing competition, he slowed us down. His older brothers weren't good role models for him, either. Like most farm boys, they were permitted to stay home to help with farm work in the spring and fall. They attended for the required forty days until they were sixteen, but their greatest interest was in disrupting the school.

One evening as school was being dismissed, one of the board members came to talk with the teacher about rumors that some of the older boys were smoking during school hours. The board member asked Helen, a second grader, and me if we had seen anyone smoking. Helen said, "Yes, they were smoking cigars."

I piped up and said, "No, they were smoking cigarettes." We didn't know that the boys were in the entry, looking through the peephole in the door and listening to us. From that day on Helen and I were not their favorite people. Helen was called "Cigar" and I was known as "Cigarette." Those were some of the nicer names they called us.

Once one of the boys came up to me at recess and called me "dumbbell" and then chanted "tattle-tale, tattle-tale—hanging on to a bull's tail" and other more profane names and threatened to knock my block off. I just stood there because I was so scared that my legs wouldn't move. But I also stood there because I really resented being intimidated by anyone, even at that early age.

Maybe the time I broke through the "rubber ice" over my knees and had to sit by the jacketed stove drying out my long underwear while the others jeered at me taught me it was best to turn my back and ignore them. Maybe something from my Swedish ancestry was passed on to me from my parents, who were free-thinking, hard-headed individualists. My father, especially, cared little about what others thought of him as long as he was comfortable with himself.

The boy was so surprised by my not moving that he just stood there, scowling at me a while, and then he turned and walked away. From that time on, the cigarette smokers pretty much ignored Helen and me. We were once again able to go to the girls' toilet and not have to stay there until the bell rang because we feared those boys.

Eva Nelson Johnson, 1923–1924, District 105, Kandiyohi County: Later Eva taught in the rural schools of Kandiyohi and Renville Counties for six years.

Super Super
Mae Barness was the county superintendent when I was a student in the 1920s. What a remarkable woman! She rode a horse to the schools and wore a big sheepskin coat. We kids loved her. She inspired us to succeed! It was my birthday. The Djerness School I attended was very close to the Pine Dale School. Here came Mae with the teacher and students from the Pine Dale School to celebrate my birthday. She had made cupcakes and nectar. In one of the cupcakes she put a ring, a knot, and other things. Whoever got what was in the cupcake, this was going to happen to them. She was liked and respected by everyone. She made me feel special.

When I was a teacher, she came to visit us at least twice a year. She knew every child in the county, called them by name, a tremendous woman. One of my sons was in the upper grades, and when he was home a few days ago, he said, "You know, Mae Barness inspired us when she talked. I remember one day during the war she visited the school. She stood up there and said, 'You know, if Hitler could see you kids here learning to become all kinds of workers, he would be shivering in his boots.'" My son remembered that forty year later.

Olga Peterson, 1924, Djerness School, Clearwater County

Memorizing Whiz
I had to stay after school one time because I didn't learn the "Preamble" to the *Constitution* and the *Declaration of Independence* the way my fifth-grade teacher wanted me to. She assigned it that day and expected me to have it memorized before I went home. I thought, "Why should I learn these so quickly? Why couldn't I wait until the next day?" Another boy who was in my grade didn't have to learn it, but because I memorized material very quickly, she assigned me to do it in one day. He went home, but she kept me after school. I had been nipping away at it all day, and in fifteen minutes I learned both of them. But I was so humiliated to have to stay after school. **Ruth Domingo, 1925, Sunnyside School, Stevens County: Ruth taught for twenty-five years, eight in the rural schools of Stevens County.**

Never Out of Style
When we went to school, we wore hand-me-downs. It didn't matter whether the hand-me-downs were from a brother or a sister. When I was in seventh grade, I wore my brother's shoes to school because mine were too small and there was no money to buy new ones. Only one person said, "My, Hannah, those sure look like boys' shoes." But I didn't react. I simply ignored the comment and continued to wear them until the end of the school year. Kids could be cruel, but that didn't stop me from wearing my brother's shoes. **Hannah Sanders, 1931, District 2, Pope County: Hannah attended country school from 1926 to 1933.**

Poetry Discipline

I'll never forget my favorite teacher. The teacher before her had used a strap. But this teacher was very soft spoken. She inspired us by her example.

There was an elderly lady who used to walk past the school to get her groceries. One noon the boys started throwing snowballs at her. We girls told the teacher. She rang the bell and called us in sooner than usual. She didn't scold the boys. She said, "Instead of the chapter in the book I'm reading, I'm going to read you a poem." She read "She's Somebody's Mother, You Know." The boys got so quiet. She'd emphasize, "She's somebody's mother, you know." She finished the poem and went on to her afternoon teaching. The rest of that winter she did not have any trouble with the boys.

She reaffirmed my decision to become a teacher. I kept in touch with her for the rest of her life—through my college days, my teaching, and all those years. I tried to do a lot of things the way she had done them. I could always see her standing there reading that poem. **Ann Hanson, 1927–1935, Melby School, Douglas County: Ann taught three years in the rural schools of Douglas and Kandiyohi counties. She taught for another twenty-seven years in public schools.**

Preservation

A friend of mine wanted to go to the outhouse, but the teacher wouldn't let him go. He had to go bad, number one, bad. So he took his color crayons out of his Prince Albert tobacco can. He dumped 'em in his desk, urinated in the can, and dumped it on the floor twice. She caught him and made him clean it up. I thought that was unfair. She should have cleaned it up. He did the right thing. He saved his pants. That was the most important thing.
Calvin Zuehlke, 1930-1934, Elmo School, Otter Tail County

Close Them All

I don't have pleasant memories of country schools. In second grade I asked to go to the outhouse. While I stood in front of the class reciting, I crossed my legs to keep from wetting my pants. The teacher just said, "Mildred, stand up straight!" I wet my pants in front of the class. How embarrassing!

We had an old maid teacher who could not control the boys, especially my brothers. Once I said "wo—a" for *who*. My brothers teased me so badly. I never did know what the right answers were because they ridiculed me and she did nothing.

When I went to high school, they set me back because I couldn't speak in front of the class. I had been ridiculed so much that I never could speak up in a group, not even today as an adult. It was a good thing they closed those schools so kids could be with more people than just their family.
Mildred Voegele Cook, 1935, District 103, Rice County

Never Again

One time the county superintendent came. I don't know why, but I was sitting on his lap and I wet my pants! I'll never forget that. I bet he never forgot it, either. **Elizabeth Predmore, 1934, District 94, near Eyota, Olmstead County.**

Spell It!

I had a pupil who was supposed to be in third grade, but he could not do the work. He was so far back that it was very hard for him to catch up. I had to start him with first grade or second grade spelling and reading, which made his dad unhappy. About the time school let out, here came his dad and he said, "I want to talk about my son. But wait until the county superintendent comes."

When the superintendent came, the father said, "There's nothing the matter with my son. He can do better work than this."

I said, "That may be so, but he hasn't been taught and he just can't do it."

The superintendent said, "Give me a third-grade speller." He said to the boy, "Can you spell this word? Can you spell this word?" He couldn't spell any of them. "Give me a second-grade speller." He gave him about five or six words, but by that time the boy was so nervous he didn't know which end was up. He couldn't spell any of them. The superintendent said, "Give me a first-grade speller. Spell cat." The boy couldn't do it. His dad grabbed the speller and said, "C-A-T! Spell cat!"

Virginia Rue Carrigan taught seven years in the country schools of Jackson County. In 1935 and 1936 she taught at a school in Russ Township, near Lakefield.

Tidbits

There were nine of us in our family. I thought school was a warm and safe place. In the first grade the teacher took us outside and read to us under the trees. I thought school was supposed to be inside, but she took us outside. That really impressed me because I thought, "Wow, you can read outside."

My brother, Haakon Hanson, Jr., got scolded at school. He was in the first or second grade. He ran to the neighbors about a half mile away, ran right into their house and hid under their bed. This was not familiar territory to him. Our neighbor found him. I don't know if he was afraid to go home. My twin brother had a hard time learning. He caused problems that he would not have caused if he had had more interest in school. He was very sick with an ear infection and had missed a lot of school.

One day our teacher said to us Hanson kids, "Come on, kids, I want to give you a ride home. I want to see your mother." We all piled in her car and ducked down. That was one of our favorite things—ducking down. When we got home, my teacher had a big bag of oranges for Harry. That impressed me. I appreciated that because my twin and I were very close, and we didn't get oranges very often.

Stella Sorbo, 1936–1942, District 16, Freeborn County

Rejected

When I was five years old, I went to school. Mrs. Olson said I wasn't old enough and I had to go home. So I said, "OK, then I'll go home and clean the shit house." **Allan Angelstad, 1943, District 51, Goodhue County: Allan's teacher was Evelyn Olson, p. 141.**

Verna Patrick attended District 4 in Yellow Medicine County from 1945 to 1953.

Fear

I was in first or second grade. My mother said I was such a happy child, and I remember that I just danced around the house all the time. After I started school, she couldn't understand why I would just lie on the couch and not say anything. I became very quiet. It was because of the way this teacher treated the class, not me so much, because I was a good kid, but she hit kids on the knuckles with the ruler. One of the boys in my grade was kind of a mouthy kid, and that's why she hit him. I had never even seen anything like that. We led sheltered lives, and my family was so gentle that I had never seen any-

Verna Patrick 1952

body hit before, let alone a teacher hit someone. It shocked me. I don't remember the teacher ever hitting me, but I remember having to stay in from recess. I don't remember what I did wrong, but it seems as though it wasn't much. My parents tried to get her moved to a different school, but it was hard to get teachers moved then. My parents had a meeting with other parents, but she didn't move. I think she had family problems and this may have come out in school. This fear of being hit and her behavior affected me for many years.

Verna Patrick, 1945–1946

Not Any More!

One day I rebelled at home about wearing the long cotton stockings and garter belts and everything that we girls were supposed to wear in those days. My mother must have given up on making me wear them and let me go to school without the stockings. I must have been in fifth grade when I started to rebel against wearing those clothes.

It was a cold winter's day. When I got to school, the teacher was aghast because I had a skirt on but I hadn't worn the long warm stockings. She made me come up in front of the room. She made me an example to the other girls. "Now look here," she said, "Verna does not have her stockings on today." I felt like she was really putting me down. I remember that to this day. It's those traumatic things you remember. I think this experience made me afraid of teachers, even in college. It made me feel I wasn't good enough. **Verna Patrick, 1949–1950**

Praise

After that, my last two country school teachers were excellent. It was a good thing so I didn't think all teachers were mean. I remember how wonderful I felt when my teacher brought a violin to school. She taught us all a little bit about the violin, but I got to play her violin for the Christmas program. I was so impressed because I had always thought the violin was so difficult so how could a kid play it for the Christmas program? I played "Twinkle, Twinkle, Little Star."

In December of 1952, we had the county music festival. All the country schools participated. I narrated "Jeg Er Saa Glad Hver Julek veld" for my school. I was proud and happy to have an important part in the program since I am one hundred percent

Verna Patrick, 1952

Norwegian. My mother taught me to sing "Jer Er Saa Glad" when I was about three years old. I remember how important I felt narrating that song in front of so many people. Then I felt so wonderful, receiving a letter of praise from Miss Thorpe, the superintendent of schools. She was strict and stern, but I admired her even when I was very young. Even if that letter was a form letter, it was very special. She must have known it would boost my self-image.

Dear Verna:

Christmas is almost here and I am thinking of you. There are beautiful thoughts that come like a gentle cloak to shield us from everything except the true meaning of Christmas. They say that one cannot truly keep Christmas unless one shares with others. When I think of your contribution to our wonderful Music Festival, I realize that you have truly shared. I want to thank you again and again to assure you that I was very proud of you.

Innocence Lost

I had a seventh grader who was a very quiet, very tender hearted. He worked hard, but he had a hard time. At the end of the year, the board decided he should go to school in Kimball for the eighth grade. His family asked me why I didn't want their son in class. I said that it wasn't that I didn't want him. The school board had made the decision. I had nothing to do with it. Perhaps the school board thought it was too much for me to have an eighth grader. They thought they had allowed him to stay as a seventh grader since the school only went to through the sixth grade. They told him he couldn't stay. He was found in the woods. He had shot himself. In my heart I feel that he solved the problem.

Mary Lou Erickson, 1957, District 3, Union School, Meeker County

Trouble

I had a sixth-grade boy move in from the cities. He said, "I've been in the principal's office more than I've been in school." One of the first graders and this sixth grader were like oil and water. They just couldn't get along. Their parents couldn't get along. He continued to pick on and tease that first grader.

Finally I decided something had to be done. One night at the end of school I said, "John, clean your desk. You're not going home until you clean your desk." It was five-thirty and he still had a mile to walk home but he finally cleaned his desk. After that he was a different student. He did his work, and he started to enjoy school. But on November 1 he moved. Later he was caught tipping over tombstones. That boy was hungry for discipline.

Marjorie Jandro, c. 1969, District 59, Dowling School, Isanti County

I Think I Can, I Know I Can
Look at me, Ted, I'm the Circus Queen.
They'll film me for the silver screen.
Twisting, turning, flipping, an' flying,
The Trapeze Darling, death-defying!

I'll be the strongman, your handsome hero,
But climbing rope, I'm just a zero.
My muscles are putty. I better rest.
Before I take the Muscle Man test.

Ted you're a whiz in every class.
With highest grades you always pass.
Together we're famous, the Wizards of Books
And I have my Shirley Temple looks.   -TM

Chapter 17

Shenanigans and Stuff

Dear Country School Teachers:

We would like to apologize for all the deceitful tricks, underhanded acts, smart-aleck remarks and clever pranks. Forgive us our chicanery and monkey business. We were rude, rowdy, and sometimes vulgar. You tore your hair and screamed "rascals and villains." For all of this we are truly sorry. Oh, but what a grand time it was!

We're Innocent

Our teachers say we were better kids
Than youngsters of today,
But we think they have lost their lids,
And memory's slipped away.

"The kids all loved us then," they mutter,
"Never fought or fussed."
Yes, we boys were sweet as butter.
And never even cussed.

The teachers were always right, you know.
We never stretched the truth.
Oh, how we loved to knit and sew,
And never act uncouth.

Like angry skunks we never stunk,
Or reeked of cigar smoke.
Those shotgun shells inside the logs,
The girls put in as jokes.

Us boys were angels, I'm not lying,
Never chewed no snuff,
Drilled no holes for biffy spying,
Or called the teacher's bluff.

The girls wanted to do some kissin'.
"Never!" we yelled, for sure.
"Boys, ya don't know what yer missin'."
But our lips we kept so pure.

Ya see, the girls caused every mess,
Actin' helpless an' refined.
Like knights of old we did confess
To trouble they designed.

What tricks and plots they did conspire,
Lookin' so demure!
Caused our teacher to retire
To Florida for a cure.

We never made our teacher fret.
You'll find the proof right here.
We boys were angels, you kin bet,
An' that's the truth so clear!   -TM

Everything we say is true, so help us Huckleberry Finn.

Note: The stories with a (T) after the name were told by Country School Students who later became Country School Teachers.

Horse Sense

My younger brother, sitting in his seat, turned with his feet in the aisle. My other brother came along and sat on his head. He hollered "ouch" so loud. So the teacher suspended him, kicked him out of school. Then my dad said, "You'll go to town to school." We had an old horse that my brother was going to use to ride to town. He wasn't a very good horse. The horse started out to school, and when he wanted to stop, he stopped, but my brother had quite a bit further to go, a couple miles. The horse didn't go like they expected him to. My brother couldn't get the horse to go any farther than the horse wanted to go from home. So my brother never went back to school. **Agnes Kosiolek, c. 1912, District 7, Minnesota Lake, Faribault County**

Pin Cushion

One of the boys had a medicine container. He carried straight pins in it. He held up his book and stuck these pins through the outer layer of his skin. It didn't hurt, but he made such grimaces and pretended to be in such pain. Then he stuck them in his left arm. He dipped the pins in his ink and tattooed himself when he stuck the pins through his arm. If he thought the teacher was watching, he just pulled down his shirt. During recess he chased us with those claws, pretending he was a strange creature.

Cecile Cowdery, c. 1917, District 1, Todd County

Disarmed

We had a teacher who taught only one year because she was a very poor disciplinarian. The boys started fighting on the playground. They were doing something that she told them not to. They were pretty good at that. They were always the bad ones, constantly causing her grief. We had a bridge between our school and the road. A lot of willow trees grew there. She got angry and went down there and cut willow branches off to whip the boys. She cut a whole bunch of them. When she got back, the big boys were out on the porch and they took the branches away from her.   **Mary Elliot Mahoney (T), c. 1919, District 3, Wright County**

Willow Weep for Me

I went to a one-room school, a joint district, which had all eight grades. Sometimes as many as fifty to sixty students attended that school. The teacher, a big, very buxom lady, was very strict. Once the bigger boys, who were all about sixteen, collected some materials to make a bomb. They put the stuff under a pail and blew it into the air. They were always up to something.

She had a hard time controlling them. Sometimes she hit them with her ruler, but most of the time she used willow switches. Willow trees lined the area around the schoolyard, and she made them go out and get their own willow branches. Then she switched them pretty good. I'm sure she wore those switches out on those boys. I always thought she was mean, but I'm certain she had to be strict to control those big boys. I was afraid of her.

Luva Wilson (T) attended District 87–181, Mt. Hope School, Meeker County, from 1921 to 1928.

Lock Up

There was a horse barn in back of the school some distance. One noon the teacher went down there to tell the boys they could not play in the barn at any time. She stayed in the barn until the last boy had run out. Then one of the boys slammed the door shut. He laughed as he locked the door. They were making noise and the teacher was hollering. The teacher was locked in there for only a few minutes because the older girls and the rest of us had gone down to see what the commotion was all about. We let her out. **Laurabelle Martin, (T) c. 1922, Great Bend School, Cottonwood County**

Foot Wet

I was walking to the lake to go school, and I had to go a mile and a half from home. Of course my mother said, "Don't walk on the lake because it isn't solid out there." But I knew where the places were that I walked before and I never went through the ice. This day I was real happy because I was going to walk across the lake. But when I got part way across, I fell in. My brother had to come and get me out. I couldn't get out. Every time I stepped, I broke off a piece of ice. I was in danger of drowning because it was pretty deep. He got me out. He fell through the ice, too when he tried to get me out, but he finally managed to crawl out. He pulled me out. He done a good job 'cuz I was heavy.

My mother found out. She said, "Didn't I tell you not to walk through the lake?"

I said, "Yes, I remember that I shouldn't walk through the lake, but it's so much closer."

She said, "Ya, and you got all wet, too, didn't you?"

I was always wishing that they would move that school away from there and get it closer to our place. But they never did that, so we always walked across the lake in the winter time and half the time we were walking in water. I walked through the water more than once. I was always foot wet.

The teacher would say, "Now you take off your shoes and put them down by the stove and hold your feet." You know it's no fun if the rest of them have all kinds of fun and you sit there trying to get dry. I couldn't even count the number of times I fell through. My mother said she was going to give me a good lickin' if I did it again, but then I did it again.

Agnes Runow, c. 1922, Wells, Faribault County

Hangin' Around

I attended a rural school about three and a half miles west of West Concord. It was so long ago that Dodge County Road 2 was just being constructed. It was supposed to have been an unusual road with deeper ditches and an elevated surface so winter snow would fill the ditches and blow across the top. Most of the power was furnished by powerful new tractors and graders. Mule teams removed most of the dirt from the ditches. In front of the school there was a crossroad so it was necessary to construct four elegant corners. Students loved to watch the progress, wave at the drivers, and ask questions.

One day the boys were playing with some rocks in the ditches when one of the them found a garter snake. The snake hunt was on! When the bell rang, one of the boys had an idea. "We'll save the snakes and see how many we can collect." Not knowing where to put them, two boys decided to hang them on the detour sign in the center of the highway. When I arrived at school, I saw the sign with five or six dead snakes hanging from it.

Every noon or recess was open season on snakes, and I must say it was a very productive enterprise. They were used to scare girls and produce squeals.The chasing discontinued as the efficient teacher was a good and fair disciplinarian. The catching and hanging of snakes continued for a few days. I didn't tell my father, who was clerk of the school board, but two mothers did! Once he knew, things began to change.

The next morning I got an early ride to school, so my father could have a private discussion with the teacher. The snakes were buried and students went back to playing ball and games at recess! **Adrienne Fleener, 1923, West Concord, Dodge County**

Forging Ahead
One of the sixth-grade boys had the job of sweeping the floors and starting the fire in the stove in my room. One morning my principal said he wanted to see me in his office. My first reaction was, "What have I done?" When I entered his office, he showed me a check he had made out as payment for this boy's work. It was a check for $6. The boy had changed the $6 to $60, and the bank had cashed the check. The principal had such beautiful handwriting that the forgery was very obvious. Someone came to talk to the boy, but I never knew what happened to him. **Alice Ekroot (T), 1925, Makinen School, St. Louis County**

So Holy!
A neighbor who lived about forty rods from the school—we had the outdoor biffy with a little window in it—well, he was so holy that he told our parents that he could see the smoke coming out of the biffy. Cigarettes weren't so hard to get in those days. We borrowed them from my father's store. Once we got a hold of the teacher's grading book and we ran halfway home and she ran after us.
John Davidson, 1926–1934, District 145, Goodhue County

Fwustwaited
My sister took me to school when I was four years old. I wasn't supposed to be there, and the boys kept picking on me. I finally got mad and threw my overshoe right up in front, right at 'em, right in front of the teacher. She told my sister Maxine, "Don't bring that little devil back to school again until you hafta." **Lloyd Steussy c. 1922, (T), Milton Township, Dodge County**

Remember how you used to count the number of people before you and then check to see which problem the teacher would ask you to explain?

Curses! Foiled Again!
One day when we were going through the multiplication tables, the teacher had the circle on the board. At that time we had to learn all the multiplication tables through the twelves.

That day she had the pointer. She was going around the circle saying twelve times one, twelve times two, and so on with one student and the student knew them right out. So then she went to the next student, and she went "hit or miss," not following around the circle.

"Well," the student said, "you darn fool! Why didn't you go around the other way?" That didn't sit very well with the teacher. **Frances Pianko Hayden (T), c. 1924, District 57, Le Sueur County**

Dumped!
Hans and Clarence were neighbors and very good friends until the "minnow episode." Hans had brought a bucket of minnows for Show and Tell. He was so proud of catching them. During recess Clarence emptied the bucket on Hans and he came in sobbing and trying to tell me what had happened. Behind him came a grinning, smirking Clarence.

I can still see him. I had to turn my head to keep from laughing. Hans was a big fifth grader and Clarence was a little fifth grader. I asked Clarence why he had emptied the bucket and he said, "I just felt like it." Of course he had to apologize and they remained good friends. **Nora Hendrickson (T), 1927–1928, District 9, near Hartland, in Freeborn County**

Albert Maas' first story appears in the dedication. In 1928, my mother-in-law, Susan Voegele Heselton, taught Albert. The following events occurred the year before she quelled the uprisings at District 114. Albert and the boys were trouble.

Just Talk

We had two teachers who didn't know how to handle children. They didn't have discipline. We learned it real quick. In the winter we'd be out for recess, throwing snowballs and everything at the school after the recess bell rang for re-entry. Five minutes later some of us would come dribbling in. She'd threaten us but she'd never follow through. And we knew that so we continued on.

In the spring as the snow melted away, it got to be mud, and we were throwing mudballs that looked real slick on a white schoolhouse. She'd holler out the window, "You guys cut that out, or I'm going to punish you!" But she never did, even after the west side of the school looked terrible. What a muddy mess it was! After one episode we had really speckled it with mud. One of the school board members lived a quarter of a mile away and he seen that. He came and had a discussion with her. I don't know what he told her—maybe that she had to have discipline or she was going to lose her job.

We came in after recess the next time, and on the way, we threw more mudballs at the school. Then she gave us a little session. She was all talk. She was always threatening but she never really punished us. It didn't impress us at all. And then she broke down crying. Well, we felt a little sorry for her. Some of us went out and tried to wipe the mud off the school, but that didn't help too much. Anyway she got laid off the job.

Albert Maas, 1927, District 114, Rice County

Albert Maas, second row, middle, looks as if he has just mud-balled the school. His teacher at the Hilltop School, which was located east of Faribault, kept Albert close to her.

She-Hulk

We had a school bully, a girl. She was always telling us that the world was going to end. She was two years older than I was and I was deathly afraid of her. I was so scared walking home from school because I was sure the world was going to end. She scared us. She didn't like a couple of the girls so for almost one year, the rest of us could not talk to them. She dominated us and we were dumb enough to follow her. She could force us not to speak to those other two girls. She ordered us and held the threat of the world coming to an end over our heads. I was terrified of her. My two friends had to sit by themselves. **Bertha Everson (T), 1928, District 111, Joint District, Freeborn County**

Bonfire

There was a creek a ways down, so we would go down during the noon hour, mostly in the winter when the creek was froze and we would skate. There were trees on the edges and roots would stick out in the creek banks. Some were the size of cigars and were dried up. So we lit them and smoked them like cigars, but, boy, were they strong! When we got back to school, we smelled like retired firemen. Teacher Ann Daleiden was curious so we told her. Then we had a bonfire, the end of our cigars.

John T. Flicek, 1929, District 71, Scott County

Toughies

I went to a school in which the kids were tough. The big guys lined up and then us little guys had to run through them. They didn't play kitten ball because that was too tame. We had one tennis ball, and then we chose up sides to see who could keep the other group from taking the tennis ball away. One of our older girls thought she had a safe place, so she put it down her pants. One of the older guys, he went right after it and he got that ball. Then the girl went in and told the teacher about it. The teacher thought about it for awhile and said, "Well, you had no business putting it down your pants."

In the spring we chose up sides to see who could get the biggest dead grass pile. We'd scratch the grass up and then we'd steal from one another. It was great sport to see who could get the biggest dead grass pile.

Sometimes we'd raise our hand to go to the out-house, and instead of that, we'd go to the grass pile and steal from the other guy. I tell you it was a great sport. We really had a great grass pile. Sometime we wrestled and fought over that dead grass just to see who could get the biggest pile of grass!

George Streich, 1929, Greenwood School, near Long Prairie, Todd County: told at Willmar County Fair, 1996

The Protector

I always watched out that the kids and the girls didn't get beat up by the bullies. I was the protector because I could handle them. Some guys were bigger than me but I wasn't scared of 'em. One of the guys was really mean and always picked on the girls. He wanted to stab the girls with a knife and I went up and I beat the hell out of him.

He would pick at them through their clothes with his jackknife. He never really cut them, but he picked them so there's a couple drops, probably. There's nothin' really to tell about the guy. He was a rouster, that's all, thought he could get by with stuff, but I showed him he couldn't.

Another time I caught him and chased him across the school yard and pert near hit him but the teacher wouldn't let me. That was the end of it for that day. He'd hide stuff from the girls, tie knots in their handkerchiefs, and tie their hands up and I'd have to get them away from him. It was just common stuff. **Marvin Dallman, Naeve Parkview Nursing Home, Wells, Faribault County**

All Tied Up

I was in the first grade, and I had a blue and white polka dot dress with long bow ties and the belts tied in the back in a bow. One of the boys sitting in the front tied one belt to the desk and the one behind me tied me back there. The teacher turned around and laughed. I never liked that teacher after that. She just laughed at me instead of punishing the boys. She thought it was a big joke.

Doris Callahan (T), 1930, Mower County

Car Rookie

We had a first-year teacher who had a 1929 Model A. The gas tank cover and the radiator cover were the same size, but the gas tank cover had a hole in it. The older boys always changed the caps around. She'd get down the road about a mile and stop. Then she had to try to get some help, but all it needed was to change the radiator cap and the gas tank cap around.

Vince Crowley, 1930, Klonberg School, Murray County

Escape

We played ante-I-over. Once in a while the ball got stuck behind the bell tower. First, we got the stepladder. That wasn't quite tall enough to reach the steps to the porch, so then we got the wastebasket and put it on the top of the stepladder. Someone held the wastebasket. Whoever was willing to risk his neck climbed up there, then onto the porch, then climbed over to the bell tower, threw down the ball, and came down the same way. One day this guy who climbed up there decided he wasn't coming back down. At one o'clock, the teacher called the students in for class and he was still sitting up there. She decided she'd fix him, so she took away the ladder and wastebasket. He jumped off the porch roof without getting hurt. He wasn't in school for the rest of the afternoon.

Walt Sommerville, 1931, District 77, Kandiyohi County

Strip Tease

When I was in the sixth grade, we were scheduled to have Mantoux tests. My older brother teased me by telling me I would have to take off my clothes to have these tests done. On my way to school, I was mulling this over, fretting about taking off my clothes in front of all those people. How was I ever going to face that thing? I was very frightened about the whole thing and I didn't want to go to school, but my mother insisted that I attend. The doctor and the nurse were already there and

Ida Haukos, c. 1946

many of the kids had had their tests taken before I arrived. They hadn't had to take off their clothes, but I still believed I had to. I raised my hand and told the teacher I had to go to the outhouse. I stayed out there a l-o-o-o-n-g time. I finally I mustered up enough courage to go back. The doctor and nurse were waiting for me. They gave me my shot and I never had to take off my clothes. **Ida Haukos (T), 1933, District 81, Dane Prairie Township, Otter Tail County: Ida taught in Otter Tail County for nine years.**

Teacher the Cat

One of the older boys hadn't passed the state boards, but he was still going to school. He got angry with the teacher in recitation. He said something really smart aleck and she scratched him. She just went at him and she scratched him across the forehead and drew blood. He yelled, "You cat!" I was probably in first or second grade and I still remember that. He could irritate her with his comments and he must have said something that really upset her. **Laverna Birkland (T), 1932: Laverna attended District 15 North near Pennock in Kandiyohi County from 1931 to 1939.**

Deflated

Our poor teacher was too old to deal with the bunch of us who were obnoxious and old enough to be out of grade school if we had applied ourselves. Everyday she drove her car and parked it near the school. During recess we let the air out of her tires and then said, "Teacher, your tires are flat, but we'll pump them up for you for twenty cents a tire." What could she do—way out miles from help—but pay us for our dirty deed?

Ed Sharkey, 1939, Sharkey School, Le Sueur County

In His Cups

Any district that could afford it had a stock of tin cups that were used for picnics and other social gatherings. They were stored in a room off the classroom. We sneaked in there and urinated a little in each cup. After the liquid evaporates, the crystals mix with the rust.

All went well until one of the girls saw two boys doing their thing and reported it to the teacher. We spent long hours and much elbow grease restoring the cups as best we could. **Hilly Gill, 1939, Sharkey School, District 32, Le Sueur County**

Lucyle Tabbert meets "the racing brothers."

"My horse is faster than your horse."/ "No, it ain't."/ "Yes, it is."/ "Your horse is ugly."/ "So's your old man!"

Ditched

Two brothers lived about two and a half miles from school. One of the boys was diabetic. It was impossible for him to walk to school, so the older brother brought them in a buggy. One of the other neighbors' children also had a team and buggy. One day they decided they were going to have a race. They were running neck and neck for a good long ways. Finally the race ended when they both ended up in the ditch. **Lucyle Tabbert (T), c. 1939, Long Lake School, Cottonwood County**

Untamed

We knew our teacher would never punish us. She never put us in the corner or anything. She never got mad. She was too kind and too good-hearted. We were just terrible. Once we got the teacher down in the basement and blindfolded her. Then we played Ring Around the Rosy. We got her so dizzy that she didn't know where she was. She wanted us to take the blindfold off. I don't think we tied her hands, so I don't know why she didn't untie herself. We did that for about an hour. Noon hour was supposed to be only a half hour so we didn't get back up to the room for a whole hour 'cuz we had her down there spinning her around.

During our half-hour noon we went skating. She'd stand there and ring the bell and ring the bell, and we'd just wave at her and keep on skating. Sometimes we decided we should walk up and down the road a little bit instead of going in. We'd wave at her and she'd stand there and ring that bell and ring that bell. We just walked right by her.

One girl brought her little Shetland pony to school. We had the outside biffy so we had to go outside. Then we'd take a spin around the schoolhouse on the pony a few times before we went back.

Florence Maas, 1934–1942, District 93, Rice County

Stuck on You

We had a well at our school. It was a regular windmill and one of the favorite tricks in the late fall or the first time it started freezing was to walk up to that steel windmill and stick our tongues up against the cold steel and do it real fast so that our tongues would not stick. If we didn't do it fast enough, a little bit of our tongue would stick to the steel. Then if it really stuck, we had to puff and blow hot breath on it till it thawed out. **Bill Herzog, c. 1937, District 22, St. Joseph, Scott County**

Whether they are Country School Students of the 1920s and 1930s or students from the 1990s, kids create their own vocabulary. While we sat in Hardee's discussing country schools, Bill Herzog asked me if I knew what spritzing *was? I didn't. Do you?*

Spritzing

The girls had the fancy outhouse. There were two in one—one for the little girls and one for the bigger girls. The seats were a little higher and the hole was a little bigger. Then the boys—well, theirs was attached to the woodshed. It was just one room. You had the high one for the big boys and the low one for the little guys. Of course everyone had to prove his manhood and see how high he could pee up against the doggone wall, and then they wrote their names up there. **Bill Herzog, c. 1937, District 22, St. Joseph, Scott County: Bill was my teaching colleague for many years. No one "spritzed" in our school!**

The Conspiracy

Our male teacher had poor discipline and poorer teaching skills. With a large class of eighth graders, his hands were full of challenges. He could not complete a full year with us.

After our hour-long noon break, when one o'clock arrived, our teacher would stand on the school steps, ringing that old familiar bell. We would not go in. We used the excuse that we could not hear the bell. We argued that the door of our snow room was pointed in the opposite direction and we could not even see the school steps.

In the winter when the teacher stood on the steps, ringing the bell for us to come in, the boys pelted him with snowballs. After that he would stay in the school and just stick his hand out and ring the bell. When it was cold, the boys sat around the potbelly stove to dry off. Then they threw firecrackers into the ash pan. You can imagine the rest.

There was a hole in the ceiling of the school. The boys used to make paper airplanes and throw them into the hole. When the school burned down between my seventh and eighth grades, my brother thought of all those airplanes in the attic which added fuel to the fire.

The boys brought a roll of coil wire from some old car engines. As we sat in our desks, we passed the wire from one person to another, stringing the almost invisible wire between the desks. Then one boy from the back row raised his hand for help. As the teacher walked to the back of the room, he tripped over the wire.

One day the school board visited. The eighth-grade girls started raising their hands, asking the teacher questions about geography and other subjects that he could not answer. He was soon dismissed and we got a nice woman teacher to finish the year. **Elaine Nelson (T), 1940–1941, St. John's Lutheran School, Sibley County**

After her interview, Evelyn Olson Dorschner took me downtown to her favorite Kenyon restaurant, The Coffee Cup, for lunch. Allen Angelstad, one of Evelyn's former country school students, was eating lunch when we arrived. Allen slid into our booth and told this story. When he had finished the tale, Evelyn exclaimed in typical teacher disbelief, "I never knew about that!"

Nippin'

J. lived north of us so he used to stop and pick us up to go to school. We were in the sixth grade then. One day in early summer the weather was nice. The three of us took off for school on our bikes. J. went out our driveway and tipped over into the ditch. He took that dive and rolled over, bicycle and all.

We didn't know what was the matter with him, but then he told us. He was crocked! He'd gotten into his dad's home brew so he brought a jug along. Of course we all got to havin' a few nips.

Out behind the toilet there was a big old cottonwood that was rotten and hollow in the middle. That's where we stored our booze and our cigarettes. So at noon hour that's where we headed. That only happened that one time. **Allan Angelstad, 1943, District 51, Goodhue County**

Slow But Sure

Our teacher was a large woman, big, very big. During the noon hour we went to a farm, which was about three fourths of a mile from the school. After an hour of sliding, our teacher rang the school bell for us to come back to school. Well, eighteen of us decided not to return just then. We knew how long it would take her and how fast we could make it.

She took off for the farm, moving all that weight as fast as she could across that three-quarter mile trek. When she got there, the kids all scattered, but one kid ran right into her. We all ran back to the school. When she finally made it back, forty-five minutes later, we were all sitting in our desks.

Mark Nasby, c. 1946, District 130, Jackson County: Mark taught junior high school science for over thirty years in the Burnsville district.

Good Times, Bad Times

Across the road from the school was this large grassy, woody swamp with lots of cattails. The grass was so tall that over the years the older brothers and sisters of the kids in the school had made passageways in the grass, long grassy tunnels. We played in those tunnels. It was kinda traditional that each year we would maintain them.

Once or twice Mr. Herzog, the county superintendent, would come to check out the school. We liked it when he came. The teacher treated it like the second coming of Christ. He usually came at noon for lunch. They ate and talked about school and we were given an hour and a half to play in our tunnels.

During the last half hour of each day, we cleaned the school. The seventh- and eighth-grade boys carried the trash out and burned it. The older boys would go over to the dried swamp, break off the cattails and light one end of the hollow stalk. That way they could smoke whatever smoke they could suck through the hollow stalk.

When I was in the first grade, we were fed spinach. Many of us didn't want to eat it, so we sat there endlessly until we were forced to eat it. Many kids sat in front of that spinach for hours, crying and whimpering. To this day I can't eat spinach.

Name withheld, St. Benedict, Scott County

Spring Fever

The teacher used to appoint one of the girls to take the class to another room to do our reading assignments. There was a little room adjacent to the main classroom that we'd go to. One day we were sitting in there. It was a nice spring day and I wasn't following the lesson too well so I flipped my book out the window and I jumped out after it. Well, Shorty Showers seized the opportunity and slammed the window shut and locked it so I couldn't get back in. So I'm outside jumping up, and all the glass in the window is soap pane except there is clear glass in the center of the big window. I'm jumpin' up looking through that clear spot, and I'm hollerin' at Shorty, "Open up that goddamned window!"

The next time I jump up I'm looking face to face at Mrs. Damey, the teacher. She's standing there, looking right at me—filling up that entire clear spot in the glass. I ran around to the front, trying to get in the door before she got there, but of course, all she had to do was just step out the door and she had it blocked. I got heck for that one.

Tom Gleason, 1945, country school at Jenkins, in Crow Wing County: Tom Gleason was my teaching colleague for over thirty years in the Burnsville school system.

False Advertising

I got suspended from school for this one. LSMFT was the slogan for Lucky Strike cigarettes. We boys had a saying that LSMFT really meant Loose Sweaters Mean Floppy T—well, you know. And so I'm sitting in the reading room again, this time quoting my new-found knowledge when Vera sends Virginia into the teacher with a note that says, "Tom's talking dirty in reading class."

So the teacher came in and really put it to me. "What did you say?"

I said, "Lucky Strike Means Fine Tobacco."

She turned to the class and asked, "Is that what he said?"

They all hollered, "Noooooo!"

She made me go through every single letter: "Loose Strife Means Fine Tobacco"—every one. She sent me home and I got a good talking to from my dad on that and suspension for one day

Tom Gleason, 1945, country school at Jenkins, Crow Wing County

Stiff

In the spring the water was running rapidly in the ditch just in front of the Cheerville School. The bridge over the creek was collecting the froth and debris while the water was running over and under the bridge. Well, us kids had to play with the water by poking our sticks at the froth and throwing stones. Gail said, "Be careful. Don't get too close to the edge of the bridge."

"Don't worry," I said. "The edge of the bridge is way over h—e—r—e," and I slipped toward the swirling water. Fortunately, I caught the edge of the bridge and the other kids pulled me out.

Fern Bock, Cheerville School

Chapter 18

The Teachers of Kittson County

The sun was barely peeking above the horizon when I crossed the county line into Kittson County, tucked away in the northwestern corner of the state. Acres of sunflowers stood stately with bowed heads, their dazzling gold fading in the late September sun. Flat prairie stretched out in every direction. Miles in front of me, a golden tornado of straw moved across the prairie. Giant combines harvesting the wheat twisted the straw into whirlwinds as the machines cut wide swaths through the fields.

It was eighty degrees that day, and puffy clouds moved lazily across the sky. However, as I passed a few country schools now converted into township halls, I wondered what a trial it must have been to teach in those tiny, uninsulated schools. What kind of people stood so tall they could confront the blizzard winds that ripped across the prairie and blasted places like Caribou, St. Vincent, Hallock, and Lancaster? Most of the people who tell their stories in this chapter were born in Kittson County, attended school there, and then headed for teaching jobs in the tiny white schools in every corner of the county.

Country School Teachers in Kittson County tell their stories with pride. Many people have asked, "Kittson County? Where's that?"

It's in the northwest corner of the state where sunflowers and teachers reach for the sky.

Alice Holm
Alice Leen Holm attended Cisco School in Polk County, where she learned discipline.

The Time Machine
Discipline was very strict. We were not to go off the school grounds. One time we went off the school grounds to slide down a straw stack. We were having a good time, but since we had gone off the school grounds, the teacher kept us after for ten minutes. When I got home, my mother was standing in the door. "How come you're late?" she asked. I had to tell her what had happened. "You listen to your teacher after this!" She knew something was up because I was ten minutes late. **Alice Leen Holms, c. 1924, Cisco School, Polk County**

Speeder
We lived in the country, but my father was a section foreman for the railroad. When it was very cold, he gave us a ride on his speeder, the machine where you pumped the bar up and down to make it go. They were not enclosed then. It was much colder on the speeder than walking but it only took a few minutes to get to school. **Alice Leen Holmes**

Alice taught from 1931 to 1938 in Halma and Beaton in Kittson County.

I'll Take That Seat

Alice Leen Holm, c. 1932

I worried about that first day. Everybody in town had told me about this boy I would have and what a troublemaker he was. "Look out for him because he is a bad one." On the first day I told them they could take their own seats and that I liked the front seats. Here this boy, who was supposed to be the bully, walked up and took that seat. I said, "That's what I like to see," and I complimented him. From then on I never had any trouble with him. He didn't have a father, and maybe his mother pampered him too much.

1932, Halma School

Kindness

I had three students who were retarded. One couldn't talk at all. They never missed a day all year long. I couldn't classify them in any class. They couldn't read or write. They shouldn't have been there, but in those days they didn't put those students in special classes.

However, their being there made me want to be kind to every student. It made me more compassionate. I tried to involve them in activities. They could color a little bit. They were there all three years I was there. I couldn't promote them so I just let them be there. One went to the day school here in town. Whenever she saw me, she said, "You were my teacher." I always stopped to talk to her.

Alice Holm ended her teaching career in 1938.

Gladys Sutherland
Gladys Sutherland taught in District 22, Springbrook, Moen and North Red River.

Er du Svensk?

In my first year of teaching, the one thing that bothered me the most was the issue of nationality. At home nobody ever asked anybody what nationality they were. We were all Americans. But when I got out here, the people said to me, "Er du Svensk?" (Are you Swedish?) I didn't think it mattered. My father was born in Pennsylvania, and my mother was born in Kansas. I was just an American. But I got the impression that you don't amount to "shucks" unless you are Scandinavian.

1925, District 22, Kittson County

No school at the North River School, 1948

In 1948, heavy rains flooded the Red River. Gladys Sutherland's school looked as if she should start gathering two of every kind of creature alive. But cancel classes? Never! This teacher from Kittson County was ready for emergencies!

Gladys Sutherland's five students meet at her home for class.

Flooded Out

The flood came with two months left in the term. All of the parents of my students were forced to leave their farm homes and go to Hallock where I lived. Of course the school was flooded as well. In order to finish the school year, I invited the students to use the large, glass-enclosed porch in my house. The students readily agreed to this and the school board and other men in the community used boats to move to town the desks, books, and whatever else we needed. I made several trips with them to get what I needed to teach. At that time I had only five students. **Gladys Sutherland, 1948, North Red River: Gladys taught for thirty years, seven in rural schools.**

Esther Hanson Mortenson taught at North Hilltown near Humboldt from 1930 to 1932. Esther's friend, Margaret Reese Johnston, taught at South Hilltown. These two Hilltown schools were rivals on Play Day, which was scheduled each spring. Esther and Margaret taught the children school yells, which thrilled the youngsters. This is one of the ear-splitting yells:

> The head of the mule,
> The head of the mule,
> The head of the mule
> Is the North Hill School!
> The tail of the mule,
> The tail of the mule,
> The tail of the mule,
> Is the South Hill School!
> Rah! Rah! Rah!

When they went to the other school, the words were reversed, tail vs. head. Play Day was one of the highlights of the school year.

Helga Foss Gillie taught from 1933 to 1938 in Kittson County near Lancaster.

Somewhere Out There

I began teaching in District 33, southwest of Lake Bronson. Usually the schools were built along a well-traveled road, but they built this school right in the middle of the section with only a trail coming to the school. The people couldn't agree where to build the school so they built it right in the middle of the district. There were no roads to the school so cars couldn't reach it. Everyone had to walk a mile and a half through mud and snow just because those people couldn't make up their minds.   **Helga Gillie**

Strange Bed Partner

In the place where I stayed, the first year the husband played jokes on me. One night I went up to bed. As I crawled into the bed, I felt something round and ice cold! He had put a watermelon in my bed. He stood at the bottom of the stairway, laughing to beat the cards. I threw the watermelon down at him.   **Helga Gillie, 1933**

Something's Not Fishy Here!

We had the custom of each family providing something that could be heated for a hot noon lunch. We had two Catholic families in our school, so on Friday the menu was to be creamed fish on toast. One Friday the mother forgot the fish. Instead she sent to school creamed chipped beef on toast. When I was dishing out the food, a first-grade boy from the Catholic family shook his head when he saw the beef. His older sister, an eighth grader, walked over to him and slapped him on

It's June 1, 1934, the last day of school for Helga Foss' District 39 Center Grove School.

the side of his face. "Eat it," she said. "It won't hurt you!" I don't remember if he ate the beef.

Helga Foss Gillie, 1937, Nordine School, six miles northeast of Hallock

Harry Sjulson

Harry Sjulson attended country school northeast of Lancaster. When the opportunity arose for some shenanigans, the Sjulson children took advantage of the situation and sent their classmates and teacher fleeing hysterically into the woods. Both Paul and Harry became teachers.

Characters in The Great Scare

Harry, second row, is waving to the camera. Brother Paul to his right is wearing his cap. The victims: teacher Alana Loer, middle with head down, Faye Balderson Lyberg, front row, third from left, Marriane Balderson, back row left, Harriet Norland, just right of Marriane.

Grin and Bear It

We lived only a few miles from the Canadian border. When we were going to country school, some of these Canadians had surrounded a woods where there was a bear. They had taken pitchforks after the bear because it had severely mauled a woman. Naturally, everyone was terrified.

So with that scare in mind, one night after school my brother and sister and I sneaked into the woods where the teacher and five or six kids were headed home. We growled and they rushed back to the school and stayed there until dark, until the person where they stayed decided something was wrong so he went to pick them up. We never told them about this until many years later.   **Harry, 1933**

Stick 'em Up

My dad, brother, sister, and I had gone to my mother's Christmas program in a horse and sleigh. We had just a little grain box on the sleigh. We three kids were in the grain box, sleeping. Mother and Dad sat up front. My mother had been paid in cash, about thirty-five dollars for the month. We had gone about three or four miles when suddenly some men came from the side of the road and yelled at them to stop. One waved a flashlight. My dad whipped the horses. We woke up. The men ran after us, but they couldn't keep up to the horses. The one with the flashlight swung it back and forth. We thought it was a holdup because they chased us. They must have known Mother had been paid in cash.

1932, Caribou School, Harry's mother's school

A Fast Learner

We lived fifteen miles northeast of Lancaster, so it was very difficult to think of going to high school. My brother was two years older, and he was scheduled to graduate. My mother asked the teacher if he would let me take the four examinations to pass the seventh grade and the four to pass the eighth grade—reading, history, spelling, citizenship, arithmetic, hygiene, geography, and grammar. I passed all but one, so I graduated with my brother and went on to high school. My mother rented a place in town so we lived with her during the week and came home on the weekends to help with the farm. Every Friday we walked those fifteen miles home. **c. 1933**

Harry Sjulson taught at the West Cannon School near Lake Bronson from 1939 to 1940 and the North St. Joseph School, northeast of Lancaster, from 1940 to 1941.

Not the Marrying Kind

Harry Sjulson and friends

The first year shortly after school began, two young ladies from the community came with some cookies and lunch and visited. I guess they were going to check out their possibilities. When I taught at North St. Joseph, one family had two daughters who were about my age. That was interesting. I took a fancy to one of them a little bit, but nothing every came of it because I wasn't in the marrying mood yet. If you look closely at the picture, you can see a hand on my left arm.

1939 and 1940, West Cannon and North St. Joseph Schools

How Embarrassing!

I was up in the front teaching when the kids started laughing. Something outside the east window was making them laugh uncontrollably. I asked a seventh-grade boy, "What are you laughing at?"

"Ho, ho, ho," he said, "it's funny. You have to see for yourself."

Outside was an older brother of two of my students. He was about sixteen. He was herding cows and had forgotten that he was near a school. He was on a new country road about a hundred yards from the school. He took his pants down and did his duty right there with his bare back-end facing the school. He seemed to have no idea where he was.

My first reaction was, "I can't laugh at something like this." But I couldn't control myself and I started laughing. After a while the boy pulled his pants up and left. It was embarrassing for his two brothers. That night when I told the people where I stayed about it, the man, who was clerk of the school board, said, "You should have gone out and yelled, 'Hey, we're having school here!'"

1940, North St. Joseph School, Kittson County

The Storm

I had a date and we had driven about three miles. All of a sudden I couldn't see anything. I thought my windshield had fogged up so I checked that, but that wasn't the problem. I opened the door and stuck my head out. The wind and snow blew my hat down in front of the car, but I managed to retrieve it. I got back in and we rolled the window down on each side about three or four inches.

We could see some grass along the side of the road so I inched along about two miles an hour. When the front wheels went down, then I'd back up and move over. The snow was so heavy I could barely see. We went till we came to a crossroads where we knew there was a house which was fifty or seventy-five feet from the road. We decided to walk there. We walked holding hands. We couldn't see any house until we got within five feet of it.

If we had gotten stuck or stalled on the road, I know we would not have stayed with the vehicle, which would have been disastrous. In those days people didn't know about the importance of staying in the vehicle. Many, many people were killed in that storm.

Harry Sjulson taught from 1939 to 1941.

Erlyce Lindberg Larson
In 1936, Erlyce Lindberg walked into her school, District 44, east of Robbins. All her dreams and the sweat and hard work to earn her teaching certificate were finally going to pay off. What a joyful challenge to teach youngsters hungry for knowledge! She never saw the thorns on the rose.

Thorns in My Side

I disliked my first day of teaching. I remember going to the window many times and looking out across the prairie and thinking, "Is this what I really want to do?" I wondered many times if I would ever like teaching.

I was in a district that was very strict. They frowned on almost all kinds of amusement, especially dances. The children were so provincial they could not relate to the things they were learning. They certainly did not want a suitcase teacher. They wanted me to stay weekends.

I had forty children and all eight grades. That year I lost thirty pounds. I lived about a mile and a half from school. That was the terrible winter of 1936. I lived in a very cold house that was poorly insulated. The living room and the kitchen were finished in wide boards. In the morning those boards were rimmed with frost.

The stress was terrible. I had so much work with forty students. The lights were so poor I could hardly work in the evening. The little kerosene lamps didn't afford much light, so I stayed at school as long as there was daylight.

The thorns arrive for class!

But the worst part was this family of six kids that was "a thorn in my flesh." I lost those thirty pounds that year primarily because of that very difficult family. They had six children in school. They did not socialize with anyone and they were really wild. The kids were absolutely undisciplined.

They didn't have money to buy shoes or overalls. One day the father came to school and said his youngsters could not start school because they had to haul trash first. When they did come, they were wild as hares. They were always tardy. The younger ones rode their horses bareback, but the three older ones stood on the horses' backs, whooping and hollering, five horses tearing into the schoolyard.

Ralph, one of the oldest brothers, was just plain incorrigible. He threatened me. He came up the aisle one day and he said, "I am not afraid of you."

I walked toward him and said, "And I am not afraid of you, either!" Then I went to the school board and they expelled him. He was old for his grade, he didn't want to be there, and he was a bad influence on all the other children.

One time I kept Dale after school. He was one of the best of them, really a very nice little boy. He brought me chocolate drops once in a while. When the grown brothers came to get him, they were very angry at me for keeping him after school. I walked out of the schoolhouse with him to make sure he got into the car OK. Then they threw a dead rabbit which landed right at my feet.

One of the older girls was angry at her boyfriend in Donaldson, so she tied a rope to a skunk and rode up and down the streets of Donaldson on her horse, dragging that skunk in front of his house.

One day I had the windows and doors closed because it was cold. As soon as this family came into the school that morning, one of the big girls looked at me and rolled her eyes. I knew what she was thinking. The school reeked of skunk odor!

First I opened a window and finally I opened the door. I said to Archie, "What have you boys been doing?" He knew what I was talking about and said, "We were hunting skunks last night and we've got 'em in the basement." They had those live skunks in the basement of their home. Imagine what that house smelled like!

Those people were like no one else. They had so little. They had a very irresponsible mother. She would tell them it was all right to steal as long as they didn't get caught. And they did steal. People told me about them. I told them it was wrong to steal and it would get them into trouble.

I won them over with love. At that time you could touch children. I did a lot of touching. It wasn't much fun touching them because they were never clean. But, nevertheless, when they succeeded, I touched them. I think I won them over by making them feel they were important and part of the group. I told them we had rules in school they had to follow. I explained that I wanted them to be happy in school, but they must listen, not use any bad words, and they must be good to each other.

We were getting ready for the Christmas program, and that was at a time when religion was part of the program. Dale waited after school one night, and I thought he ought to be on his way. He sat in his seat in the middle of the room.

I said, "Aren't you going to go home, Dale?"

He said, "I want to ask you something. Who is Jesus?"

I told him the story and why it was part of our Christmas program.

Erlyce Lindberg Larson, 1936, District 44, east of Robbin, Kittson County

Myrtle Trudeson

How would you have liked a teaching job in Caribou during the Depression years? Never heard of Caribou? Can't find it on the map? Locate Birch in the northeastern corner of Kittson. Follow Highway 4 up to the Roseau River. You should be within a stone's throw of Caribou. Myrtle taught in Caribou from 1937 to 1938.

A Toboggan Pickup

I was way up near the Canadian border in Caribou. The people there were very friendly. We had square dances at the community center and the kids would pick me up with their toboggans and horse-drawn sleighs. They would take me to the square dances. They were such wonderful kids, even if they lived in the boondocks. Recently I met one of the students from that school. He said, "I'll never forget the night my parents had to borrow your car to take me to the hospital thirty-five miles away for an emergency appendectomy."

Myrtle Trudeson, 1937, Caribou School, Kittson County

SOS

One winter day one of the little girls, a first- or second grader, went to the outdoor toilet at the end of the path across the yard. She closed the door, hooked it, then couldn't get out because the outside latch had crossed over. I didn't miss her for some time. Then I looked out the window and saw her scarf dangling through a small window opening in the door. I sent one of the older girls out to get her. She was very cold. **Myrtle Trudeson District 8, North Red River School**

When I located Caribou on the map, I asked Myrtle, "Wasn't teaching there a lonely, miserable existence?" The tears welled up in her eyes and she said, "Those were such wonderful years. I loved those children so much."

Bits and Pieces from Kittson County Teachers

Sheepish Gift

A big farmer in the area drove his sheep past the school every day. One old sheep could not keep up to the group, so he gave that old sheep to the school. We had to give it to another farmer who lived nearby. **Gunda Hanson Larson, North Star School, Lancaster**

Man Hunting?

I went with a friend to apply for a job. As soon as we entered the board member's home he said, "Oh, you're here looking for a man."

"Noooooooooooo!" I exclaimed.

However, I married a local fellow.

Clara Hoyum Loer, 1933

Stuck

One of my first graders was walking home on a warm spring day after the snow had melted and the fields were very wet. His home was close to the school so he just cut across the field. I looked out the window, and there he was stuck in the mud. He couldn't move. I plodded through that muck and pulled him out. **Clara Loer Laude**

Smallest School?

I taught for two years in a school west of Hallock that had two pupils, one second grader and one eighth grader. A third came in the spring for six weeks as a kindergarten pupil. The district wanted to keep that school open. **Marie Sandberg Erlanson**

Tiny Bits

1. We got our drinking water from a hand-dug well in the school yard. The water looked oily and tasted different. They cleaned the well during the summer but the water still tasted bad. That well was full of lizards.

2. The teacher asked the boy what his name was. He answered, "My name is Johnny Taylor, the Great Commander, Shot a goose and killed a gander, Alexander Taylor." The teacher was not happy with his answer.

3. A youngster had a black spot on his hair on one side and another black spot on the other side. The teachers asked, "Do we have a Holstein here?"

Ellen Vik, c. 1920, told these stories to Clara Boyum

Student Stories from Kittson Country

Too Tough

One boy was continually lifting our dresses and one day he tried to pull our pants down, too. We girls ganged up on him and literally buried him in the snow. I'm surprised he didn't suffocate.

Helen Sylvester, Rose School, north of Orleans, Richardville Township

A Sinking Feeling

One of the boys dashed out of the school to catch his ride home. It was spring so he had to cross the snow in the ditch to get across the road. He sank right into the snowbank and the suction held him there. No matter what he did, he couldn't get out. Finally the teacher came and pulled him out.

Glen Gunnarson, Garfield School, Tegner

Skinny Dippin'

In the spring the boys went skinny dippin' in the pond just kitty-corner from the school. They thought they had it made because they were sure the teacher wouldn't come for them. But she picked up their clothes and made them come out.

Lois Laude Peterson, school east of Kennedy

Ouch!

We had been sliding down a big snowbank off the school grounds where we were not supposed to be. The teacher told each of us to get a stick of wood from the entry and bring it to the front of the room. Then she made us sit on it, facing the other students. My stick was pointed at both ends. One boy brought a big chunk covered with snow that was split in half, so it was about six inches by twelve inches. The snow soon melted and ran down the aisles.

Another punishment was to carry wood from the woodshed into the entry. The teacher determined the number of sticks we had to carry by the seriousness of the rule which we had broken. She counted the number of sticks we carried as we passed the window and checked off our names listed on the blackboard. **Martha Poole Lindholm, District 45, Washington School near Kennedy**

Sopped

We had a contest in the late fall when the water was frozen on the top but still flexible. We crossed the "rubber ice" on the coulee back and forth until it weakened and someone broke through. Then, sopping wet, the kid sat in front of the stove to dry out.

Floyd Nelson, District 30, Dahlgren School, west of Kennedy.

Drippings

After drowning several ground squirrels, the boys pitched them through a broken window in the gable in the front of the school. One day when we came to school, we found maggots dripping from the ceiling. All the desks and most of the floor was covered with maggots. Our teacher, Olive Nelson, sent us girls out to play and made the boys clean up their maggot-filled squirrels in the attic and then clean the schoolroom. **Martha Lindholm Nelson, District 45, Washington School east of Kennedy**

Today it's my turn to be Country School Teacher!

Chapter 19

On Top of the World

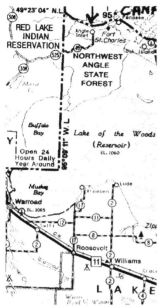

"Teacher Wanted: We have an immediate opening for a young, enthusiastic, and dedicated Country School Teacher. This teacher must be self-reliant and resilient in order to to cope with both the mundane and the extraordinary quirks of humanity and nature. This position will be especially rewarding to someone who seeks solitude and introspection. Salary and living conditions are average, but the beauty and unpredictable personality of Mother Nature are priceless. Starry nights, majestic forests, and wild animals make this position the envy of teachers trapped in urban turmoil."

This fictitious job description of the teaching positions at the Angle Inlet and Oak Island Schools tells only part of the truth. The advertisements fail to consider one inescapable truth: Mother Nature is schizophrenic and her mood swings are dramatic, even dangerous, in those two isolated spots forty miles from the border separating the United States and Minnesota from Canada. When she is isolated, she can be very fickle, working magic on the people she visits.

Although Helga Smith and Elsie Mason taught in this isolated outpost, their stories are very different. Helga, born in 1911 in Beltrami County, was twenty-one when she taught on Oak Island in 1931. Elsie Mason, born in 1914 near Pine River, was fifty-four when she taught on the Angle Inlet in 1970. Elsie had never been in a country school until her teachers training.

Helga Stebakken Smith

Helga Smith was born in 1911. She attended Carp School in Beltrami County from 1917-1925. She taught at the following schools in Lake of the Woods County from 1930-1936: Hay Creek, Oak Island, Dollarhide, and Germanson.

Helga and her twin sister were about a year old when fire devastated the area where they lived. Their parents took the babies down to the Rapid River in order to survive the ordeal.

Forest fire again interrupted her life when the fire of 1931 burned the Hay Creek School during her first teaching assignment. Then in the fall of 1931, she

Helga Smith, age 21

boarded a boat for Oak Island, east of the Northwest Angle. She taught there from 1931 to 1933.

Welcome!

The first day I went was the third of October and the weather was just beautiful. The lake was like glass. I got off at the Oak Island Store, and Ivan, the son of the family I was going to board with, came to meet me.

There was a bunch of guys there and later one of them told me Ivan said when I landed, "Well, I guess I'll have to go and face the music." He had an old touring car that was terrible. There was no top on the car and the roads were terrible. I bounced around. I thought I was going to fall out.

I had a friend who was teaching about eight miles from the Angle at American Point. This fellow had a saw mill at American Point and he paid the teachers. We used to get together. Sometimes we would walk to American Point from Oak Island for the weekend. That was eight miles across the ice. There was no road to the Angle as there is now. The only way we could get out of there was by boat or across the ice by car in the winter.

When we went to the island from Warroad, they had to put planks across the cracks in the ice because it was so risky. Sometimes they had car trouble out there on that lake. It was a cold, dangerous forty miles from Warroad to Oak Island.

The Seasons Just Go Round and Round

One day I was having language class, and we were studying the seasons. I asked this little boy, I think he was in the second grade, what the seasons of the year were. "Oh, yes," he said as he raised his hand, "I know—freeze-up season and hunting season and break-up season and fishing season. And, oh, yes, there's duck season."

In the spring during break-up season, we couldn't get any mail or anything for three weeks. I had no contact with anyone—no mail or telephone.

Seeing Red

Gangsters from Chicago sometimes used the Northwest Angle as a hideout. One of the most interesting of these visitors was Dakota Red. He appeared one day, wearing his .45 Colt. No one knew his true identity.

Certainly no one pried into his business. For a while Dakota Red volunteered as a cook at a fishery. He lived at the Northwest Angle for a few years until he headed for Arizona to make his fortune mining gold.

Dakota Red and Helga

Although it looks as if we knew each other very well, I didn't really know him. I met Dakota Red once at a friend's house. An Indian woman had given him a dress she had made to wear at pow-wows. Someone suggested I put it on and so I did. The frills on the dress were made of narrow strips of tobacco cans.

Crabby Teacher

One day I came home from school and Mrs. Earl, the lady I boarded with, said, "You better look in your room, especially in your bed. My husband, son, and hired man were in there before they left for Warroad with their load of fish." When I reached under the covers at the foot of my bed, something bit me. They had put a big crab in my bed. They found it when they lifted their fishing net. Another time they balanced a pile of pans and kettles against the door. When I came home from my date, they crashed to the floor. We made our own fun up there!

I've Been Shot!

I was boarding with this family. One night I was sitting at the table with Mrs. Earl, my landlady, stringing beads. The men had gone hunting deer—out of season, which they did all the time—and when they returned, they leaned the rifle against the door jam. Their eight-year-old son reached around to get a drink of water and knocked the gun to the floor, right into the dining room where we were sitting. Bam! The gun went off, shot me in the ankle, not with the bullet, but with the jacket of the bullet. The casing splintered and part of it hit me right in the ankle. It was one of those big bullets used for deer hunting. It was one of those bullets that had a copper jacket and that splintered.

I yelled, "Oh, my gosh, I've been shot!" Mrs. Earl was hit, too. There was a doctor nearby but he was an eye doctor. The men took the boat and got him anyway. All night long he took his jackknife and dug in that wound to get all the pieces of that jacket out because he was afraid I would get poisoned. I had to keep the wound open and keep it moist. At noon I had to put on new moist bandages.

Usually I had to walk a mile through the deep woods to get to my school, but obviously, I couldn't walk. So they took me over to Center Island, which had a resort, and I went by boat to teach every day.

Helga Smith taught on Oak Island from 1931 to 1933.

Helga Smith and friend, Oak Island, 1931

Elsie Mason

Elsie Mason attended Woman Lake School in Cass County from 1921 to 1927. She received preparation at an early age to become a Country School Teacher.

Home School

We played school all the time. There was no school until my folks built one on our property. Before I went to school, I knew the alphabet. I could read. I could count. I went through all the books in the school for the first three years in one year. From the time I was two years old, my sisters and brothers had been making me go to school. That's all we played at home. At age six I could read most of our books. They must have taught me phonics. They got after me until I could do it. **1921**

Diggin' the Teacher

Our teacher, Jesse Moffett, took it into her head one day that because it was real bad weather with a lot of snow, she could cut the distance from her home to school in half by walking across the lake and cutting across the bay. She got almost all the way across, but she couldn't climb up the bank. She sank into the snow drift, and we had to dig her out. She had wallowed around, trying to get out till she was buried to her hips. The more she fought, the deeper she settled.

We took our shovels and our sleds down the bank. We dug her out, pulled her out, rolled her onto a sled, and pulled her up to the schoolyard.   **c. 1925**

Bed Linen Curses

We had a German family that spoke rather broken English. They would get mad and accuse us of cheating, only they'd say, "You sheet!"

We got back at them by calling out to them "You pillowcase!" That was our big fight. "If we're sheet, then you're pillow case."   **c. 1925**

After graduation from high school, Elsie attended normal training at Pine River from 1931 to 1932.

1931: Teacher Training

At noon we studied in the room, but first we went down to the store and bought bags of salted peanuts for ten cents a pound. We just sat there, studying and eating peanuts. Our teacher came in and said,

"Oh, salted peanuts. They just nauseate me." We got kind of a kick out of it. Then we got to doing it more just to aggravate her. One day every one of the twelve of us had our sack of peanuts, and she walked in. She said, "When the cat's away, the mice will play."

I pulled out my sack of peanuts and said, "You want to play, too?" And she took some. When I first said that, I thought, "Whew, she'll clobber me good." She took some and never said anything about the odor of peanuts again.

Elsie attended Miltonvale Wesleyan Junior College and graduated with a bachelor's degree in theology. She then married a minister. Because Elsie was also an ordained minister, she became the pastor of a church. When her husband was seriously injured in a car accident, the main responsibility for earning a living fell on her. She decided to use her teaching degree.

At the age of fifty-four and burdened with her husband's doctor bills, Elsie signed a contract to teach in the Angle Inlet School for $6,800. For the next three years Elsie stayed in a teacherage, a small, one-bedroom home next to the school while her husband cared for their ill son in California. Unfortunately, Elsie's husband died during her second year of teaching.

Success

K. was supposed to be in the second grade. He had been in kindergarten two years and first grade for two years. He was older than the others, and his baby brother was coming to school with him. But poor K. could not do any school work. Oh, the agony of watching that boy! He just couldn't read or write. He would contort his face in pain and turn and twist his body in anger and frustration. I stressed phonics and I sat with my back against the board, so I could write the words. When he came to a word he didn't know, I wrote it phonetically and told K. and the other students the phonics rules—the simple rules.

Elsie Mason, 1970

One day I took them out to see the steamer, the *Bert Steele*, which came from Warroad with the mail. We went on the launch for a field trip. Bert, the owner of the boat, told them stories, and K. was just thrilled. It was a beautiful trip out on Lake of the Woods. Then the students wrote a story. I was so proud of that kid. What an improvement!

Two years before, he was supposed to write a story about a picture of a boy on a pony. Below the picture he had written LLMPGLLGKETDMZOFL. The letters just didn't make any sense. Down at the bottom he had written ITMESASOMD. I finally figured out what he was saying: "It makes me so mad." He was so frustrated because he could not write or spell a word.

This paper was quite an improvement for a boy who could only write LLMPGLLGKETDMZOFL.

After we had worked with phonics on a first-grade level for six weeks, I noticed that when he read, he looked up at the board. He saw the way I had written the words phonetically. Then he said the word. Pretty soon he abandoned the board and read by himself, sounding out each word.

One day the principal came out and watched me teach for the entire day. She came on a Friday when we were reading stories. K. got up in front of the entire school, and he read slowly and deliberately just—like—this—all—the—way—through—the—story. He figured out every word.

It wasn't a beautiful reading, very monotone, but he was reading. Afterward the principal said, "What did you do to that child? He can read." When they took him into town school in the middle of the year, the school put him in the average group.

Even at the top of the state, politics, bias, differing educational philosophies, jealousy, vindictiveness, and all the demons that confront teachers anywhere sprang out of the North Woods. Elsie also experienced these frustrations.

K.'s younger brother C. was a capable student, but he was a handful, a real challenge. Every one thought that he was "cute." Elsie walked a tight rope, trying to challenge and protect K.'s self-image and at the same time teach and discipline his younger brother.

A Stinky Deal

The family moved because the younger brother was a little stinker. Because he was younger and a capable student, I never let him give any answers to K. to keep him from making K. feel small. But every time C. was stumbling, I let K. tell him if he could, just to build up K.'s self-esteem. It was impossible to damage C.'s ego. His nickname was Fragrant. Sometimes he came to school with his clothes dirty. The next week he'd come to school with his clothes turned inside out. He wet the bed, dried out the clothes, and wore them to school. Ugh! That's why they nicknamed him Fragrant.

But the other kids put him up to all sorts of things. One day he would not stay in his seat. He would not be quiet. He would not do anything. They had evidently come to school with the plan to "keep something going." He knocked books off his desk or somebody else's desk. He switched his desk around. Every time I walked by, he went "Puuuuuut! Puuuuuut!" I couldn't get him to stop. He just jumped around and hopped his desk around.

Well, I tied him in his seat. Then he bumped it and banged it around until finally I had his older brother take him home. The parents kept the two home for the rest of the day, and the next day they kept all five kids at home. Then the whole family moved. They never said anything about it. But that was about half the school.

Although the school board was pressured by two influential families to maintain the tradition of keeping a teacher for only two years, they hired me for a third term and again offered me a contract for a fourth year. They signed the contract and all I had to do was sign it as well. By this time I had paid my bills. I drove to the board meeting and told them I had decided it was time to move on. I asked if I could keep the contract. They said, "Why?"

"Just to prove that I could have if I wanted to."

At age fifty-seven, Elsie Mason left the Angle Inlet the same way she had arrived. She climbed into her trusty car and fought the slimy roads and deep ruts to find a new life.

Chapter 20

Four Student Storytellers

When I began my journey to tell Country School Teacher's story, I did not intend to tell Country School Students' stories as well. However, everywhere I met Country School Teachers I also met the students who were the centers of the teachers' lives. Students, too, said, "Hey, what about us? We have a story to tell also. Listen to this one. One time...."

Describing Country School Teachers is considerably easier than describing Country School Students. Telling Country School Students' stories is like throwing a rock in a still pond and then trying to grab the ripples and hold them.

Sometimes students speak reverently about cherished teachers or deceased classmates. They laugh about shenanigans kept secret for decades. Many pontificate with absolutely unflappable certainty about what's wrong with education today. "Kids minded their teachers and parents in those days. Country School Students in those days got a 'real' education. There was no fooling around back then, I can tell you. Country School Students were more ethical and more moral. Child psychology was simple."

How different were Country School Students from today's children? If you can catch the ripples, you can answer those questions easily by reading their stories.

Cecile Du Frene Cowdery

Cecile was born on May 17, 1909, the seventh of thirteen children. In addition, Cecile's parents took in another thirty-nine children over the years, including a fifteen-year-old girl from the Orphan Train.

Cecile attended District 1 near Long Prairie in Todd County from 1915 to 1921. She excelled in all her classes and won every art award until she told the teacher she wasn't entering any more contests. "It didn't seem right that I should be awarded for what came so easily to me and so hard to others."

In the 1970s, Jackie Cowdery, Cecile's granddaughter, was a student in my honors English class. Twenty-two years later Jackie and I sat at her grandmother kitchen table and listened to Cecile's stories. At the same time she peeled the meat off a boiled chicken for chow mein and laid out a spread with all the fixin's.

The Play's the Thing!
My mother had great instinct. She was a very unusual person. She taught at Osakis and wrote plays for her students. Mother wrote original plays for the school or bought plays from Dennison. She made all the costumes for us. The school was the center of the universe. The people from Long Prairie came as well as all the farm people.

Cecile Du Frene, age six, upper right, 1915

Word spread and the people from Eagle Bend asked if we would put a play on there. At first the actors were all school children. Then if she wrote a play that had old people in it, someone from the community played that part. We took those plays to other towns and charged each person ten cents. Dad took the lumber wagon full of people. Some of the roads were corduroy—logs laid across the road and filled with dirt. All twelve or fifteen kids would say, "Ahaaaa, haaaa, ahaaaaa, haaaaa" as those wagon wheels bumped over the logs. What fun we had! However, the noise was awful. I don't know how my dad stood that racket. Mile after mile of that.

The plays were often about the South because Mother wanted to have roles for all those gentlemen and gentlewomen in them. I played Topsy in one and Suzanna in another. All the money went to buying things for the school.

Mom cast characters to teach a particular child something, to develop some skill or aspect of the child's personality. If she could enhance one skill, it helped not only the child but also the whole family.

For example, we had a German family. They knitted all the time in school. They studied their lessons with the book open on their desks and those needles just flew under the desks. They knitted all the caps, scarves, mittens, and stockings for the eleven children in that family.

They could knit, but they couldn't pronounce English words properly. Mom knew this would hold them back, so she wrote parts for them in the plays. She would help them pronounce the words correctly as they practiced. All those children learned English by participating in those plays, and they really enjoyed learning by acting in the plays.

She tried to include parts for everyone because what were the other kids going to do but watch in envy? Sometimes she wrote small plays which we could put on during recess when the weather was bad. She was never paid for this. Most teachers welcomed Mom's help. We did have one man teacher who never used plays or anything Mom used. Whether he was incapable of it or it was a woman treading on his private property, I don't know. He just did what he was hired to do. Other teachers welcomed her help, but he seemed to resent it.

Better Have Him Checked!
The man teacher who wouldn't accept any help from Mom or use her plays took delight in telling her that my younger brother was not very bright. He told Mom that he colored everything brown and didn't know any better.

The teacher said, "I think you ought to have him examined." Mom said she would see what the problem was. She was gentle and always took the roundabout way of finding out things. She said, "Your teacher seems to think you don't know your colors because you color everything brown."

He said, "Well, Mom, by the time they get to me, brown is all that's left." The teacher really thought he "had something" on Mom. She could have poked fun at him because whenever he had some free time while the kids worked, he spent his time tatting lace for handkerchiefs and crocheting doilies. But Mom wouldn't make fun of him.

c. 1917, District 1, Todd County

Mother Magic
One day a nine-year-old boy was running from the school building onto the porch, and he tripped and fell. He was carrying a pencil that didn't have an eraser. When he fell, his mouth flew open like it does if you are going to scream. The metal part cut a cookie right out of the roof of his mouth. He bled terribly. We lived a quarter of a mile from the school so the teacher carried him to our house so Mom could do what she could for him.

Our home was the place everybody ran to because both Mom and Dad were very quick witted. We had thirteen in our family, so they had to know what to do. For example, Dad was scything the grass around the chicken coop and my sister fell and the scythe cut off her finger. Mom grabbed the end of the finger, ran into the hen house, and grabbed an egg. She took the skin inside of the egg and wrapped it around the reattached finger. My sister's finger grew back beautifully.   **1917**

Spell "Hormones"
In the spring of 1918, our regular teacher got the mumps. We had a substitute. I'll call "Leggy." We were having a spelldown at the Little Fox School. The teacher marched up and down the aisles, giving the words, which was not what we were used to. Then she stopped at the boys' desks and put her foot up on the seat and showed that leg. She gave them as good a look as they could possibly get. Then she always gave them a really easy word. Of course, they always got it right.

Ingenuity
At that time the girls all wore corsets. That was so smart. One girl who lived south of us past the woods was very poor. She sewed pieces of cardboard together with binder twine and wore it to school. When we were in the outhouse, she showed it to us. I felt pity for someone who was denied the simplest thing that everyone else had. People told me things they wouldn't tell others because they knew I cared and wouldn't ridicule them. It was sad, but I was proud that she had the ingenuity.   **1918**

Unforgiving
Our teacher urged us to buy war bonds, so we brought small amounts of money to school and bought $.25 stamps, which we licked and pasted in our small books. When we filled a book, it was

taken to the Little Sauk State Bank. Eventually they were converted into bonds. At the end of the war, the banker absconded with his bank's total assets. Dad wrote to him in prison and told him he was a good man gone wrong. He never repaid us, so we kids weren't quite so gracious as Dad.   **1918**

X-ray

The biggest privilege in the school was to ring the school bell. We had a big bell with a rope that hung down into the vestibule. Of course, only one person could ring it at a time. I wanted to ring that bell so badly, but the teacher wasn't sure I was big enough to pull the rope. That rope had a lot of power and that's why I wanted to ring it. I saw one of the big boys ring it, and when his arm went up, the rope pulled him a long way. I knew if I grasped the rope as high as I could reach, it would lift me right up as the bell turned over and it would be like flying. I hung on with both hands, and that bell pulled me right off the ground several feet into the air. Then Henry, who was such a pest, bent over and peeked at my

Cecile Du Frene Cowdery, age seven, 1917, and her nemesis, Henry

bloomers and hollered "X-ray, X-ray!" I let go of the rope and let the bell go on its own. Mother had just made me those bloomers out of X-ray flower sacks. "X-ray" was written right on the seat of my pants. Those darn letters were on so tight you could not bleach them out. Whenever one of the boys said, "X-ray," I knew Henry had snitched.

Playing "Home"

There were heavy, deep woods south and west of the school. The kids built shacks with downed lumber and cardboard boxes. If the weather was nice, then the seventh and eighth graders played in the woods. If the parents and the teachers had ever known what went on in those shacks in that woods, they would have killed the whole batch.

They played "doctor" and "home." They had intercourse. They were playing husband and wife. They were doing what they saw at home. They didn't know any better. Those that were abused by their fathers didn't know it didn't happen in every family. It's the way things were.

Nobody paid any attention to what was done in the woods. The teachers never checked. I'm not sure why. The teachers ate lunch. I imagine they were sick of kids and they relished every moment they were without kids.

We were French, and I thought it was those German, Norwegian, and Swedish kids who were different than us. We didn't go into the woods or play with them. Those were the big kids' games. They never let us get near them.   **1915–1921**

Talking Phone Poles

We always felt a little left out because we were French. The other kids talked to each other in German, Norwegian, and Swedish and we couldn't understand a word of it.

About that time the telephones came. Dad got an extra job putting in poles and stringing the lines in our area. We discovered if we laid an ear against the pole in cold weather, we could hear all kinds of weird things, humming and clicking, and all sorts of strange, mumbling noises.

One day my sister Franny and I stood on each side of the telephone pole near the school. We jabbered in nonsense language. The kids looked at us to see what we were doing. We kept up this jabbering, and they were completely baffled.

They asked, "What is it? What's happening?"

"No, no, we can't tell ya. We're not supposed to tell ya," we said.

We let them worry and wonder for a day or two. Then we said, "You listen."

"Ya, but what is it?" they asked. Then Franny and I would jabber and jabber.

"But what is it?"

À LA TOUCHE LA LAVEC
FOUCHE
EAU DE COLOGNE
C'EST LA GUERRE
COUPE DE GRAS
VIVA LA FRANCE
MONSIEUR
CAFE AU LAIT

"We aren't supposed to tell, but it's the people in Paris giving us the war news. Our French Dad has been hired to help the government during the war, and they are sending him war messages in French. We can understand it, but we aren't allowed to tell." We kept that up for two years. They never figured it out what we were listening to.   **1917–1918**

Graduation Gala

I graduated from country school when I completed the sixth grade at age twelve. The teacher asked me if I would like to take the examinations with the eighth grade. I came out with the highest score and they didn't know what to do about that. So the state sent out another examination and I took it in the court house in the superintendent's office.

Mom let me choose the material for my graduation dress, pale blue batiste at eight cents a yard. The dress required one and a half yards. We bought three yards of lace at ten cents a yard and a four-cent spool of thread. With hours of mom's work, the dress cost $.46 and my slippers cost $.49.

Mom and Dad drove me eight miles to Long Prairie in the surrey. After the ceremony they took me to Dodd's Ice Cream Parlor, where I ate two scoops of ice cream from a fancy glass dish while Mom and Dad had one scoop. My mind automatically went into gear. At five cents per scoop, that would have been the equivalent of four dozen eggs. But we had our own chickens and Mom and Dad sold eggs, so what the heck. What a wonderful day for me and my parents!   **1921**

Too Soon

I started high school and went for one year. It was hell. I was neither pup nor dog. I didn't belong anywhere. Country kids were not accepted by the town kids, especially me. I had to come eight miles to school.

The town kids thought we were dumb and stupid no matter how old we were. Some of them may have been resentful that a twelve-year-old made them look dumb. I was very timid. They called me "country bumpkin," "cow," and "pig," any animal's name. The girls were always meaner than the boys. The girls picked on me by doing something like shooting spitballs and then telling the teacher I had done it. The girls pointed their fingers at me. The teacher sent me out in the hall. Those big boys who had done something were also sent out into the hall. We'd sit there and they'd tease me. They were having fun, but someone would tell the teacher I was fooling around in the hall.

Some of those boys were twenty-two years old. I was like a teddy bear to them. They felt bad that I

Hi, I'm Cecile. I'm in the first grade and I can read. Can you read? My sister's name is Merry Christmas. What's your name? I like to draw. I know my a, b, c's. My mother writes plays. Can you act? We have a big family. Someday I'm going to draw pictures.

173

was getting teased. The more attention I received, the angrier the girls got because those guys were their boyfriends. They were looking out for their own property. I suppose those girls were jealous. I was not the proper age to be accepted anywhere. Mom allowed me to stay out a year and go with my own age group. That year Mother taught us about the stars. She was a silver medalist in elocution, so she taught us all speaking skills. It was a very rich year. She was a seamstress and a musician. She was a midwife and I helped her that year. Throughout my life I have delivered babies, too. It was much easier to go back when I did. **1921–1922**

From the time Cecile could hold a pencil or crayon, she drew on anything she could find.
In art class I won every contest until I was ashamed to compete. It wasn't fair that something so easy for me should be compared with some kid's struggle to succeed. My sixth-grade teacher excused me from regular art work and brought beautiful art paper and paid me to make personal cards for her.

Cecile did not flatter Der Fuhrer. Permission granted to reproduce Cecile's envelope by USM Publishing, Lakeville.

Envelope Art
During World War II Cecile's husband was drafted and stationed in California. Cecile wrote to him, illustrating her envelopes to show her husband that she loved him and missed him. Her son published these letters in *World War II Envelope Art*, and her granddaughter Jackie presented the book to President Clinton aboard the *U.S.S. George Washington* during a celebration to commemorate the 50th anniversary of World War II.

Jerrold Ellis
Jerrold Ellis is an eighty-nine-year-old poet and storyteller. In 1975 he published a collection of poems called *Written Thoughts*. In the introduction Jerrold says, "I have enjoyed poetry ever since I was a child. I loved the old poets like Longfellow, Holmes, Whittier, and Lowell."

Jerrold often recites his favorite poems on his daily walks. In the middle of one of his stories, he stopped, looked me in the eyes, and then recited one of the many poems tucked away in his memory.

The leprechauns live by the hundreds in his spirit. As he tells and retells stories of his youth, he can't control his impish laughter. He tells each story as if he just remembered what had happened over seventy-five years ago.

The first poem in Jerrold's book is "Words." The last stanza reads

> There are words of comfort, anger and hate,
> But the saddest words I recall
> Are the kind words someone waited for
> And they were never spoken at all.

Jerrold began school in 1916. He went to First Oak Lawn for a year. He then moved to South Long Lake, then to a school near Brainerd. He graduated from a school near Pine River in 1926.

> The Old Country School
> Most country schools have long disappeared,
> But one remains with us still.
> It stands on the fairgrounds just out of town,
> And we pray it always will.
>
> Once it stood by the road at South Long Lake.
> It was the township's pride and joy.
> Generations of children entered the doors
> Of the school where I went as a boy.
>
> The teachers were many who taught at school.
> We learned our letters by sound.
> I remember the fun at recess
> As we played on the old school ground.
>
> A basket social was held every year
> To buy candy for each boy and girl.
> The Christmas program we practiced for weeks.
> Left our minds in a whirl.

The Christmas program was always held
In spite of the wintry weather.
Each of us had to speak a piece
Though our knees were knocking together.

Each year we had a school picnic
With a dinner and homemade ice cream.
Sometimes I wonder was I really there,
Or was it just a dream.

Now I think of these bygone years,
The years of the Golden Rule.
It makes me proud to be one of the crowd
Who attended that Old Country School.

Jerrold Ellis, age seven, front, second from left, 1917, District 3: Jerrold seems to be distracted by events in outer space!

People who know Jerrold Ellis would knight him "Giver of Words, Giver of Joy." Perhaps when you are out walking in Brainerd, Jerrold will pass you reciting Longfellow, Poe, or Lowell.

A Geography Lesson
I have many happy memories of those childhood days. We sometimes had two and a half miles to walk to school, but we had fun on the way. We left home early and joined the neighbor children on the way. Sometimes there were nine or ten of us. One time on the way home I was teasing one of the older girls, and she hit me on the head with her geography book. I had wholesome respect for her after that.

History Whiz
I was never too good at spelling or arithmetic, but I loved history and geography. One day when I was in sixth grade, the teacher gave us two pages of history to study for the next day. I took my history book home and stayed awake for hours memorizing both pages. The next day when the teacher called our class to the front of the room, she called on me first. I recited both pages from memory. When I got done, she said, "Sit down, Daniel Webster."

I Never Said a Word!
My teacher is now ninety some years old, and her memory is gone. When I had her for a teacher, I was six or seven years old. At recess time the older boys were settin' there talkin'—we had double seats—and this one boy had on just his rubbers and wool socks, and when I run by 'im, I grabbed one of his rubbers and run outside.

Him and another guy chased me and caught me. They were gonna take my pants off. One of the girls run in and told the teacher. Her name was Meg, and she come rushin' out there, and she got them in there, and oh, man—they had busted the button off of my pants—and she took their hands and hit 'em with a ruler.

Then she made 'em sew that button back on, and they had to stay after school three or four nights. But she never did know what I done. I never said anything. But when she described what had happened, she said, "Some of the older boys was being mean to Jerry. This girl come in and told me," so she went and got 'em, but she said, "I made 'em sew that button back on," and she went on and on. I thought it was so funny because she didn't know that I had done anything. She was quite a girl.

Jerrold has always been a teller of tales, some considerably more colorful than others. He loved retelling nursery ryhmes and fairy tales.

Not According to Jerrold
My nephew went to the same country school I did. When he was little and started school, I told him crazy stories. I told him nursery rhymes and changed them around. I taught him the "Little Red Riding Hood" story: Her and her mother were eating peaches and they couldn't eat it all, and she said, "Throw it in that bag and take it to your grand-mother. She'll eat anything." The first day he went to country school, the teacher read about Little Red Riding Hood. When she got done, he jumped up and said, " That ain't what my Uncle Jerrold said!"

I seen her afterward uptown and she said, "What do you tell them kids?"

A Strange Bird

My younger brother never learned to spell. One day he was mad at one of the little boys so he wrote him a note. He wanted to call him a "damn fool," but he spelled it "dame fowl." This kid brought the note over to me and asked, "What's a 'dame fowl'?"

I said, "I don't know, but that's what you are." I thought afterward it was a good thing that he spelled it that way. If the teacher got a hold of it....

My brother was twenty years in the Marine Corps, and when he'd write us a letter, we really had to figure it out. He just couldn't spell.

It's Who You Know

I just loved writing stories, but I had my brother read them 'cuz I couldn't read them without laughing 'cuz I had this crazy stuff in them. The teacher'd scold me about them, but she had us writing them every day and that was out of the ordinary, so I think she kinda liked them. She made it sound like she didn't, but I think she enjoyed them.

She had kept a lot of them, and she said, "I'm going to give them to the superintendent, Mrs. Hartley, and then you'll find out. Well, my mother knew Mrs. Hartley. She came one day, and I was settin' there next to the aisle. She knew me 'cuz she came to our place. So she sat down and said, "How is your mother?" Well, the teacher was surprised! After Mrs. Hartley had left, I went up by the teacher's desk. She pulled out this drawer, and I said, "Oh, there's all them stories. I thought you were going to give them to Mrs. Hartley."

"Never mind!" she said.

Ya, she was a good teacher.

Safari with Friends

Our teacher was goin' with a guy named Henry Fleshhogger. We thought that was a funny name so we put it in a story: I and my brother were over in the jungles of Africa hunting tigers and we finally captured one. We skinned him and we made some leather shoestrings and sent them to my mother for Christmas.

As we were walking out of the jungle, who should we meet but my good friend and companion, Henry Fleshhogger.

Then she got up and said, "Don't use people's names." I suppose I was in the third grade when I started writing those stories.

My Charlie Chaplin Routine

We had an outside toilet, and you raised your hand to go out. So I went out there. We all wore bib overalls. I let out my suspenders, so my pants hung way down low. Then I put my shoes on the wrong feet. Then I came in. She was busy up in front with the little ones so I sat down real quiet, but the kids were all laughing.

She turned and said, "What did you do?"

I said, "I didn't do nothin'," so she went off. I was gonna change them, and then she called our class and I had to get up in front of the room.

She said, "Jerrold, you've got your shoes on the wrong feet."

I looked down. "Oh, I have?" She didn't say anything about my pants.

But then three guys come in that was on the school board, and she got so nervous she didn't know what to do. So she set a big box in front of my feet. I had to stand there all the time while she was talking to them. She never said anything to me about it later.

You Promised

Our teacher was deathly scared of mice. She said, "You know, if I saw a mouse, I'd faint." So my brother found a field mouse outside in the woods, and he come in and she let a yell out of her, and he said, "Oh, I thought you were gonna faint."

Jerrold, second row left, his hair combed over his eye, is in constant motion. He's "hamming it up" for the camera and tormenting a first grader. Jerrold's brother Lyell, his hair parted down the middle, is sitting in front of the teacher. This picture was taken in 1925 when Jerrold was in grade eight.

Christmas Stuffing

We had an awful lot of fun when we were practicing for the Christmas program. The teacher had all those little kids to take care of, so she told us older ones, "You can help me now to get them ready for the program."

This one little guy had a wonderful memory, but he was a little skinny. He was supposed to be a little fat boy, so she had given me a bunch of stuff and he had a slipover sweater. "Now you make him look heavier," she said. So I took him back there and I kept stuffin' stuff in 'im.

He said, "I think that's too much."

"No," I said, "she wants you fat." I kept stuffin' more and more stuff in 'im.

Then she called him to come out. He didn't want to go so I gave him a little push. Well, he fell down and he couldn't get up. He just kept rockin' back and forth on that huge soft belly.

Oh, my, she was mad! Then she come—but I thought afterwards when I grew up—that sweater, sweaters were cheap, you know, that sweater was hangin' down to the kid's knees. I bet his mother liked that.

My Christmas Poem

The teacher said to my brother and I and them other big boys, "You guys just find a nice poem to recite." So we did. I think the one I learned was "Dangerous Dan McGrew"—not a very appropriate poem for Christmas. I remember all them older guys—Pete Johnson and all of them—were settin' in the front and they laughed until they cried 'cuz it took me quite a while, ya know, and she was behind the curtain shakin' her fist at me. Old Pete Johnson said that was the best part of the program.

Gertrude Linnell

Gertrude Linnell attended District 2, Birchwood School, Cook County, from 1921 to 1928.

My grandparents came to the northeastern corner of Minnesota and established a little town called Mineral Center about 1909. Mineral Center is about six miles from the Canadian border and six miles from the Grand Portage Indian Reservation. One of the men was certain the land was rich in minerals. They would all become rich as they developed this mineral industry. They built a school as the families moved in. My mother was the very first school-teacher in this new town. She taught some of her brothers and sisters. This was the school I went to for seven years.

Smoke Gets in Your Eyes

Things were a little boring in school, so the mischievous boys thought it was time for a day off. Very early before daylight, they stuffed gunnysacks into the chimney. The teacher started the stove and smoke poured into the school. She was frantic because she thought the building was on fire. So she dismissed us and we were sent home.   **1922**

The Worst Boy in School

Arnold was the most mischievous boy in school. He always wrestled with the goat. In those days if a boy liked a little girl, he never went about telling her. He just pestered her. He was as mean as he could be to the little gal that was the "apple of his eye." I came home in tears many times. If I was swinging, he gave me an extra hard swing that almost sent me over the top of the bar. He called me names like "Sweetie Pie." I came home crying one day when my grandma was at my house. I told her the story of Arnold's behavior. "Huh," she said, "you'll marry him some day." If I would have dared sass my grandma in those days, she would have heard a thing or two. He would have been the last man I would marry. Of course, later I married him.

c. 1925, District 2, Birchwood School, Cook County

Still Bad

We had a male teacher who wasn't beyond whipping the students. He loved to lace you good and proper with a switch, which grew in the back of the school. Part of our punishment was to go out and get our own willow switch, which really laced you around the legs. How that stung!

One day Arnold did some heinous thing which merited this type of punishment. The teacher looked over the top of his glasses and said, "All right, Arnold, you go out and get yourself a switch so I can punish you." Arnold went out and came back with the sorriest looking scrubby branch that ever there was.

The teacher took one whack at the floor and the switch was so rotten it fell into a million pieces. Then he said, "This won't do. Get me a real switch."

"This is the sorriest looking branch that ever there was!"

I think Arnold made about three trips before he came back with a satisfactory willow switch. The teacher was a very serious man, but I think even he could see the humor in the situation. Then he took Arnold out to the entryway to give him his switching. Of course, Arnold made the loudest noises as if he were being murdered.

After completing teachers training, Gertrude returned to Birchwood and taught there from 1935 to 1937.

The Town That Was, Isn't

Times were very tough in 1934 and I considered myself very lucky to be able to go back to that little school to teach. I was teaching there when the government decided to enlarge the reservation. They bought up the property of the people who lived in Mineral Center and added it to the Grand Portage Indian Reservation. This happened in 1937. I was the last teacher. **Gertrude Linnell taught for thirty-four years. Mineral Center can be found on very detailed Minnesota maps.**

John Otis

John Otis' paternal grandfather settled on the shores of Sissebakwet Lake. Four generations of the Otis family have found peace and solitude on the lake. From 1936 to 1942, John and his twin sister Jane attended the "new" Sugar Lake School, located southwest of Grand Rapids.

Private Chauffeur

My father was a "flying nut." We had a golf course and a potato field in the 1920s. When my father got the flying bug, he plowed up this land and made an airport out of it. We were too poor to have an airplane, but he did buy a hanger. He would hanger these planes in exchange for flight lessons. He offered anyone who landed on his airfield a fried chicken dinner. In 1938, Babe Allsworth, a barnstormer from Fairmont, came to Grand Rapids. He had a 40-horse Piper Cub tandem. We hangered the plane for him in the winter and he gave my father flying lessons down on the lake. Of course, forty horse-power isn't much to get two people off of the lake with all the ice and snow.

Sugar Lake School was about a mile from our place. One day Babe said, "I'll go over there and pick them up." There was a potato field next to the schoolhouse where he could land. So Babe flew over the field with this little Cub on the skis. He landed, put my sister and me in the front seat, lifted us out of the snow, and flew us home.

Barn-stormer Babe Allsworth chauffeurs the Otis twins, Jane and John, home to Sissebakwet.

My dad thought that was really something. Because he was a publicity hound with a circus orientation, he enlarged upon this event in 1941.

We didn't have an airplane so he got Miller Wittig from Hibbing to fly over our school with a three-place Piper Cub with skis. Then he got a photographer from the Minneapolis *Tribune* to come up. Miller put us in the airplane and we flew over to the school again. The photographer drove over.

We had ten kids in the school at that time. Somehow my father got the teacher to turn all ten kids out of school to help push the plane down the gravel road and into the front yard of the school. The photographer took a picture of all ten kids in front of the airplane with my sister and I being handed our lunch buckets by the pilot.

On February 23, 1941, in the rotogravure section of the *Tribune*, here was this big spread about the Otis twins flying to our rural school. The caption said, "Big Blizzards Come but It Doesn't Bother the Otis Twins. They Just Have Their Pilot Roll Out Their Airplane and He Flies Them to School." That really stunned us because we were "dirt poor." The reader was led to believe we had our own pilot just waiting for a blizzard to come along so he could fly us to school.

From that time on, whenever a plane came along on skis or on wheels, my dad said, "Could you go over and pick the kids up at school?" A few times he would have the pilot taxi down the road and through the gate. Then the kids poured out of the school and he'd get some more photos.

My dad convinced those pilots to land at the school periodically until 1942, when the school closed. So the Otis twins would be flown the one mile to school by "their pilot" in "their airplane."

John Otis taught a variety of literature and writing courses at Mankato State University from 1963 to 1991. Retired, he now spends his summers at Sissebakwet Lake, reading, writing, and enjoying life without correcting student compositions.

Mary Heinen Plumier
One late fall morning I went in search of Mary Plumier. I turned off the blacktop road connecting Milaca and Foreston and headed north on a sloppy, greasy gravel road. After slipping and sliding for a few miles, I pulled into Mary Plumier's home and studio. Mary is an artist for all seasons. She is a storyteller, writer, and painter. She creates with a feverish passion. Tacked to her studio walls are paintings of the country schools in her area. Next to the unfinished sketches lying on her

Mary Plumier, c. 1961,

drawing table are books and memorabilia detailing the history of Benton County.

In 1961, Mary Heinen Plumier, a three-foot, eight-inch, forty-pound bundle of energy dressed in her red plaid, pleated skirt and white blouse, joined her seven sisters and three brothers on the half-mile walk to Wildwood School in Benton County. The only fear she had about going to school was the bear that had been sighted a mile or so from her farm.

Made with Love
Everyone brought their lunch to school. Metal syrup pails were often used and perhaps even some of my family used them. However, my lunch pail had once contained lard! I can still see that lovely yellow bucket with the fat red pig on it.

On the day before school I saw my dad in the milk house. He stood by our metal cooler. I was too short to see him working on top of the cooler. He had my yellow lunch bucket. He took off the metal cover. With his hammer and a nail, he punched a series of holes in the lid, writing out MARY. When he showed me my name, I was filled with awe at how neatly it was written. This memory fills me with love.   **1961**

Peek!
Once a month the Mothers Club met at school. Often times our mothers would have us compete for prizes. I still feel guilty about that October Mothers Club meeting. Mrs. Bauer blindfolded me and her daughter, my only classmate. She then instructed us to draw a pumpkin on the sheet of paper she had placed on our desks.

The competition between her daughter and me and between our families—they had thirteen children and we had ten—was just too great for me. I really wanted to win! So I cheated. The teacher hadn't put the blindfold on tight enough or something because I could see my pumpkin. My pumpkin drawing sure looked good. Maybe a little too good!

I might not have felt quite so bad about this pumpkin incident if Mrs. Bauer hadn't asked me if I peeked, and then I lied to her on top of all my sins. At that time I rationalized that it was her fault for not putting the blindfold on me properly.

Today, thirty years later, I now believe that she

must have known that I was lying to her because she had thirteen kids of her own. When I won the Halloween treats that day, they sure didn't seem to taste quite as good as they should have. I had a stomach ache all afternoon.

Red Jacket Surprise

Every morning we filled the water crock by pumping the water from the well outside the school. One morning when we were pumping the water an enormous yellow and black-striped garter snake came streaming out of the pump instead of the expected cool, clear water.

That pump spout must have been warmed up like a rock for the snake to slither up and crawl into it as the night's coolness settled in.

We were so startled by the snake's aggressiveness that we scattered away, screaming so loudly that the teacher came running out of the school. We finally chased the snake off our playground. ("The Red Jacket" was the name given to the hand pumps used at the country schools.)

Mary and her brothers and sisters believed in the old adage, "The early bird gets the worm." Since they also liked school, getting to their favorite place early in the morning seemed to be a wonderful idea. They soon discovered that "letting one's hair down" has more than one meaning!

She Let Her Hair Down

Wildwood School was one large rectangular room with a small entryway. Off to one side was a small room for the teacher to sleep in. Our teacher, Mrs. H., was an elderly woman. She slept in that little room all week and went home only on the weekends. She always wore her long brown hair very tidily rolled up into a bun on the top of her head. She used lots of bobby pins so there was never a hair out of place.

One morning my brothers and sisters and I arrived much earlier than usual. We always came to school early, but for some reason that day we were very early, too early.

When we caught Mrs. H. unprepared, she screamed at us for arriving too early. Her red, angry face scared me. She screamed, "Your parents don't know how to raise you properly! Never arrive early again." We never did.

Siesta

Mrs. H. could be a very grumpy old lady, and she certainly had little compassion for us noisy kids. One day we were playing on the slide. One of the girls, S., was carelessly throwing a chunk of concrete around the playground. My older sister, being protective of the younger kids, grabbed the chunk from S. as she was going down the slide. My sister threw the chunk away. Unfortunately, S. found another, slightly smaller, chunk of concrete and chased my sister.

My sister tried to run into the school to alert the teacher, but she became a trapped target for S. between the outside door and the locked inside door. Mrs. H. was sleeping in her little room and didn't want to be disturbed. S. hit my sister in the forehead with the chunk of concrete. She was quickly covered with blood that spattered her favorite dress and tee shirt. S. felt terrible and she and my sister were both crying.

The teacher, who had to give up her nap, seemed more concerned about the work involved in cleaning up the mess in the entryway than she was about my poor sister. None of this would have happened if the schoolhouse door had not been locked for Mrs. H.'s nap. But because of Mrs. H.'s naps, we often extended our recess time. If we played very quietly, we extended it by many minutes.

The Cherished Gift

At Christmas we exchanged gifts. One year the shabbiest dressed, poorest boy in the school got my name. His father had died very young of a heart attack. As a kid in a family with ten kids, I was drawing on the back of junk mail because we never had enough paper.

How I cherished his gift of an 8½-by-11-inch chalk blackboard, a red sponge eraser, and a little box of chalk. He gave me the opportunity to draw hundreds of pictures. I'll never forget him or his wonderful gift. It is the only present I can remember receiving. It was the best present anyone could have given me. The fact that he knew how much the present would mean to me says a lot about him.

If you drop in to visit Mary in her studio on 140th Avenue in rural Milaca, you will find her drawing and writing with passion. Decorating her walls are wonderful, detailed drawings of country schools, especially her beloved Wildwood.

Chapter 21

We Never Missed

No matter what degree or clime,
To school we made it every time,
Bundled up with little exposed,
Just our eyes and runny nose.

Dressed in long johns, a wooly itch,
We faced the cold, an' drifted ditch.
If Dad thought we'd lose our way,
He brought the horse and runnered sleigh.

Snuggled 'neath blankets 'n' woolen
    frocks,
We warmed our feet on heated rocks.
But mostly those chilly miles we'd walk
An' pass the time with teasing talk.

We didn't know nothin' about wind chill,
As we bucked the blasts across our hill.
Many a time we almost froze,
Saved at last by a blazing stove.

Through rain, tornado, or clouds of dust,
'Bout nasty weather we never fussed.
We knew the teacher was waitin' at
    school,
With readin', writin', and the Golden Rule.
                                        -TM

In 1921, Vera Wessman Olson was a Country School Student in Lake of the Woods County where the Canadian winds blistered down from the north.

Hear Those Sleigh Bells Jingle
When I was in the first grade, a man picked up the kids with horses and a sleigh. My brothers had to walk. They had a cab built on the sleigh in the wintertime. We sat around a little wood stove. It was warm in there. The ones who lived over four miles were boarded near the school. Their board was paid by the district when the weather was real bad. The first year I went to school I froze my fingers so much that my finger nails fell off so I couldn't write. They were green and blue and swollen. I got excused from writing. **Vera Wessman Olson, 1921, Carp School, Lake of the Woods County**

Brothers often fuss and argue with their older sisters, but Knute Nelson had one good reason to treat his sister like a princess.

Like a Deer
My oldest sister went to school just one year when I did, but she saved my life. Our parents never came and got us in winter weather unless it was really bad. But this time we were going home in a storm and they didn't come to get us.

My sister and I cut across the woods. This happened over seventy years ago. I was in my first year in school. It was so cold my hands were froze. I had no feelings in them. My feet were froze. And before we got home we cut across the field up to my folks' place. My feet were so cold they just wouldn't work anymore. She dragged me like you would a dead deer across that field. She grabbed me by the hand and slid me about an eighth of a mile. The first thing we hit was the barn. If she hadn't been there, I would never have made it. I had no control of my feet or hands. They were numb. We got to the barn and that's as far as we got 'cuz it was warm in there.

When I thawed out, oh, boy, did that hurt. My dad said it was storming so bad he didn't know where to begin to look. My brothers and sisters took the road home, but we cut across the field.
Knute Nelson, 1922, Chase-Brook School, District 20, Mille Lacs County

In 1919, Vi Fleischer moved from Wheaton in Traverse County and attended a country school. In 1923, while she was in the eighth grade, she experienced an event that would prepare her to cope with the emergencies she would later encounter as a rural teacher.

Camping in the School
Our neighbor, driving his sled pulled by horses, took our whole neighborhood to school. On the way a terrific blizzard began. Mr. Roman continued to the school. We knew the weather was going to turn worse. Mr. Roman unhitched the horses because he

thought they would go home, but they stayed right by the schoolhouse. The teacher was there when we got to the school. She got a telephone call—we were one of two schools in the county that had a telephone. Someone called to tell the teacher about a little second-grade girl who was walking to school on a high grade with a ditch on the side and a section of prairie on the other side.

We were all worried because we didn't know how this little one was going to get to school. She had several brothers who went out after her. They found her clinging to a telephone pole. Her cap and her mittens were gone. It was a few days before Valentine's Day and she was carrying her valentines, which also blew away. Her brothers took her back home.

Mr. Roman stayed in the school. We had a coal bin built into the school so we didn't have to go outside to get the coal. The snowstorm got worse and worse later in the afternoon, so we had to stay overnight. All we had was a little milk and water and a little rice, which we tried to cook up for the little kids. When it got dark, we found a couple of kerosene lamps but they didn't have any globes. The teacher cracked out the bottoms of some jars and used those for chimneys for the lamps.

When it came time to put the little ones to bed—we had students from first through eighth grades there—we got the younger children onto the double-seated benches and covered them up with our coats. The teacher continued firing the furnace. But it grew very cold and keeping the children warm was difficult.

My mother had been in the hospital and had surgery the day before, so my dad was very worried because there were three from my family in the school. But our parents telephoned the school every few hours to see that we were OK. The next morning the neighbor men followed the fence as a guide and took us home. **Vi Fleischer, 1923, grade eight, rural school near Wheaton in Traverse County**

Dust
When I was in country school during the Dust Bowl years, it got so dark in the schoolhouse that we were excused at noon. The dust started blowing in the morning, but by noon it was so dark in the school we couldn't see. All we had were those little kerosene lamps on the walls. Dust was blowing

through the window sills into the school. A group of us always walked home together. The wind blew the tops off our syrup pails. The dust blew so hard and it got so dark we could barely see, so we held hands until we got to our mailbox. All the kids came into our house. It was so dry there was little grass. That wind blew that top soil so hard the sky was black.
Joyce Huebner, 1933, District 63, Stevens County

When Martha Witt and her siblings left for school, they looked like creatures out of an early science fiction movie.

The Loving Inventor
In the winter time my dad walked us to school. He used white feed sacks and he cut a hole in those so we could see out and then he put some kind of a flexible glass in it so the wind wouldn't blow in our faces. It kept our faces from freezing. He walked us to school every day. He came back and walked us home. He did that for three years. **Martha Witt Cederholm, c. 1930, Good School, Koochiching County**

Tornado
One year while having an end-of-the-year district school picnic, a tornado struck. All the folks were eating outside in the yard when we sighted the dark cloud coming right at us. It lifted right over us, but the next district was wiped off the map. That evening we went back to clean up the dishes and food that people had dropped as they ran to their cars and drove away.
Margaret Kopecky, c. 1938, District 86, Jackson County

She's No Girl Scout
My first-grade teacher was not a Girl Scout. She could not build fires. Our janitor was an older boy. When the temperature dropped to thirty or forty below, his alarm clock didn't seem to go off. He always came to school late. The teacher boarded at our house and I walked to school with her. My mother worried about the school being ice cold because the teacher couldn't build a fire. So my mother packed my lunch and a sack of wood that went under her six-year-old daughter's arm. There was birch bark and kindling in there.

Since my father was sick, she couldn't leave him, so there she was wondering what was happening to me also and whether I was getting the fire

started. But she always checked on me. If the wind was from the east, she walked out to the road. If the smoke was going across the road, she knew everything was OK. She told me about this years later.
RuBelle Towne, 1936–1943, Boone School, nine miles south of Baudette

Rescued

When I was a kid going to country school, a blizzard came up suddenly in the late morning. Our teacher, Nora Hallberg, told us to save some of our noon lunch because we might have to stay in the school overnight. In early afternoon a team and sleigh driven by two brave fathers arrived. They had warm robes and warm bricks and stones for us to put our feet on to keep us warm for the trip home. I was the only pupil living south of the school, so they took me home first. It was lucky as my mother was just getting warmly dressed for the half-mile walk to school with a basket of food. I shudder to think of what might have happened to her as she faced the storm.
Leone Hedlund, c. 1930, District 78, Kandiyohi County

Winter storms often endangered the lives of teachers and their students. Fortunately heroes and miracles turned many potential disasters into stories with happy endings.

Hanging On

Our country school was about a mile outside a small town of about one hundred people. The blizzard hit with a vengeance! I can still remember sitting in my desk and hearing the old building creak and groan and turn colder. The old coal stove couldn't produce enough heat. The kids in the floor above us said they could feel the building swaying and hear the American flag fluttering. The wind blew through the cracks in the boards and windows.

The two teachers made a long "crack the whip" line, big child, small child, big child, small child, with a teacher on each end of the line. Holding hands, we weaved our way into town, clutching each others' hands desperately, depositing children as we went by their homes.

The wind literally lifted the smaller kids right off their feet, and the older kids hung on for dear life. Everybody got home safe and sound, thanks to our caring and resourceful teachers.
Rene LaValley Carr, c. 1940, District 190, Otter Tail County

Pioneer School, District 61 near Holt: Betty Berg is second from the left in the front row. The neighbor boy who nearly froze to death is third from the left.

The Statue

We had three miles to walk and it was about thirty below. My father took the three of us children to school on a stone boat pulled by horses. We had our blankets on. We got about halfway to the school when we found our neighbor boy who was just standing frozen because it was such a cold morning. He was so cold he couldn't move. First Dad thought he was just watching us, but when we got there, Dad took a hold of him. The boy couldn't move. He was frozen stiff. We put him into the stone boat and covered him up and took him all the way to the school. The teacher had started the fire and thawed him out. He was fine once he got thawed, but if we hadn't come along, he wouldn't be living today.
Betty Berg, first grade, 1940, Pioneer School, District 61

A good comic knows to look at tragic or serious situations to find the absurd side of life. To Gordon Ostby, all the world's a stage.

No Joy Ride

After the snow melted, the roads had ruts a foot deep. Then our neighbor used his Model T Ford to take us to school and pick us up in the afternoon. The tires had wooden spokes. One night he came to pick us up. We got about twenty-five feet from school and the wheel broke. The whole front side dropped down. The car sagged to the front left. We were riding on the hub and the spokes. There we were, sitting at that angle going thump, thump, thump down the road on the spokes.
Gordon Ostby, 1937–1945, District 67, Swift County

Chapter 22

Dragon Slayers

"Country School Teachers, what did you learn about your personality and character during those years you taught in the rural schools?"

A chorus of teachers replied, "One thing we learned was that we had courage and determination. We could persevere. Sometimes our determination was nothing more than bullheadedness, but we weren't going to quit."

Stories of Country School Teachers' perseverance are legendary. They defeated the dragons of weather, green firewood, unruly students, and a host of other scaly demons that made teaching in those country schools a daily battle.

Many Country School Teachers had learned years earlier to persevere as Country School Students, and they carried this determination with them to the other side of the desk. "Townies" also learned the weapons they needed to survive as Country School Teachers. Dragon-slaying in the rural schools was not for the faint of heart.

Lillian Balke was born in 1901. In 1906 she began school in Plumber in Red Lake County.

Sit Still

I started school in 1906 when I was five years old. The first day I climbed up on my desk and sat on top and put my feet on the seat. My sister quickly pulled me down and showed me how to sit in school. I didn't have any books, but I remember some big charts in the front of the room with letters on them. The teacher pointed at them and we were to read them. At recess the older girls wanted to play school with some old desks that were behind the schoolhouse. I ran away from them because I had enough of sitting.

That may have been the last time Lillian ran away from school. She taught for forty-seven years, thirty-seven in the country schools of Becker, Polk, and Mahnomen Counties.

In her first year of teaching, Lily learned that the dragons of teaching are a fickle-hearted lot.

Betrayed

I slept on a mattress on the floor. They had a bed. I was lying in it but the people I was staying with got company, some of their relatives, and they asked me to sleep on the mattress on the floor. I did. You would think they'd decrease my rent but they didn't.

Lillian Balke, 1918, Osage, Becker County

More Grief

I taught at Pine Hill School in Clearwater County for twenty-seven years. During those years I experienced a blizzard, a "Peeping Tom," a girl who broke her leg, a slow student who colored constantly on her desk but couldn't talk to me or the other students, the death of one of my students, a daily lunch diet of four eggs, and a hearing-impaired student who had her own language but learned to read and write just from watching me teach the other students.　　**Lillian Balke**

Lily Johnson

When I called Lily and asked her if we could meet before 8 a.m., she told me that would be no problem. Lily awakens every day at 3 a.m., says her prayers, eats her oatmeal, and then goes back to bed until 6 a.m. When I arrived, she served me a heaping bowl of oatmeal and entertained me by playing the same songs she had played on the piano for her students fifty years ago. She certainly hasn't lost her touch.

Lily Johnson, age 20, c. 1927

Lily Johnson taught at the O'Leary Lake School in Itasca County from 1927 to 1928.

Bug Ball

Perhaps the worst thing was that there were bedbugs and cockroaches. One night I was sitting at my table, writing to my girlfriend, who was teaching in Forest Lake. I told her about the baseball game that the cockroaches were playing by the chimney. They were making home runs constantly, running all over my room. I burned my kerosene lamp all night to keep the bedbugs from roaming around. I tried everything to kill them.

They were in my bed clothes and in my mattress. The ceiling of my room was slanted because my room was a lean-to. I could see the bedbugs crawling on the ceiling. Coming from an immaculate home, I was shocked by all this bug activity.

Lily Johnson, 1927–1928, O'Leary Lake School, Itasca County

Lily Johnson's students pose in the spring of 1928.

Eggs and Oatmeal

When I went to teach at O'Leary Lake School, I didn't go with the idea of cooking my own meals. I thought I would board with the farmer and his wife, but they chose not to board me. They let me take saunas, but they didn't want to bother with the meals. The woman was partly crippled with arthritis. I paid two dollars a month for my room.

That first week Mother had put part of a loaf of rye bread and an orange in a bag and that's all I had. But every day for noon lunch the children brought oatmeal and that's what we ate all year long, oatmeal. I did buy eggs from the farmer, and I fixed them in the morning. For supper at night I had an egg sandwich. I had to walk two miles to the school and I was always hungry by the time I got to school. When my folks came to pick me up that Friday, we had corn on the cob. It was so delicious!

Lily Johnson, 1927–1928, O'Leary Lake School, east of Bigfork, Itasca County

In 1926, Janet Gustafson began her career in District 50, west of Adrian in Nobles County.

Concentration

Working with Tom, an unmotivated reader, I noticed his attention was wandering. So we quit working on the lesson, and I proceeded to talk quietly and sincerely to him about the value of learning to read. Tom's attention was focused squarely on my face and was I proud. He was looking

Janet Gustafson, c. 1930

me straight in the eyes. I was hitting home. I paused to think of more reasons for being a good reader. Suddenly, Tom said, "Do you know you got a brown spot in the blue part of your eye?"

So much for teacher's pride. **Janet Gustafson**

Armed with renewed idealism, Janet took a job in Judson, where everyone was Welsh.

Spelling Lesson

I'm full-blooded Norwegian, and I had never encountered names like Maldwyn, Llewlyn, Mavaunwe, or Myfanwy. I couldn't pronounce the names, much less say them with the beautiful lilt the Welsh language has. And spell? Shouldn't a name be spelled like it sounds? Shouldn't Maldwyn be spelled Maldwin? One first grader informed me when we were practicing penmanship and spelling using their names that he could already write his first name, so I suggested he use his middle name. "What is it?" I asked.

"Theophilus," he replied.

"What?"

"Theophilus," he repeated.

I didn't know how to spell it, but I tried. That day I sent them home with their name-writing assignments. The next morning Earl came running in. "Ma said you spelled it wrong!"

I learned that the Welsh language is not easy to spell or pronounce, and that Theophilus is spelled with a *ph*, not an *f* and ends with *us* and not *is*.

Janet Gustafson, c. 1926, Judson, Nicollet County

Like hundreds of other Country School Teachers, Janet Gustafson was undaunted by minor defeats. She was bursting with perseverance, willing to confront whatever teaching obstacles she might face. Since there was no specialist to help her with a needy student, Janet became a speech therapist. With no training, she devised her own tactics.

Enough Is Enough

I had an eight-year-old who had a speech impediment. He couldn't pronounce words with the *s* sound. Not having been trained in speech correction, I simply started a conversation with the boy. When he ran into trouble, I stopped him and we worked on it. I tried to break the word into separate sounds and begin pronunciation from the last sound and work toward the first.

It was close to Easter and the boy said, "I fixed up an Easter basket and lined it with raw."

"Whoa! Look at me carefully. Raw?" I asked him.

"Raw," he repeated.

"Tuh-raw," I instructed. "Tuh-raw" I then said it correctly with great emphasis, "Stuh-raw."

Looking directly at me, he thought a minute and said, "I think it was hay."

He had had enough.

But Janet Gustafson did not have enough. She was a Country School Teacher. Bring on the next dragon!

In 1930, Doris Sather Erdahl taught in District 51, Ridge School, in Stevens County. The following year her cousin taught at the same school, and Doris challenged her to be more successful than she had been.

Double or Nothing

One of the boys could read one word—*t-h-e*. I tried to get him to work in school but he just slept. His dad ran a still. This was during the moonshine days. His dad made the liquor during the day. People came to their house to pick it up at night. There was a lot of activity at night so he got no sleep. He probably had to help his father. As a result, he slept right on his desk. At the end of the year, he still could only read one word—*the*.

The next year my cousin came to teach at that school. When I told her the boy knew only one word, she said, "Boy, you're a poor teacher!"

I said, "Well, you work hard and tell me how many words he can read at the end of this year." He learned one more word—*are*. But he married a teacher who did his reading, writing, accounting and he became quite successful. That's the secret about education: you can never tell about a person who can read just two words.

So when people ask me if I taught everyone to read, I say, "No." Once someone told me about a teacher who had not taught everyone to read. Then she asked me if I thought that woman was a poor teacher. I said, "No, she was an honest teacher."

Doris Erdahl taught for ten years in five different Stevens County schools.

Sometimes Country school teachers had to battle the dragon to win a job and pass through the the schoolhouse door. Al Carrigan and Virginia Rue attended Lakefield High School. Al completed teachers training in 1932 and Virginia in 1933. Then their adventure began.

No Stopping Love!

You couldn't teach if you were married. When I signed my contract in the spring, the board asked if I had any intentions of getting married. Well, we couldn't afford to get married, so I said, "No, I have no plans to get married." I got the school.

Al got a different job that summer and we said, "If we don't get married when we can't afford it, we'll never get married." In the meantime his father died, and he had five younger brothers and sisters at home that he was supporting. We thought that if I could teach, we could get started.

So we ran off and got married. We didn't tell anybody. We kept it a secret. I was living at my folks and Al was living at his folks. We didn't live together until January. I didn't tell the school board until Christmas time, and they said, "We knew it all the time. We read in the paper that you had bought a license." What a surprise! My school people then had a shower for me.   **Al and Virginia Carrigan**

Clara Rasche began her teaching career in 1933 at Liberty Bell School, District 34, in Cottonwood County. Perhaps the nastiest fire-breathing beast facing Country School Teachers was named No Benefits, No Health Insurance.

Keep the Dream

I began teaching in 1933. That winter I got terribly sick with the same thing my brother got two years before. My dad had died in November and my brother died in February. He urged me to never give up my dream of going to college.

When I got sick with a mastoid, the same thing that had killed my brother, they took me to the Slayton hospital. We had cared for my brother at home during his illness, but they treated me in bed in the hospital for a whole month.

Of course, during that time they hired an experienced substitute, and when the year was over, they hired her instead of me. But that didn't stop me!

Clara Rasche also taught in Murray County. She taught a total of forty-two years, eleven in the rural schools.

During the 1930s, an insidious group of educators sought to eliminate the teaching of phonics from the state's reading curriculum. Evelyn Koetke confronted this evil force eyeball-to-eyeball in 1934 and 1935. Why would an inexperienced teacher challenge the most ferocious administrative dragon which breathed smoke and ashes—Thou Shalt Not Teach Phonics?

War

Those of us who were trained to teach in the 1930s were taught not to teach phonics but to teach the whole word and sentence. I could not comprehend learning to read this way, as phonics had taught me well. So, I taught phonics to my lone first grader, and she was doing well in reading.

One day in the middle of the term in comes the superintendent to observe me. When I dismissed the pupils for recess, he came to me and asked, "Were you taught in college to teach phonics?"

"No," I said.

"Then why are you doing it?" he asked.

"Because my little girl is doing very well and because she can help herself when she approaches new words," I replied. Now being young and shy, I thought, "There goes my job." As the superintendent departed, he said he was recommending me to a town school for the coming year, and later I was hired. I believed in teaching phonics.

This battle was fought during Evelyn Koetke's first teaching job in District 39, Pickerel Lake Township, Freeborn County, approximately two miles west of Albert Lea. Obviously, Evelyn the Wonderful won this scuffle.

Luva Wilson encountered a secretive, stealthy villain whose innards smoldered and smoked.

Blowing Smoke

I had a teaching partner who smoked. She smoked during school time. We had those double furnaces in the basement. She would light her cigarette, open the furnace door, puff on her cigarette, and then blow the smoke into the furnace.

Luva Wilson, 1933, Union School, Meeker County

*Bang! Bang! Bang!—On the first day....
Not even Country School Teachers in isolated areas escaped the Science Civil War Dragon.*

And the Beat Goes On

This happened the year we started teaching science as science. We had to say the word *science*. We had to get new science books, and on the label of that book was written *Elementary Science*. We had to use that word which was a dramatic change.

The directors of the Christian school decided that *science* was the devil's word because that was Darwin's theory of evolution. That's all they tied to. That's what they thought science was. So we got these new textbooks, and we started teaching.

I had one man who came to my doorstep every week. He scolded me about science. I said, "We've been teaching science all the time only we called it nature study. Has anything changed because it has a different name? Nothing."

Eventually his children left and went to the Christian school because we used the word *science*. I stuck up for what I was doing because I thought I was right. We had state laws and I expected to obey those laws. I knew there was a word *evolution*, but I didn't learn about it until much later.

I went to Pipestone to take off-campus courses from Mankato and we had to take nature study. The word *evolution* came up. The lady who was riding with me was a Christian school teacher, and she believed it was not "morally correct" for a teacher in a Christian school to be riding with a teacher from a public school. She said to me point blank, "Do you believe in evolution?"

I said, "Yes, I do. Evolution is change, and the earth has changed considerably since the Lord created it. And that's evolution!"

1935, name withheld by request

When dragon beasties climbed into the ring with Country School Teachers, they assumed their opponents would stay down for a ten count. How little they knew about the teachers' spirit!

'Twas Just a Scratch

I went out of this boarding place where I lived and I stepped on an icy sidewalk. My feet shot out from under me and I hit my head on the sidewalk. I picked up my dinner bucket and my book bag and went to school. If there ever was a time I wished I didn't have to start a fire it was that morning. I got such terrific headaches and then they would die down. Then I'd get a spurt of headache and it would die down again. The pain was terrible. I felt dizzy.

The children said, "What happened to the back of your head?" My head had swelled up in a knob. The little bit of flesh back there swelled up.

When the children went home at 3:30, I went back to my boarding place and laid down. Then I realized I was an invalid. I had jarred the muscles in my neck and shoulders. After I had once laid down, I could not use any muscles to get up. I had to roll to the edge of the bed and get down on my knees and then get up that way. It was just like I was paralyzed. It gradually wore away. I didn't go to the doctor. It was something that just had to take time to heal but it took a long time. **Leona Simonson taught for thirty-five years, fifteen and one-half in the rural schools of Meeker County. The dragons never knocked out Leona.**

Scaly beasts slithered through many country schoolhouse doors, expecting to find naive, weaponless damsels in distress. How little they knew about Country School Teachers! How surprised they must have been to meet Joyce Heubner, the master of an ancient weapon.

Lung Power

One night after school I was checking papers when this man I had known for a very long time came into the school. He wanted to sell me insurance, but I told him I wasn't interested. But he kept trying to sell me that insurance. I had a mile to walk and I was getting scared. He just would not leave. I headed for the door, but he stood in front of it and wouldn't let me past. I was getting very frightened. He was an older man, in his forties, and I was just eighteen in my first year of teaching.

I screamed and yelled until he came to his senses and moved out of the way. I told what had happened to the people I stayed with. The husband was on the school board. I thought they should know about this. Nothing ever came of it so I imagine they told him. **Joyce Heubner, 1940, District 18, Stevens County**

Too Clever

I put my daily schedule on the inside of the outside door, so when the superintendent came in she would see the program. The first thing she saw was phonics. She turned around, stared at me, and said, "Get that down! Get that down! Get it changed! You are not to teach phonics." I was very intimidated by her and her position because it was the first time I had met my new superintendent and the first month in my new school. So I took the program down. However, I just incorporated phonics into my reading lessons.

Martha Kruen began teaching in 1926 in Rock County

Martha Kruen taught in a school between Woodstock and Edgerton in Pipestone County in 1940.

Florence Hartwig wrestled with a few mouthy dragon whelps in order to help one of her students master his weaponry.

Smooth

I had a boy in seventh grade who was smaller than most boys his age. He stuttered so badly that he couldn't express himself; in fact, he would go into tears many times and just stop talking because his tongue got stuck on the top of his mouth.

The children were cruel and teased and mocked him. He couldn't read orally but he could read everything silently. He got along pretty well in school after I had a long talk with the children about how we all had many problems that we had to overcome in life. I told the children we had to give him more time to say what he was trying to say. From then on the children didn't mock him or tease him openly, although I doubt whether they stopped entirely. Because he was the only one in his grade, he could take his time in saying what he wanted to say. Then he got along beautifully. In the state board examinations, he was the only student I ever had that got a perfect paper in math. He overcame his stuttering, mastered public speaking, and became a lobbyist in the federal government. I was very proud of him. **Florence Hartwig, 1943, District 72, Buck School, Dodge County**

Just about any food fueled the dragons' fire, but none as tasty as Eloda Wood's oil barrel.

Well Oiled

I had always taught at schools that had wood-burning stoves. When I got an oil-burning stove, I thought, "How wonderful! Now I will not need to carry wood and bank the fire." About Christmas time I told the school board officer that our fuel barrel was getting low. He said he would he take care of it. He was a procrastinator and did not contact anyone until the stove went out. During vacation the person delivered the fuel oil.

When I walked into the school in January, the floor was swimming in fuel oil. Here I had waited all my teaching career for an oil-burning stove and the result was a disaster. That wooden floor just soaked up that oil like a sponge. They mopped it up and cleaned it as well as possible, but that oil smell never left the school. It was a terrible odor, especially in the winter when we could not open the windows. I had to teach in that stinking mess all year. At the end of the school year, I ran off and got married so I escaped the oil that way.

Eloda Wood, 1946, Bateman School, Fillmore County

What happens when Country School Teacher finds she has sent smoke signals beckoning the dragon to make its home next to the school?

Smoke Got in My Eyes

One fall day after school I took the garbage out to burn it in the ditch as we always did. Then I returned to the school to correct some papers. I had the windows open. I heard this crackling, but I never paid attention to it. Then I smelled the smoke. I looked out to see the whole school yard on fire. I grabbed my wool jacket, ran out there and whipped and whipped my precious jacket on those flames. I

finally got it out. The entire school grounds was black. I worried what the school board and parents would say, but instead of criticizing me, they sympathized with me. They also laughed at me, too.

Veronica Blees Smith, 1956, District 63, west of Donnely, Stevens County

Hie Thee Hither
A Eulogy for You Can't Do It—As Slimy a Teacher-Hatin' Beast As Ever Blew Doubt and Vacillation Out Fire-Breathin' Nostrils:

You Can't Do It,
   that dragon beast,
Tried to make me its daily
   feast.
Somedays the battle
   looked mighty grim,
Chances of winning were
   spider-web thin.
The snow piled up, the
   mercury dropped.
My fraction lessons
   always flopped.

In the window I saw it
   blinkin'.
His scaly eye at me
   was winkin'.

"Kid, you haven't got the
   the wit
You're this little dragon's
   tremblin' twit.
Your will power's wilting
   bit-by-bit.
Pack your bags and say, 'I
   quit?'"

But teaching has made me
   dragon-tough.
I stared him down, called
   his bluff.
"I can do it, you blustery
   pain.
Why, you'd be whipped by
   Dick and Jane!"   -TM

Dragon sleuths report that You Can't Do It continues to prowl in today's classrooms, preying on teachers. He was last observed in Minnesota, starving and begging forgiveness for his sins.

Chapter 23

Sisters

Mining stories from sisters who were Country School Students, and especially sisters who became Country School Teachers, is like going to the circus. Sisters, like performers in the center ring, tell their own stories, but at the same time they are part of the one big show. Like two jugglers they spin their stories back and forth, one sister grabbing a word or phrase in midair, adding more vital details and flipping the tale back to her sister juggler.

At times they are trapeze artists, lifted to heights by the power of stories too poignant and tragic to touch the ground. Overcoming their hesitancy to throw themselves past social propriety, one leaps into time past, spins out hidden tales, and just at the crucial moment is plucked out of fearful telling and rescued by the other sister, who twists and turns, catapulting her story in another direction.

Like ventriloquists, they throw their voices into each other's stories. When one pauses or mixes up facts or dates, the sister ventriloquist throws her voice into the narrative. Having traveled years and miles through The Tunnel of Love together, each sister performs her act with humor, respect, and compassion for her partner.

Meet the performers: Margaret Lauritson Chenoweth and Eleanor Lauritson Wilson met in the Clementson Lutheran Church near Baudette; Theresa Topic Stemmer and Eleanor Topic Trnka starred in Theresa's home near Prior Lake, and Ruthe Rosten Dahlseng and Liz Rosten Braaten performed in the Nodland Cafe in Starbuck.

The Lauritson Sisters

Margaret Lauritson Chenoweth and Eleanor Lauritson Wilson grew up near Baudette in what was then Koochiching County. They lived on the banks of the Rainy River, a mile and one-half from school. Margaret is seven years older than Eleanor, and although they are sisters, some of their memories of their country school days are very different. What was student life like for children of the northland during the 1920s?

Margaret Lauritson Chenoweth was born in 1916 and attended Williams School from 1922 to 1928 and Border School from 1928 to 1930 in Koochiching County.

Like their companions, they walked to school with shiny syrup buckets and sailed the great rivers of the world in their imagination.

Sailing Buckets

We walked to school. There were no roads so we walked along the river, across creeks, across fields, and through the woods. In the fall the creek wasn't too deep. We stood on the fallen trees and set our dinner pails in the water.

The pails were five-pound syrup pails, not regular lunch buckets. Halfway down the creek someone was supposed to catch them, but often they didn't. Often the lids popped off and the pails sucked in water and sank.

Sometimes five or six of us sailed our buckets. If we were brave enough, we ran down the creek, hoping to catch the buckets. Many times we fell into the creek, but usually we just walked on the logs that hung over the creek, trying to catch them as they floated by.

Some days we had no lunch and no pail to bring home. When we came home without dinner pails, mother asked if we had forgotten them. "No," we had to admit, "the bucket is somewhere in Junkwood's Creek."

Williams School, 1927: Margaret Lauritson second from left, laughs with sisters Nora and Edith, front row to her right. Sister Eleanor, seven years younger, is not yet in school.

Warm Feet

Mother knitted us woolen stockings for school, and Dad, who was a farmer and trapper, made us moccasins. He made different sizes to fit everybody. They were primarily made of deerskin. Sometimes he used moose hide. He tanned the hides, which takes a lot of work. Then he cut out the moccasins. Walking to school was very cold, but with those wool socks and moccasins our feet were never cold.

A Wolf Is a Wolf

My brother and I set trap lines. I was my brother's "brother" and where he went, I went, whether it was fishing or hunting or whatever. We checked the trap lines after school or on Saturdays. Once he trapped a wolf, and, of course, we hadn't carried any kind of firearm to shoot it.

The wolf was still alive, so we went home to see if my brother could get a gun to shoot the wolf. Mother was very reluctant but she did give in. We went back and shot the wolf, which was really a coyote. But I did whatever he did. I followed him everywhere. I was a classic tomboy.

Eleanor Wilson Lauritson was born in 1924 and attended Border School near Baudette from 1931 to 1938. She lived long before the days of women's athletics in public schools, but those who remember her as a young girl talk about her gifts of running and jumping. Country school also taught Eleanor about temptation and the importance of a good ruler.

You Big Bully!

We had Field Day with three schools: Border, Birchdale, and Lower. We got together for one day in the spring and held contests. I think I won the blue ribbon all eight years. I could run fast and I could jump high and far.

I competed against girls, but there were mixed races, too. I did pretty good against the boys. They called me a bully. I wasn't very big, and they weren't too happy with me. They wanted to win and they didn't want a girl outrunning them. I won most of the races against the boys.

When I ran and won, I wanted to be best at something. I wasn't the best honor student. I wanted to excel at something, so I put all my energy into my long legs and I ran. I wanted to be really good.

Eleanor was not fast enough to outrun guilt.

Candy Bar Guilt

My girlfriend and I stole a candy bar from our classmate. He was a storekeeper's son and he always came with candy bars, and he sat there in front of us and ate 'em.

One day we thought, "We'll fix him." We went into his desk and took his candy bar and ate it. He got upset. He didn't know who did it, but he went and told the teacher.

We didn't say anything for several days, and finally I said to my girlfriend, "We've got to tell the teacher. I can't even sleep at night." So the next day at noon, we told the teacher, "We ate Eugene's candy bar."

She said, "I'm proud of you for coming and telling me, but don't do it again!" That finished him bringing candy bars to school because she said to him, "You eat your candy bars at home."

Imagine how guilty we felt. If the teacher would have looked at us, she would have known we were guilty. I never did tell my parents. I probably would have had some sore spots to sit on. I learned that you don't take things that don't belong to you.

Country School Students would have found this invention a rare treat. This cylinder phonograph is on display in Verna Ziegenhagen's school, District 57, Le Sueur County.

A Powerful Ruler

We had a boy that was full of mischief, not the nicest kid. On the first day of school, he was going to show off to the new teacher. She came over and picked him up by his hair and took him into the cloakroom. She warmed his behind and brought him back out, sat him down and said, "Now you know who is boss around here."

That kinda put him in his place for the rest of the year. When she picked him up by the hair, it made an impression on the whole room. Everybody was dead silent. We didn't have to worry about who was boss. Other kids tried things but she always won out. She never hesitated about using the ruler. She always took them into the cloakroom. She never hit them on the knuckles or the face, but they sat down gently when they came back.

She was very good with the ruler!

Up to His Armpits in Trouble
At Halloween the same boy who we stole the candy bar from was going to play a trick on us girls at school. He had gone over to the school and moved the girls' outhouse, and then he put grass and everything over the pit, hoping that one of us would fall in. The next day we were playing ball and he forgot what he had done, and guess who got the dunking? He went down into the outhouse pit clean up to his shoulders. He said, "Oh, my garsh!" I'm sure he also said something worse that we didn't hear. Some of the other kids had to pull him out.

The teacher said, "You're not coming into our school. You go down to the river and get cleaned up." He knew if he went home his mother would really lay it on him. He was one stinky kid.

Margaret and Eleanor have never strayed from the north woods they love. Margaret Lauritson Chenoweth lives in rural Birchdale, and Eleanor Lauritson Wilson lives in Baudette.

The Topic Sisters
Eleanor Topic Trnka and her sister, Theresa Topic Stemmer, are the proverbial "two peas in a pod." They taught at schools so close that they could challenge each other in spelling contests or play baseball against one another by walking across a few fields. They planned their lessons together and rode to school together. Later they earned advanced degrees by attending Mankato Teachers College—together.

No Smoking
Miss Erickson was our teachers training teacher. She always wore the same maroon knit dress with a little piece of her petticoat showing in the back. And Miss Erickson smoked—our teacher smoked!

Teachers were not allowed to smoke in those days. That was dreadful! We'd be working on a project and she'd walk out to have her cigarette. I almost lost my job the first year because my cousin came from Wykoff to visit me. She smoked in the outdoor biffy. There were ashes on the floor and the kids accused me of smoking.   **Theresa**

Hot
One night it was so cold that I really built up the fire. The next morning there was still a little flame, but it was so hot in there during the night that each student's crayons had melted together into one big lump.   **Eleanor, 1936, District 95, Rice County**

Eleanor and Theresa Topic: Eleanor completed New Prague Normal School in 1936, and Theresa earned her certificate from New Prague Normal School in 1938.

The Birds
I had this family of four children. Apparently the children were left alone a lot, and so they created a language of their own. It sounded like little sparrows ("cheep, cheep, cheep") talking among themselves. "Cheep," I want a scissors. "Chee, Chee, Cheep" would probably mean "I want a drink of water" or "I'm thirsty."

I thought they spoke this way because the parents really didn't take good care of them. The mother did laundry and the father—I don't know where he was. The kids were left on the farm. The neighbors said those four little kids were left alone from the time they were little.

They were in grades one, two, three, and four. They had never heard people speak English, so their language was a combination of Czech and their own creations. They understood each other because I'd point to something and then they would point to something they wanted. Eventually I learned what they were saying and I'd say, "Glass, glass, glass" or "book, book, book."

They stayed after school until they could say some words. It wasn't easy, especially for the fourth grader who had spoken that language for so long. The students played games with them and helped them with the spelling words. One of them learned to spell *arithmetic* by saying, "A rat in the house might eat the ice cream." The oldest became quite prominent in his town. He told me, "I didn't know how to speak when I first came to your class, but you really helped me."   **Eleanor**

Country schools were gathering places for many social events. Parents participated in many school events. However, Theresa Topic gave student-adult participation a unique twist in 1938.

Theresa Topic won the hearts of her District 68, Rice County students when she let them shivaree nearby newlyweds.

The Wedding
When I taught at Foley School, their daughter was getting married. Usually in those days, people got married on a Tuesday. The kids in my school and I had a shivaree. The Foleys were having a reception in their backyard and we came banging on stuff and singing all the songs we sang in school. They didn't expect us, but we all had a great time.
                    Theresa's first job, District 68, Rice County

1 + 1= 0
I had a boy in the eighth grade who was seventeen, and I was just eighteen. He told me he really liked me. He said, "You're cute," and other things. He hung around after school when I was busy. He'd do anything like bring in water. He was my helper. When he realized he didn't have a chance, he said, "Miss Topic, I have a brother nineteen, who lives in St. Paul." The poor kid, he had such a tough time with mathematics. He really liked me, but he couldn't even pass his state boards.   **Eleanor**

Humiliation
When I was in Veseli, after school we had to register the people for rationing books during World War II. When it got dark, they still came to get their stamp books, and all we had were those kerosene lanterns. The people had to register for shoes, gasoline, and we had to do all that registering and checking. We did all the paperwork. First, they had to register and show proof that they lived in the district. Then they had to tell how much sugar they had on hand. We had no way of knowing if they were honest, so we had to ask them, "Do you have any at home?" Having to pry into their personal lives was very embarrassing. We didn't enjoy that job.
                    Theresa and Eleanor

Trendsetters
When we first started teaching, it was a "no-no" to go to a dance. To dance in public was strictly prohibited. But Theresa and I changed all that. Dad was a musician. He played at dances, so we went along. During my first year of teaching, 1936, the first wedding dance was held at Herman's Hall in Lonsdale. I was getting ready to go when Grandma Tikalsky said in disbelief, "You're going to the dance?" I danced with the brother of one of my students. If the word would have gotten out that Theresa and I were at that dance, we would have lost our jobs. Then things started to change. Other teachers started going to dances.   **Eleanor**

Crunch!
We also played softball during recess. I loved to play. That's how I broke my nose. I was in the outfield and one of the boys hit the ball really high. I jumped up to catch it and so did Dick Krenick. The ball hit me right in the nose, but I still caught it.
                    Theresa

You're Out!

Theresa had a baseball team at District 25 and I had a team at District 108. In the spring we played each other for several years. We were two miles apart so we walked from one school to the other. I pitched and Theresa umpired. Who won the game depended a lot on the umpiring. Enough said.   **Eleanor**

Frustrated

One little boy I had didn't know much English. If he had to go out to the outhouse, he stood on the porch and went—right off the porch. If a car went by, he ran in saying, "Ford go by. Ford go by!"

I had another first-grade boy who didn't know English very well, either. We always taught a unit about the family. Every book had Dick and Jane and baby. One day I asked John, "What did your father do today?" The poor boy had a very hard time. He said, "I—the—woods—" and he was demonstrating with a sawing motion.

He sawed back and forth, trying to think of the word. He grew more and more frustrated. "In the saw—, In—the—," Finally he said, *rezat*, a Czech word that means cutting. He was trying to show me his father was cutting wood, but he didn't know how to say the English words.   **Theresa**

Eleanor Topic Trnka taught for thirty-two years, seven in the country schools, and Theresa Topic Stemmer taught for thirty-nine years, nine in the country schools.

The Rosten Sisters

Ruthe Dahlseng and Liz Braaten are two of ten children—eight girls and two boys. Five of the children became teachers. Ruthe and Liz attended District 33, Pleasant Hill School, a Norwegian public school in Pope County. Often four or five of the family were in school at the same time. All twenty-eight students in school were cousins.

Ten

We were a large family of ten children, living with the school practically in our backyard. All the kids thought we were so lucky to be that close to home. Twenty years separated the oldest member from the youngest, so by the time we younger ones started school, the older ones were in high school or out working. None of us carried the syrup pail with sandwiches. Dear Ma cooked our noon lunch. **Ruthe**

Style

Once we had a program in which I was really embarrassed. I thought I had a pretty nice outfit on. My mother had made it from some of my older sister's clothing. It was kind of a suit. Of course we always wore bloomers made from Pillsbury flour sacks. You could probably still see the "Pillsbury Best" on them because it took a long time to wash out. It never completely disappeared.

By the time the three of us had them worn out, the sign would finally be gone. Underneath the bloomers we wore long underwear. One time I got up in front with the class to sing a song and one of my older sisters was looking at me and she was so ashamed. I never noticed my bloomers were falling. She said, "Liz, didn't you know that the elastic in one leg of your bloomers had fallen down?" It hung over my knee. It got longer and longer but I didn't notice it. I just kept singing.

When I was in the third grade, I thought I should have nicer stockings. So my grandmother knitted one red pair and one gray pair of wool socks that barely came over the knees.

We had an inner tube that we cut apart and made ourselves garters. But I kept pulling and that stocking kept falling. You can imagine what it was like when we went outside. It was full of snow in that wool sock. It was just like I was pilled with snow ball on my socks. For dress I had a pair of high black shoes that were passed on many times. That's why I think I ended up with a lot of bunions and corns. My shoes never did fit.   **Liz**

However, Liz and Ruthe had an even greater pain than those on their feet.

Her Majesty

A heavy-set school teacher roomed at our house. We had only three bedrooms upstairs and, of course, no running water for bathrooms. So we girls slept together with two in each bed in one small room, and our brothers slept in a small, cold room at the end of the hall. My mother really had to do a great deal of extra work, making special meals in the evening as we now had a guest. Then mother went out in the barn after supper to milk cows.

The teacher only paid about fifteen dollars a month, which wasn't much for all we did. This treatment was a far cry from what I would later experience when I became a country school teacher. In one place where I stayed, my room was in a cold, unheated upstairs room. I brought my night clothes downstairs to warm them and undressed behind the oil heater in the dining room. My bathroom was a wash dish in the kitchen. I ducked so I had some privacy. The stool was in the outhouse.

Ruthe Dahlseng

Oh, the Pain of It All!

We had to carry water up to the teacher's room and empty her "everything" and carry it down again. When she ate, she crunched on hard bones. We couldn't stand the sound of it. We looked at her and thought, "Why don't you just quit eating?" Every night my mom said, "We have to have pie tonight," and I was the one to make apple pie.

The teacher sat there and said, "Do you like to bake pie, Elizabeth?" and I said, "I sure don't." She just laughed because she thought she was giving me a bad time. We had to carry a cake pan with hot dinner over to her.

I don't think she could have carried it because there was so much snow that it went right over the plum thicket. She was real heavy. She would stomp down in the snow. Once she fell through and sank up to her thighs. My dad used a sling rope to pull her out of the snowdrift. She had legs like spindles and a body shaped like a barrel. We really didn't care much for her. We were glad when she went home for the weekend so we could use her combs.

Liz

"Let's hurry, you guys. Her Majesty is waiting. Grab an armful, Ruthe. And Liz, will you stop practicing your Christmas solo long enough to carry a load of wood. Do I have to do everything around here? You're off-key, Liz."

Can you bake an apple pie, Lizzy dear, Lizzy dear?
Can you make it through the snow, charming, Ruthie ?
Oh, I'd love some steaming lunch,
Something I can really crunch,
I'm afraid in the snow I'd fall and smother.

During the 1942–1943 school year, Elizabeth Braaten poses with her six first graders in District 33, Pope County.

If They Could See Me Now

My sister had become a teacher. I wanted to be a teacher so bad because I loved the smell of that sweeping compound. I had a skirt with pleats on the bottom. I thought, "This is really like a teacher." Then in seventh grade my mom got me some shoes at a fire sale. They had high heels. I wore them to school—just to be like a teacher. I got to sweep the floor after school and I swept around with that broom, thinking, "Gee, isn't this fun!"   **Liz, 1934**

Liz Braaten and Ruthe Dahlseng taught for more than a half century. Liz taught in three rural schools in Pope County. Her dream of becoming a teacher and having her own floor to sweep came true. She began throwing sweeping compound on the floor of District 70, the Lowry School, in 1941. On Friday afternoons, a red dust cloud hovered over her school as she swept with ecstacy.

Innovators

One winter we had an unusually large amount of snow. I had three small first-grade girls. They did not like to put on their outdoor wraps and go to the outhouse. One noon hour, these three little girls asked if one of their dads could bring a big pail, so they could use that for their potty instead of going outdoors. I wished I could have said yes, but that would have created more problems.   **Ruthe, c. 1940**

The Visitor

When I came to school one morning, nice sunshine was coming in. But there in that sunshine a skunk lay sleeping by my desk. I knew I couldn't have school, so I drove to one of the school board members and told him about the skunk. I said, "I don't want to rattle him so I think we'll just have to leave school for the day."

One of the kids had crawled in through the basement window and found the skunk down there. He shot him with his BB gun. Then the boy went up into the school. We don't know how the skunk got up there, if the boy carried it up or what. But the odor was so bad that we had to close the school for three days.

Liz Braaten, c. 1947

Country School Teachers rarely drove models off the showroom floor. That did not keep them from improvising or sending up a cloud of dust as they hurried to be on time. Sometimes they ended up in the ditch.

Stranded

Ruthe and I were teaching in a two-room school about fifteen miles from the closest town. In April a freakish snowstorm came up shortly after lunch. School was dismissed shortly after one o'clock.

The parents picked up their kids, and my sister and I set off for home. The roads were slick ice because it had rained first and then turned to snow. My sister had driven our big old Buick that day.

We got close to an airport where we slid off the road. What were we to do in such a blinding storm? We had no blankets and the seats were covered in that slippery, plastic-like material.

We decided to follow a netting fence on the other side of the road. We didn't know where it would lead us. After we had walked about three-fourths of a mile, we were thankful to see a barn and a farmhouse. We made it to the farmhouse, and the lady of the house took us in. The warmth was good, but the house was filled with strong barn odors, and it was very disorderly. We were thankful to get out of the storm, but the odor was so terrible.

The farmer's wife made us some tea, but I could never drink tea so I made a trip to the bathroom and carefully emptied my cup while my sister sipped hers.

They must have had about ten children, one who was very retarded. She sat on the floor and constantly did naughty things for which her mother scolded her. Her name was the same as my sister's, so every time her mother scolded her, my sister got the giggles.

The cats ran around the house, which certainly added to the excitement. Then two more people who were stranded came in. The farmer had no telephone, so we could not let our parents know where we were. We were stranded.

About five o'clock the lady of the house said she'd make us supper. She had no meat, she said, so she boiled potatoes and made baking powder biscuits. My sister asked if she could make the biscuits because she thought maybe they might be more appetizing.

About the time the biscuits were done, a snowplow went by because a school bus had slid off the road. What music that was to our ears! We put on our wet coats and rode back to town in the snowplow with the two others who were stranded there. Yes, we were thankful to find this farmhouse for shelter, but we were also thankful we could leave and get back to our families.

Elizabeth Braaten, c. 1964, near Glenwood

In the heart of every teacher lies the the anxiety of having a hostile, incorrigible student who is ready to battle the world.

The Rebel

I had a boy in the fourth, fifth, and sixth grades who felt very rebellious because his widowed mother had moved from a town only four miles away to this village, smaller than one hundred people. He carried a chip on his shoulder that I felt as soon as he walked into the room.

All he could do was talk about how great the larger town was and how he detested moving here. He set up a fence between himself and the other students who thought their school and teacher were wonderful. I struggled with him, trying to help him in his troubles. His younger sister had adjusted well, made friends, and done a good job in school.

As time went on, I thought he had accepted the school and me. One day we had a lesson in health class on how to deal with problems and troubles that were on the the students' minds.

The pupils were encouraged to write down their troubles and get them off their minds. Then they were to crumble the papers and discard the papers into the waste basket.

All the children who had a problem proceeded to do this. I then dismissed the children for recess. I came back to my desk and there sprawling on the top of the wastebasket was a large scribbled note: "I hate this school and Mrs. Dahlseng too. I want to burn down this stupid school."

Anger seethed within me. Since there was no principal to go to for help, I had to go it alone. When the children came indoors from recess, I called him to the door and asked him to go home for the rest of the day because his feeling about the school had to be dealt with.

I went in and gently closed the door. He came in and refused to leave. I took him by the arm and ushered him to the door again, but he came in again. He was a small sixth grader, so I picked him up bodily and carried him down the flight of stairs, while he kicked and squirmed.

I carried him through the outside door and shoved him out, but a " bad penny returns," so in he came again. Finally, I reluctantly gave in and told him he could stay the rest of the day. After school I called on a school board member, told him the story, and showed him the note.

Kindly old Mr. Grimley said that he would go to the boy's home that evening and have a chat with the family. He told me to keep the note in a safe place.

The next morning the boy and his mother showed up at school. The boy returned with a different attitude and a smile, forced, I am sure.
Ruthe Dahlseng, 1965, northern Pope County

Elizabeth Braaten taught for thirty-one and one-half years. Ruthe Dahlseng taught for twenty-three years.

And then we'll go to teachers training together. We'll teach right next to each other and plan our lessons together. My team can play your team in baseball. But you can't umpire. We'll take dad's car to the dances. Remember, Billy is mine. We'll help each other put on our Christmas programs.

Sisterly Advice
My sister taught three miles away.
We savored life in every way.
Paste and tales we shared with glee.
She was my gift, a part of me.

"I can't teach phonics well," I said.
"From splitting wood I'm nearly dead.
I've no control; they run about.
What can I do but scream and shout?"

"Have patience, but be firm," she said.
"Let every child with love be fed.
Praise them all and sing the day,
'bout troublemakers this I say.

"I set them down in desks like these.
'Be quiet now. Don't even sneeze.'
But 'Wiggle' is their middle name,
For this they'll make the Hall of Fame.

"Their day is long; the school is cold.
Their stomachs growl; the cheese is old.
Just when they act like alien creatures,
They'll smile and say, 'We love you, teacher.'"
-TM

Chapter 24

1933-1940

1933
Franklin Roosevelt begins the first year of his twelve years as President of the United States, and Adolf Hitler begins his twelve-year reign as dictator of Germany. Country School Teachers and Country School Students will live their lives in the chaos of those twelve years. The influenza virus is identified, Bordens produces vitamin D whole milk, DOW Chemical is founded, and Phillip Morris begins making cigarettes. Americans fantasize with songs like "Let's Fall in Love," "Paper Moon," and "Everything I Have is Yours." *Duck Soup*, starring the Marx Brothers and *I'm No Angel* with Mae West help them escape hard times. "Jack Armstrong, the All-American Boy," saves the day for many Americans in distress.

Orville Olson

Orville Olson taught in Goodhue County at the following country schools from 1933 to 1940:

Orville Olson, age 19, 1933

Underdahl, Belvedere Mills and Trout Brook. Orville volunteered his time guiding young people in scouting and religious education for more than fifty years. When he signed his first contract, he thought he was young and idealistic. He thought he would be teaching the lessons. Little did he realize that many people were waiting to teach the teenage school master a few things.

Orville became a Country School Teacher in the fall of 1933 when he walked through the door of the Belvedere Mills School in Goodhue County. The teacher learned his lessons well that year.

Lesson 1

I was nineteen when I got my certificate. When I applied for my first school, my dad and I drove out there. There was an awful hill. The mud was seven or eight inches deep. I tried to get back up the hill. I saw a young farm boy coming along with a team of horses. I thought, "Gee, he's an intelligent young man. He's coming here to help pull me out of this." How mistaken I was!

When he got up to where we were, he said, "Hello, are you stuck?" and proceeded on his way. I didn't think he was so smart then. He was kind of dumb, walking behind a horse instead of riding him. But, nevertheless, I found out he was an awfully nice person. I had him in the eighth grade that fall. He was a great kid.

Lesson 2

That fall the superintendent of schools and her assistant came out to inspect my school. That was a terrible day for me! One kid had never been in a rural school before, so he needed help. One of the fifth-grade girls became ill and vomited all over her desk and the floor. I had to clean that up. I sent her home with her third-grade sister, so then I had no third grade.

Lesson 3

I was upset because my schedule was all mixed up. I'd had one nosebleed in my life when I was a little kid. The superintendent walked in while I was working with the first-grade kids in reading. Suddenly I got a nosebleed. I had to go outside and stop it. I came back in and apologized and told her what had happened previously.

Lesson 4

When she left, she said, "You are doing a marvelous job." Her assistant agreed. But I wasn't sure how sincere she was. When we got outside, she said, "By the way, this is election day. Are you going into town?"

I said, "Oh, sure."

"I hope you know who to vote for," she said. She was running for re-election, and it was the first time she had any opposition.

I said, "Oh, yes, I do." But I didn't tell her I wasn't old enough to vote.

1933, District 30, Belvedere Mills School, Goodhue County

In 1936, Orville moved to District 54, Underdahl School, and quickly challenged several traditions and a few school edicts.

Standing Ovation

When I was planning my first program, everybody

said, "Put everything on the walls way up high. The kids will tear around. They'll just tear it all to pieces."

I said, "No, they won't; they'll be just fine. In fact, they're going to put the program on all alone."

"Oh, you can't do that. That will be terrible, a disaster."

Usually the kids practiced their things at home, but they kept the whole program secret, *Orville Olson, 1936, on the Underdahl School steps*

especially the fact they had learned a Norwegian song, which one of the mothers taught them at school. Previously, they were not allowed to speak Norwegian on the school grounds. That was ridiculous. Why forget their native tongue?

I sat out in the audience. One little fifth grader took charge of announcing. Each had their own piece. When they sang their Norwegian song, the parents were so happy and pleased that the kids had to sing it three times before the audience would quit clapping. It was just wonderful!

1936, District 54, Underdahl School

"And, And, and And"

Many of the students spoke Norwegian better than English. I spent one hour and twenty minutes trying to teach a boy to learn the word *and*—how to recognize it and know what it meant. He simply could not grasp the meaning of the word *and*.

He'd always said "dah." He read "red dah orange."

Then I asked, "What's this word?" "Dah, dah," he said instead of *and*.

I had him say several times "and," "and." He said the word every time I asked him to.

Then he'd read it, "red dah orange."

"Now what's this word?" I asked.

"Dah, dah," he replied again.

Finally, it was just like a light bulb lit up. He realized what *and* meant. He said, "Oh, I know. That means we should use both red *and* orange." He finally caught on.

A few years later I was in a ski tournament. This great big hulk of a guy came up and said, "Bet you don't know me."

I said, "I'd know you any place, Harland." That was the same kid. "Dah!"

1936–1938, District 54, Underdahl School

Cloakroom Magic

One little girl in the second grade tested me. We had flash cards: 1 + 4, 2 + 6, and so on. Two plus three was the one I showed little Betty. She said "Two."

"Betty," I said, "two apples and three more apples equals how many?"

"Two."

She kept saying "Two." Then she said "four" for awhile. Then she said "six." I knew she knew the answer when she skipped five. I said, "Betty, I think you and I should go in the cloakroom...."

"Five!" she shouted.

I saw her a few years later, and I said, "Betty, are all those kids yours?"

"Yes," she said, "and now I know what you went through with me. I was awful!"

Orville Olson taught a total of seven years in the country schools of Goodhue County.

Luva Wilson

Luva Wilson attended District 87-181, Mt. Hope School, in Meeker County, from 1921 to 1928.

Willow Weep for Me

I went to a one-room school—a joint district which had eight grades. Sometimes as many as fifty to sixty students attended that school. The teacher, a big, buxom lady, was very strict. Once the bigger boys who were all sixteen collected some materials

Luva, second from left, 1928

to make a bomb. They put it under a pail and blew it into the air. They were always up to something. She had a hard time controlling them.

Sometimes she hit them with her ruler, but most of the time she used willow switches. Willow trees lined the area around the school yard, and she made them go out and get their own willow branches. Then she switched them pretty good. I'm sure she wore those switches out on those boys. I always thought she was mean, but I'm certain she had to be strict to control those big boys. I was afraid of her.

Mt. Hope School, 1921–1928, Meeker County

"Blubba, Blubba, Blub"

My husband started school when he was six years old, on April 28. He spoke only Finnish, so his father taught him three expressions in English: "George Wilson," "Casper Wilson," and "six." Then he told him they were the answers to three questions the teacher would ask him: "What is your name?" "What is your father's name?" and "How old are you?" His older brothers went with him to make sure he matched the right answer to the question asked.

The teacher would put words on the board that didn't mean anything to him. Then she'd come and wipe them off. The other kids would take a piece of paper and start writing. He couldn't imagine what they were doing. They were doing their spelling.

George was the third of seven boys. The two older ones would come home from school and say, "Blubbba blubba blub" and make all kinds of sounds, and he thought they were speaking English. They were talking nonsense to tease him and confuse him. And it did confuse him because it made it difficult for him to learn English.

Well, the teacher thought he was a dumb boy or that he was retarded, so all he did for the rest of the year was put colored wooden pegs in holes. Knowing that everybody was laughing at him embarrassed him so much.

Later anything that had anything to do with pegs or pickup sticks, anything like that, blew him right back to first grade.

Once he learned English, school was easy for him and he loved it. He completed school when he was thirteen and in seventh grade.

Luva Wilson telling about her husband, who attended District 43, Pleasant Grove, Meeker County.

What Luva wants, Luva gets!

There Was No Stopping Me

I completed the eighth grade during the Depression. My parents thought we were much too poor to go on to high school. I wore the same dress to high

Luva Wilson, c. 1933

school every day until Thanksgiving. On the weekends I laundered that dress and ironed it and then wore it again every day the next week. When my parents saw how serious I was about going on to school, my aunt made me some more dresses. The times were so hard. I walked three and a half miles to school in Kimball. Sometimes if I got to the neighbor's house by 8:30, I could get a ride with them, which was wonderful.

But I loved school and I loved education. I wanted to get an education, so I could make some money and help my parents. Nursing or teaching were the only options. A friend of mine in St. Cloud helped me find a baby-sitting job in St. Cloud.

I learned love from my parents and grandparents, and because I was the oldest in that generation, loving children seemed to be natural.

Puff!

When I went to practice teach, I was put in a room with a smoker. In those days, smoking just wasn't done. She eventually got into trouble. I wanted to graduate so badly that I just couldn't put myself into that situation. I don't know if she ever completed school. I know they threatened her with not graduating. I did everything I could to separate myself from her. She must have really been addicted. I don't know how she could take that chance. Her career was riding on every puff if she were caught. But still she puffed. She opened the window and then blew the smoke out. Sometimes it got very cold with the window open. **1932, St. Cloud Teachers College: Luva Wilson taught in the country schools of Meeker County from 1933 to 1937. From 1937 to 1938, she taught at the Willing Workers School in Stearns County.**

Frances Pianko Hayden

With single-minded passion many aspiring teachers studied at teacher training centers

Frances Pianko Hayden

under respected, experienced instructors who taught them course content, lesson planning, and discipline. Many of these young people followed the prescribed social rules and all the "thou shalt nots" their instructors preached as absolute truth. However, for some the drum beat a different rhythm. They marched a bit more freely than the less spirited.

Frances Pianko Hayden was born in 1909 on a farm south of Belle Plaine, one of eight girls and four boys. There was no room for wallflowers or people who did not speak their minds in the Pianko family, not if one wanted to be heard.

Frances wanted no part of small town teachers training programs. She headed for St. Cloud to take a few classes and enjoy the social life. However, Frances soon ran into a thorn, Miss Pribble. Frances was a strong-willed farm girl used to having her say and convincing others that her philosophy was right. Miss Pribble was an inflexible academic authority figure. She tried to control Frances' future and interfere with her acrobatics to juggle a lively social life with the task of earning a teaching certificate. The battle was on!

The Bubble Hits The Thorn

I had a teacher who would give you a zero or an A for every day, and four zeroes for the quarter flunked you, so I had to be very careful. I used to get into arguing matches with her.

She was so strict that nothing could move her. I had to be careful because I had her for math and English. I knew I was getting pretty close to those four zeroes and the quarter was only half over.

One day she gave me a problem to teach. She made me go the board and teach this problem to her. She pretended to be a rather ignorant student in a country school.

So I proceeded to the board, and I knew how to do the problem. I was doing it in a way I thought was pretty darn good, but she'd just keep saying, "I don't understand that! I don't understand that!

Next I had to explain it another way. Then she said, "Now that's what you're going to encounter when you get out there. Kids are not going to understand everything you say from the beginning."

And so I made a few more valiant tries to teach her that stupid problem that was so easy to see.

Finally it just got to me. I said, "Miss Pribble, I hope I never get a kid in school who is as dumb as you are because I'd quit the first day." Well, I didn't get many zeroes after that.

She did the same thing with the other class I took. One time I went to the president of the college to complain. I said, "I want to talk to you, Doctor."

And I said to myself, "God, imagine me coming from the farm and going to the president of the college!" Nobody talked to him because they were all afraid of him. I wasn't afraid of him.

I said, "I want to talk to you."

I told him about Miss Pribble, and he patted me on the shoulder and said, "I had her, too. Just do the best you can. She's all right."

I said, 'No, she isn't!" I was so gutsy.

Frances Hayden, 1928, St. Cloud Teachers College

Trouble at the Red Barn

I probably could have been a good student, but I wasn't. I didn't pay too much attention. I loved the men teachers, hated the women teachers—loved the men teachers except one—Dr. Brainerd, a history teacher. I didn't get along with him.

We were not allowed to go just any place. We had to be on the straight and narrow or get caught.

There was a place called the Red Barn in St. Cloud where they held dances. Of course, we were not allowed to go to the Red Barn, but I went, not once but quite a few times. I loved the dancing and fun.

One time I was there all primed to have a good time. I went to the bathroom, and when I came out, who do I see standing there by the door but Dr. Brainerd. Guess where I spent the rest of the night? In the bathroom! I would have been kicked right out of school if he had caught me. **St. Cloud Teachers College, 1927–1928**

In 1928 Frances finished the teachers training program at St. Cloud and headed for the country schools in Le Sueur County. She taught with the same love of life and sense of humor she possessed as a student. Her stories are punctuated with bursts of laughter. Students seldom got the upper hand with Frances.

However, sometimes Frances became so engrossed in her teaching that she lost track of time. Free from her discipline, two students used this time to work and "chew on" a good topic.

They Were Probably Studying!

When I was at the Sharkey School, I had two brothers in class. There was a basement in that

Frances, schoolmarm in her winter finery, c. 1934

school. These two boys were being very helpful. They always wanted to go down to the basement and chop some wood for my stove, so I let them go. What a mistake! They were experimenting with what their older brother had taught them. They brought a little bit of snuff to see what it tasted like. I told them, "Ten minutes is all you can stay down there," but since they couldn't tell how long ten minutes were, they said, "Will you call us when ten minutes are up?" But sometimes I forgot about them, and they stayed down there half an hour or an hour chewing snuff like crazy and chopping wood.

Like all teachers, Frances encountered situations in which she had to decide whether to do what she thought was best for her students or follow the directions of someone else. What does Country School Teacher do when Mother gives an order? She never thinks twice about spilled milk.

Dump It!

I had a little child in class whose mother was very proper. The kids were brought up very well. The mother wanted the kids to be healthy so she put cod-liver oil in their milk. The lunch buckets sat behind the stove on the shelves. Obviously it was very warm there, and you know what warm milk tastes like, but can you imagine what it tastes like if it has cod-liver oil in it?

The little girl's sister told me that her sister wouldn't drink her milk. "Well," I thought to myself, "if the mom sends the milk, what's the difference if it's a little warm. She should drink it." Then I opened it up, and oh, that smell!

I dumped it. Then I wrote her mother and told her not to put cod-liver oil in the milk. "The child can't drink it," I said. "I threw it out." **c. 1934**

Early Day Care

"The parents were really good—well, all but one, who didn't like me. She never said anything to me, but she told everyone else.

Her child was a small kid. She dropped him off at school with the rest of her children. He was not supposed to be in school at all, but I thought, 'Well, so he comes, let him do whatever he wants. Maybe she just wanted to go someplace for the day. He came back the next day and the next day and the next day!

So I thought to myself, "Kid, if you come here, you're going to learn something." I told him to come to the front of the room and sit in the small desks, but he didn't want to. I said, "You've got to do what the rest of the kids are doing."

There were three other children in first grade. But he didn't come. So I thought, "I'll just bring you here, kid." When he saw me coming, he flopped his little belly on the seat and hung on tight. I put my hand under his little tummy and lifted him up.

He wasn't in school the next day. He wasn't old enough to be in school and I thought, "Good, let his mother baby-sit him."

Most young teachers who taught in the county school put the coming of the county superintendent at the top of their anxiety list. One described the superintendent as "sniffing around to find out what was wrong with my teaching." Some actually feared these visits.

Not Frances Pianko! She had faced her most intimidating opponents at the family dining room table. Her sisters were far more formidable critics. Frances, who had fought and won the battles with Miss Pribble, the college president, the Cod-Liver Oil Mother, and the Day Care Delinquent, certainly was not going to lose the battle of nerves every time the superintendent visited. Generally she won both the battle and the war.

Tables Turned
The county superintendent came to observe me once a year, the only supervision I had in the country schools. He came the day I had a math problem in the eighth grade that I couldn't solve. I simply could not work out that danged problem, so I thought I would ask him to work it out. "Mr. Poehler, would you work out this problem and show me how to do it?" I asked.

Well, he sat at that desk working on that problem, and I was teaching. Of course, he wasn't watching me at all. Finally he said, "I can't get it. Send it to the book company and ask them to solve it." Tables turned and battle won.

Frances Hayden moved to a city school when the country schools closed. She continued her teaching career at St. Joseph's Catholic School in Hopkins. She retired in 1978 after teaching thirty-three years.

1935
The Soil Conservation Act and The Social Security Act are passed by Congress. Alcoholics Anonymous is formed, the Richter Scale is invented, and sulfa is used in chemotherapy. Ginger Rogers and Fred Astaire dance away America's Depression in *Top Hat* and Olivia de Havilland stars in *Captain Blood*. Benny Goodman's Band, The Hit Parade, *Tortilla Flat*, *Mutiny on the Bounty*, and Monopoly appear this year. Only ten percent of all rural homes have electricity, but the newly formed Rural Electrification Administration will light up farms and schools across the country.

Evelyn Ogrosky Hande
Evelyn Hande completed her teachers training at Winona State and began the search for a job. Like many parents during the Depression, Evelyn's mother was anxious for her daughter to become employed as soon as possible. However, Evelyn was not about to take just any position.

No, Thank You!
One time I was offered a job up north at the school at the Angle Inlet on Lake of the Woods. I didn't  want to go there and my mother was quite anxious that I should get a job because I needed one. I got the application and the application asked, "Do you smoke?" and I put down, "no." "Do you drink?" and I put down, "no." The next question asked, "Would you be willing to abide by any decision the school board would make about this?"

I wrote, "I will not drink or smoke for anybody!" I didn't want the job, and naturally I didn't get it. I never told my mother I had done that, but I did send in the application as she wished.

Evelyn Ogrosky Hande age 19, c. 1933

Evelyn Ogrosky was nineteen when she signed her contract at Witoka School in Winona County. She discovered that although she was close to home, she had entered a much different world.

Dinner Pangs
Most of the parents invited us teachers for dinner. We knew it was an effort for many of these people to have us in their homes. The thing that really surprised me was that the father and the mother and maybe the two older kids sat with the teachers and the rest of the kids stood around and watched. It was an uncomfortable time because we didn't know the parents. We knew the kids, but they didn't act the way they did in school. They just stood and watched us in awe as if we were strangers. They stood in the corner, and then they ate later if there was anything left over.

One family had eleven or twelve children. Some older ones who were helping the father farm were allowed to sit with us. There was another teacher there with me. All the rest watched us eat. The children just stood there looking at us. Afterward when we moved into the living room to talk, the kids ate. I felt that if I ate too much, the kids wouldn't have enough.   **1935–1937**

What's in a Name?
One of the girls asked, "Miss Ogrosky, would you please name Elnora's baby?" I had the younger kids from both families in school.

"I don't understand," I said.

"Well, she had a baby and she doesn't know what to name it, so she wants you to name it."

I said, "Oh, I'd have to think about that."

"She wants to know today what to name it."

"Harold would be a nice name," I said. "That's my brother's name." And so they named the baby Harold. I thought that was quite an honor. It isn't every day a teacher has a chance to name someone else's baby.   **Evelyn Ogrosky, c. 1935**

A Touching Story
I wore silk or nylon stockings. Evidently that was something that the kids were not used to. I sat in the big chair and the class sat in smaller ones. It was not uncommon for one of the kids to come up without thinking or saying something and feel my legs. I just wanted to hoot! They did it because the silk was different, smooth, and interesting. That happened many times. I assumed their mothers wore cotton stockings. I imagine it looked strange!   **1935–1937**
Evelyn Ogrosky Hande taught for twenty-four years.

Gladys Schmidt

Gladys Schmidt, 1953, and her District 53 students

Gladys Schmidt attended the teachers training program in New Ulm from 1933 to 1934. She taught one year, 1935 to 1936 in District 4, near Searles. After raising her two sons, she returned to teaching in 1948.

When her colleagues and students start telling their tales, Gladys says little. She just goes to her photo album and takes out the picture that shows her standing on top of a snow drift as tall as the telephone pole. 1936, District 4, Brown County

The Weather Outside Was Frightful!
The giant snowstorms hit Minnesota in 1936. Teachers and students tell stories about how powerful the storms were, how hard the winds blew, and how high the drifts piled up against the buildings. Men shoveled snow from one tier to another before the horses could clear a path for the snowplows.

The Spelling is Close
In the book it said that we empty our bowels every morning. Well, this little girl didn't know what bowels were because we hadn't had that lesson yet, but she said, "Oh, yes, my grandma washes those bowls every time we eat our Rice Krispies."

1936, District 4, Brown County
Gladys Schmidt taught for thirty-six years, twelve as a Country School Teacher.

Eva Markuson Jasken
In 1932, Eva Markuson's world began to shrink dramatically. After graduating from Minneapolis Central High School, she left the big city to attend teachers training in Mankato. After completing that program, she signed a contract to teach in a rural school two miles east of New Auburn in Sibley County.

Winter Wonderland

Eva Jasken frolics above, but in bad weather she often rode to school. On rare occasions she took the reins. c. 1935

No Exceptions to the Rules

Some of my students were nearly as old as I, and several were much taller. This became a problem when one boy said, "I don't think I should have to clean and wash the boards anymore. I'm too old for that." I told him the other students would have to agree to that since they would have to do what he had been doing. Needless to say, the other students thought he should still have to do his share. But for anyone as grown up as he was, I can understand his embarrassment when he was doing the work of grown men at home. **Eva Jasken taught for twenty-six years, two years in rural schools.**

Mildred Kampert McAdams

Mildred Kampert McAdams grew up on a farm near Fairmont. "I came from a long line of teachers: my grandmother Pennington was a teacher, my aunt Eunice was a teacher, and my mother was a teacher. My dad had five sisters who were teachers. I was born to be a teacher."

Mildred's mother and Aunt Eunice hitch up Daisy and leave for their schools. c. 1912. Only a few years earlier Mildred's grandmother had driven Daisy to school.

Mildred Kampert McAdams

Mildred went to the same country school in two different places. The year is 1922. Imagine being a five-year-old coming home from your first day of school at District 51, located in an idyllic place called Rolling Green Township in Martin County. It's only a half mile north and west of your home, just a short stroll. You chatter with your parents about that wonderful first day and go to bed dreaming of the next day. You step out of the house, turn toward the school, and discover it has vanished overnight.

It's Gone!

When I got up the next morning, the schoolhouse was sitting in a pasture straight west of my home. I didn't have to go to school for two weeks until they moved it to its new location. Four bachelors had filed an injunction to keep the school from being moved, but the judge dissolved the restraining order.

Men from the southern part of the district used poles and tractors and moved it during the night because they wanted the building more centrally located. Miss Rouse, the teacher, asked the board, "Where will the school be tomorrow?" **1922**

Donovan is a name Mildred will never forget!

Watch Mildred!

My mother and our neighbor were great friends. We lived three miles apart. They had taught together and we ate Sunday meals at each other's houses. One summer, Donovan, our neighbor's son, was very ill. It was time to can green beans, so my mother sent me with our pressure cooker to can beans for Donovan's mother. I spent the whole day there. I held Donovan at noon while his mother fixed lunch. The next day they came to my home and Mrs. Donovan said to my mother, "You'd better watch Mildred. We have just come from the doctor and Donovan has infantile paralysis."

A Contract's a Contract

By the 1930s, most of the state's schools used a standardized, two-page, typed contract outlining all the teacher's duties. Official contracts were usually notarized and signed in duplicate before they were official.

Mildred's contract was handwritten on a six-by-nine-inch piece of lined paper, ripped out of a tablet. She probably wondered what the board had eaten at their "meating." And how was it possible that the "cleark" lived in Iowa? Mildred honored the unusual contract and taught in Districts 119, 9, and 90 in Martin County.

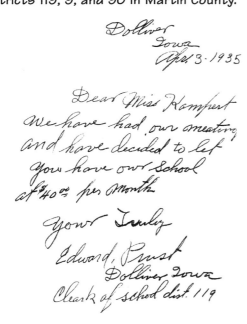

*Dolliver
Iowa
Apl 3 · 1935*

*Dear Miss Hampert
We have had our meating
and have decided to let
you have our School
at $40.00 per month

Your truly
Edward Prust
Dolliver Iowa
Cleark of school dist. 119*

Arlo

Arlo, 1936

One day Arlo, a first grader and one of ten children, was naughty so I sent him out in the hall. The hall door hit against the wall and cracked the plaster a little bit.

While Arlo was out there, he picked all that plaster off around the wall. When it came time to read, I went to bring him in. I scolded him for breaking that plaster.

Then he began to cry. But I said, "OK, Arlo, it's time for your reading now."

Then he bawled, "I (sniff) can't (sniff, bawl) read because (bawl) I'm crying." **1935, District 119**

Years later my son met Arlo's son. Through him I contacted Arlo and sent him some pictures. He wrote to me:

Dear Mrs. McAdams,

Thank you for the pictures. I went over and over them. It really brings back the memories. I sure was a dirty rag peddler. In fact I appeared to be among the homeless and living out of the dumpster.

I can understand it though because I don't know how mom did it as well as she did. I am 64 and have to baby-sit for the grandchildren a lot of the time.

I have found out what a lot of work these mothers go through and I honestly ask myself how they do it. I wish the men would wake up to see their duty in this.

Thank you very much. Arlo

Donovan, Again

Donovan had overcome great obstacles. He wore a brace on his leg. He was an excellent student, but he

Mildred McAdams c. 1938

was also very ornery and difficult to discipline. I bought a new car in 1938. One day the car was covered with a very thick coat of dust so Donovan took a stick and scratched the word DIRT in my car. Another time he drew a picture of me and under it he had written FATSO. He was always doing something he shouldn't do. It seemed as if every time I turned around he was causing trouble.

In September of 1995 I went back to a reunion of my students. Donovan was there, and he apologized for how he had acted. **District 9, Meeker County**

Strange Animal

One day I was teaching geography, and I was talking about Yellowstone National Park. I asked the students what a geyser was. One of the boys said, "Some kind of an animal like a bar."

Mildred McAdams taught in the country schools for twelve years.

Selma Tietel

Selma Tietel completed her teachers training at New Ulm High School in 1934. She taught from 1936 to 1938 at Grass Valley School, District 16, near Franklin in Brown County. Then she worked as a private tutor from 1959 to 1961. From 1961 to 1965 she taught in District 506 in Lafayette, in Nicollet County.

Selma Tietel, c. 1936

Selma attended District 11 in Watonwan County. She may have forgotten a few obscure facts and how to figure square root, but she recalls the following two events quite vividly.

History on the Radio

When I was in the elementary school, we walked to a neighboring rural school to listen to the first inaugural speech of a President of the United States broadcast on the radio. Our teacher excused the lower grades and invited those of us in the upper grades to take our lunch pails and walk the two miles to the other school. We arrived just in time to hear President Warren Harding's inauguration ceremony. The students sat there just like they were glued to the radio. Our parents didn't have radios.

There were several people from the district there who came to listen—parents and students from other schools. Then we ate our lunch and walked home. It was a grand occasion because we were part of history. All this was done without the consent of the school board. But what an education! My parents were surprised when I came home early, especially my dad, who was on the school board.

That was an extraordinary experience I'll never forget. We saw a radio and heard the address.
1924, District 11, Brown County

Chit Chat

Usually the teachers stayed in the school during the noon hour. However, we had one teacher who didn't do that. There was a farm across the road from the school. The tenants had several grown men in the family. My teacher, who was single, discovered this. So she came out at noon.

She watched for these men who were working in the fields. She spoke to them over the fence. That was fine with us because we were playing ball. Many times we had a longer noon hour than usual. The conversations must have been quite interesting! But she didn't marry any of them. **c. 1929, District 11, Brown County**

Selma is the studious young girl in the dark dress, second from the right. It's teeter-totter picture day at District 11.

Selma signed her first contract in 1936 without unanimous support from all the board members.

Tiny But Powerful

I had an offer in April to finish the year in a school in the corner of Brown County, a long way from home. My brother took my instructor, Ida Kock, and me to meet the school board. We went from one to the other because they were out in the fields working. I got the position, but I found out later that one of the board members said to the others, "Why in the world did you bring that little thing when we have already had three bigger people in here this year?" One of the three was a man and he couldn't take it. I never heard the reply.

District 16, Grass Valley School

Most stories about school board members portray them as manipulative penny pinchers, trying to squeeze the life out of every coin and conniving ways to work their teachers to exhaustion. Selma's board had other qualities.

School Board Shenanigans

My boyfriend, who eventually became my husband, and I had been going together for two years. However, since I had to live in the district, I stayed with a family in Franklin, but I went home on the weekends. My boyfriend picked me up on Friday and brought me back on Sunday. The board noticed that I was leaving, supposedly with my big brother.

The board challenged a young fellow in the district who didn't have a girlfriend to see if he could persuade me to date him. One day after school the young man came to the house. My house parents were surprised when the man asked for me. I knew him, but I didn't expect to be invited out. He wanted me to go to a dance with him and his sister.

Then my "recall" kicked in. Our teachers training instructor had told us to mingle with the people in the district. This was a good opportunity, so I accepted. He left to get his sister. My house parents were shocked because they had met my boyfriend many times. However, I went. Then they turned out the lights and went to bed in case my boyfriend came. They could pretend they weren't home. They didn't want to talk to him.

The dance band was from my boyfriend's hometown so they informed him the next day that they had seen me with someone else at the dance. When he came to take me home on Friday, I made a full confession. However, I found out later from my house parents that one of the school board members had challenged the young man to ask me out. They had dared him.

We were told in teachers training to be sociable! I probably shouldn't have gone, but I was very young, naive, and dumb! **1935, District 16, Grass Valley School, Brown County**

Panic

I lived with a farm family that first year. In the spring of 1938, I had decided to get married and give up teaching. During this year a brother of the man of the house where I stayed came to live with his brother on the farm. The men worked together, but the brother who owned the farm got sick and passed away rather quickly. His son then came to help on the farm. Then he became ill and passed away quickly like his father.

The State Health Department came to investigate. They discovered the brother was a typhoid carrier. We were all given tests to determine if we were infected.

During all that time I sat across the table from the infected brother. My life flashed before my eyes. I wondered if I had a future, would ever fulfill my plans to marry, to live. My tests showed I was not infected. The brother who had infected his own brother and nephew had to be put into isolation. **1938, Spring Valley School, Brown County: Selma Tietel taught in the New Ulm public school system from 1965 to 1978.**

Orpha Oelkers Siffing

Orpha Siffing attended Gates School in 1923 and

Orpha Oelkers Siffing

finished her elementary education at Bee Hive School, District 69, Isanti County. According to Orpha's memories, things really buzzed at the Bee Hive school. As a young girl at the "bee hive," Orpha learned many lessons about discipline and survival from her Country School Teacher. However, some of her teacher's tactics were quite unorthodox. Orpha's teacher taught her to recognize the color red and how to "pull her weight."

First Shave!

The big boys caused a lot of problems. One of these boys was really an aggravating kid. The teacher, a large lady, was a strict disciplinarian. She had her ways. One boy always talked when he wasn't supposed to. With thirty-six in school, you can't be talking. So she taped his mouth shut with adhesive tape. He didn't talk much after that. He was old enough, so that his whiskers were starting to come in. She only kept the tape on for about a half hour, but when she took it off, she ripped it off. He was humiliated by the tape and the ripping.

c. 1926, Bee Hive School, District 69, Isanti County

Teacher Was a Redneck
They had Mothers Club in that district where the mothers mulled over things from school quite extensively. They often criticized the teacher for what she did. We always knew when they had been there. When she came to school the next day, we could tell she was upset because her neck would turn turkey red. She'd put us all in our seats and then she'd stand up there and really give it to us.

She Had Pull!
One boy who lived close to the school had to stay after school. He decided he wasn't going to stay. He grabbed his coat and left. The teacher went right after him. I can still see them. He got home first and grabbed one of the posts on the porch. She pulled him off the post and dragged him right back to school. He had a real crabby father, so I thought she was really brave doing that.

c. 1928, Bee Hive School, District 69, Isanti County

Orpha completed normal school in 1936 and that fall taught in District 36, the Bergdahl School. From 1939 to 1940 she taught in the Green Lake School. Both schools were in Isanti County.

First-Year Miseries
I usually went out at noon and played ball with the kids because it was big deal for the kids to strike out the teacher. But one day I didn't go out. When I looked out the window, I could see they were having a funeral for a gopher they had killed. They went through the whole procedure. They laid the gopher in a box, dug a hole, and had a graveside service for the dead animal. Another time in the spring, I didn't go outside either. There weren't any windows on the south side of the school. I thought it was awfully quiet. I walked outside to see two of the boys had a tub and they were rowing across this

really big pond, which was next to the school. They had a couple sticks and they were rowing right out into the pond. I ran down there, hollered at them, and they came back. That really scared me!

1936, Bergdahl School, District 36, Isanti County

The Kid Stinks!
A second grader was the cause of me quitting teaching for several years. He was the minister's son and the worst kid. When his father came to school, he said, "You can do anything you want with him. I cannot straighten him out." I couldn't either, but I tried. The day the county superintendent came that kid crawled into the wood box. He peeked out all day. I didn't know what to do, so I let him sit in there all day. I was so humiliated. All I could see was the top of his head.

When he came to school, he walked down the rows, clunking the desks with his lunch pail, saying, "SKUNK! SKUNK! SKUNK!" He kept a ruckus going all day long, irritating everyone. I suggested to his father that the boy not be allowed to come to school because he might not like that. That didn't work. He enjoyed those two weeks at home.

One day I said to him, "I'd surely like to see you when you grow up to be a man and see what you look like and how you act." Years later when I was sitting at my desk, this man walked up and said, "Well, Mrs. Siffing, I came to show you what I look like!" He had turned out just fine. 1939, Green Lake School, District 19, Isanti County

In 1946 Orpha signed a contract at King's School in Isanti County.

Jingle Bell Romance
One spring we were getting ready to rake. One of the girls put her little bells in her desk and one of the boys took them. I didn't know he took them and the girl wasn't sure, but she thought it was him, so she told me she thought he had taken the bells. In the morning I told the rest of the students to go outside, and I took the boy inside. I said, "I think you have the bells." I knew he had the bells because he jingled them in his pocket. I said, "If you'll admit it and give them back and tell the girl you're sorry, I'll forget the rest," and he did. He didn't intend to be mean, but he liked her and that was his way of showing it. **1946, King's School, Isanti County**

A Safe Place

I had a girl and a boy who lived in a very bad situation. The mother and the man she lived with ran a beer joint. Those two kids had to sleep in the basement, which wasn't finished. I could smell that they were sleeping where there was wood piled. I could also tell they were not treated very well. Every morning when I came to school, the girl, a third grader, was there waiting for me on the steps. I don't know what time she came, but she came early. She must have wanted to get away from home. Of course, I needed to prepare and get things on the board. But she would say, "Oh, teacher," and laugh. She was so happy just to be there. Evidently she just wanted to talk to someone and be away from her home under the beer joint down in the basement.

1946, King's School

When Orpha's husband joined the Marines, she became Rosie the Riveter at Consolidated Aircraft in California. She returned to education, working twenty-nine years as a principal's secretary.

Edward Maher

Edward Maher taught from 1936 to 1938 at Gunderson School in Carlton County. From 1938 to 1939 he taught at the Howard Gensen School in St. Louis County. Some Country School Teachers dolled out heavy-handed discipline. Ed had a reputation for creative discipline.

If I Had a Hammer....

There were two schools, the Mud Creek School and the Gunderson School. The clerk of the school asked me if I would take another student. At the Mud Creek School they had this kid who was playing King of the Hill, and he tossed a little kid down the hill and broke the kid's leg. The neighbors wanted to put him in Red Wing. They wouldn't take him back in the school. The clerk said the only choice he had was to move him to my school.

Ed Maher, c. 1936: Ed was Mr. Country School Teacher for three years, 1936 to 1939.

I said, "OK, send him over." He was a big guy. The teacher at Mud Creek told me how terrible he was. He controlled the school because he was so obnoxious and so big. He constantly moved his desk around. He never sat still. I decided he was going to behave and not move the desk. He was going to sit still. I took a hammer and a couple of tenpenny nails and spiked his desk right to the floor. I put something over the nails, so he couldn't see it was nailed down. He never figured it out. The other teachers could not understand how I could keep this kid from moving his desk around. I never had any trouble with him at all. He certainly didn't move.

1936–1938, Gunderson School, Carlton County

Snake Eyes

Some kid found a garter snake and put it in my desk drawer. I went in there to get a pencil and here's this snake opening his mouth. Everyone knew about it. They were waiting to see what I would do. I reached in there and grabbed his tail. I snapped him and his head flew off. I just left the head lie where it landed and threw the rest in the wastebasket and kept right on going. From that day there wasn't any trouble of any kind in that school. That was an easy school to teach in. **1936–1938, Gunderson School, Carlton County**

Country School Teachers had no MEA/AFT bargaining power. Many were intimidated by tight-fisted conniving school boards which knew teachers would never say "no." Not Ed Maher!

Horse Dealing

My salary had risen to $100 a month when I applied for this job at the Howard Gensen School. The teacher who was there before me was getting $85. Mr. F., one of the board members said, "We're never going to pay a $100 a month. No teacher is worth $100 a month!"

I said, "If you got two horses and one is worth $100 and the other is worth $85, which is the best horse?"

"Well, any fool knows that, the $100 horse."

I said, "I'll tell you what. I'm a $100 horse. Good night. I'm going home." The next day one of the other board members called and said, "You got the job. I'll send you the contract." When I got the contract, I noticed that Mr. F. hadn't signed it. He was mad and refused to sign it.

In the spring he said, "Bring your contract over and I'll sign it."

I said, "I don't care if you sign it or not. Maybe I won't stay next year anyway."

He said, "No, I changed my mind."

I said, "My mind isn't made up yet." **Ed Maher 1938–1939, Howard Gensen School, St. Louis County**

Absentee Supervisor

To get my college degree I had to take time off to practice teach even though I had taught all that time. My supervisor needed to make some more money. So he took a job at the steel plant in Duluth. I had more experience than he did. He said, "Don't tell them about this at the college. You don't need any supervision." So he worked there instead of supervising me. He would stop in once in a while. I don't think UMD cared either.

In addition to his three years in the rural school, Ed Maher taught for thirty-five years, most of them in the Cloquet public school system.

1938

Glen Miller and his band begin touring, putting America "In the Mood." Thornton Wilder shows life in *Our Town* and Katharine Hepburn and Cary Grant help everyone escape in *Holiday*. Teflon, fiberglass, and nuclear fission of uranium make the news. Woody Guthrie supports the labor movement, singing "Hard Traveling." Neville Chamberlain naively says, "I believe it is a peace of our time, peace with honor." Country School Children meet the *500 Hats of Bartholomew Cubbins*. Country School Teachers rejoice at the invention of the ballpoint pen, and, like the Seven Dwarfs from *Snow White*, Bernice Huston whistles while she teaches in Wright County.

Bernice Houston

Bernice Huston

Bernice Huston completed her teachers training in Buffalo in 1937. Bernice taught in the following Wright County schools: Paddon School, Stockholm School, Hanover School, Carlson School, and Hasty. Bernice Huston taught for a total of eight years.

Piggish About My Salary

One year one of the school board members, who was so proud of the fact she had a master's degree from the University of Minnesota and held it over everybody's head, said that they couldn't give me any raise because the price of pigs had gone down. I thought that was quite leveling! **1938, Paddon School**

More Than Reading and Writing!

In my first year of teaching, the homes were very poor and many had poor sanitation. The children in several families had scabies so bad; naturally I was the teacher and the janitor, so every Friday night I washed the woodwork to try to keep the disease down. I never expected teaching to include this.

These people were farmers who were very poor and operating on a shoestring. Their clothes were poor. One little boy came to school wearing a girl's coat. Naturally some of the older boys made fun of him. I realized my goal in teaching was not just to teach them reading and writing, but to teach them concepts of life as well.

I immediately knew what was going to happen, so somehow I arranged it so that this little boy wouldn't be present when I talked to the kids. I told the children that it didn't make any difference whose coats they were wearing as long as it was warm. The kids just didn't have warm clothes. My little talk took care of the situation and we never had any further problems.

1938, District 135, Paddon School, Wright County

Composure

One of these little boys came to school on the day the Pope had died. They were very staunch Catholics. He had no understanding of geography and the father didn't either. The boy said, "Dad said if we had a better car, we'd drive over to the Pope's funeral." I had to have real presence of mind to handle that without putting the kid down, but it was pretty hard not to step aside and laugh.

c. 1940, District 135, Paddon School, Wright County

'Tis a Puzzlement!

I had a fountain pen that had been given to me by a school janitor when I was in high school, and it was something that was quite precious to me. One day after school the fountain pen was missing. I thought it must have gotten knocked off my desk into the wastebasket or on to the floor. I searched everywhere, but I couldn't find it. The next morning when I came to school I searched again, but I couldn't find it. At the end of that day I did something which I think now was a very risky thing. I said, "Now, somebody has my fountain pen, and we won't go home until the pen is laid on my desk."

And we sat there. Finally one little boy said, "Can I take my brother up to the front of the room and search him?"

I said, "Yes." Well, he took his older brother up to the front of the room and searched him and pulled out the fountain pen. The brother just went right up to the front and let his younger brother search him. I felt terrible for what I had done to that brother, but he learned a lesson about life and I learned a lesson about life, too. I'm sure all the kids did. Think of the courage that it took to say, "Can I take my brother up to the front of the room and search him?"   **c. 1940, District 135, Wright County**

Who Needs a Chart?

I had this little girl who was quite shy, and she had parents who were quite old when she was born. The father was brilliant, but he was quite odd. The little girl was so bright that she knew how to read as a first grader, but I didn't know that. I had put up color charts on the walls with the word *red* after it so the students could learn the word *red* that way. I showed her a little flash card and said, "What does this say?"

She said, "red."

I said, "Well, how did you know that?" I thought she was going to say she had matched it to the color chart.

She said, "Well, r—e—d spells red, doesn't it?"

This little girl went on to receive several master's degrees. She became a teacher, and when she was commissioned as a missionary in Quito, Ecuador, I was honored as her first-grade teacher. That was my proudest moment as a teacher.

The Convention

Bernice had other moments as Country School Teacher which were not quite as fulfilling. When the weather turned cold, the field mice spread the word that it was again time to hold the annual School Rodent Survival Convention. The chilly critters headed for the country schools. Bernice's chapter was very productive.

Mitten! Mitten!

Many times I stayed at school late working on lesson plans and doing the janitor work. One night I was washing the boards, and I must have been interrupted. Perhaps someone came to get me, and I left the pail of water next to the stove where we always hung the mittens to dry.

The next morning I looked in the pail, and I saw these five points sticking up in the pail. So I said to myself, "Oh, one of the kid's mittens must have fallen in." I reached in to bring out the mitten, but what I grabbed was not a mitten but five mice!

Mickey and Minnie's Music

Music has always been a big part of my life. I had a lot of music in the country schools. The parents really appreciated that because the Depression was a time when people needed music in their lives. But we never had any equipment, a piano or anything like that.

When I was teaching in one of the country schools, the people in my hometown said they had a piano that we could have. So the school board brought it to the school. Oh, we were so happy to have that piano!

The first day we had the piano, we could hear these little tinkling sounds. I thought, "That was the piano. What made that sound?" Well, the piano was full of mice. It was never of any value because the mice had eaten all the felt off the keys.

Bernice Houston taught in the rural schools for eight years.

1939

World War II begins in Europe. Seventeen percent of the American work force is unemployed. The atom is split for the first time and Albert Einstein alerts President Roosevelt about A-bomb opportunity. Americans are reading *The Grapes of Wrath* and *Uncle Tom's Cabin*. Judy Garland stars in *The Wizard of Oz*, the Dinah Shore Show premiers, and Frank Sinatra joins the Harry James Band. Batman appears. Pocket Books sell for 25 cents. Fluorescent lights go on. The Baseball Hall of Fame is established and Lou Gehrig retires. Jimmy Stewart and *Mr. Smith [Go] to Washington*. Country School Teachers who oversleep can still fix a nutritious breakfast with new five-minute Cream of Wheat or quick-cooking Quaker Oats.

Vivian McMorrow
Vivian McMorrow taught in Wright County from 1939 to 1940. The school was located between Howard Lake and Cokato on Highway 12.

The Name Dilemma

Vivian McMorrow

On the first day of school I called the roll for the first graders. I called the name Michael (last name), and he said, "That's not my name." Then I realized he was brought up by his grandparents. He thought his mother was his sister. But on his birth certificate, which I was using to call roll, it used his real father's name. I decided it was not up to me to tell this kid his background. It was a touchy situation so I just let it go and called him by the name he wanted to be called by. His grandparents were nice to me and he had a good home life with them.

He was a smart kid. He learned to read with no problem. At the school picnic in the spring, he won a book as a prize. He said, "Why did I get a book? I don't know how to read."

I said, "Yes you do. You read in school all the time."

"But those are school books," he said.

"Look at this. Open it up." He was just amazed that he could read something besides school books. So evidently at home he had no books. He thought you could only read in school.

One time he asked me how old I was. I told him I was nineteen. He said, "I like girls who are nineteen. Will you wait for me? I want to marry you." He was a darling boy!

Teachers training prepared Vivian for the academic battles, but it did not teach her how to confront a lecherous school board member. However, he was no match for Vivian McMorrow!

Country Casanova

I lost my job at this school because I wouldn't go to the church that one of the school board members wanted me to attend. He sent me notices of meetings and church events, telling me I should go. But I didn't go because I had my own church.

I also think part of the problem was that he would have loved to have had an affair. He stopped at the school on any pretext. Because he was on the school board, he could legitimately come in and ask, "Did I need this or that for the school? How are things going? How are my kids doing?"

But he always came after the kids had gone when I was alone. He chased me around the school enough so that I knew what he was after. Once he put his arm around me. I told him I didn't want anything to do with him. He was married. I had his kids in school. I was only nineteen, and he was probably in his early forties. I had a boyfriend I knew I was going to marry. I was naive, but I knew I didn't want anything to do with that old farmer.

Finally, I just got tough and told him about my boyfriend. Then he stopped coming. It was such a sensitive issue because he held my job in his hands. This was during the Depression, and there were so few jobs. I didn't want to antagonize him, but I had my principles. He was one of three who voted me out. He was probably afraid I would say something. The county superintendent told me later I was lucky to get out of there and that I would be much happier in a different school.

I never told that story to my boyfriend. He was my boyfriend from sixth grade on. He was killed during the D-Day invasion. We were married for almost two years, but we only got to spend about twelve weeks together before he shipped out. I was a widow at twenty-four.

Casanova's Offspring

That farmer's second-grade boy slashed my tires. He wandered around for no reason whatsoever. I told him he had to stay in his seat, so I put an empty shoebox next to him so when he got up, he would kick it and remember to sit down. That made him mad.

I looked out at recess and there he was, slashing my tires with his jackknife. He had slashed the first one and was working on the second one. I went outside and stopped him. I couldn't do much about it except call my dad to come and fix the tires. It was the Depression. There was no use going to his folks because they didn't have any money. I told them about it but they didn't offer to fix my tires.

213

From 1940 to 1941 Vivian McMorrow taught in a school two miles south of Howard Lake.

Arms Filled with Love

In my second year I had only seven students. One of the boys was ten years old but only in his fourth year in school. He couldn't read anything. He had no concept of numbers. His mother had died when he was born, and according to the father, this child could do no wrong. The teachers who had him before I came were constantly exasperated. He came to school sporadically.

The county tested him and told me if I treated him like a four-year-old, his mental age, he would do better. With only seven students I had the time, but I didn't have the training.

I got him so he could say a couple of sentences in a row. He loved to come to school and never missed a day. I never taught him to read that year, but he did talk. He could look at a picture and tell me a three- or four-sentence story. When his social skills improved, he quit hiding behind his mask. One day the superintendent told me I was doing a good job with this boy and that made me feel so good. I could never be honest with that father and tell him the boy wasn't up to par. I just said he was improving. The father couldn't accept the truth. The boy went through eight grades and later became a good farmer.

The year after I had him in class, I was at the county fair. When he saw me, he ran up to me and threw his arms around me. It was the first time he showed any emotion that he really liked me.

During the 1941 to 1943 school terms, Vivian McMorrow taught in the Corvuso School. The octagonal school was located between Litchfield and Cosmos.

Fender Bender

I had a 1930 Chevrolet that was high off the ground. The farmers all had newer cars that were lower to the ground. They would wait until I got to school in the morning before they started out because I could go through the snow with my car and make a track for them.

One day the brakes gave out and I hit a telephone pole. After that the fender always flopped up and down and made lots of noise. The oil pump often froze up during the day. I would park my car over a hole in the snow when I came in the morning. Then I would take a burning log and put it under the oil pump to thaw it out. In the spring there were burned-out logs scattered all over the schoolyard.

The next year I was driving home in the dark and the fender fell off. I thought I had hit a cow or a pig or some wild animal.

Grace Swanson

Grace Alm Swanson, 1940

Grace Swanson completed teachers training in 1939. From 1939 to 1941 she taught in the Collins school, District 56, six miles south of Dassel in Wright County. She then married and raised five children. In 1962 she returned to teach in District 66 in the Ellsworth School in Meeker County. She taught there until 1969. When Grace began her teachers training, her instructor lectured her with this admonition: "Do not expect to pass the course if you sleep more than four or five hours a night!" Her threat was accurate. Grace often worked into the early morning hours.

Grace and her classmates managed to cope quite well with the rigorous academic demands. However, a few situations required creative problem-solving skills. Perhaps these difficulties prepared her to solve the trials of teaching in a rural school. For example: What does one do when things get really "hot" or when students are spoiled rotten?

Grace's teachers training class at Litchfield in 1938 to 1939: For their Hollywood glamour pose, they stuck out their legs and rolled down their stockings. Grace is first on the left.

Star Trek

I lived with my cousin Doris during teachers training. Once we had a dozen rotten eggs. We'd forgotten them in the warm closet. The fall days were hot and our upstairs room was very warm. Of course we had no refrigerator. What were we do do with them? We waited till very late one night to go for a walk under the stars, carefully carrying our rotten eggs. Soon we found an empty lot and disposed of our stinky problem. What a smelly mess!

Grace (left) and her cousin Doris lived in the house behind them to the right. They had no refrigerator.

Creative Thinking Exam: Teachers Training 101: What does an aspiring teacher do in the heat of the night when the thirst for cool water becomes overpowering and no ice cubes are available? To survive as Country School Teachers, Grace and her roommates relied on chicanery.

To the Power Cubed

One evening it was so very hot and uncomfortable. We wanted something cold to drink, but our drinking water came from the bathroom sink and was never cold. This same sink is where we washed our dishes. We were desperate for a cold, cold drink and thought of a plan.

We went downtown to a cafe called The Black Cat. We had been told they always brought a glass of water filled with ice cubes. So we went in, sat down, and sure enough—the waitress came with ice water. We quickly drank the water, wrapped the ice cubes in the napkins, and stashed them in our purses. We went to the lady at the cash register and told her we were sorry but an emergency had come up and so we had to leave. That evening we had some ice cubes in our pitcher of water.   **1938–1939**

The Master Builders

The school had a beautiful oak recitation bench across the front of the room where the children sat for their class time. However, in my class of one-year teacher training, we were taught that was not good and that we should have a small table and chairs for the class discussions. When I asked my school board members for a table and chairs they said there was no money for that.

So after school one day I had the big eighth-grade boys saw down the legs of an old kitchen table. Then I got wooden apple crates at the town's grocery store, and we cut off the one end and the half sides to make four small chairs.

The boys sanded and painted this furniture. Then I let them chop up the recitation bench (not knowing how valuable that antique would be today). We burned it in the stove. Those boys had been troublemakers for the previous teacher, but I believe this eighteen-year-old teacher won them over with that project for I never had any troubles. The school board members never said a thing about it, but the next year they ordered a small table and chairs and gave me a raise in salary.

District 56, Dassel, 1940

Horsing Around

I remember so well my first school picnic. I came to the picnic wearing an outfit called "Farmerettes." It was like a bib overall. My school board members said they had never had a teacher come wearing slacks or pants. They expected to see a dignified teacher dressed like a lady. I was only eighteen years old and they liked to tease me.

Before the picnic, I asked the school board how the picnic meal would be served. The picnic was to be held in a neighbor's pasture where there were horses and cows. I asked if we'd be bringing tables for the food, but they said, "No, we'll just lay a couple of boards across some horses." I thought they were talking about the real horses in the pasture. When I got to the picnic, someone talked about the sawhorses. However, I never let anyone know how ignorant I'd been.   **1941, District 56, Dassel**

Flushed

I had four children who got off the bus around 4 p.m. each day. I knew they'd have so much to tell me when I got home, and I knew I'd also have to make supper, do laundry and other housework. So I stayed in the school to study for my off-campus classes, which I was taking for my degree, and to do my lesson plans for the next day.

There always seemed to be lots of mice in the Ellsworth School. It was so quiet, but as I sat at my desk, the mice came out from behind the piano, the bookcase, and the space heater. Before I went home, I set traps. There were always dead mice in them the next morning. I didn't dare throw them in the wastepaper baskets for fear the boys might find them and chase the girls with them.

Instead, I flushed them down the toilets. One year we had a plumbing problem. The plumber wondered what had plugged the toilets. "Could it be the mice?" I wondered. I didn't dare say anything.

Sparky

When I signed my contract to teach at the Ellsworth school in 1962, I had a very unusual condition in my contract. The contract stated that I must let a dog named Sparky, a black Labrador, come to school. Years before, the dog as a puppy had come to school with his boy owner, Hugh Smith, and the teacher let the dog lie at her feet under the desk. The following teacher refused to let the dog come to school. Sparky's owner locked him in the barn. He

Sparky

tried to tie the dog to a pole or tree, but Sparky just went wild chewing down the barn boards to get out. He wanted to go back to school to play with the kids.

So when I came, Sparky came to school, also. The children taught him to slide down the slide. There were twenty-six pupils who would line up, go up the steps, sit down, and then slide down. Sparky did the same, and after sliding down, he always went to the end of the line for his next turn.

He lay on the steps outside so no one could enter the school except the children or their parents because Sparky knew them. When a telephone repairman came one time, I had to go out to let him in. At noon Sparky was allowed to come inside where he ate the sandwiches the children didn't like or he ate some extras they had for him. Then they would say, "Sparky, go play the piano," and he would go up and down the piano keyboard with his paws.

The Minneapolis *Tribune* came to take a picture of Sparky at the slide and they wrote a full-page feature article about him. After that the article was published in *The Stars and Stripes*. We received letters from serviceman stationed all over the world, so we used this as a teaching tool. We marked the places on our big world map. Many soldiers told us about their dogs at home. **1962, Ellsworth School, Darwin, Meeker County.**

Grace Swanson was a Country School Teacher for nine years.

Many of the teachers who began teaching in the 1930s saw the end of the country school when the rural schools consolidated. However, for generations, Country School Teachers filled schools like the Fifty Lakes School in Crow Wing County with dedication and passion. What stories these old buildings could tell!

Fifty-Lakes School, Crow Wing County, south of Emily

216

Chapter 25

That's Life!

Edith Korsch Clafton lives a few miles north of Grand Rapids. We had just finished our interview and I was packing my equipment into the car when her husband said, "Ask her about *Life*."

I grabbed my video camera and tape recorder and went back to the house. "Edith, please tell me about *Life* magazine."

"Did he tell you to ask that? I wasn't going to mention it."

What a tale it is! Edith taught in a country school for only two years, 1938 to 1940. Her life was much like most other Country School Teachers until shortly after school opened for the new year. On January 22, 1940, Philip B. Sharpe of South Portland, Maine, wrote a letter to the editors of *Life* magazine. He announced that as a kid he didn't like school any more than other kids, and then came his startling news: he had discovered why and he decided to tell the world.

Mr. Sharpe mentioned that he had been giving instructions on firearm safety in an unnamed state. Working for that state's board of education, he had addressed approximately 1,500 teachers. He claimed that only four or five of the women in this group could be considered attractive. He concluded that most of the women would scare children. No wonder they didn't learn.

Mr. Sharpe assumed that some attractive girls become teachers, but where were they? What happens to them? Do the good-looking ones marry? Are there any attractive teachers? Then like the classic flim-flam man, he invited attractive teachers to send him their photographs. Unless these beauties could change his mind, he would continue to hold his ugly-teacher theory.

Life was deluged with letters from irate readers. Two hundred and forty-five people included photos of attractive teachers. Parents, sweethearts, friends and relatives challenged those Sharpe words. Many teachers sent their own pictures to *Life*, defending themselves and their profession from this Sharpe attack.

On February 12, 1940, in its "Speaking of Pictures" section, *Life* published twenty-six photographs and noted in bold print that *Life's* readers had chosen these teachers for their looks. *Life* also wrote that many teachers mentioned it was difficult to look like a movie star on an average salary of $1,200 a year and that many of the prettiest teachers marry and then lose their jobs because married women aren't hired.

Twenty-year-old Edith Korsch's photograph was on page thirteen in Life magazine.

Because of the Depression, few farm families in Edith's home area subscribed to *Life*. However, Edith's mother took the magazine to make certain her children knew what was happening in the world and who was making the news.

"This Is Your *Life!*"

My mother and my eleven-year-old-brother Don sent in my picture and a letter. I was teaching in the Arbo School, District 318, in Itasca County. I was seven miles from town. No one in that area even knew about *Life*. They were very poor. Any money went for food or clothes, not for entertainment, certainly not for a magazine.

When I went to town, a stranger walked up to me and said, "Your picture is in *Life* magazine." I couldn't believe it so I bought a copy. Sure enough. There I was! There was no one I could tell. I couldn't even call my parents because they had no phone, so I wrote a letter home.

JUNEAU-YOUNG HARDWARE COMPANY

HARDWARE · SPORTING GOODS · PAINTS
BUILDING SUPPLIES · STOVES · RANGES
FURNITURE · RUGS · LINOLEUM

JUNEAU, ALASKA

March 11 - 1940

Hello

Saw your Picture in Life along with a lot of other Goodlooking Teachers and seeing that you were from my old Home town thaught I would Say Hello. I am not trying to get fresh or act funny but it has been So long Since I have Seen or heard from there that I just got kinda lonesum So if you ever come up this Way look me up the name of the Company that I work for is on the top also will Send you a Picture of my self & truck.

Best Regards.

George, the swain from Alaska, tells his pickup that he's lonesome for "back there" and that he has written to an attractive teacher. "You know, old buddy, we may move back there, or maybe she'll come up here." Edith wasn't interested in either Alaska or George.

Illinois State Penitentiary, Menard Division

THE DEPARTMENT OF PUBLIC WELFARE

NO CRIMINAL NEWS WILL BE PERMITTED UNDER ANY CIRCUMSTANCES

Dear Miss Worach:

I am writing to you asking, if you will help me with my present difficulty.

I know you come in contact with many a people. I've had a parole since April 28, 1937. I need a job + sponsor. Working for a farmer $15 a month room + board. Or if you know of some one in town who needs some one. These parole papers got to be sign before I can go free. If you can help me please write to me right away and I'll send you a set of parole papers to be sign. Remember your not responsible, all your doing is helping me to get a new start in life.

I and Illinois. I was then 17 years old. I was paroled once. June 15 1935. Return for parole violation, for possession of a stolen car. Aug. 13. 1936. My Mother + Father have passed away. I've learned my lesson. I can do most any kind of work.

Hopeing you will lend me a helping hand. I will prove myself trust worthy to you.

I wish you.

Good Health

Lots + Lots of Happiness

+

Good Luck

Always

Letters, I Got Letters!

Edith received a letter posted February 23, Fort McDowell, California.

Dear Miss Korsch;

Maybe you will be surprised at receiving a "blind date" letter of this kind on the other hand you might have received dozens of them already.

Now if this sort of thing is distasteful please forgive me and forget it. On the other hand if you would like to be kind to a lonely soldier then answer and we will proceed with a correspondence which I will try my very best to make interesting.

I am five feet eight inches tall, weigh about one hundred fifty three pounds. My hair is blonde and my eyes are blue. Light complected and not exactly an ugly duckling. I won't bore you with likes and dislikes after all you may not be interested.

As I mentioned I am a lonely soldier in the good old U.S.A. I have been for quite a long while and expect to be for quite a long time to come.

I really enjoy letters and I sincerely hope you will sit down, and permit me one of yours.

This letter from a soldier destined for long-term loneliness did not move Edith to strike up a relationship. The postmark on another letter of February 23 was stamped Pike Road, North Carolina.

Dear Miss Korsch,

Hope you'll not be surprised to hear from some fellow you never dreamed of, but you see while taking a look through *Life*, I happened to see your picture. Gee, It will be dreadful If I happen to be writing to some fellow's wife won't It? but you will excuse me just one time won't you Miss Korsch.

Miss Korsch your picture reminds me more of a Teacher Friend I used to go with here at home than any girl I ever saw and of course I thought she was real nice looking. If you answer this letter send me a picture of yourself and I will send you one of mine if you care to have one. I am 30 years old, five feet eleven inches in higt wt 173. I quess as ugly as the general run of the Boys.

Now that you are getting tired of reading this terrific writing I will say good nite. Bye write soon.

About February 28, a letter postmarked Chattanooga, Tennessee, really warmed up Edith's mailbox with southern hospitality.

Dear Miss Korsch:---

I hope this letter doesn't strike you as being bold or from some crank. I'm not a crank, and my friends think I'm rather sound.

For the next five pages the writer argues that the man who said teachers were ugly was wrong, gives Edith a verbal guide of Chattanooga, and documents the area's role in the Civil War. Then he returns to the real business of the letter.

I am manager of a hardware store and hope to have one of my own soon. I know the business and the folks in my neighborhood—oh, I forgot, of course, I'm single and judging from the way they had your name I took it for granted you were. That seems about all I can write—please don't disappoint me and I'll be expecting a letter from you next Thursday, a week from tomorrow, it'll take about two days each way. Hope to hear from you soon.
    Sincerely Yours,

"The Dynamo of Dixie"

The other half of the "Dynamo's" photo has been carefully cut off.

One of the letters was postmarked January 27, 1941, Halifax, Nova Scotia.

Miss Korsch,

Just a line or to this Morning to asked if you Would Like to do some Correspond With me this year. A Friend of Mine told me about you, and how nice A Lady that you Was, so that is—The Reason I am Writing this Love Letter to you. My Love, I am a Truck Driver, and I may say that I Like the Job Very Good. In your Love Letter that you Write back to me, I Wish that you Would tell me your age, and if you would Like to have me to write to offten. Say have you any pictures of youself. If you have. please send me one in your next letter My Darling—

Dear. Miss Korsch.

*Jest a line or to this. —
Morning. to arked if you Would
Like to do some Correspond with
Me this year. a friend of mine
Told Me about you. and how nice
d Lady that you Was. so That is —
The Reason I am writing this Love
Letter to you. my Love, I am a
Truck Driver. and I may say that
I Like the Job very Good. I'm you
Love Letter that you write back to.
me. I wish that you would tell. me.
you age. and if you would Like
to have me to write to you often
say have you. any picture of yourself.
If you have. please send me one in -
you next Letter. my Darling. —*

And I Will send you one of mine. My Home is in the Annapolis Valley—Was you ever down in Nova Scotia it is a very nice place. Well, I hope that this Love Letter Will please you enought so that you may answer all of mine—Love Letters. Edith. And May God-Bless you allways My Dear————From your true Loving Friend

xxxxxxxxxxxxxxxxxxxxxxxxxxxxx

*And I Will send you one of mine
My Home is in the Annapolis. Valley
Was you every down in. Nova —
Scotia. it is a very nice place.
Well. I hope that this Love Letter
Will please you enought so that —
you may answer all of mine —
Love Letters. Edith. And May God.
Bless you allways my Dear. —
From. you true Loving Friend..*

xxxxxxxxxxxxxxxxxxxxxxxxxxxxx

Edith did not give up her job and move to Nova Scotia, nor did she become the writer's "Darling." No letters were posted from Arbo School, Itasca, Minnesota, to Nova Scotia. All the "my loves," "my darlings" and "my dears," could not persuade Edith Clafton to rush off to a Halifax.

The letters kept coming. A woman in Oklahoma wrote, "I am interested in finding out whether we tally at all physically and if we do, how different our minds may be. It might be interesting to trace back and dig up whatever race type makes us look alike."

Another man from Massachusetts wrote, "Dear Miss Edith, I have seen your picture in life book as a teacher. so please excuse my writing to you but it is just an idear i got when i seen your picture to drop you a few lines. Here hoping we can exchange letters that is if you care to answer. As pen-pals."

An Army major in Washington wrote, "I am at present in negotiation for a small tract in the Lake region of Northern Minnesota where I plan to buy a sort of a 'dream castle' and watch 'the rest of the world go by.' I assure you it will be quite proper for you to tell me where Brook Park is located, as I am single, under forty, and do not have the habit of writing to pretty school marms."

The major's use of a popular song could not win Edith's interest. She was unimpressed with the pitch to "build a sweet little nest out there in the West and let the rest of the world go by."

Edith received one other romantic proposal, this one from a man from the Shanghai Race Club. When he saw Edith's picture, he wrote, "I am being bold enough to ask you if you would care to correspond with me." His reason for "electing you as the recipient of my first attempt to write to a lady who is a perfect stranger is that I hail from the "Show Me State." Edith was not interested in moving to China, nor did she move to Alaska or become a social worker for the prison inmate from Illinois.

Edith received many other letters from people who thought they might be long-lost relatives or people who thought Edith looked like a friend: "One of our customers brought in a clipping from *Life* because he thought you looked enough like our bookkeeper to be a sister. I am enclosing a snapshot of her.

Edith Clafton did not stray very far from Grand Rapids, and if her husband had not given her secret away, she would have let me drive away without telling me her *Life* story.

Chapter 26

Stormy Weather

The weather gods were cruel to us,
Snow and icy rain.
We had no fancy yellow bus.
Walkin' was a pain.

Windy blasts from North Dakota
Blew Hallock a mile east,
Froze up half of Minnesota,
That snarling Winter Beast.

The room each day I got to school,
Was forty-eight below.
The stove just took me for a fool.
I couldn't make it glow.

The fields blew through the window sills,
Throughout the Dusty '30s.
Shovelin' an' sweepin', I had my fill
Of everything that's dirty.

Then one day the flood washed in,
Things looked so damned grim.
Sandbaggin, we tried so hard to win
'til the books began to swim.

Golden times, we reminisce
And sigh, ah, such nostalgia.
Brought us joy and peaceful bliss,
Neuritis and neuralgia.

-TM

He Swept Me off My Feet

The railroad depot lay in the lowest part of Freeburg. There was a creek on the other side of the railroad tracks. In the spring the creek overflowed and flooded into the depot. The water was probably a foot deep. That happened one night when I was to take the train home. We mailed our mail at the grocery store where the mailman took it and got it ready to throw into the train. Usually he was in the depot room, but this time it was flooded. I got a ride in a horse and buggy as far as the depot, but I couldn't get very near to it because the water was too deep. I wanted to get home so badly. The mailman, Mr. Welsh, came over to the buggy after the train had whistled and was coming in. He picked me up and carried me to the train and set me on the first step. I got home.

Julitta Schmitz Pearl, 1922, Browerville School, one and one-half miles east of Freeburg, Houston County

Ingenuity

The roads were so muddy and slippery that everybody got stuck. My sister and I were teaching out in the country. One night I got stuck in a mud hole. I looked in the car to see what I had. I had some cardboard boxes and I broke them up and laid them in front of the back wheels. Another time it was so slippery that I couldn't even get the car out of the garage. I had some flowerpots, so I dumped out the dirt under the wheels and got out of that spot, too.

Evelyn Comer, 1922, District 2, Atwater, Kandiyohi County

Mountain Climbing

In April we had a terrific snowstorm. Emil Bach, who owned the house where I boarded, sent their hired man, Bill White, with a bobsled and a team of horses to get me at school. We went up and down the mountains of snow. When I went to the school the next day, the top of the furnace was covered with snow, and inside the whole north wall was plastered with snow. There certainly wasn't much insulation in that school.

Regina Starken, 1924, McLeod County

Dirt, Dirt, and More Dirt

The worst experience I had in my twenty-four years of teaching was a dirt storm that came up in the middle of May in 1929. I was going to have a Mother's Day program the next day. At four o'clock I was putting up some things for the parents to see. The storm came like night. I got on my knees and cried and prayed because I had fourteen kids who had just left school.

Some had ridden horses. All I could see was the top of the flagpole. It looked like night. Two little girls walked across a plowed field and luckily found a brooder house. They stayed in there, which saved their lives.

A girl who lived close to the school said to her dad, "I'll bet you Miss Likehart is scared," so they set off in that terrible weather to rescue us. It certainly was a life-threatening situation. It was so dark they had difficulty seeing the person in front of them. To keep from getting lost, they followed the fence across the road to the schoolhouse, and we followed the fence back to their house. I stayed there. The storm lasted for four hours, and the dirt blew as high as the fences. People had to go out there with road graders to clear away the dirt.

My husband-to-be was out in the fields and all he could see was the back of the horses' feet. He couldn't see well enough to direct the horses, but the horses were smart and had great instinct and took him right to the barn.

When I went back to the school, my books were buried because the ventilating room carried in fresh air from the furnace and that blew open as all that dirt from the plowed field blew on my desk.

Those two years of dust storms destroyed many farmers. My parents lost their farm. For those two years they couldn't even take a binder out. There was no crop. They had to get feed loans. My sister and I helped my parents for six years to put groceries on the table and pay off those loans.

Hattie Likehart Hallaway, 1929, south of Alberta, Kandiyohi County

Muck, Muck, and More Muck

I had to travel thirty-five miles from Northome to Effie. The highway was Number 1, but the funny part of that is that the name of the highway was Park Avenue. It was named after an alcoholic doctor who lived on Park Avenue in New York and came out here to recover.

I was home for spring vacation. My brother and a friend were going to take me back to my boarding place, which was about forty-two miles. The weather wasn't too bad when we started but it grew worse. We had a terrible time because of the soggy conditions which turned the road to muck. It took us from seven in the morning until seven at night to go to Bigfork. The roads were clay mud. They practically pushed the car through that sticky, slippery clay all those thirty-five miles. I steered and they pushed. I called a logger who came with his logging truck to take me the seven miles out to the school.

Ruth Gould, 1930, District 1, Itasca County

Sandy

There had been a windstorm on Sunday. When I got to school on Monday, the window sills were an inch deep in dust. The kids were coming in half an hour. I couldn't sweep it because it covered everything.

I thought, "What am I going to do?" The window sills wouldn't be too difficult because I could take the dustpan and scrape it off, but I knew I could never clean the floor and the desks.

So I thought a minute and decided I would wait until the kids came and see if they knew what to do. They had the same thing happen in their houses.

When they came they said, "Oh, we had that, too. You know you're not supposed to take the broom dry. We hafta put water on it. We know it's gonna make a mess, but we hafta do that cuz you can't sweep it out dry."

So they sprinkled the floor. They wiped the dust off their desks right on to the dustpan. We washed the desks and seats with paper towels. Sometime during the morning a parent came and asked how we were getting along, and by that time we had the mess pretty well cleaned up. With the kids' help I got through that mess.

Ida Welter, 1932, District 52, Scott County

In 1935, Phyllis Van Buren Rupp, who had never attended a rural school, got a job in a school on the prairie between Breckenridge and Fergus Falls in Wilkin County. Life on the prairie was not the same as life in town.

Dust

People were so poor out there on the prairie. None of the farm buildings had been painted for quite some time. All of the trees and any kind of shrub and grass had died because of the drought and the dust storms. The prairie was wasteland. The walls of the classroom and the windows were smoky because of the heavy winds and the dust blowing across the prairie. The women washed them before school started but they smoked up again.

Phyllis Van Buren Rupp, Wilkin County

Pheasant Under Grass

Even though everybody was so poor, I had pheasant in my lunch every day until the middle of January. The pheasants came to the barn and picked in the straw piles. The boys had made some holes in the barn through which they shot them whether it was legal or not—I suppose it wasn't—and their mother fixed me pheasant lunches until January. Then the birds were too thin.   **Phyllis Van Buren Rupp**

Cool, Cool Water

Many years before, my grandfather, who was a well driller, had drilled a well on this school property, and he struck a vein so that we had a flowing well that ran all year long. We always had fresh water. Out on the prairie all the trees had dried up and died in the drought, but right by the school near that well was a big willow. Three of my students rode to school on a horse. They tied the horse in the shade by the tree and she could drink there.

Phyllis Van Buren Rupp, Wilkin County

Fashion Setter

I was teaching southwest of Mountain Lake in 1936. So much snow fell that the mile south of

Elsa Kettler

Highway 60, which ran toward the school, was closed. The banks of snow reached to the telephone wires. At the neighbor's place, only a few inches of apple branches were visible above the snow. For awhile travel was impossible. Many farmers joined together to bring the children to school by bobsled. Sometimes the snow was so deep that the horses had to be dug out, too. I had a very difficult time getting to school. I had to walk a long driveway and then a shorter stretch to school. Here the snowbanks were so steep I had to negotiate them by crawling on my hands and knees. The drifts made it impossible to walk.

Women's apparel did not include snowpants or slacks so to face the cold, I got a pair of men's overalls. My landlord cut rubber bands from an inner tube, which I used to secure the pant legs around my ankles. This kept the freezing winds off my legs.

A long time later, I was told that David Tieszen, who lived near the school, climbed the windmill to see if I got to the school door safely.

Elsa Kettler, 1936, District 65, Cottonwood County: Elsa taught for forty-five years, eighteen as Country School Teacher. She taught in the Mountain Lake public schools for twenty-seven years.

Trapped

I knew a storm was coming. I was hurrying to get the children home when one of the boys threw another boy's cap up on the roof. I said, "You have to go home without the cap; there's a storm coming." I went to the coal shed to get some cobs for the next morning's fire. Then the building started to shake. I hung on to one of the two-by-fours. Suddenly the roof blew off the corncrib across the road. I was terrified of being trapped in that coal-shed, but the school protected the shed from the worst of the storm. I hung on and prayed. I was scared to death when the roof blew off.

Mildred McAdams, April 30, 1936, District 119, Lake Belt Township, Ceylon, Martin County

District 119, Mildred McAdams' school, 1935 to 1937

A Sinking Feeling

The winter of 1936 was horrible. The board decided if it was twenty-five below, there would be no school. The temperature never got above zero for the entire month. My dad's sheepskin coat saved me. I walked two and a half miles across the river to the South School, but most kids would rather have been in school than at home. It was warmer in school because we burned coal.

One morning my landlady's daughter and I were walking to school. The wind and snow were constantly shifting. Normally we could go down the bank of the Yellow Medicine and up the other side, but the snow had drifted. I took a step and sank into a snowbank over my head. I was terrified. I thought I was going to die.

The daughter ran to the next farm and told Mr. Torgeson that I was trapped. They came and dug me out. That winter we had 126 inches of snow. In the spring when the river overflowed, the board hired another teacher to teach in the South End School because the children could not cross the river.

Gail Palmer, 1936, District 2, Lyon County

The Power of Music

On a hot May day in 1936 in late afternoon, I noticed a severe storm approaching. The light in the school grew dim. I suggested to the students that we should take a break and go down to the basement to play singing games. We all marched to the basement and started our games. I urged the children to sing as loud as they could. When the storm passed, we went upstairs. We looked out the window and saw several trees had been uprooted. Only one child suspected that it was storming. I was so thankful that he kept still because I would have had thirty-one panic-stricken students.

Leone Sandstede Anderson, 1936, District 64, Rock County: Leona taught for thirty-eight years in Rock County, sixteen in the country schools.

Thermia

I found a teaching job about five miles from my home, so I boarded near the school. During the last year there, I had an elderly car. One night about 5 p.m. I couldn't get my car started. Someone started it for me. I was on my way home into a blizzard. I was not dressed properly, no slacks in those days nor the right kind of boots. One-half mile from home my car refused to go on. I began walking. The blizzard hit me right in the face. After one fourth of a mile, I squatted down. It felt so good to take the stinging off my face and legs, but I knew I must get up and go on. I had no memory of walking the last half mile. My mother heard a bump against the house. I could not talk coherently. Thermia came very close to ending my life. **Vera Flategraff, 1936, District 2, Maple Grove, Cass County**

Befriended

The day started as a beautiful fall day. Then the storm hit. About one o'clock one of the parents came to pick up all the youngsters living southeast of the school. Later, another parent came for the rest of the students. I was left alone, but not for long. One of the parents got me by bobsled. I spent the next four days with their family. Four of their children were my students. We huddled together in the kitchen while the older sons and dad brought in ducks and geese from the ponds to thaw them out. We slept upstairs with no heat, but we were warmed by feather beds. Now I reminisce about the storm and how they befriended me. **Bernadine Mattson, 1936, District 33, Pleasant Lake School, Scott County**

Making Hay!

Often a greater challenge than teaching was the problem of getting to school. When County Road 2 was constructed past our farm, I had definite problems. On one of my many backroad routes I had to cross Hay Creek. Imagine my consternation when I discovered that most of the bridge was gone, and I would either have to cross on a few planks or drive several miles to get around it. With my heart in my throat, I chose the planks and gave a prayer of joyful thanksgiving when I crossed safely.

Lillian Nelson, c. 1936, Roseau County

Snowbound

I remember very well the November storm. It was raining in the morning, and I was caught at school with sixteen children. There was a creamery quite close to the school, about a quarter of a mile. The buttermaker and his helper managed to get to the school; they knew no one could go out in that storm. They made two trips and got all of us over to their house. I didn't lock the schoolhouse when we left. I left the door open because if anyone was stranded, they could come to the school for shelter.

We managed to put them all to bed. The boys slept downstairs and the girls upstairs. The buttermaker's wife and I stayed up all night and baked bread, so we'd have something to feed them in the morning. The parents came after them in the morning. When two of the fathers saw their children were safe, they cried.

Florence Miller, 1940, Faribault County

Tote That Bucket

After the Sunday Armistice Day blizzard, I got out to my school on Tuesday. The rural schools had a vent to let in the fresh air. My stove was piled high with snow. I carried out sixty-five pails of snow and then I got tired and lit the stove. I thought I could mop the snow up. **Leona M. Kelly, 1940, District 32, Lac Qui Parle County**

Snow Ghosts

After the blizzard that Sunday, we didn't get out to the school until Thursday. We had a tin roof on the school and cold air vents on the sides. The wind was so powerful it blew in around the tin roof. The wind blew all those vents open, and wherever there was a crack, the snow blew in. The rows of desks were mounds like ghosts full of snow. Where it hadn't mounded on the desks, it was seven inches deep throughout the whole school. I went to one of the school board members, and we shoveled until noon and then again all afternoon. We built a fire to melt the snow. After supper we mopped up the water. On Friday I had perfect attendance. We got rid of those seven inches of snow in a hurry.

Lola Prigge, 1940, District 21, Brown County

Mud Doll

One night Delores was waiting to take the bus home. It was so muddy in front of the school that she fell off the boardwalk and got covered with mud. I cleaned her up the best I could and sent her home on the bus. I thought, "Oh, what will her dear mother say?" I tucked a note in Delores's coat to explain the incident. Her mother replied the next morning, "Oh, we just said, 'Oops, another accident.'" **Lois Davy, Freeburg School, Houston County**

Stir-Crazy

A terrible snowstorm swept in off Lake Superior. The snow was then covered with a crust of ice that closed Highway 61.

Esther Norhar Babiracki c. 1942

Nothing could open that road. Another teacher and I lived with a woman who ran a resort. We were snowbound for two weeks. We had no telephone, no radio, no electricity. She had forgotten to bring in the kerosene lamps from her tourist cabins that fall and no one could get to the cabins because of the snow. We had one candle. We rationed that candle so we could have light. Every night we went to bed about six o'clock. When we ran out of fresh meat, we ate canned herring balls. Every day we had fish balls and whatever else she had canned. One day a man crawled on his hands and knees down to Beaver Bay to work. He crawled so he wouldn't slip or break through the icy crust. In his mouth he carried his lunch bucket.

Esther Babiracki, 1943, Beaver Bay School, Lake County

Abandoned

In 1951, I was supervising student teachers. On the last day of their teaching assignment, a terrible storm came up. One of the student teachers was out at Barnard on Otter Tail Road. The clerk told the students and teachers to hurry home because a bad storm was approaching. The regular teacher left, but the student teacher stayed because her father was coming to get her.

The storm was so bad her father couldn't get there. Even though there was a farm family across the road they couldn't get to the school, and the teacher couldn't cross the road to the farm because of the wind and the drifts. They didn't even realize someone was left in the school. My student teacher stayed all night, keeping the fire going. The next day her father finally got her.

Later I realized I had five students who could not get home for Easter, so I invited them to our place for a big meal. While we were eating, the paper boy came by and threw our paper against the door and made a terrible racket. The girl who had been trapped in the school over night screamed something fierce. She was so frightened by any little noise. Then I realized how terribly frightened she must have been that night. After the scream and the terrible fright that went through the group sitting at my table, they began to giggle. That was the best thing they could do to cope with that fear. **Annette Kjaglien was a teacher training instructor in Otter Tail County from 1948 to 1960.**

How High's the Water, Teacher?

We were in class one day when one of the children shouted, "Mrs. Wangen, the flood is coming!" I was scared stiff. A great big lake was coming toward us. It had been raining for several days and nights, but none of us realized a dam had broken or what had happened. In minutes, a flood of water surrounded our school. Soon parents came in hip boots and carried the children from the school to the road. The water rose about hip high and then it moved on. The next day the water was gone.

Ardus Wangen, 1950s, Mower County: Ardus taught in Freeborn and Mower Counties for eighteen years.

Chapter 27

You Did *What?*
Student Stories

Country School Students with laugh or grin,
Told many a story; your hearts they'd win.
Stretched-out facts came at their biddin'
Sneaked past Conscience; Truth was hidden.

The words flew out of mouths so serious,
Tickled the teacher, made her delirious.
Secrets they told, the very worst,
Teachers' girdles nearly burst!

Kisses stolen, beans so hot,
Some tales were and some were not.
Lickin's and huggin's and birthin' rumors,
What a gift, the children's humor!   -TM

Note: Those people with a (T) after their names grew up to become Country School Teachers.

Esther Babiracki, left, in Mexican sombrero, c. 1935, District 68, Embarrass: Esther is developing her teacher skills.

Panting
We had sixty students in grades one through eight and just one teacher. In them days the teacher wasn't supposed to give a spanking. But once in a while our teacher would give a spanking with a little stick across the fingers, which was really no good. The rulers used to have a little lead on one side. He'd turn that ruler around and hit 'em across the knuckles. Later he got a buggy whip. That smarted.

One day the teacher was going to give this kid a spanking. At that time he didn't have no strap or stick or anything so he pulled his belt out of his pants. He tried to put the kid across the bench, but the kid fought him.

When the teacher just about had him across the bench, the kid started pulling the teacher's pants down. He had to let the kid loose and grab his pants. Then he grabbed the kid and tried to lay him across that bench again. By the time the kid had got 'em so far that the teacher was in danger. He had to quit again and pull his pants up. Finally the teacher just gave up. The kid never did get a lickin' that day.

Ed Schroeder, 1916–1924, Courtland Township Lutheran School

Gettin' Even
I went to school near Chatfield. There were twins in that school the same age as me and they used to flog me, beat up on me. They were mean and ugly as could be, always fightin'. You know how it is with kids that age. They git an idea in their heads and they bet ya. You still got an idea you're gonna get even. I couldn't handle two of 'em. Finally I caught 'em one at a time. I got even. Ya know, them was the two best twins in town. I slapped 'em up good.

Wilford Horman, c. 1916, Chatfield, Fillmore County

Sam Who?
My twin brother and I started first grade in Morris. My mother was a widow so we moved to town for the winter. Then the Spanish influenza got so bad the schools were closed. In the spring we went to a country school. One day my mother came to visit. I suppose the teacher wanted to show something special so we sang a song called "Cheering the Sammies." My mother was Norwegian and she thought we were singing "Shearing the Sammies." She wondered what "shearing the Sammies" meant.

Doris Sather Erdahl (T), 1918, District 56, Stevens County: Doris became a country school teacher in 1929 and taught ten years in rural schools.

Mothering
In Spring Valley there was a little boy that liked me. I was so bashful, and he'd follow me home every day. I told my mother that I didn't like him following me home and picking on me. She said, "I'll take care of it." One day she walked up that way and set behind a tree. I knew she was there. We got right

to that place, and he was picking on me. She jumped out and hollered, "What're ya doin'?"

"Ahaaaaaaaa! Nothing," he said. And that was the last time he picked on me. **Alice McNeil, 1919, Spring Valley School, Fillmore County**

Button, Button

We had a hill near our school and in the winter we slid down the hill on our sleds. One day we talked our teacher into going with us. She took a little run and belly-flopped hard on her sled. Just as she flopped down, all the expensive buttons on her coat popped off. That was the end of our sliding for the day because she made us hunt for every one of those special buttons until we found them.

Alice O'Neil, 1920, Fountain School, Fillmore County

"I hate my name! It's too hard to spell." What can a first grader do if she doesn't like her name?

What a Marvel!

I started school at the age of four. I wanted to go to school so badly and there were no restrictions at that time. One day I visited the school. The teacher held me on her lap and read me a story. I thought that was so great. I fell in love with school then. I went through six grades and read all the books. My dad got furious with me for reading so much and crying when I read books like *Uncle Tom's Cabin*.

My first name was spelled *Marvelle*. And *Shaughnessy* had eleven letters, much longer than anyone else's name. I was furious that everyone else could write their names faster. The first day I told my mother, "When I get married, I'm going to marry someone with a short name." And I did. Then I dropped the *le* in Marvelle in the lower grades.

Marvel Shaughnessy Rice (T), 1920, Kerry Lake School, Sibley County

Croquet Anyone?

My father and mother had a store at Clementson, just one block from the school. I was late almost every morning for six years. Then we moved and I attended the Williams School. I walked the three miles and built the fire for the teacher, and then I was never late.

Although I may have been late for school at Clementson, the boys at the Williams School soon learned I was not a passive angel. We played croquet at lunch and recess. One day one of the boys interfered with my playing and I hit him with the mallet and cut his head. From that day on no one messed with Elida Farber.

I saw him years later and he said, "I can still think even though you whacked me on the head."

Elida Farber Berg (T), 1923, Williams School, Lake of the Woods County

Froggie Went a-Courtin' and He Did....

I went to the Sugar Bush when the Indians at Grand Portage were tapping the maple trees. I knew a lot of the Indians who were working there. This one place was making maple cells. They had little forms that they poured the syrup into to make maple candy.

I had a few pennies in my pocket. I said, "How much can I get for this amount of money?" She went and got a little bit of a do-dinger full of the maple candy. I started eatin' on it, and there was a frog leg in it! It was cooked right in there. I threw it as far as I could throw it. **Donald Peterson (whose family homesteaded in Mineral City), c. 1925, Cook County**

He Kept Me in Stitches

In the last years I went to school, I was one of the biggest boys there. When they had the Christmas program, the school board always brought in a box of apples. We had a man teacher who said, "They just drove in. Will you go out and get those apples?"

Now my folks were immigrants. We had a big family and we were hard up, so we wore hand-me-downs. I had a nice suit, but I had outgrown it. I picked up that box of apples and I set it on the floor. Rip—there went the seam in my pants.

The program was supposed to start at eight o'clock and this was a minute before eight. I was so embarrassed. I hated to say anything about it to my teacher. I was very shy. I went to the teacher and said, "I just ripped my pants wide open." There was a gap wide open and I don't suppose I had on very good underwear, either.

He said, "That's no problem. Come on. Let's go."

I said, "The program's supposed to start now."

"Well, it can't start until I'm here," he said. He boarded down across the field and he had made a path through the snow, and we run down to the teacher's house.

"Take your pants off," he said. Well, you can imagine how much a kid that age hates to take off his pants in front of the teacher! I took them off and I wondered what kind of underwear I had on. He threw the old pedal sewing machine open. He was good on that machine. He just zoomed on the seam there. He sewed them up and I put them back on. He was about twenty-five and I was thirteen and we just ran across that old field. Nobody even knew we were gone. The program went on as usual.

Knute Nelson, 1928, Chase-Brook School, District 20, Mille Lacs County

Hair Today, Gone Tomorrow!
There was a boy who sat right behind me. All of a sudden he gave my hair a good tug and he held up two great big hairs. He said, "You got gray hairs." He was holding up two great big horse hairs. I didn't believe him because they were too long and I knew I didn't have gray hair.

Laureen Churchill (T), 1929, District 53 near Grand Meadow, Mower County

Double or Nothin'
We had one bully of a kid and two or three others with him. It was such a fearful thing to go to the outdoor biffy during recess or noon hour because they had no mercy on us. They pelted rocks against the wall or opened the door and threw the rocks inside. Sometimes they peeked through the knothole. So I raised the two fingers during school a good share of the time.

Edith Ailie (T) attended Little Swan School, District 21, in Meeker County from 1929 to 1935.

Nosy
The kids helped milk cows, and when you milk, it leaves a brown ring around your hand from the milking. Some of the kids didn't wash their hands too good and that odor of cow milk and cow made a stench that you could smell. So this young teacher wrote a note home to the parents to see if they could get the kids' hands washed up a little bit better.

So the old dad he sat down and wrote a note to the teacher and said he appreciated the note about the boy and that they would get his hands cleaned up. He said they appreciated what she was doing and they wanted to cooperate, and then he said, "If it's all the same to you, ma'am, why don't you teach him and not smell him!"

One of Cal Zuehlke's (T), Country School Teacher friends told Cal this story. Cal taught from 1930 to 1934 in the Elmo School in Otter Tail County.

Wishing!

Mmmmmmmmmmm!
I kissed my first girl in a country school. Little Jane was a pretty gal. She was moving out of her seat, leaning way over, and I couldn't help myself. I just had to get over and kiss her on the cheek. Mad, she got mad! She was going to tell the teacher, and I couldn't hide. Her cheeks tasted like soap. Her mother scrubbed her good that day. She had neat clothes and curly hair. I was a clod. What a circus!

Cal Zuehlke (T), 1930–1934, Elmo School, Otter Tail County

Strange Vocabulary
My husband once asked me what the phrase "Brattlebo" meant. I told him I didn't know. His teacher said "Brattlebo" when another student was reading. Then the reader stopped and another student began. He finally figured out the teacher was saying "That'll do." **Luva Wilson (T), Meeker County**

District 21, located near Dassel in Meeker County, was better known as Little Swan School. The school was located in a beautiful, secluded spot, surrounded by woods. Unlike most country schools, it was not located on a road or intersection. The center of attraction was Little Swan Lake. It probably would not inspire a magnificent ballet, but to the students of District 21 it was heavenly. Little Swan was the center of their world during noon hour and recess.

Country School Students loved water. Some swam with the fish and leeches. Others tried leaping across creeks. Some paddled wash tubs across ponds. However, in the spring of 1935, Wally Nordstrom and his buddy Bob Boreen decided to play Huck Finn and Tom Sawyer on Little Swan Lake in Meeker County.

Carp—eted

In the spring we visited the bogs and stream just east of the school where we could find flowers, and someone would invariably fall in. Bicycles were also a large part of our activities in spring and fall. We rode on the road along the lake as far as the north end of Little Swan and sometimes we rode to Big Swan Lake. It was on one of these noon-hour adventures that Bob Boreen and I found a sunken boat along the lake shore. We managed to pull it out and get it floating again. This was in the spring when the carp were going out of the lakes into the surrounding streams to spawn.

We paddled the boat around the north end of the lake where we watched the fish swimming. The next day we brought spears to school and used the boat again to go out where the fish were spawning. When we speared a fish, we threw it into the boat. Before the school bell rang, we had half a boat full.

The weight of the fish made the boat ride so low in the water that we couldn't get to dry land because we hit the bottom too soon. We had two choices: either stop to take off our shoes and be late for school or walk to shore, getting wet but getting back to school fast. I chose the last approach, and with my weight out of the boat, I think Bob made it without getting wet. This story intrigued my dad, so he went to check it out. He found the boat more than half full of carp and called his brother who ran a mink farm to come and get the fish for mink food.

Walter Nordstrom, c. 1935, grade seven, Little Swan School

Bag Lady

One year I was asked to thank the lady who donated the paper bags the ladies filled with nuts, candy, apples, etc. for the Christmas program. So I thanked her for her bags. I don't remember anyone telling me to say paper bags or paper sacks. I was so embarrassed and surprised when everyone laughed.

Carol Hunkos Kack, c. 1935, District 49, Madison, Lac Qui Parle County

Is Today the Fourth of July!

Leona Nelson survived the bean attack to become the leader of the band. c. 1942

In 1938, I was in fourth grade. We brought hot lunch and put it on top of the furnace. Somebody brought three cans of baked beans but forgot to open the cans. As we were getting close to noon, BANG, one of the cans exploded. Beans covered the ceiling. We didn't dare go up there and get the other two. Then BANG, BANG—the other two cans exploded. Brown spots covered the ceiling. We all sat there at our desks but nobody studied much after that. I don't know who cleaned it up. It could have been the teacher because she might have been embarrassed. She should have known that the cans needed to be opened. Maybe a student had this job and forgot to check the food. Later it rained beans.

Leone Nelson (T), grade four, 1938

Alphabet Paste

We were doing a group project and we were cutting letters and pasting. Somebody dropped one of the letters, and one of the little boys hollered, "Get the H out of the paste! **Edith Salvervold (T) 1939, District 57, the Buzzle School, Beltrami County**

What should we do during recess? In 1927 and 1928, these students from District 88 in Brookston, St. Louis County, built a log cabin near their school. All the children are one hundred percent Finnish. Aare Suomela, grade two, top left on roof, is one of four Suomelas in the photo.

Horse Sense

Meribeth Peterson, a second or third grader, rode her pony to school each morning, a good mile's ride. At school she'd dismount, give him a pat, and tell him to go home. The horse would promptly take off for home.

The Minneapolis *Tribune* came to school to write the story and take pictures of Meribeth's arrival at school, but they were too slow. The pony beat them back home, so they were unable to film him going down the road back to the barnyard.

The horse was smart but not brilliant! Meribeth's parents had to pick their daughter up at school each day because they could not teach the horse to go back to school to get her. **Grace Swanson (T), c. 1940, Collins School, Wright County**

The Best of Times

All seven of my siblings attended our school. We lived just down the hill from the school—out of our desks, past the pump house, over the farmer's lime pile, through the apple orchard, and into the house.

We could actually wait until the first ring of the school bell, slurp up the last spoonful of Campbell's Tomato Soup, rip through the orchard, scooping up a fallen ripe apple from the ground, jump the lime pile, run up the gopher-holed hill, avoid the pump house, and slide into our wooden desks before the bell tolled its twelfth dong.

Marge has many memories of her days as Country School Student.

Taking turns, we cranked the RCA Victrola on Friday afternoons. Soon there was enough electricity to play at least one record, a thick, black, scratchy 75 rpm. "I've Been Working on the Railroad" was our favorite. We never knew why someone was in the kitchen with Dinah; guess all they ever did was strum the old banjo and sing.

My father built an enormous sandbox (six feet by six feet). Unknown to the teacher, some of us invited a stray cat to spend several "overnights" in the school. On Monday morning the sandbox reeked of a peculiar odor. Some of the first graders playing in the box wondered why the strainers wouldn't strain the sand as they had done the week before. The sand was kinda lumpy and smelly.

We older kids kissed the boys behind the school next to the coal chute. That was quite exciting! **Marge Lelwica, District 23, Birch Lake School, White Bear Lake, Ramsey County**

Forever Young

It was Mrs. Kenthoph's birthday and my son Wayne said he would bring a cake to celebrate her birthday. Together we made a fancy birthday cake. He wanted candles on the cake, so checking to see how many I had, I knew I had to go to the store. I asked Wayne how old his teacher was, and he answered, "Why, Mother, don't you know you have to be five to be in kindergarten?" So Mrs. Kentoph had five candles on her cake because to Wayne she was five years old like the rest of the kindergartners. **Donna Kersting, c. 1956, District 218 near Cohasset, Itasca County**

The Ostrich Kid

Naturally we had few sports. We played a little baseball, but that was all. I knew nothing about football. When I moved to Wisconsin for the fourth grade, they played football. Since I had never learned to play in Forest Center, I hid in the ditch and buried myself under the leaves so they couldn't see me. They found me though and I had to play. **Mike Langer, 1963: Mike went to a two-room school in Forest Center, a logging camp about fifty miles northeast of Ely. Nothing remains today except a sign and a huge rock.**

Come on, Mary Lou, take it easy. Please miss. How's igonna look if I lose to you? You already have all my cat's eyes and my best steelies. A girl's not supposed to be so good."

Chapter 28

1940-1960

The teachers in this section all began their teaching careers in the 1940s. Many continued teaching in country schools until the schools were consolidated and closed.

1941

On January 6, President Roosevelt calls for the Four Freedoms: Freedom of Expression and Religion as well as Freedom from Want and Fear. Hitler proposes the Final Solution. The United States sends one million tons to food to Britain in the Lend Lease Program. Food prices are 61% higher. Cheerios is introduced by General Mills. Dumbo flies across the screen and Curious George makes his appearance. Americans are watching *Citizen Kane* with Orson Wells and *The Maltese Falcon* with Humphrey Bogart. We are singing "Lili Marlene," "There'll Be Blue Birds over the White Cliffs of Dover," and "We Did It Before and We Can Do It Again." On December 7, the Japanese attack Pearl Harbor, and the country goes to war.

Like students all over America in 1942, Bertha Everson's classes in Waltham School in Mower County answer the President's call and collect scrap metal for the war effort.

Esther Norhar, St. Louis County, shows her school's effort.

Mildred Sandell's students have stuffed their feedsacks with milkweed pods to be used in flotation devices. The military later abandoned the use of milkweed, but the students found other ways to help. Mildred's students lived in Mower County.

Yvonne Gagnon

Yvonne Gagnon completed her teachers training in 1941. She taught in Carver and Wright counties. Every teacher can recall at least one specific event in which students initiate the novice. Yvonne's came on a beautiful September day in 1942. Fortunately, she had a wise mentor.

Demon Rum

It was September of my first year of teaching. We were having our last recess of the day. I was playing with the children. One of the boys found a whiskey bottle someone had thrown in the ditch—the school was right on the corner—and he showed it to me. I looked at it and said, "Would you please throw that down the toilet." I went on playing with the children and forgot about the incident for the rest of the day. The next morning the boy's uncle came to school, stood at the back of the room, and said, "Do you know what you did yesterday?" I didn't know what he was talking about. He said that the boy had not put the whiskey bottle down the toilet. He had hid it, and when school was out, he got it. On the way home he drank the little bit of whiskey that was left in the bottle. By the time he got home, he was smelling of whiskey and not acting just right.

His uncle, who was on the board, told me this in front of all the pupils. It was my most embarrassing moment. I felt terrible. I had known this man since I was a little girl and he could have told it to me privately, but he said it out loud.

When I got home, I started to cry. My father asked me what the trouble was. "Don't feel bad about that," he said. "Did you remind him that his child made two mistakes? He disobeyed you and he should not have drunk the whiskey because he knew that was strictly forbidden." But I still felt terrible.

1942–43, District 38, Carver County

The students were not the only ones who taught Yvonne the "teaching in a rural school" facts of life. The school board educated her quite early about one "fact" about country school boards' hiring policies: "Let's be realistic, Yvonne. What would a woman do with so much money? You're not the main breadwinner in the family."

Gender Gap

The year before I came to this school, the board paid the man teacher ninety dollars a month. Two

families in the district had boys who were very troublesome, and when I applied, the board told me they didn't know if I could handle these boys. I thought I would try it because ninety dollars was a lot of money. They informed me that they would hire me, but they would only pay me seventy dollars because I was a woman and I didn't need

Yvonne Gagnon, c. 1941

ninety dollars. I took the school and then got lucky. During the summer the two families with the troublemakers moved away, so I was left with ten very nice little children. I had a great year. I thought I would be hired there for the next year and also get a raise. When I asked for a five dollar raise, the board's response was, "Well, why do you need the money? You're a woman." My home school offered me ninety so I left.

1943, District 38, Carver County

Ask Country School Teachers if there was one student they will never forget, and their eyes will light up and they will clench their teeth. Mention the name "Gordon" to Yvonne and watch her face.

No Dancing Tonight!

One Friday afternoon about 2:30, it started getting cold in the school. I was giving a spelling test, so I asked Gordon, who was sixteen years old and very

tall, to get a "little" chunk of coal and put it in the stove. I really emphasized "little" because that's what I wanted. It was Friday night, and I wanted to leave, so I wanted the fire to burn out quickly.

When I heard the kids laughing, I looked up. A huge chunk of coal was stuck in the door of the

stove. Then Gordon dashed across the room. I hollered, "Don't!"—but it was too late. He kicked that huge chunk into the fire. He was tall, about 5' 11" and he kicked it with his long legs. I knew what he was going to do, and that little devil knew exactly what he was doing, too! They all knew it

Sir Long Legs

was Friday and I would be getting out of school early. They knew that settled it.

My father came to get me. Well, it was dark and we were still sitting there waiting for the coal to burn, so it was safe to shut the draft. I can see the humor in it now, but I couldn't then. I was going to a dance that night and I wanted to get home.

Yvonne Gagnon was a Country School Teacher from 1942 to 1948.

Wilma Harthan

I had planned a four-day trip, interviewing teachers from Grand Marais, Hibbing, Grand

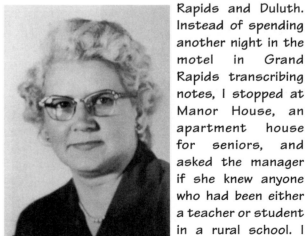

Rapids and Duluth. Instead of spending another night in the motel in Grand Rapids transcribing notes, I stopped at Manor House, an apartment house for seniors, and asked the manager if she knew anyone who had been either a teacher or student in a rural school. I

Wilma Harthan, c. 1941

spent two hours that evening listening to tales about Wilma Harthan's life as a Country School Teacher. Wilma taught in the Dorholt School near Deer River in Cass County and in District 318, Heywood School, in Itasca County.

Trick or Treat: What a Blast!

I expected to be tested in my first teaching assignment, but it wasn't really the students who decided they were going to test me. Some of the young people in the area thought they were going to get the best of the new teacher at Halloween. They had warned me that they were going to "tear the school to pieces." But they were in for a surprise. My husband went over to the school and waited for them and he brought his shotgun. About the time they started gathering around the school, he walked out on the steps and fired a blast in the air. That shook them up, let me tell you. They just tore out of there, and I never had any problems after that.

1941, Dorholt School, Cass County

Love and Sacrifice

The first year I didn't take enough time to have fun with the students, to laugh with them, to really get to know them. I was so intent on getting the material across and making them good little boys and girls I really didn't take time to enjoy them. Well, that changed. Two remarkable things happened that opened my eyes about how they felt about me and how I felt about them and made me love them. One

Keith, left, gave the best part!

of the little boys wanted to show me how much he loved me. His mother had made chocolate chip cookies. He picked the chocolate chips out of his cookies and brought them up to me and said, "Teacher, I love you," and gave me the chocolate chips. He gave me the very best part of his cookie.

Another day one of my youngsters said, "Teacher, your daddy must love you an awful lot because you always have fruit for your lunch."

It made me stop and think. I came in 1941, just after the Depression. Those kids were from very poor families. I didn't take sandwiches for my lunch like they did. I always took a piece of fruit. I realized they didn't have fruit. They had lard on their bread. That made me feel bad. From that day on I didn't take fruit, either. I took a sandwich.

1941, Dorholt School, Cass County

Bambi Stays Here!

During hunting season the kids were out playing, and all at once we heard hunters from across the road driving a deer. That deer ran out of the woods and stood in the midst of those kids in the playground. The men all hollered, "Chase 'im out! Chase 'im out!"

The kids all said, "No, we're not going to chase him out." That deer just stood there. Finally the men got discouraged, turned around, and walked away.

1949, Heywood School

Power of the Poem

I had given my students eight lines of poetry to memorize and this mother came a-roaring to school. "I need my kids to help me at home. They don't have time to learn poetry. What's the use of it anyway?"

I sat down and said, "Did your mother ever recite poetry to you? Did you ever learn any poems?"

"No," she said.

"Well, my dad did," I said, "and he taught me a love of poetry. I believe every child needs to learn a few lines of poetry and to appreciate at least one poem."

She said, "Well, if you can show me what's good about it, I'll let 'em learn it." I got a poem. I don't remember the name of the poem I read to her, but before I was finished, she was crying. She said, "I see what you mean." That was it. The children learned the poetry. **1949–1950, Heywood School**

1943

The war rages on. Bill Mauldin creates Willy and Joe and tells the story of our GIs. Italy surrenders! Pay-As-You-Go appears. For the first time taxes are withheld from workers' wages. Americans are told to "Use it up, wear it out, make it do, or do without!" Cheese and shoes are rationed. The sale of sliced bread is banned and there are no sneakers to be bought. Gym floors are scarred with black heel marks from recycled rubber. DDT is sprayed, *Oklahoma* is staged, *The Little Prince* is written, and the United Nations is born. Country School Teachers sing "Comin' in on a Wing and a Prayer" and "You'd Be So Nice to Come Home To." Country School Students try to figure out what "Mairzy Doats" means.

234

Zola Reese
Zola Reese taught at District 7, Opsahl School, Freeborn County; Christensen School, Waseca Co; District 72, Coulter School; and River Point School in Steele County.

Bed Partner
I roomed and boarded with a family that lived a mile and a half from the school. Every morning I took a bath, but they had no bathroom so I had to bathe in the living room. The house was very cold so I had to bathe where there was some heat. I got up in the wee hours of the morning to take my bath by the oil heater. I heated the water and did a quick sponge bath. But I was used to that because I had grown up without running water and an indoor toilet. However, I never got used to the cold water.

When they had company, overnight guests, there really wasn't any room for their little boy, who was one of my first graders, to sleep, so he had to sleep with me. When he got to be a grown man in his thirties and forties, every time I met him and he was with some other fellows they'd say, "Do you know Richard?"

I always said, "Yes, he slept with me when he was younger."

Don't Mess with Me!
The Opsahl School was named after an old bachelor, who lived down the road a ways from the schoolhouse. The school was located right on the edge of a big woods. Old man Opsahl had pigs in that woods, practically wild pigs, which ate the acorns and foraged in the woods.

I had to leave that schoolhouse and go down the road about a half a mile to meet the bus. One night I started to go down the road and there were two or three pigs out on the road and they were angry. They started after me so I ran back to the school. I didn't know what I was going to do. How was I going to meet the bus? But the bus driver figured something was wrong, so he came down to the school to get me.

The next morning I sent one of my pupils down to Mr. Opsahl with a note, telling him that his pigs were out and I was scared of them because they looked ferocious. I wrote that I didn't dare go down the road to meet the bus and would he please see that they were penned up.

He stood there and read the note. Then he told this little girl, "You know, I don't think your teacher knows what she's talking about. Those pigs wouldn't hurt anybody."

This girl, a fifth grader, got so angry. She looked up at him, put her hands on her hips, and shouted, "MY TEACHER DOES NOT LIE!"

1945, Opsahl School, Freeborn, County

Someone Said That....
Because I got married on September 10, there was one family that said, "Oh, oh, that teacher had to get married." I remember how embarrassed I was that spring when the county superintendent, Mr. Steele, came out to visit my school, and he really had a mission. He even had the papers with him that said that I would gladly resign from teaching because I was going to have a baby before school was out, which wasn't true at all.

He was a bachelor and didn't know anything about married life or babies. It was such a hard subject for him to talk about, but he did it as delicately as possible. He said something like this: "Mrs. Reese, I have kind of a delicate subject I want to talk to you about. One of the mothers in your district has informed me that you are going to have a baby before the school term is up. I have a note of resignation that I have typed up for you if you'd like to use it."

I told him that I was expecting my baby at the end of July. I told him that if I resigned I would have to find another job. He was so apologetic, so sorry he had even mentioned it. He told me I did a beautiful job of teaching and that I should keep right at it. My baby was born at the end of July. That business put a sour note into my first year.

1945, District 7, Freeborn County

Turtle Trauma
We had some baby turtles that we kept in a small aquarium. One morning when I came to school, the turtles were frozen in ice. The students were so concerned because they had become fond of those little creatures. They said, "Mrs. Reese, we think they're dead."

I said, "Oh, I don't know about that. Let's put the aquarium on top of the oil burner. To protect it, I put something underneath it. Well, I forgot about the turtles. When I thought about them, the water was practically boiling, and the turtles were dead. One of the children said, "Mrs. Reese, you murdered the turtles." **1947–1949, Christensen School, Waseca County**

Michael

Michael was in the second or third grade. He walked to school, about a half mile. I noticed in September that he was walking very unsteadily. I got so disturbed about it that I went to his family and told them about how poorly he was walking. They never did anything about taking him to a doctor. I didn't suspect a brain tumor, but I knew something was radically wrong. I said, "If they don't take Michael to a doctor, I'm going to take him." His parents did take him to a doctor, who discovered that Michael had a malignant brain tumor. They gave him treatment at the University of Minnesota, but the tumor was too far advanced.

When we had our Halloween party, I called his mother and asked her if it would be possible for her to bring Michael to school. She said that she would. I went out to the car to get him, and I carried him in, so he could be with his class. I knew that he wouldn't live long. About a week later he was dead. Of course, we all went to the funeral. The church was just across the road from the schoolhouse.

He was such a darling little boy.

Zola Reese taught for thirty-six years: fourteen in the rural schools and twenty-two as a fourth-grade teacher in Albert Lea.

Corrine Johnson and Helen Gresko

Corrine and Helen became friends when they roomed together during their teacher training in Litchfield from 1942 to 1943. Their teaching careers and marriages took their lives in different directions. Years later when they were both widowed, they met on a bus tour. Since then they have renewed their friendship.

Helen Gresko, left, their roommate, and Corrine Johnson

Teachers Training Blues
by Corrine Lesteberg Johnson

Living with three roommates in a two-bedroom upper floor of an old house may seem like the ultimate life style for an eighteen-year-old freshman. There were fun times, but there were also lonely times, so Helen and I took to writing letters to fellows serving in the armed forces.

We had friends on all fields of battle in World War II. Some of them were family. Some were former boyfriends or classmates, and others were new-found friends or pen pals. In all, I believe I wrote regularly to more than ten servicemen.

Corrine and Helen wrote to the men in service during teachers training from 1942 to 1943. This photograph shows Helen Arbogast Gresko at her desk.

In early fall I was encouraged to write to a lonesome buddy of one of my roommates' boyfriends. At first the letters were factual and friendly but not too personal. The letters came more and more frequently and they got more personal. I began to get a bit nervous.

Then unexpectedly a framed eight-by-ten photograph appeared. I became alarmed! Was this becoming more than a means to pass my spare time? Were my letters of encouragement to a stranger from Texas resulting in a romance I had no intention of pursuing? I began to worry.

Then the letter came asking for permission to come to Minnesota to meet me on his leave. I was excited yet mortified! I just couldn't continue. I wondered how I ever got myself into such a situation. What should I do? I'll never know what the outcome could have been because I returned the photograph and politely discontinued what had begun as an innocent act of kindness.

Corrine Lesteberg Johnson

Corrine Lesteberg Johnson
Corrine attended District 40 East near Murdock in Swift County from 1931 to 1938. Those years were not always happy and carefree.

Corrine learned a few childhood lessons about teaching which she never forgot. The fragile thread of self-esteem wound its way through her mind during her own teaching experiences.

Up in Flames
I didn't get to go to school in September because my father stuck by the rules. I wasn't six so I couldn't go, but my sister brought me books that pacified me. My six-year-old sister, who was three years older than I, was the aggressive one. I followed along. She taught me English. She couldn't speak English when she went to school. She spoke just Norwegian.

Corrine Lesteberg Johnson **becomes a teacher, 7-31-1944.**

When she came home from school the first day she said, "We must speak English in this house!" I could read and write before I started school. My older sister brought home the books, and I asked my mother what the words meant. I was a sight reader. She finally got tired of telling me. I had a sister born February 5 so I started school February 1. They didn't have time for me because now they had a baby in the house so off to school I went.

Then a parent brought her child who had her birthday two or three weeks after me in May. School ended in May and I was six in May. The mother argued, "If Corrine can go, then my girl should be able to go, too."

But the girl didn't have the background. She was just like a spring primary student and couldn't go on. Well, the mother said, "OK, I want to hear Corrine read. So I read out of a book, and she wouldn't believe it. Then she found another one. I read that one, too. Then she said, "Why, she's memorized these." She would never admit that I could read. Finally she picked one I had never seen before and I read it, but the mother never would accept that

I could pass the second grade and her daughter had to stay in the first grade. I think these rejections all contributed to my loss of self-confidence. **1931**

Innocence in Flames
We all knew that our second-grade teacher had never lived in the country. So we had a feeling that she thought she was better than the rest of us. I started at Christmas time making valentines. We had a long Christmas vacation, six weeks off, so what was there to do during that time but make valentines. I loved that kind of creative stuff.

I used foil from the Christmas cards and the laced doilies that my mother had bought. I made the cards so they were three-dimensional. You could open them up. Oh, I really worked on those cards. On Valentine's Day I passed out all my beautiful cards. I made a special one for my teacher.

At the end of the school day after everybody had looked at their valentines but before school was even out, my teacher opened the door to the furnace and threw all the valentines into the fire, including my beautiful card. That really hurt me. I had worked so hard on that valentine. If she didn't want to keep them, why didn't she wait until we had all gone home. Then I never would have known. I never really had a lot of respect for that teacher after that. It broke my heart. I cried all the way home.
1932, District 40 East, Swift County

Children of school board members had the ultimate weapon: "I'll tell my dad. He's on the board." However, when Dad had to make a decision the kids didn't like—well, let Corrine tell the story.

Grudges
We had big banks of snow after the plow had gone through, tall banks on the sides of the road. This was the main road people took to Benson. During recess we slid down those banks out onto the road—down and down and down. Then somebody said, "I'm going to bring a sled tomorrow." We went up the hill to where we got the water and slid down the hill on the ice-packed snow. Oh, my that was fun! It was the biggest thrill we had.

My father, who was on the school board, wrote a note to my teacher and said, "This must stop. The danger is too great. People are coming over the hill and those kids are right in front of them." It didn't

237

matter to us that it was dangerous. What mattered was that my father put a stop to a lot of fun. I was ostracized from the group. Oh, I wished he wasn't on the school board. The kids said things like, "Ya, if it wasn't for that school board's kid over there!" I wasn't allowed to play with them anymore. They made me feel like I was the cause of the whole thing. But they didn't hold their grudge too long.

1936, District 40 East, Murdock, Swift County

Corrine Lesteberg Johnson taught in District 54, Swift County, and District 102 and District 15 South in Kandiyohi County. She signed the standard contract for $155 per month. However, Miss Lesteberg had to make one concession rarely asked of other teachers.

Once Is Enough

SECOND.—With respect to vacations during the school year:
THIRD.—**With respect to holidays: *teacher to be out at night not more than one night a week.*

FOURTH.—That the teacher shall arrive at the school house, each school day, in time and remain long enough to perform all services herein agreed upon, and not later than *8 O'clock* and to remain until *her work is finished*

FIFTH.—This contract is subject to all the provisions of the Teachers' Insurance and Retirement Fund Law.

IN WITNESS, WHEREOF, We have hereunto subscribed our names this *31* day of *July*, 19*44*.

My contract stated that I could not stay out more than one night a week. The board didn't want me out on the town. Who knows what it meant? They didn't want me going to social events. That didn't worry me one bit because my boyfriend was in the service. It didn't bother me to sign that. I would go out with the people I lived with when they visited their relatives. They made me feel as if I was part of the family.

One day in October there was a knock on the door. There stood my boyfriend in full uniform. Unbeknownst to me, he came home on furlough from California. He had come home on an emergency leave because of his father's illness and imminent death. He said he would be back at four o'clock. Before he returned to his post, we were engaged. We went out more than one night a week for three weeks, but nobody called me on it.

1944, District 104, Raymond, Kandiyohi County

My Little Run, Run, Runaway

My first day of school was probably the most frustrating day of all my years of teaching, not because of the amount of work to do but because my first-grade student ran home. It was too long a day for

him so he ran home about one o'clock. One of the big boys said, "Oh, I'll go get him on my bike." Well, the boy cut across the field and the boy had to follow the county road at a right angle. He couldn't get him to come back.

I didn't know what to do because I had no telephone. That night I called the parents to see if he was OK. I didn't know that some teachers had only half a day of school the first day.

1943, District. 54, Swift County

Religious War

There was a teachers' crisis in 1951. School board members came from several different churches. Kerkoven had a conflict between the Lutherans and the Catholics. Murdock was Catholic and Kerkoven was Protestant. That's the way it was. There just wasn't any trust between the people.

Living in Kerkoven was a strong teacher who was asked to teach, but when the board interviewed her and discovered she was a strong Catholic, she didn't get hired. The board was afraid she wouldn't lead the students the way they wanted her to. In the middle of the second week of September, they still didn't have a teacher. When I signed my contract, I was told that I must lead the students in Bible reading and prayer every day. We would also have a moment of quiet time. Sometimes we did a unit in prayers that everybody knew. **1951, District 102, Raymond, Kandiyohi County**

Corrine Johnson taught in St. Paul from 1961 to 1962 and in Burnsville from 1964 to 1987. She taught for twenty-eight years.

Helen Arbogast Gresko

Helen attended grade school in District 37 in Meeker County from 1930 to 1936. She completed teachers training in 1943 at Litchfield. She began her teaching career in District 40 in Grove City in 1943. Helen taught in Districts 40, 27 and 90 in Meeker County.

Who Needs Luck?

I was eighteen on the first day I taught. I was to have five first graders and one of them was the daughter of a person I knew. The mother came in and said, "This is Mary, one of your first graders." Then she shook my hand and said, "Well, good luck!" And she kinda chuckled as she left. I was so naive. I thought that was really strange, wishing me good luck. I was a trained teacher. But by the end of the day I knew I needed lots of luck. It was overwhelming. Mary was a really strong little girl who liked to suck her thumb, and when she got mad, she pouted and wouldn't talk to me for a week.

Day One, 1943, District 40, Grove City, Meeker County

A Scrap of Paper

Helen Arbogast and Corrine Lesteberg, 1944

I had one child who went home for lunch. When she came back, she had a little note from her mother, and all it said was ITALY HAS SURRENDERED. That tiny paper made such an impact on me. I still have that little scrap of paper in my scrapbook. We were so isolated, and she had heard it on the radio and knew that I would want to hear that. We studied about the war as much as we could. Kids brought in letters. I had one little boy whose father was in the service. The other kids had older brothers and sisters who were overseas. I didn't know at that time that my future husband was in Italy that day.

1943, District 40, Grove City

I Should Have!

One day we saw an official government car go down the road and the Feds took a boy who was a conscientious objector off to jail. I couldn't talk about it to the class. The little brother was in my class at the time. I talked to the little boy about it and explained that his brother was living up to what his parents had taught him and that he was standing up for what he believed. I told him that the other children felt that his older brother was going to be taken away, and the little boy said, "Yes, he was." And I wished him well. They were lovely people. The little boy wasn't expressive about what I said. He just listened. I would imagine he had been told not to discuss it. It was a very emotional moment for him. I should have hugged him. I don't think I did. We didn't hug kids then anymore. We used to hug them all the time. The boy stayed in school. The other kids accepted his brother's arrest and didn't make any to-do about it. **1944, District 40, Grove City**

Out of Place

I was sweeping the floor when a car drove up. This great big kid, not quite sixteen, who hadn't finished ninth grade, got out. He was being forced to finish school. He was living on a farm near where I was teaching. I said, "Well, I'll have to get the school board to put in a desk. Do you know what grade you're in?"

"Ya, about the fifth."

Here was this great big kid, bigger than I was, sixteen years old and I was nineteen. Then on Friday night I saw him drinking beer up at Mannana—where they had the Friday night dances. After that I wasn't so scared of him. He seemed more like the other guys. He came to school a couple days, then he was absent. I think in all he came six days. Then his parents moved.

He knew he was out of place in that school. The kids didn't know how to treat him. He wasn't a kid, but he really was at the third-grade level. I didn't dare put him there. I was afraid of what the other kids would say to him. I tried to help him. We did get the desk—a big one.

Reading to Cook

One of the girls had a great difficulty with reading. She couldn't comprehend what she read. Her mother wanted to know if there was something she could do to help her at home. I encouraged her to let the girl bake cookies and cakes if she could read some recipes. Then maybe she would become interested in reading other things. The girl loved to cook, and right away she started bringing me cookies she had made. Her big sister said, "And she read the recipes!" This carried over into her schoolwork. Reading wasn't such a mystery to her any more. That was very rewarding for me.

1955, District 90, near Litchfield

Helen Arbogast Gresko taught in the rural schools for five years. Then she moved to Eden Prairie where she taught for twenty-five years.

A desk in the corner, alone and
   sad,
The teacher placed one day.
Be good, dear children, and
   never bad,
Back here there is no play.
        -TM

Chapter 29

Smitches and Smidgens

Tricks and treats, playing games in a ring,
Teachers who try but squeak when they sing,
Walking to school 'cross fields hand-in-hand,
Hopscotchin', rope jumpin', to beat the band.

These stories are smidgens, pieces and bits
'bout students who often gave teachers fits.
Some smitches are sweet; some are tart.
Others may touch a place in your heart.

-TM

Not for Me

I was born in 1893. I started school in 1898 when I was five, and when I was thirteen I had all my grades done. Then I couldn't go to school no more. I had to herd cows and herd pigs and do all kinds of chores around the home. I couldn't go any further. We had to drive horses, and that was six and a half miles. They couldn't drive the horses that far. Nobody went to high school. When I was going to school, I had chores like carrying wood, corn cobs, carry water, all kinds of chores on the farm when we were not in school. **Agnes Sonek, Naeve Parkview Nursing Home, Wells**

Sliding

There was a hill behind a building. A bachelor poured water on the hill to make it nice and slippery. We'd slide down and go all the way out on the lake. The big boys made a rink. We didn't have any cars to go around in so we used to do a lot of skating. We took our skates to school. At noon they gave us an extra half hour to skate. Then the teacher rang the bell. **Elvice Bloom, 1900–1908, Chisago Lake, Chisago County**

Croquet Anyone?

When I went to school, we didn't have a kitten ball to play with at recess, so we used a croquet ball. The pitcher threw the ball and when I hit it, it glanced off the bat and hit me right in the mouth and knocked out my teeth. Oh, that was a bad one!

I bled just like a hog. Ya, Ya, we were using a croquet ball. Imagine what a wood ball feels like. **Bertha Schwarz, c. 1905, District 139, Blue Earth County**

Frog Fry

Our teacher was so liberal. She let the big boys do just about anything. At recess the older boys caught frogs. Then they would build a fire and fry frog legs on a stick in the back of the school. Then we ate them. **Beatrice Torrey, c. 1910, Madison, Lac Qui Parle County**

Up on the Roof

We played ante-I-over over the outhouse. We used a beanbag because we didn't have a ball. Nobody had much money, but we could make a beanbag and put corn in it. That was our ball. Once it got stuck on top of the outhouse, and since I was the little one, the big girls put me up on the roof, and I had to get the bag down. **Rose Nilson, 1915, District 98, Jackson County**

An Early Start

In 1915, I started school at District 57 in Le Sueur County, when I was four years old. My brothers and sisters were going to school, and I cried when they left home. I followed them, so my dad said, "Let her go. She won't stay." I went and the teacher made a pet out of me. I had my fifth birthday on Halloween, but at that time there was no limit as to when you could start school.
Elizabeth O'Connell, c. 1916, District 57, Le Sueur County

Cut Ups

They brought the cordwood in. We burned wood, ya know, in them days. They had to bring the cord wood in four-foot lengths and then us kids, we'd have to take a bucksaw and cut it up into two-foot lengths to get it in the stove and then cord it in the woodshed. We come to school to do it and we had to do it. **Wilford Horman, 1914–1922, Hardscrabble School, Fillmore County**

The School Shack

We had our Christmas program in our home. Everything was in the homes in those days. We had our school in a gentleman's homestead cabin. He deserted and went back to Sweden, and we picked it up. He got disgusted with it and left. He had a difficult time making a living so he just packed up and took off. We got permission from his two nieces and we just moved into this old shack. The father of the Palms made the desks. Two kids sat in each desk. There wasn't any money for anything. The cabin burned in the 1931 fire. **Evelyn Erickson, 1918, Hay Creek-Rapid River, Beltrami County**

The Launch
They dug this drainage ditch past the school so the ditch was on the school side of the grade. The ditch had quite a bit of water in it. We all had a vaulting pole and we'd start running from the school door, up over this grade, poke the pole into the ditch, and vault over the ditch onto the farmer's land on the other side. Then we had to go down to the bridge and walk back. **Leora Brown White, c. 1917, Benedix School, Beltrami County**

World War Flu
We had a Christmas party. All the parents and children came. My dad came but my mother was sick. He came and got us children just as soon as the play was over. We were the only ones in the neighborhood that didn't have that terrible flu. They thought we didn't get it because we didn't mingle. As soon as the program was over, we went home. The other people stayed until ten o'clock. We did not eat any of the lunch. It was called the World War flu. The neighbors lost two boys. We had six kids and none of us got it. I was in the second grade. Whole families died of that flu. **Alma Ahrens, 1918, District 10, Martin County**

Stubby Pencils
We did our homework around the big dining room table which was covered with oilcloth and had a kerosene lamp in the center. Dad would be reading and we did our homework. It seemed none of us could ever find our pencils, so Dad would reach down into the pocket of his bib overalls and pull out enough short stubby pencils for each of us. With a smile, he would say, "Here they are, children. Be sure to leave them on the table when you are finished with your homework." And we did just that because the next night the same thing happened. **Ann Burns, c. 1920, District 7, Le Sueur County**

Erasers, Suckers and Ram-Riding
I had a teacher who had a sawmill and all he taught us about math was board length. I just couldn't get math because he didn't teach it right. He would get

so upset he would throw anything he could at us—erasers, books—whatever would come sailing at us.

We had sheep and one day they came down to the school at noon, so my brothers decided they were going to ride the old ram home. Well, when they got home they didn't dare get off him because he was so mean. I don't know how they got off. The ram chased them when they finally jumped off. **Hilda Hendrickson and Leora Brown White, 1922, Benedix School, Lake of the Woods County**

All Wrapped Up
Once, four of us girls ventured out on the pond next to the school. Hilda broke through the ice and really got soaked. We went into the school and the teacher made Hilda undress in the girls' cloakroom.

When Hilda came out, she was dressed in the teacher's long coat. To dry the clothes the teacher hung them over the registers. Her flannel bloomers were stretched over the wall register. When the bell rang, there were some grins and sly glances. The boys thought it was quite a sight—the hanging bloomers and Hilda sitting in her seat all afternoon wearing the teacher's coat. **Laurabelle Martin, c. 1922, Great Bend School, Cottonwood County**

Woe to the fools who insisted on putting their tongues on the windmills and pumps in the depths of winter. Pity not those daredevils. Stories of this winter ritual can be found in every corner of the state. But Laurabelle Martin has a variation on that theme called "Second graders dread the trip to the outhouse."

Stuck
In second grade we went to the Christmas program. I wore a brown satin dress with fancy embroidery that my mother had made. I made my first stage appearance with my brother Harvey, acting out a song that the older girls were singing. After the program I had to go to the bathroom outside. The snow was very deep. As I was plodding through the banks coming back, I fell. When I put my hands on the knob to open the door, my hands stuck. I started to cry. Luckily for me a gentleman was outside and heard me. He came and put his warm hands on mine. The door soon opened. As we came in, the treats and gifts were being distributed. **Laurabelle Martin, 1922, Great Bend School, Cottonwood County**

The Awakening

One time I was playing physical education. We were playing ante-ante over at recess time and I threw the ball over the roof. It didn't go the way I wanted, and I swore a dirty word. The teacher called me in. She didn't say anything. Then she hauled off and slapped me. She gave me a bloody nose. She said, "Listen, son, you can play in phy. ed. and recreation and do anything, but you can't swear, and you can't be dirty. You can't do things like that!" She started making a man out of me about that time. She set the rules down and she carried them out. **Lloyd Steussy, Milton Township, Dodge County, 1922–1930: Lloyd became a teacher and coach. Lloyd is a member of the Minnesota Basketball Hall of Fame.**

Too Cruel

One time one of the boys used to pick on another boy. They picked on him so much that the parents of the boy who was being picked on kidnapped the boy who was tormenting their son and hid him down in the woods. They got mad at him because he was picking on their boy all the time, beating him up. They left him there until his parents came to find him, but they had a hard time finding him. That incident was a tough deal. **Lloyd Steussy, 1922–1930, Milton Township, Dodge County**

"No Teaching for You!"

I wanted so bad to be a schoolteacher. I envied those women when they came to teach. They had such beautiful clothes. I said, "I'm gonna be a school-teacher so I can buy clothes like that."

Well, my dad ran the sawmill. He wouldn't let me go to high school. He said, "You'll go in there and get in with the crowd." He thought I'd end up in a gang or something. There weren't any gangs in those days. I don't know what he saw because he was the only one who ever went uptown. We were sixteen miles out of town. Imagine, join a gang.

Leola Brown White attended Benedix School in Beltrami County from 1917–1927.

Good Times

Our school was on a plot of land from my step-father Casten's cow pasture. We used the east side for ball games and prisoner's base. The west side we girls made into a playhouse, simply outlining the rooms with sticks that we picked up from nearby pasture trees. Our *couche* we covered with moss. The Buffalo Creek ran at the foot of the north slope by the school. The boys found a grapevine long enough to swing across the "crick." Of course, the younger boys and us girls were the audience that made it worthwhile.

Adela Eibs Belz, 1923–1929, District 13, Sibley County

Early Driver

I was the oldest of eight kids. When I got up each morning, I had to help my mother. My father had a school bus, a home-built one with canvas over it, drawn by two horses. I helped him hitch up the horses. When I was eleven, I drove that bus, even in the winter time. I picked up the kids, and I drove it to school. There was a little barn by the school house, and I unhitched the horses. They stayed there all day. I fed them at noon time. I hitched them up after school, started the fire in the school bus, and drove the kids home. I marvel now that my parents gave an eleven-year-old all that responsibility.

Marjorie Earl Badde 1924–1928, Lake of the Woods County

Helping Hands

My father, who was a steel worker, lost the use of his right arm. He had to make his living for seven with the other arm. In 1925, we moved to a small rented farm in Minnesota. It was very difficult in the 1920s and 1930s. Later we moved to a mortgaged farm and I entered another country school. I went to school and taught in Jackson County. There were five of us in an eight-year span. Everyone wanted to go to college at the same time. We all earned our own way. I helped my younger sister, and she helped my brother and so on while our parents were paying for the farm.

Margaret Kopecky, c. 1925–1933, District 86, Jackson County and District 58, Nobles County

Bad Day

One day when I was in the first grade I had to walk to school alone because my brothers had to stay home to help with the farm work. As I walked, the wolves began to howl in the woods. I was so scared, I tiptoed, so the wolves wouldn't hear me. After school I didn't dare go back that way, so I walked way around the woods with some other kids.

Helen Lepisto, 1927, District 178, Hintsala School, Otter Tail County: Helen escaped the wolves and taught for twenty-six years, five in the rural schools.

Skinny Dippin'

Hanson Lake was just over a big hill in the woods, which in those days were full of bears and wolves. Some of us boys and girls decided to go swimming. We didn't have swimming suits, so we just went skinny-dipping right in front of the crowd, but the girls left their bloomers on. When I got back to school, I thought, "What's that crawling on my leg?" We all had bloodsuckers crawling around between our legs. **Aare Suomela, c. 1927, Boys Camp School, Brookston, St. Louis County**

How can a teacher be both an intimidator and heroine at the same time? Miss Rubell, attired in smocks, starched and stiff, made a lasting impression on Hazel and Hannah Tvedt.

Heroine

Miss Rubell, my eighth-grade teacher had three smocks—tan, green, and blue. She wore those three all year, and she starched them so stiff that we could always hear her coming if she approached us from behind or from any direction for that matter. She also wore leather boots up to her knees. She was very, very strict. Now I see her as a heroine. She was independent and she has done a lot of good in her life. But at that time we didn't think that way. **Hazel Tvedt Amlie, 1929, Gracks School, Swift County**

Doghouse Blues

Miss Rubell was a very large person. She was overly religious. My uncle and aunt were moving and there was a farewell party at their house one night. We went to this farewell party so we were tired in school the next day. And of all things, they danced at the party which the religious teacher very much opposed. We got home late that night so we were very sleepy in class the next day. Boy, we sure were in the doghouse that day. Every one who had been there was in the doghouse. Her name was Rubell but we called her "Rubble" instead. **Hannah Tvedt Sanders, 1929, Gracks School, Swift County**

Mighty Mouse

We had a young lady teacher who just could not handle the parents. If something went wrong, two or three families yammered at her. Then we got this man teacher. It didn't work that way with him. This little kid swore in class and he made him stay after school. His dad, who was broad, big, and tall, came

to the school, figuring he could beat up the teacher who was about five foot, four inches tall. The teacher said, "OK, let's go out on the road." He wouldn't fight on the school grounds. The guy took off for home. That man taught there for eleven years. We liked him and we learned. **Lorraine Schroeder, 1929, District 57, Lime Prairie School**

Yuuuuuuummy!

We had a big crock—about two or three gallons. It was a clay crock and in it was this gray paste, and when you needed some, you just went up and got it. I don't know what the big attraction was but we ate that stuff. It was made out of hogs' hooves and that kind of stuff. All the kids loved it. There was a steady stream up to that crock. My sister said, "Oh, yes, we ate that paste like it was going out of style. We just stuck our fingers right in. We shared it. The teachers were aware of it. They didn't think it was going to hurt us. Paste was probably the biggest thing on the budget." **Bill Herzog, c. 1937, District 22, St. Joseph, Scott County**

I Remember

I was a tomboy, even in the first grade. During recess we played in the cemetery across from the school. We climbed around on the tombstones and read the names. Some of the kids wouldn't go because they were superstitious. In the fall the boys played football, and I told them I wanted to play. One of the boys, who was sixteen, said, "Well, let her play." He hiked me the ball, and then he picked me up and ran with both me and the ball. **Anita Peterson, 1940–1941, Otter Tail County**

Ordella Lecy attended District 5, Riverside School near Echo from 1920 to 1928. No other teacher or student I interviewed told this story of religious education. Her account of the Norwegian Congregational Church using public school time captures the power of the local Norwegians' belief in the Biblical phrase "all things whatsoever I have commanded you" and the effect of that belief on the surrounding public country schools.

Norwegian Month

We had parochial school for one month of the year. We had only seven months of public school and one month of parochial education. This took place in January, February, March, April, and May. During the month the parochial teacher was teaching in the district, the teacher and students who did not attend the parochial school had vacation. The teachers knew that when they were hired.

We were one of the first ones to have this. There were five school districts in our church area. Rock Valley Church, which is located six miles north of Echo, hired a parochial teacher to teach one month in each district. It was more important to go to church school, especially when you got to be confirmation age, so you might go two more weeks in another district to get in some more religion.

The church hired these special teachers who taught religion and Bible study. They taught us how to read and spell Norwegian. A little Norwegian reader, Luther's small catechism, Volrath Voight's Bible history, which we had to memorize, and the *Bible* were the main books. We memorized the Ten Commandments, the hymns, and the Bible stories word for word. We also studied music and spelling in Norwegian. Everything was like the regular school except in Norwegian.

At the end of the season when the teacher had taught five months of parochial school, all the students from these five districts put on a *barnefest*, a children's program which was all in Norwegian.

Some people objected to using the public schools for parochial education. Two of the board members opened a granary where they could have the parochial education. The parochial education ended when the state required nine months of school. When the churches went to English services, the parochial schools ended.

Jim and Ordella Lecy, Granite Falls

Dreamin'
Smitches and smidgens can also be dreams,
Wrapped in youthful haze.
Far-off places were closer it seems
In Country School Student days.

The town kids bragged, "It's great to be free,"
And mocked us with many a yarn,
But they never read in a dreamin' tree,
Or cracked homers over a barn.   -TM

244

Chapter 30

Schnibbles

In 1958, I began my teaching career in New Prague. Because I was the rookie teacher on the staff, I was assigned many duties which were anathema to the old-timers. Heading the list of undesirable assignments was senior class advisor. The seniors were responsible for putting on the Winter Dance, which meant providing the tree and decorating the gym with snowflakes, twisted crepe paper streamers, and tons of cut-up, shiny glitter.

After the dance the majority of the students took off and left a few generous volunteers and their naive advisor to clean up the mess. We grabbed the janitors' brooms and headed toward the gym. It was at that moment that LaDonna Pint exclaimed, "You guys, we've got to clean up these schnibbles." Although I had a college degree in English, I did not know what a schnibble was.

LaDonna patiently explained, "They're all those little bitty pieces of cut-up stuff that don't have regular size or shape. Schnibbles are just bits and pieces without names. Sometimes you can barely see them, but they are there."

Some of the following schnibbles glitter. Some do not. They were left lying around after the big "book-writing dance," waiting to be included somewhere.

Schnibbles: Part 1
I'm Blushing!

The storytellers in this section asked not to be identified, so their stories became schnibbles.

Buy You a Beer?
I was having trouble with a difficult sixth grader. I told her to sit down and she threatened me. She told me she would get her brothers to beat me up. I was staying with a family who owned a store. I was told the brothers were at the store. I went there and bought them a beer. We talked and got along very well. The next day I told the girl she had some very nice brothers. She didn't know what to say. She looked at me with open-mouthed awe.

That was the only beer I ever bought in my life.

The Great Duel
For three or four years the boys had contests. At recess we would go into the six-holer. We would line up on one side and see how high we could pee up on the opposite wall. We learned systems on how to get higher. I was one of the younger kids and I could outgun any of them. If you weren't circumcised you could have a system. You could hold the end of it and build up a reservoir. Then you opened and you could squeeze the reservoir. That's how I got the name Squirt Gun.   **c. 1924**

Brown, You Say?
I taught a lesson to my first graders about squirrels. We talked about where they live and how they bury their acorns in the fall and dig them up in the winter. We talked about gray squirrels and brown squirrels. Then I gave each of the children a squirrel to color. They were all excited about coloring the squirrels. Now in those days we were more intent on having the children do what was real than using their imaginations, so the children began to color their squir-

245

rels brown since that was the color we had we talked about the most.

But this one little fellow was coloring his squirrel pink. I said, "Oh, so you've got a pink squirrel?" He just nodded his head. I said, "I guess we were talking about most of them being brown and some being gray. Do you suppose you'd like to color yours that way? Everyone else is coloring theirs." I stopped at his desk and mentioned it a couple times more. I guess he felt he had been heckled enough and was plumb disgusted with me because he looked up at me and said, "This son-of-a-bitch is gonna be pink!"

1940s, someplace down 35W where people know Spam

Tricked

When he went to country school, the boys drilled a little hole in the outhouse, so they could peek when the girls went to use the outhouse. During recess him and his buddy would hide behind the outhouse, and the other ones playing would let them know when a girl was coming so they could peek at her. The other boys played a trick on him and his buddy one day. They waved that a girl was coming to the outhouse, but it was the teacher who went in there, and they really got into trouble.

An aide at Parkside Nursing Home in Wells

Schnibbles: Part 2
Potpourri

The country school was a Festival of the Senses. If one were to imagine that a character such as Country School Room Nose lived and was willing to write its autobiography, what a story it could tell! Throughout the book are many stories that will trigger recollections of odors and aromas that wafted throughout those rooms—bouquets of spring flowers, lunches cooking on the stove, burning wood and coal, smoke, unwashed clothes, overshoes placed too near the stove, battles with early morning barnyard chores, teachers' perfume, hectograph worksheets—a dizzying, dazzling aromatic potpourri.

The following stories are a few of Country School Room Nose's favorites. Nose had a reputation for discerning and labeling the most offensive odor to the most heavenly sublime aroma. However, some question Nose's "taste" in stories.

Pea-U

Kitty-corner from our school the Green Giant Company owned a pea-viner which at the end of the harvest contained a large stack of silage. In the fall the silage was parceled out to the local farmers who would haul it with horse and wagon or trucks throughout the winter months.

During one noon hour period after we had finished eating our lunch, six or eight of us guys climbed the pea silage stockpile for the sheer joy of some rough play. When we returned to the warmth of the school, it didn't take long and the whole school reeked of the smell of silage. From that time playing on the silage stockpile was forbidden.

Alvin Dietz, c. 1936, District 81, Le Sueur County

You know what's going to happen now don't ya, Stinky? Country School Teacher and Country School Students, those skunkopaths, are going to tell stories about us. I wish somebody would come to interview us about them.

The Uninformed Skunk

If you pick up a skunk by the tail, it can't spray you. That's what I had heard as a kid, and I believed it, for a while. One day the kids in my school chased a skunk into a culvert and got one of the naive third graders to agree to catch it. They came running into the school house, "Oh we're going to get this skunk. We're going to catch it." The third grader said he would catch it by the tail. They took long sticks and poked at the skunk, and when he came out the boy picked him up by the tail. Well, it didn't work. The skunk didn't know he wasn't supposed to spray. The boy got as far as the steps of the school, and I said, "No, you've got to go home. I don't want you in the school." I had a Model A, but I wouldn't put him in my car. His sister walked home with him and they washed him in tomato juice.

Burton Kreitlow, c. 1936, District 75, Highland School, Wright County

Just west of Wells stands one of the most colorful one-room schools in the state. The school and outhouse are painted a bright pink, which catches the eyes of motorists coming from both the east and the west. Across the road just north of the school lives Dale Yonke, who keeps a watchful eye on District 40, Faribault County.

According to Dale, he spent many hours of his grade-school years in the front cloakroom for what he now calls "disciplinary problems." I persuaded Dale to squeeze into one of the desks that might have been his and tell one of his tales.

That Ain't Perfume

I was in the sixth or seventh grade and I was trapping skunks. I didn't have a gun, but I had a baseball bat, or a softball bat. I killed the skunk with the baseball bat. You know what happened then! I got sprayed. Of course, it didn't seem so bad to me, but when I came into school after I had run my trap line, the kids just about jumped through the windows. I spent the whole week out in the hall just by myself, in that cold hallway because I stunk so bad. I couldn't sit in there with the kids. There were probably worse crises than that, but I don't remember.

Dale Yonke, District 40, Faribault County

Dale Yonke is fourth from the left in the second row.

Natural Gas

There were three big boys who were kinda unruly, and I had all eight grades. I had three little girls up at the blackboard. I was teaching them arithmetic, and I was working with them so it was real quiet. One of the boys was real obnoxious. If he wanted to "gas-off," he'd do it. It was just as quiet as could be and sitting on those wooden seats, "wang" it went. Those poor girls got cherry red and they couldn't think. They couldn't do anything, and I had to let them sit down. They were so flustered.

After school, I told the three boys to stay in— C., W., and L. I dismissed the school. I knew that L was the one who was doing the "gassing-off." I went down there, folded my hands, and looked at L. I never said a word to him.

L. said, "I didn't do it. W. did. C. saw it. C. saw him raise up and let it go."

In 1930, when Knute Nelson of Milaca was helping a former country school teacher who had back trouble, the teacher told him this story.

Schnibbles: Part 3
Serendipity

Serendipity—fortunate discoveries made by accident. Before I set off to interview people, I took great pains to inform them about the kinds of stories I was looking for. I carefully planned my itinerary to have time to drive from one town to another. Mining for stories demands careful planning. But sometimes Serendipity can be a wonderful companion for a story miner. I would turn a corner, start a conversation at a gas station, visit a county fair—there was Serendipity, mining a story, waving at me to hustle.

After finishing an interview in Hayfield, I headed up Country 56 for a 5:00 interview in Dodge Center. As I did often when I had some time, I stopped at the senior citizens home and asked the activities director if she knew anyone who might be interested in telling stories about going to a country school. By a stroke of luck, I met Wilford Horman.

By Jimminy

When we were at war, Kaiser Wilhelm was fightin' and we won the war. We rung the bell twenty-four hours, us kids did. We changed off all night and all day. We rang the bell when they signed the treaty, 1918, wasn't it? We rang the bell all day and all night because the war was over. And I wrote a poem about it, but nobody ever paid any attention to it.

Wilford Horman, 1918, Jordan School, Fillmore County

I asked Wilford if he still had a copy of the poem in his room. He looked at me and tapped his forehead three times. Then this wonderful eighty-nine-year-old historian-poet recited his verses from memory. He never missed a beat.

By Jimminy

The Kaiser sat in his old arm chair
With foam on his lips and lice in his hair,
And his voice rang out in the morning air,
"I'll lick the world, by jimminy!"

He started his army on for France
And met the Belgians by chance.
He scratched his head and with a glance,
Said, "I'm checked here, by jimminy!"

He started in to sinkin' American ships
And Wilson got mad and gave a frown.
"Now old Kaiser you'll lose your crown.
We'll lick you bad, by jimminy."

So Wilson trained an army so very fine,
Crossed the ocean, marched up the Rhine,
Met the Kaiser just in time,
And took his crown, by jimminy.

Wilford Horman, c. 1918–1920, Jordan School, Fillmore County

When I got home that night, I typed Wilford's poem. Then I took it to the basement, cut a mat, mounted the poem, found a piece of glass, and framed it. If you pass by Wilford's room, stop in and see his poem. Ask him to recite it.

Francis Pianco Hayden is my sister-in-law's aunt and a wonderful storyteller. While she was telling stories about her own experiences, Serendipity freed the following story about her older brothers.

They Didn't Know English

When I was a little kid, we spoke Polish at home. When I went to school I didn't speak English. I was a stutterer because I had to speak English in school and I didn't know how to speak it. My little brothers didn't speak English very well either. One thing that happened to them was just terrible. We had teachers at that time—if you misbehaved, you got it. Our teacher had a ruler that was an inch thick four ways—a twelve-inch ruler, and she used it. That ruler was still there when I taught there, unless there were several new ones brought in, but I don't think it was ever broken on anyone. Then something happened during Halloween time.

The teacher had a favorite book, and instead of teaching the kids their regular lessons, she read from her book. On Halloween night someone broke into the school and spit snuff and chewing tobacco on her book and all around.

And worst of all, someone went to the toilet on her chair. She had feces on her chair to contend with the next morning.

When the children arrived, she asked everybody if they were in school the night before. My brothers, Jack and Tony, thought she had said, "Were you in school the day before."

So they said "yes." She took that ruler and she beat and banged their poor little hands until they were black and blue and swollen.

My brothers misunderstood because they knew so little English. They were small, little guys. She should have known that they couldn't have done it. And my brothers were so young at that time. They did not know what snuff and chewing tobacco were. And my ma and pa would never let them get out at night. The teacher should have known that.

Dad was a good disciplinarian, and he didn't want anyone to misbehave in school and not mind the teacher. But this upset him so much that he went to a board member and told him they should get rid of that teacher. But at that time it was hard to get teachers. They did talk to her about it, but they didn't get rid of her.

Frances Hayden, c. 1920, St. Thomas, Le Sueur County

Better Off in School

I had a very nice little boy who was in the second grade. His father passed away. The next day he came to school. I said, "Are you sure that you want to go to school today?"

"Oh, yes," he said, "Mother said it's better for me to be in school because I'll talk to the other kids and won't be thinking about Dad." I talked to him years later and he remembered that day very clearly.

Elida Farber Berg, c. 1940, Hagen School, Lake of the Woods County

When I went to Cambridge to interview Marjorie Jandro, she mentioned that her mother had taught in country schools during the 1920s. Unfortunately, age had stolen most of her mother Edna's memories. Edna sat in the hallway, behind a door while her daughter told me stories.

248

When Marjorie mentioned the word *Depression*, Edna leaned forward and told the following story with great passion. The look on her face told us the moral in case we had missed it: "What a great gift! The man gave me his prized possession."

A Gift

It was during the Depression and nobody had much food. I had a little first grader who wet his pants. Then he went out and buried them. I didn't know what to do with him. I didn't want to embarrass him. I sent another boy up to the neighbors to get some underwear for him. The next day his father came and wanted to know what was wrong. I told him what had happened. The following morning the father came and brought me a great big potato for caring for his son and not embarrassing him.

Edna Erickson Gerkin, c. 1924, Isanti County

I followed the directions carefully to Laverna Bergland's farm near Willmar, but no one answered when I knocked. As I was leaving, I saw two men near a machine shed. I introduced myself and they said, "Oh, yes, mom is down at the house waiting for you. She may have the radio on." We talked for awhile, and as I was leaving, I asked them if they had any stories. Laverna's son Rod was a Country School Student. Laverna'a stories appear in other chapters.

November 22, 1963

I was eight years old the day President Kennedy was assassinated. We had Mrs. Moline for our teacher. She got so upset when she heard about the assassination that she immediately shut down class. She was weeping as she walked us across the road, approximately a tenth of a mile to Arnold Olson's farm. We watched it play out over and over again on a little round black-and-white TV. There was just dead silence. I shivered, listening to it over and over again. I'll never forget the reactions of my classmates and my teacher. She seemed to be in shock.

Of course, we were younger, and we didn't quite understand what was going on in her head. But she was so sad. I just remember it was windy, and she was wearing a long dress and the wind was blowing her dress as we were walking to that farm.

Rod Bergland, grade eight, 1963, Kandiyohi County

I Never Knew Humans Could Be That Cruel!

Every day we played with a pet dog during our recess breaks. We got to know this dog quite well, as any kid would. One day one of the neighbors came to the school and shot the dog. We were outside, but we didn't see him shoot the dog because he came up from behind the school. But we did hear the shot.

Then the man tied the dog around its front legs and then he tied it to his car. He dragged the dog down our county road. That really devastated us kids to witness that. We loved that dog. You don't forget something like that.

I think that was the first time in my life that I saw cruelty. I grew up on the farm and my dad had cows. And every once in a while he'd lose an animal, but this was different. I loved dogs. At one time we had thirteen dogs on our farm. I'm sure if you were to ask anyone who went to school at that time, they would remember the dog being dragged down that gravel road. It was so cruel. This man overreacted. He had three kids in school, and he may have thought his kids were in danger.

Rod Bergland, grade eight, 1962, Kandiyohi County

Schnibbles: Part 4
Bless the Beasts

We know about that lamb of Mary's,
And how it went to school.
It must have made her teacher contrary,
Breakin' all her rules.

Sometimes the room became a zoo
When animals came to class.
But teacher knew just what to do
And wouldn't take that sass!

Sometimes the mice just came to read,
The skunk to raise a stink,
The goat to wrestle a boy in need,
Or just to rest and think.

They squeaked and squawked, nibbled and
    drooled,
And loved the one-room school.
They stayed in class when we said,
    "Scram,"
And passed their state exams.   -TM

Lunch Guest

Walter Hintz raised sheep, and he had a buck sheep which annoyed me. It chased me whenever it saw me on my way to and from school. Walter said it was my lunch that attracted the sheep. I was afraid of it and ran all the way to school, but it still chased me. One day the pupils and I heard the girls' entry door open. We heard a strange noise in the cloak-room. We thought it was the county superintendent coming to visit. The noise got louder, so I opened the door. The big buck sheep looked right at me. He had opened some of the dinner pails and was enjoying the lunches. I must have startled him because he dashed out the door and ran home. We shared our lunches that day with those whose pails had been robbed! **Malinda Heaney, 1924, District 118, Sunnybrook School, Faribault County**

Missing in Action

In the spring and fall I cut through the pasture to shorten the distance to school, but I was always par-alyzed with fear because Old Ferdinand the Bull gave me the "glad eye." At the neighboring school one of the fathers driving by the school stopped to check why the children were playing outside during the school hours.

When he discovered the teacher had not shown up and that she had left her boarding place in the morning, he became concerned. He found her up in a tree where she had sought refuge when the bull in the pasture she cut across charged her. I would have been in great trouble if that had happened to me because I could never climb a tree. Even though I crossed a different pasture and faced a different bull, from that day on I took the long way to school.

Helen Merville, c. 1929: Helen taught in Brown County from 1927 to 1931.

Dash

My school was three miles away by road. Usually I drove my little Chevy coupe. However, one spring day the roads were impassable, so I had to ride Dash, the family pony. She was black with a well-padded tummy. She was very difficult to catch. If I had a treat, she would let me catch her. With no treat, I would think I had her, but then she would kick up her heels and speed for her fenced-in domain in the apple orchard. Fortunately, I caught her easily. We took the shortcut across the pasture, and I left her at my Uncle Timmy's farm, the

halfway point. She delivered me safely to the neigh-boring farm, and I walked the rest of the way through the terrible mud. **Esther Nordland Lickteig, 1935, District 78, O'Leary School, Freeborn County**

The Visitor

The school grounds were in my great uncle's pas-ture. He had a barn on the upper part of the pasture, which was enclosed with a fence. He had some goats and most of them stayed put in the old red barn up on the hill about a block from the school, but it was still part of the school grounds.

He had one old goat that was very belligerent. He would come down and check on us every day to see how things were going. The boys used to wrestle him the way people wrestled bulls in the old western days. They would hold something in front of him to torment him.

"Ok, rookie, jump on. I'll send your tailbone to goat heaven! Did you learn the word nemesis in school today? Hop on."

This goat was not averse to visiting the school if the door was open. He would walk down the aisles and the kids would stick out their feet and try to trip him. They tried to irritate him just to cause a commotion. One day he came in and checked us out. We had a big water crock and he was nuzzling the button that controlled the bubbler. He got to poking around and dumped the wastewater pail into which the wastewater drained. The teacher called on the boys to get the goat out of the building before he wrecked everything. Of course the boys had a field day wrestling him down. Then he would jump up again. He was a belligerent old fella. He didn't take any nonsense from anybody. But he never seemed to get angry. I think he enjoyed being wrestled as much as the boys did. But that wasn't the end of his visits. He came back many times. **Gertrude Linnell, c. 1934, District 2, Birchwood School, Cook County**

Baaaaaaaaa!

One year the children thought it would be real exciting to have a live lamb in the Christmas manger scene—have a little one in a box and when the shepherds came, they could have a lamb with them. Everyone promised not to tell. Then it would be a surprise. It worked pretty well. However, we forgot a little lamb would bleat before it came on stage. "What's that?" everyone asked. It was funny anyway. **Viola Loftness O'Day, c. 1933, District. 133, Loftness School, Marshall County**

Viola's class, 1932-1933

Robert Burns' "wee, sleekist cow'rin, tim'rous beastie" was no friend of Country School Teacher.

A Mouse a Day Keeps....

One day we caught 125 mice. We caught them every day. I had two traps which I set every night. I hoped I wouldn't have a mouse in the morning, but if I didn't catch one, I just knew it would be running around the schoohouse. It was hard for me to set the traps because I couldn't stand to look at a mouse. I put a paper toweling over the trap while I opened it. Then I put the mouse in the furnace.

One day we had a very active mouse doing his best to distract everyone. He was so busy that the students couldn't concentrate. Finally I said, "All right, boys, pick up any weapon you need and get that mouse."

Grabbing the broom, stove poker, coal shovel and blocks of wood, all the boys started after the mouse. The girls were on their desks and making their share of noise.We couldn't hear the knock on the door and in walked our dignified county nurse. It was bedlam, but after I explained the situation, she was very gracious.

Virginia Rue Carrigan, 1936, Jackson County

"Clank, clank, clank went the ...."

One day we heard a clanking in the fresh air outlet attached to the huge indoor heater. Several of the big boys and I went to investigate. A beaver had moved in. We took the beaver back to the stream and then we ate our lunches right there. Two days later the beaver was back, clanking in the outlet. We couldn't figure out why the beaver had moved away from the stream and his dam. We checked the encyclopedia and discovered that when a beaver refuses to work with his peers and family, he gets "booted" out of his home. Since he couldn't live in our air duct, we took him several miles down stream. **Celia Wiedenhoeft, c. 1937, Grattan School, Itasca County**

The Invasion

One year we had a major army worm invasion. The school was an old building and the worms just came up the cement foundation. Every time someone had to go to the outhouse toilet, I got the broom, swept the worms off the steps, and then swept a path, or one of the boys took a shovel to scoop out a path to the outhouse. They were a foot thick. Then we swept them out of the outhouse.

The kids dug a hole a couple feet deep to see how long it would take for the worms to fill the hole. In a couple minutes it was full. The school yard was covered with them.

There were car accidents because the highway was so slippery from those crushed worms.It was just like winter. They crawled along the telephone lines. We couldn't play outside. When the students came in the morning or when they went to the outhouse, one of the older students or I stood at the door and brushed the worms off as they came in. "Shake your coat, brush your pants, clean your feet." This lasted three weeks.

Margaret Pickering, 1952, Balsam School, Itasca County

Walking Partner

I had a mile an a half walk to school along a country road. There were timber wolves all over. One wolf walked with me every day. He walked back just far enough so I could see that tawny coat. He walked when I walked. When he got close to Highway 65, he turned around and left. He was a lobo, one of those big males ostracized from his family.

Margaret Pickering, 1941, Hansen Lake School, Itasca County: Margaret outlasted wolves and worms and taught for forty years.

A Captive Audience

We had a run-in with a rabid skunk at the school near the Merton Store. It kept circling the outhouse and occasionally took a trip around the school. All twelve students felt the need to use the outhouse, but how could they with danger lurking so near? The girls relented and used a pail, but the boys thought that was "sissy" stuff, so many managed for a number of painful hours until a nearby neighbor came to our rescue.

Evelyn Olson Dorshner, 1957, District 4, Steele County

Schnibbles: Part 5
Father and Son

If one of your molars is giving you trouble and you decide to visit Dr. Bruce Trulson at his dental clinic in Stewartville, you are in for a sentimental journey. Dr. Trulson has turned his waiting room into a country school museum.

If you haven't gained too many pounds over the years, you could squeeze into one of the desks and reminisce about your days in the one-room school. Enlarged photographs of classes from the Thorson School, District 56, southeast of Chatfield, hang on the walls. A painting of the school as well as photographs of the building also decorate the clinic's walls.

Bruce held an open house and had invited people from the community to visit his museum. He extended a special invitation to anyone who had attended the Thorson School in order to help him identify the students and teachers in the photographs. While the party was taking place in the lobby, I met with Bruce's father and we mined a few stories. Later Bruce told his favorite story. Both father and son were Country School Students.

Bad Timing

I was twelve years old, and since it was winter, many of us brought our sleds to school so we could slide at recess or on the way home. The road to our home went down a steep hill, which was known as Bendickson Hill, a very long hill.

My sled was a beauty. I had been admiring it in the Grasskamp Hardware for weeks before Christmas. The store owner, detecting my love affair, suggested I might get enough money at

Christmas to buy the sled. I made arrangements with the store owner that I would come back after Christmas with the money. He let me take the sled home. I found out later my folks were upset because they planned to give me the sled for Christmas.

Well, one day after school my friend Ervin Rathbun and I pulled our sleds from school to the top of Bendickson's Hill. Often we would give our sisters a ride home down the hill. My sister Ruth would lie on top of me and Ervin's sister rode on top of him. But for some reason we decided not to give them a ride that day. I went first. The road was gravelly and icy. There was a bend in the road so I couldn't see the bottom from the top of the hill.

As I flew down the hill and cut around the bend, I saw Ted Torgeson coming up the hill with his team of horses and sleigh. He was coming home from Preston after hauling a load of meat to town. I yanked my sled and just missed the horses.

Ervin, who was right behind me, couldn't turn his sled on the icy road and slid right under the horses. The horses wore sharp-shod shoes, which are special horseshoes with sharpened knobs to grab the ice. The horses "spooked" and tromped on Ervin. They broke his left leg in three places. Mr. Torgeson stopped the sleigh immediately, picked up Ervin, put him on the sleigh, and headed back to Preston to Dr. Grimmel.

Odin Trulson, c. 1926, Connelly School, Fillmore County

Odin Trulson, thirteen, back row, second from right, stands in the Connelly School yard, District 145, a mile and one-half east of Fountain in Fillmore County on April 30, 1926. Odin's sister, Ruth Trulson, with the dark dress and bangs, is on the far right in the front row.

Odin's son Bruce attended the Thorson School, District 56, which is located seven and one-half miles from Chatfield in Fillmore County. Bruce's favorite story is much different from his father's.

Bruce Trulson, front and center, is holding the sign, identifying his class of 1954.

Uninhibited

I had memorized a poem called "A Present for Daddy" for my part in the school Christmas program. The Pilot Mound School, which was about three miles away, also had a Christmas program. The families from their school attended our program and we attended theirs.

We had had our program and my parents and my four brothers and I went to the Pilot Mound Town Hall for their program. I thought about my poem as I listened to those children perform their songs, skits, and poems. I was sitting in the front row, wearing my four-buckle boots.

At the end of the program the teacher said, "Now, I hope I didn't miss anyone? Did anyone else have a part that I didn't call for?" I raised my hand. Not wanting to embarrass me, the teacher asked what I had. I jumped up on the stage and recited my poem. This brought the house down. I was told later that not only was everyone in the crowd surprised because this was not my Christmas program but that my recitation was the best piece in the program.

A Present for Daddy

I'm going to buy a present
Just for Daddy dear,
But, gee, you'll think it's funny
When my secret you will hear.

My daddy's gettin' older
He's going on thirty-seven
But acts just like a kiddie-
A kid of only 'leven.

You'll never guess that present
Though you should tax your brain,
So I will have to tell you
It's a 'lectric train.

You see my daddy's crazy
'Bout things that run like that.
Like engines, trains, and such things,
He's crazy as a bat.

But that's not all the reason
I'm buying it, you see.
It's 'cause we play together,
So it makes more fun for me.

Bruce Trulson, c. 1954, Thorson School, Fillmore County

Schnibbles 6:
We Learned Something in Those Country Schools!

This I Know for Sure

I was kept after school once. I had to write down on the board "Manila is the capital of the Philippines." And I learned that it was.

After the second campaign and a big buildup of forces, we were headed for the Philippines. I got a note that said "Corporal Maas, report to the first sergeant right after breakfast." We were on New Caledonia. He said, "Here's the slip. Get these three guys. Tell them to pack their duffel bags and you pack yours and be back here in an hour."

"Are you transferring us?"

"No."

"Where we going?"

"I don't know."

That's the army. They didn't know. We went to New Guinea and stayed there a month. The four of us were medics and we had to work with the National Guard to get them physically fit. We drove trucks, dumped off the supplies, and unloaded the supplies. After a month we got on board the troop ship. We headed north. The other three medics asked, "Where we goin?"

I said "Jeepers, cripes, we're going to the Philippines or Japan. We're going north."

"Well, how do you know that?"

"I've been in combat and through three campaigns."

Albert Maas, Geography Champ

We were playing cards one afternoon. A plane was flying above our ship. I heard that plane, and I knew it was Japanese. I quit playing cards, and I looked up.

"What the heck is the matter. You look scared," one of the other guys said.

"I'm not scared, really. I'm alerted. There's a Jap plane up there."

"Oh, hell, no. It's ours. It can't be a Japanese plane. The sirens didn't sound."

"They will," I said. Almost as soon as I got it out of my mouth, the klaxon started and they announced, "On deck, all troops." As medics we were assigned. Of course the navy gave their men the breaks. One fellow and myself had to guard the gunners at the fantail, at the rear of the ship.

Here come this kamikaze pilot out of the sun about three o'clock straight at our ship. Fourth shell got him. I was scared. I took a quick glance, and I could see him coming. And the sound. Holdy cripe, he was closing in fast, full speed! And the shell just blew it all to hell! Pieces fell all over.

Some pieces fell on the ship, and the men down below opened the hatches, run up and got a piece to make bracelets out of it.

The next day those three guys said, "How're you so sure we're going to the Philippines?"

I said, "Jeepers, cripes, man, we've been on the ship two days and we are heading straight north all the time." I said, "I know one thing for sure: Manila is the capital." All three of them looked at me. "How the hell do you know that?"

None of them had to write it down one hundred times in school like I did.

Albert Maas's words of wisdom were spoken in 1943.

Schnibbles 7: School Is Almost Out
Final Recess: Nosey Nellie

Nosey Nellie
Nosey Nellies were
    made of wood,
Strings and canning
    jar rings.
Catching the loop on the
    nose was good
It made us laugh and
    sing.

Mother said, "It will
    teach you grace,
Even though your head
    gets dizzy.
Hook a loop on Nosey's
    face
And dance into a tizzy."
                        -TM

Sweepin' Up
The kids are gone; the school is quiet.
Not much happened, just one riot.
We set the schoolyard lawn on fire,
Don't think it's me next year they'd hire.

Today our hearts all wore a frown.
Next year we go to school in town.
I better sweep up, just once more.
Tomorrow forever they'll lock the door. -TM

254

ONE ROOM SCHOOL

I remember the Buzzle School House
  With windows all in a row;
The double desks, carved with initials,
  Filled with children, all aglow.

Do you remember the flag pole?
  And the pump, which sometimes froze at night?
The washstand in the cloak hall
  That wasn't always right?

Do you remember that big old stove,
  With the ink spot on the ceiling up above?
Since it was never washed away
  It was something we had to learn to love.

I remember those frozen sandwiches
  Packed in pails from syrup or lard,
And stacked outside upon the porch
  While we children played so hard.

I remember the Pledge of Allegiance,
  And those early morning songs,
Like" Yankee Doodle Dandy"
  That helped keep us from wrongs.

The early morning aerobics,
  For necks and legs and arms;
(Almost as good for our muscles
  As working on the farms.)

I remember those long, straight ink pens
  That always scratched and spattered;
We students doing our penmanship
  Found our writing couldn't be flattered.

Do you remember our silent whispers
  While other children were in class?
And the teacher would call on every grade
  As the daily chores would pass?

I remember the clock upon the wall
  Which ran from year to year,
With the steady sound of tick and tock
  Resounding loud and clear.

Do you remember recess
  With sleds and skis on the run?
The cabins, towers and wigwams
  That were really built for fun?

I remember the faded overalls,
  Sometimes patched or torn,
And the lovely gingham dresses
  Starched before they could be worn.

If you remember our country school
  You'll probably say its true
That present-day open classrooms
  Are not exactly new.   by Conrad Stai

Conrad Stai attended the Buzzle School from 1924 to 1933.
From 1939 to 1942 he was Mr. Country School Teacher in the
Northern Rural Consolidated School in Beltrami County.

Chapter 31

Once Upon a Time:
A Story in Two Parts

Part I
In the Magic Land of Dale

Great teachers are great dancers. Life's music fills their spirits and they dance whether or not they can hum the melody or name the tune. Great teachers dance their students and other partners through life's joys and pains. They could no more stop dancing than they could stop loving. Great teachers dance the formal, prescribed steps, but they excel when the music allows them to improvise.

Lincoln School

Leona Doty Davison Buttermore is one of those extraordinary people who has heard life's music clearly and filled her life with dancing and loving. This is the story of Leona's special dance with another person who has also devoted his life to songs of the spirit.

This story begins in the spring of 1924 when Leona Doty completed the one remaining credit she needed to earn her high school diploma on the same night she completed her teachers training. Moments later she signed her first teaching contract. That fall she began her teaching career at Lincoln School in Wabasha County. She was just seventeen, but the music of teaching beat passionately, and Leona never hesitated to join in the dance.

When I Was Seventeen

I had five big, seventeen-year-old boys in my first school. They hitched the horses to the sleds and those boys and all my friends from Zumbro Falls and I went to town to dance. They put the horses in the livery barn. Sometimes we went to the hotel at midnight for oyster stew and then back to the dance hall. There was never any drinking, and no one left the dance hall. If someone would have, well, that would have been a mark on their back. We danced till morning and then we got in the sleigh and went home. The next day I had them all in school. Even though I was seventeen and those boys were seventeen, there was no romance, and they were never a particle of trouble. They just loved to dance and so did I. We had a wonderful time.

I Remember

In 1928, Leona married and signed a contract to teach the eight students who attended Dale School. Although neither person could hear the music, this dance began when Wendell Buttermore, a twelve-year-old farm boy, wearing overalls and a long-sleeved shirt, put on his horn-rimmed glasses, slicked back and parted his hair, and headed to school that fall. Leona remembers Wendell Buttermore and another boy named Doug, who discovered Wendell was a sharp guy!

Class of 1928, Dale School: Back row, third from left, Wendell Buttermore, next, Doug. Teacher Leona Davison is standing next to Doug, third from right in the back row.

Rocket Man

At that time many of the farmers had boys from the Owatonna Orphanage and the farmers worked those boys to death. They just took them in to have help, but they did send them to school. Doug was so much older and bigger than twelve-year-old Wendell. Doug was a bully who took advantage of Wendell and did awfully mean things to him. One day the anger built in Wendell and he couldn't take it anymore, so he reached under the desk and jabbed Doug with his compass, the ones with the needle-nose for making circles. I saw Doug shoot into the air like a sky rocket.

Shall We Dance?

At the end of the school year in the spring of 1929, Wendell moved to Kansas, where he married, became a Wesleyan Methodist minister, and raised his family. Leona stayed in Wabasha, where she became a teaching legend. She taught for forty-five years. They would not meet again for sixty-six years.

In 1995, Alvina, Wendell 's wife of fifty-five years had heart bypass surgery in Rochester. When their three grandsons from Kansas came to visit their grandmother, Wendell wanted them to meet "his favorite teacher."

After reminiscing about the one-room school days at Dale, Wendell and his grandsons returned to Rochester. Alvina became suddenly very ill and died that evening.

When Leona, whose husband had died sixteen years earlier, learned of Alvina's death, she sent Wendell a sympathy card. One year later he wrote and thanked his former teacher for the card.

Mr. and Mrs. Buttermore

Suddenly the music that had played unheard in 1928 swelled and swept Leona and Wendell into a romantic waltz. Leona wrote back the following day and the "Miracle Letter File" began. Soon they were calling each other two or three times a day. On August 30, 1996, Wendell mailed the final miracle letter and proposed. Three minutes after she had received his proposal, Leona called Wendell and said, "My answer is yes."

On November 9, 1996, eighty-year-old Wendell Buttermore married ninety-year-old Leona Davison in the Dale School, where they had first met sixty-eight years earlier.

Early in our interview, I asked Leona if any of the five seventeen-year-old boys had ever made romantic overtures toward their seventeen-year-old teacher and dancing partner. Leona laughed and pointed at Wendell.

A Picture Is Worth....

That's the only romance, and I don't know if it was really a romance. He took a picture of me the first year I went to Dale when he was an eighth grader. He took that picture and he saved it all these years. He doesn't know why he saved it, but we call that our first date. He was twelve and in the eighth grade, and I was twenty-two, married and teaching. He thinks there was a little spark that was kindled. I guess he thought I was just about right.

Wendell laughed and told his version of the first date.

Favorite Teacher

I had saved up enough money from trapping gophers to buy my camera—one of those accordion models, and very likely, it was the first picture I took with it. Under the photograph I wrote, "My favorite teacher." There was no romance in it at all. She was just a great teacher. She turned my life around in the eighth grade. She had such a positive way of teaching.

Well, it was in the spring and she was kind enough to stand by her Model T Ford. I have no idea why I kept that picture all these years. When we started writing, I found the picture. I've got both now. I've got the picture and I've got her!

If you happen to stroll down 8th Street in Wabasha, don't be surprised if you hear the music of two hearts dancing.

Part II
In the Magical Town of Centerville

In 1855, three men from Connecticut traveled to the Territory of Minnesota and staked their claim on 320 acres of land south of Zumbro Falls. They called their new home Pleasant Prairie.

By 1885 several other families had settled in the area, and the people decided they needed to educate their children. Since the school was built on Simon Dale's farm, it became know as the Dale School. To make the school safe for their children, the builders added a cyclone cellar directly under the school.

The Cyclone Hits

In 1928, a cyclone named Leona "blew into" the Dale School, and for the next twenty-two years, this storm of energy blew imagination, compassion, and knowledge into the students of Dale School.

At that time few school boards hired married teachers. However, they must have seen something special in Leona. Although she had recently married, the board offered her a contract to teach the eight students who attended the Dale School.

Usually cyclones destroy towns, but Cyclone Leona built a town named Centerville—inside the walls of the Dale School.

Centerville

First, we named the aisles—streets, avenues or boulevards. The pupils' desks became their homes, complete with house numbers and signs to identify their addresses. In order to change their seats, the students had to sell their homes and buy another. To do this, we needed a real estate developer to handle the transactions. The realtor also acted as an appraiser and placed a value on the desks. For example, a desk near a certain boy or girl might increase in value.

on January 15, 19 40 I sold my other 2 bungalows for $800.00 and traded 1 occupied bungalow for the telephone Exchange. I took possession at once. We allowed the January rent to make necessary repairs

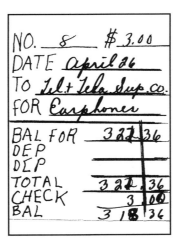

With all the money being exchanged from the sale of homes, we needed a safe place for the money, so we created a bank. The tellers were seventh and eighth grade pupils, as there was no room for error. Occasionally the bank examiner, the teacher, was called in to right a wrong.

In art class we made the necessary bank items such as deposit slips and checks. The students drew with a hectograph pencil, and we duplicated the items one page at a time on a gelatin hectograph. It was a laborious task, but a very rewarding one.

In mathematics class the students balanced their accounts. These activities were so real but the students thought of it as play rather than arithmetic class. Of course, the bank inspector checked the pupils' work as there was no room for error.

We stressed such values as courtesy, neatness, and respect. We thought it would be fun if each pupil took a new name such as Mr. Owen, Miss Bank, or Mrs. White.

Centerville Becomes a Boom Town

Once the bank was built and prospering, Centerville sprang to life. Geography, composition, art, history, arithmetic, spelling—every facet of the curriculum found its practical application in Centerville's bustling activities.

The Mail Must Go Through

Each business was constructed from cardboard boxes. The buildings were movable, and we changed their location in Centerville. Our post office was a busy place. All the students' papers went through the post office. After I had graded their papers, I mailed them back to the students. All special items such as our *Weekly Readers*, Valentines, Christmas and birthday cards, special notes, all written communication, went through the post office. During special holidays such as Christmas and Valentine's Day, we put on extra help in the post office to take care of the influx of mail.

For stamps we used the stamps that came in the Publishers Clearing House mail. To cancel the mail, we made a stamp with the logo DALE SCHOOL, DIST. 53. We pressed the logo stamp in the ink pad and stamped each item, just the way it was done in the real post office.

Reality was never sacrificed, even to "Old Glory," which graced our post office. At the close of each "business" day, the flag was taken down and the post office closed.

The Centerville Store

The heart of village was the Consumers' Cooperative of Centerville. Early in the year the students were working on a class story. When they began working on their stories, they discovered they had several different kinds of theme paper. "Why can't we have a store of our own and then this won't happen again?" asked one student. From that question the cooperative was born.

The students interviewed officials of local cooperatives, ordered a book of laws and regulations, and wrote articles of incorporation. During recess and noon periods they built showcases, shelves, and counters. They installed a light and built a vault. They hired a manager for five cents per week and clerks for three cents per week. We sold shares in our store and soon we were selling such items as pencils, tablets, combs, crayons, pens, and candy. I purchased the products at the Oslo Drug Store in Rochester.

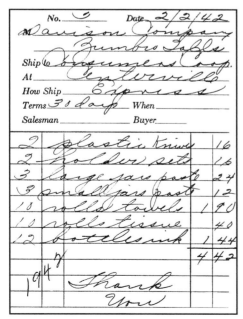

Teachers in the area schools sent in orders for their students. Parents put in orders for such things as paper towels and soap. We had quite a supply of merchandise. During the Depression, the students never had to worry about having a pencil or tablet. They could always come to our store. They knew we would always have fair prices.

I delivered the orders from other schools on my way home (the Davison Express). We could always make a one or two cent profit on each item. The students used sales books like the ones used in most restaurants.

The students constructed each business from cardboard boxes. The buildings were movable, and from time to time we changed their location in Centerville.

The children's enthusiasm fairly bubbled. They checked invoices, marked goods, and placed them on shelves. They worked during the noon period to keep the store clean.

Even the smallest youngsters knew that the success of the business depended upon the efforts of the pupils themselves. They were living a real life situation. They were engaged in an enterprise where real, not make-believe, problems presented themselves to be solved.

"May I Speak with Wendell, Please?"

The students wanted a way for their businesses to communicate with each other. The science class came up with the solution. By using a dry cell battery and a doorbell, the students constructed a switchboard and created another business that required employees, billing, and payment. Again, by adding just one more business, the entire town was affected.

Each pupil had a call, such as one long and two short rings for the banker. If I wanted to call a student, I rang the number on the doorbell, and they could hear it outside. We made a telephone directory to aid the telephone operator. Each student paid rent for the convenience of having a number. That precipitated business for the bank and the telephone bills were sent through the post office.

Fortune and Fame

Word of the creative cyclone whirling inside the Dale School spread rapidly. Students published the *Centerville News*, using the trusty hectograph. The *News* sold for two cents a copy.

The county superintendent of schools often brought visitors from the State Department of Education and Winona Teachers College to visit Centerville. Leona was invited to Chicago and Milwaukee to attend educational seminars and describe rural education in Centerville. One day the county superintendent brought the head of the rural schools in Switzerland to visit the Dale School and Centerville. All this notoriety had little effect on the students. According to Leona, "The kids just loved having the dignitaries come. They got so accustomed to having visitors it didn't bother them a particle."

Leona Davison Buttermore taught in her beloved Wabasha County for forty-five years. In addition to her years as Country School Teacher at Lincoln and Dale schools, she taught five years in Zumbro Falls and sixteen years in Kellogg. Leona retired in 1970.

Christmas, 1940

At Christmas we stocked a few little gifts the kids could buy for their parents. At Christmas we made calenders for all our customers. This is a facsimile of the original card.

Compliments of the
Centerville Bank

The Last Bell

When I was a child, I spent many summers on my grandparents' farm. Every meal was a banquet of stories. Of course, the stories I liked best were the personal anecdotes—how my grandfather built the county road and how my mother and my aunts hid in the cornfield and laid branches across the field road and waited for the steel wheels of the manure spreader to crawl over them and slam down against the road. The spreader thumped down, spewing manure into the air and showering the hired hand, who cut loose with a string of Polish obscenities. I learned who these people I loved were through their stories.

I have always loved stories. I love to tell them as well as listen to others spin out their tales. This passion led me to major in English and teach stories for thirty-two years. However, nothing quite compares to the adventure of mining for stories.

Every journey begins by stepping on some kind of threshold and moving into a new world. Whether we travel to an unfamiliar land, enter a closet to open a magic door, fly over the rainbow, or confront the demons in our mind, we step over the threshold and enter an untraveled world.

My story mining journey began when I stepped on the threshold and walked into Verna Ziegenhagen's school. I put my foot in the worn groove where my grandfather stepped the first day he started school. We both began our adventures by stepping on the same threshold one hundred years apart.

Seldom do quests go the way they are planned, and often we reach a different destination from the one we circled on our map. Often the adventure shines more light on us than we have ever seen, brilliant, wondrous light. If we are fortunate, we find the source of the light not only "out there" but also in ourselves.

The goal of my journey was simple: I had no one to guide me, so I began like Don Quixote, charging windmills. Armed with my video camera, tape recorder, maps, tripod, notebooks and miles of audio- and videotape, I crisscrossed the state. Monday, head for Caledonia and Freeburg. Tuesday, type up stories. Wednesday, meet Ordella Lecy in Granite Falls at 8 a.m. Thursday, type up notes. Friday, take off at 4 a.m. for Brainerd. For one and a half years my white '84 Olds streaked across the state from one interview to another.

I wasn't really positive about why I was mining these riches or whether the mines would surrender their treasures. But every time I interviewed one of the people in this book, I became more intrigued by the storytellers and I became hungrier for their stories.

Soon I was scheduling overnight trips: a three-day jaunt to Kittson County, two days in Morris, Madison, Appleton, and one or two more stops on the way home; and one four-day excursion from Grand Marais to Ely and on to Hibbing, Virginia, Coleraine, Bigfork, Grand Rapids, Cloquet, Proctor and Two Harbors. Frantically, I chased stories throughout the state.

After each mining, I laid the treasures out before me. Soon I realized I was in the presence of heroes, forgotten heroes, but heroes, nevertheless. Who were these people whose precious nuggets glittered as we panned for treasure? How could teenagers be so courageous? Why would they choose to live in such harsh conditions? Why did they teach? Would anyone endure such hardships for so little pay if they didn't truly love children? Do today's teachers know how much they owe these educational pioneers? What do Country School Students remember about those "good old days"? What stories would they like to tell?

After interviewing one hundred teachers, I turned around one day and saw History following me, wondering what I was doing. But History moved cautiously and kept its distance. It didn't take me long to discover that Country School Teachers had been sadly neglected by History. The more people I interviewed, the more I realized that Country School Teachers may have been one of the most important figures in America's history for well over one hundred years.

But History has silenced these heroes by not listening to their stories, by not writing them down, by not passing them on. History's apathy had allowed Country School Teachers' stories to die, and so I decided to fight a personal war with History.

I wasn't naive when I went to battle. I knew most people would say, "Who cares? It's too late. Why go running all over the state? Why spend all those hours in front of that computer?"

Some would say, "The task is too great," and others would say, "What difference does it make?" My only allies would be the Country School Teachers and Country School Students. But they could only say, "Here are my stories. Time has taken away my fighting spirit. You will have to do this alone."

I also knew that History can cast a spell of apathy, ennui, and indifference so powerful it can silence the spirit of the most passionate crusader.

But some fire inside me told me, "Hey, listen to your heart. You have to do this." I knew the main goal for Country School Teachers was to tell their stories and be recognized for who they were and what they had given.

Finally, after the first few interviews, I knew that this quest would be just like all the others in my life. It would not be the book at the end of the labyrinth that would matter most, it would be the journey that would lift my spirit. Meeting the storytellers made the adventure so rich that I always knew I was in the presence of magical, mystical, moments, poignant moments that cannot ever be repeated.

However, mining can be an impossible task if the guardians will not yield their treasures. Country School Teachers as well as Country School Students gave their treasures enthusiastically. They are proud of their gifts, and they know they provided better lives for thousands of farm children. They know that History snubbed them, shrugged its shoulders, and elbowed them aside. When the noble and worthy have been ignored, they tell their stories with passion.

When people give a story from their treasury of precious experiences and say, "Here, you take this gem. I want you to have this story. No one else knows it. I have saved it all these years because its brightness touches my spirit," they have given you gems embedded in the Holy Grail. Often the "telling" is as precious as the story. Unfortunately, seeing stories on the printed page doesn't tell the reader much about the location and trip to the mine—tires crunching the gravel driveway to Pearl's farm, the walk through the care center to Elvice's room, the door opening to Emma's well-lived-in home, Harry's collection of coffee grinders, or Lois sitting on the steps, telling the history of the Freeburg school.

"How did you find 170 country schoolteachers who wanted to tell stories?" History asked me.

"No problem! You can't miss. Take Highway 11 east out of Baudette until you get to Birchdale, turn right and then take a right just past the fire observation tower, then turn right into the gravel driveway. Knock on the screen door, walk through the entryway filled with her art projects and go into the living room. There you'll find Lu Rud."

After listening to a few history makers tell their stories, you just face the wind and it will blow their stories to you. Stories seek out the one who comes to listen.

The "giving of the story" is often as magical as the place where the storyteller lives. Unraveling Country School Teachers' personalities meant mining every kind of story, especially those that show vulnerability and weakness. When they said, "I really shouldn't tell this story," I knew I would be hearing a story that would reveal Country School Teacher from saint to mere mortal.

"I really shouldn't tell this, but the day was so hot I couldn't wait to take off my garter belt. I threw it on the desk."

"I don't know if I should tell this, but I tackled as hard as I could one of those boys who had broken all the windows. They didn't break any more windows that year."

Those are real people talking, "giving nuggets from the mines."

The printed page can't capture the sounds of the storytellers' voices—the laughter, the pain, the sarcasm, the tenderness. The marks on the paper don't pause, whoop and holler, tremble and weep. But I am blessed with the gift of seeing the storytellers and hearing their voices every time I reread their stories. A triple blessing!

Describing the "giving of the stories" would require another book, but I must tell one story because it touched me so deeply and because it shows the power of the human spirit.

I was invited to speak to the Strokers Club at

the Courage Center, a support group for people who have had a stroke. While I put away my equipment and after most people had left, one of the men shuffled up to me and said, "Haaaave.......IIII-IIIIII got........ a stoooooory for youuuuuuuu." His words slurred together and were very difficult to understand.

I asked him if I could tape record his story, but he said that I would not be able to understand him. We were both a bit uncomfortable at first. I asked him to repeat himself often and that increased my anxiety. However, he made certain I got every word. Nothing was going to stop this man from telling his story. When he gave the punch lines, we both roared.

"Do you have another one?" I asked. We spent an hour together. He told one story after another about his life as a Country School Student. We forgot our anxiety. At the end of each story, we laughed and I asked him for more details. We became two ordinary guys, one telling great stories and the other loving every word. What a courageous man! What a fantastic hour!

Only a book of one thousand pages could describe the emotions of the storyteller's eyes, mouth, and hands—the language of the body! Frances Hayden's story is told in the book, but the reader cannot see this eighty-five-year-old dynamo fold her legs underneath her and wave her arms and hands as her eyes glow when she hoots and laughs about having to spend the evening in the ladies' room of a St. Cloud nightspot because her professor stood in the door.

As I re-played the videotapes of the storytellers in this book, I watched and listened again and again to the magic and power of how another person's stories can put us in touch with the music of life. We may not hear it loudly all the time, this music of love, loss, hope, and tragedy, and re-birth—the songs of life. But we all dance to the music and if we don't know the name of the dance, all we have to do is look into the story-mirror and we will see ourselves dancing our lives.

I want to thank all the wonderful people I met in this journey. Thank you for welcoming me into your homes; thank you for the meals, coffee, and every wonderful, fattening dessert.

Many of you received phone calls that began, "Hello, Lily, Bill, or Frank! My name is Tom Melchior and I'm working on a book about Country School Teachers...." Thank you for welcoming a stranger to your table. Thanks for helping me mine your stories. But most of all, thanks for the dance.

To you Country School Teachers I missed who have stories yearning to be told, please find a way to make them known. Perhaps the next dance will be ours.

And now Country School Teachers, you can forget about those compositions, turn off the kerosene lantern, and rest. There will be no school in District 1 ever again. Before you rest, take a glance at History. He's slinking off into the shadows. Don't you think he looks a bit guilty?

And Cecile, dear heart, thank you for this love affair so late in our lives. You can put away the pencils and watch your characters frolic across the page. This part of our journey together is over.

Memory Page

How many of you had Mothers Clubs?

Who had a hot car in 1942 like Bertha Everson's?

Name all the recess games.

Who loves Oskosh, B'gosh?

Burt Kreitlow taught boxing? Anyone else?

Esther Norhar wore white. Did you wear white stockings, too?

Ruth Domingo wore white. Who romanced the school marm?

Name all the occasions for "lining up"?

Did you have a sister sitting behind you?

264

Index